BATMAN '66

VOL. 4

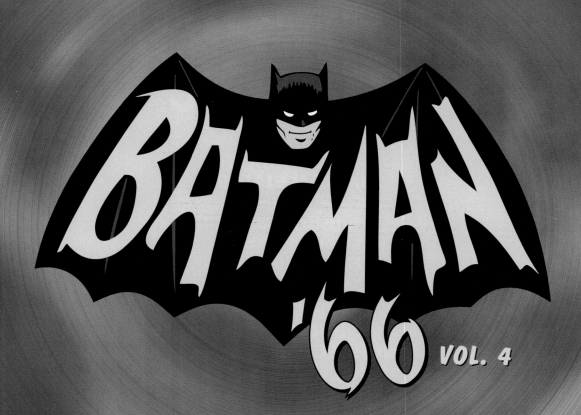

BATMAN '66

VOL. 4

Written by
JEFF PARKER
HARLAN ELLISON
LEN WEIN
MIKE W. BARR
TOM PEYER
ROB WILLIAMS

Art by
JOSÉ LUIS GARCÍA-LÓPEZ
JOE PRADO
MICHAEL AVON OEMING
SCOTT KOWALCHUK
DAVE BULLOCK
RICHARD CASE
LEONARDO ROMERO
RUBEN PROCOPIO
SANDY JARRELL

Colors by
ALEX SINCLAIR   SCOTT KOWALCHUK
TONY AVINA   JORDIE BELLAIRE

Letters by
WES ABBOTT

Cover Art & Original Series Covers by
MICHAEL & LAURA ALLRED

BATMAN created by **BOB KANE**

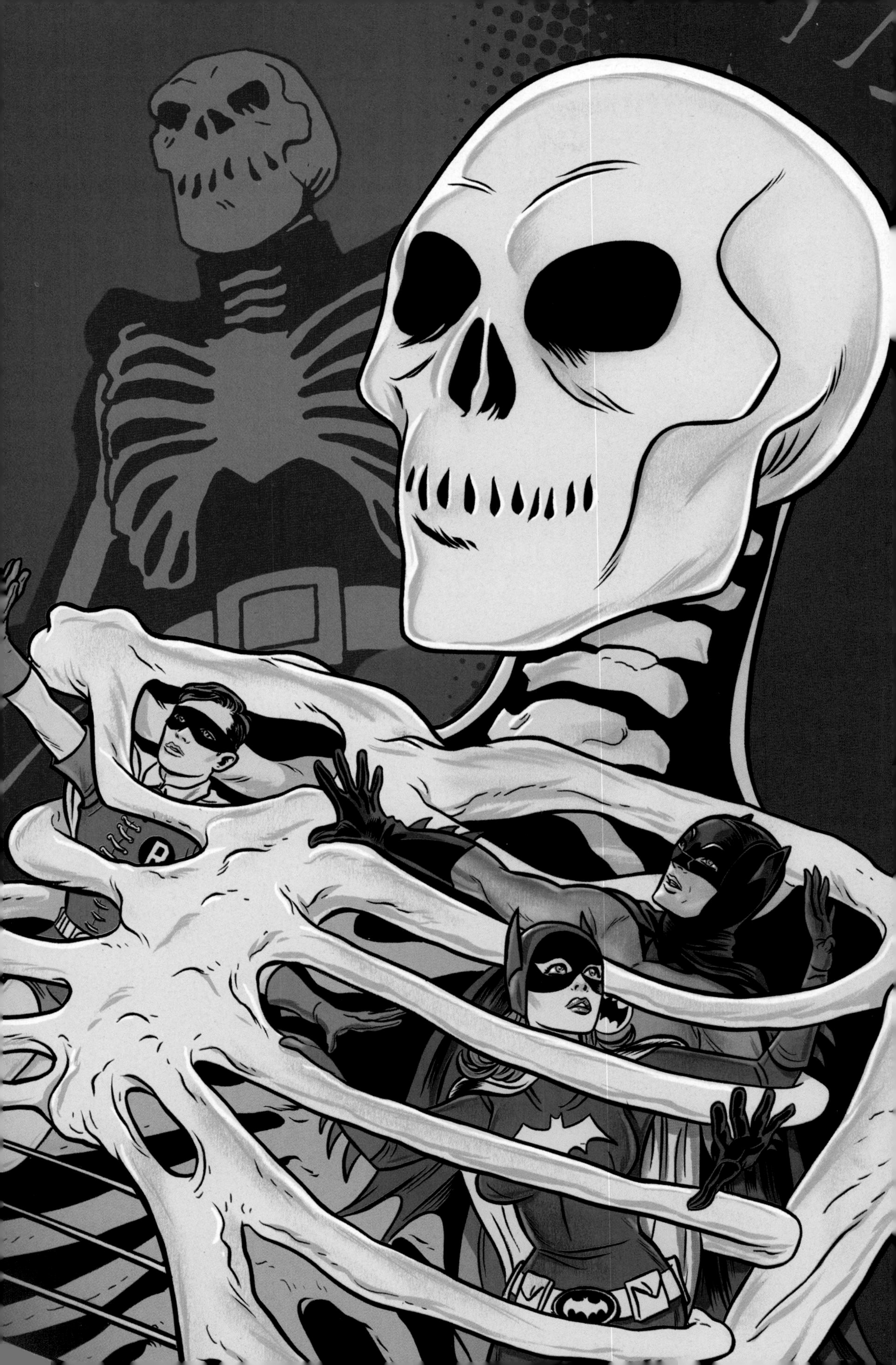

TABLE OF CONTENTS

IM CHADWICK
Editor – Original Series
NIZ ANSARI
Assistant Editor – Original Series
EB WOODARD
Group Editor – Collected Editions
AUL SANTOS
Editor – Collected Edition
TEVE COOK
Design Director – Books
URTIS KING JR.
Publication Design
OB HARRAS
Senior VP – Editor-in-Chief, DC Comics
IANE NELSON
President
AN DIDIO and **JIM LEE**
Co-Publishers
EOFF JOHNS
Chief Creative Officer
MIT DESAI
Senior VP – Marketing & Global Franchise Management
AIRI GARDINER
Senior VP – Finance
AM ADES
VP – Digital Marketing
OBBIE CHASE
VP – Talent Development
MARK CHIARELLO
Senior VP – Art, Design & Collected Editions
OHN CUNNINGHAM
VP – Content Strategy
ANNE DEPIES
VP – Strategy Planning & Reporting
ON FALLETTI
VP – Manufacturing Operations
LAWRENCE GANEM
VP – Editorial Administration & Talent Relations
LISON GILL
Senior VP – Manufacturing & Operations
ANK KANALZ
Senior VP – Editorial Strategy & Administration
AY KOGAN
VP – Legal Affairs
EREK MADDALENA
Senior VP – Sales & Business Development
ACK MAHAN
VP – Business Affairs
AN MIRON
VP – Sales Planning & Trade Development
ICK NAPOLITANO
VP – Manufacturing Administration
AROL ROEDER
VP – Marketing
DDIE SCANNELL
VP – Mass Account & Digital Sales
OURTNEY SIMMONS
Senior VP – Publicity & Communications
IM (SKI) SOKOLOWSKI
VP – Comic Book Specialty & Newsstand Sales
ANDY YI
Senior VP – Global Franchise Management

BATMAN '66 VOL. 4
Published by DC Comics.
Compilation and all new material Copyright © 2016 DC Comics.

All Rights Reserved. Originally published in single magazine form as BATMAN:
THE LOST EPISODE 1, BATMAN '66 17-22 and online as BATMAN '66 Digital
Chapters 46-57. Copyright © 2015 DC Comics. All Rights Reserved. All
characters, their distinctive likenesses and related elements featured in this
publication are trademarks of DC Comics. The stories, characters and incidents
featured in this publication are entirely fictional. DC Comics does not read or
accept unsolicited submissions of ideas, stories or artwork.

DC Comics, 2900 West Alameda Ave. Burbank, CA 91505
Printed by RR Donnelley, Owensville, MO, USA. 4/8/16. First Printing.
ISBN: 978-1-4012-6104-7

Library of Congress Cataloging-in-Publication Data

Parker, Jeff, 1966-
  Batman '66. Volume 4 / Jeff Parker, Harlan Ellison, Len Wein, Mike W. Barr,
Tom Peyer, José Luis García-López, Joe Prado, Michael Avon Oeming.
      pages cm
  ISBN 978-1-4012-6104-7 (pbk.)
  1. Graphic novels. I. Ellison, Harlan. II. Wein, Len III. Barr, Mike W. IV.
Peyer, Tom. V. García-López, José Luis, illustrator. VI. Prado, Joe, illustrator.
VII. Oeming, Michael Avon. VIII. Title.
  PN6728.B36P375 2015
  741.5'973—dc23
                                                            2015031177

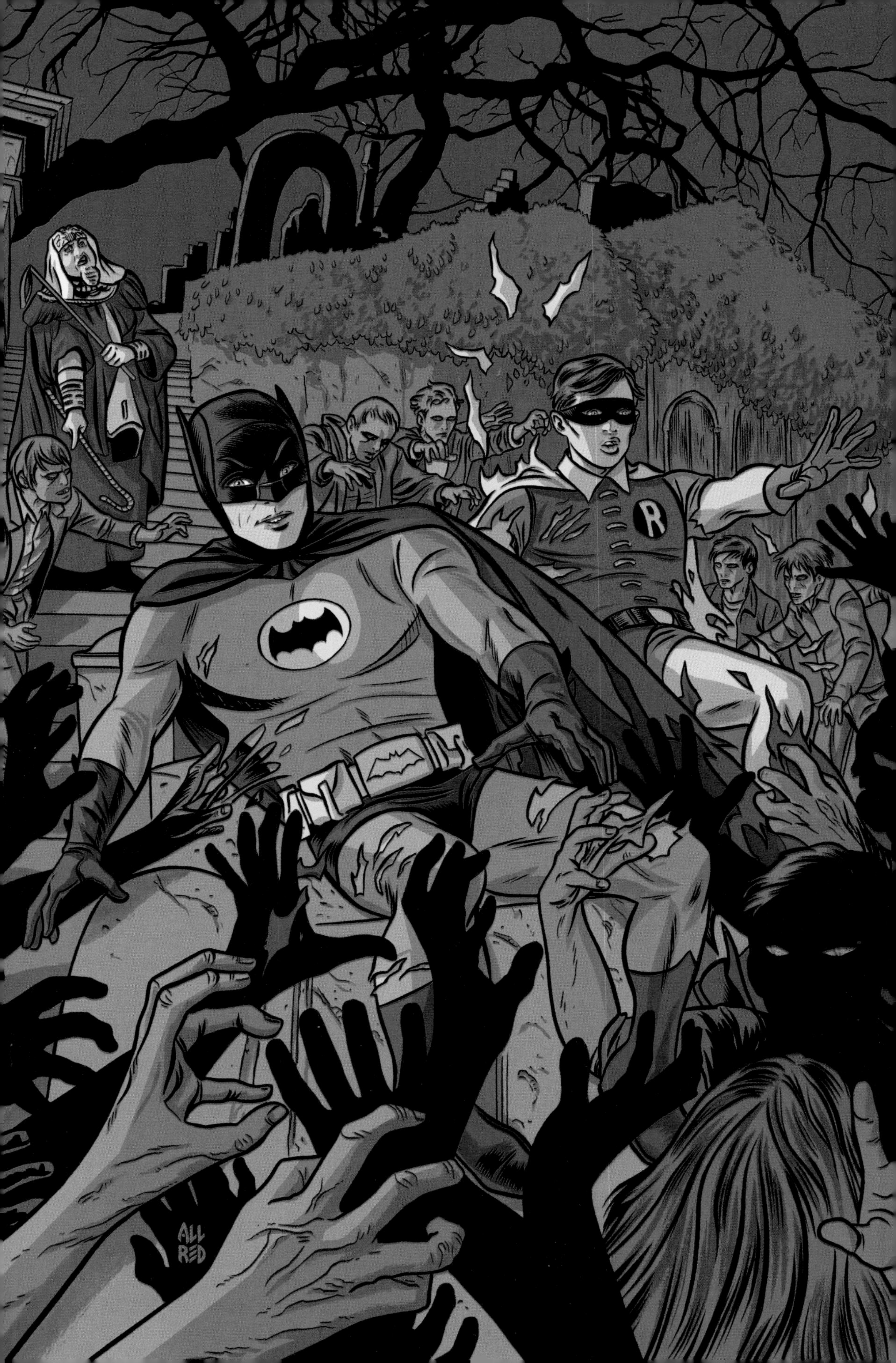
ALL
RED

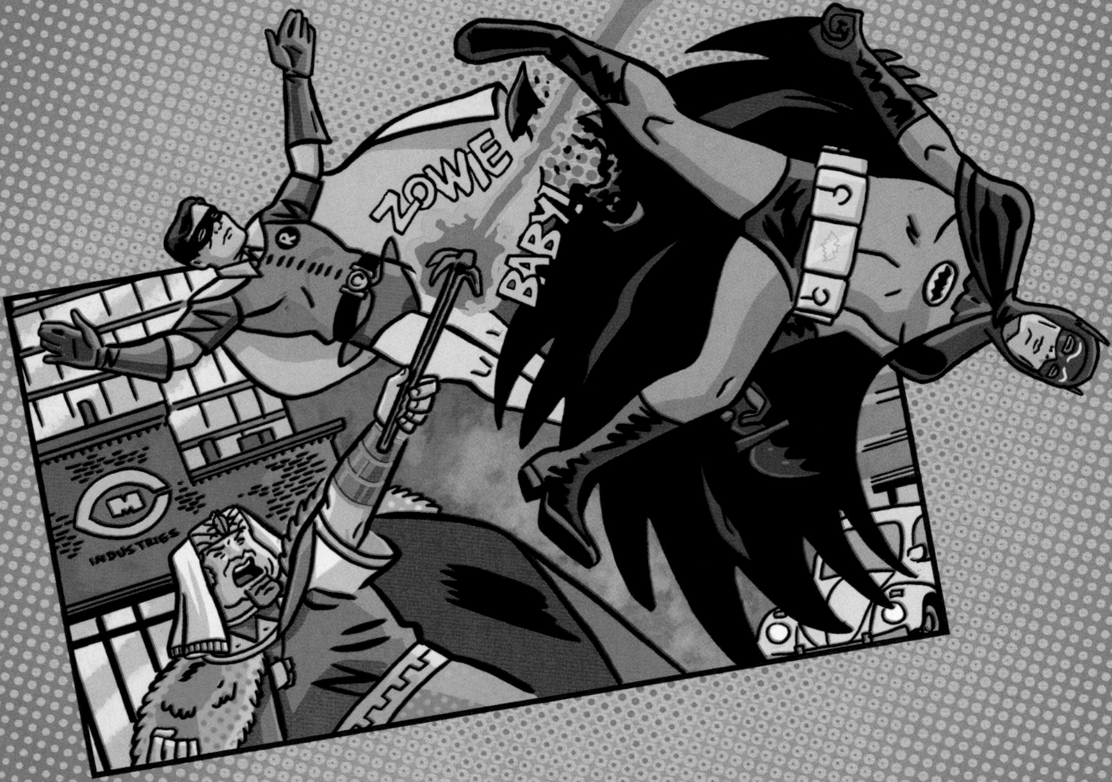
ZOWIE
BABY!
INDUSTRIES

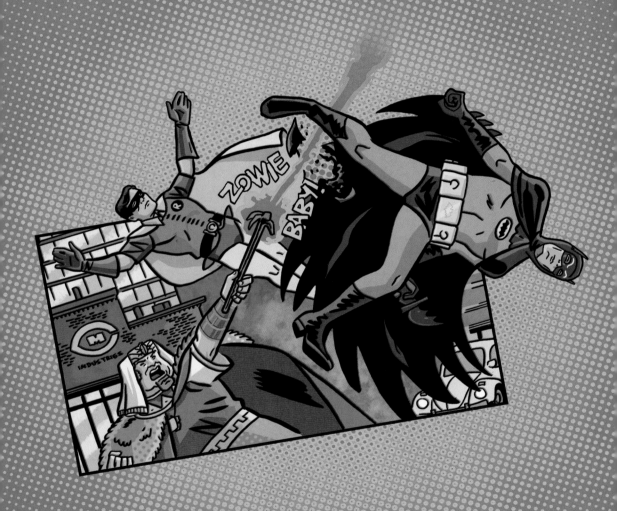

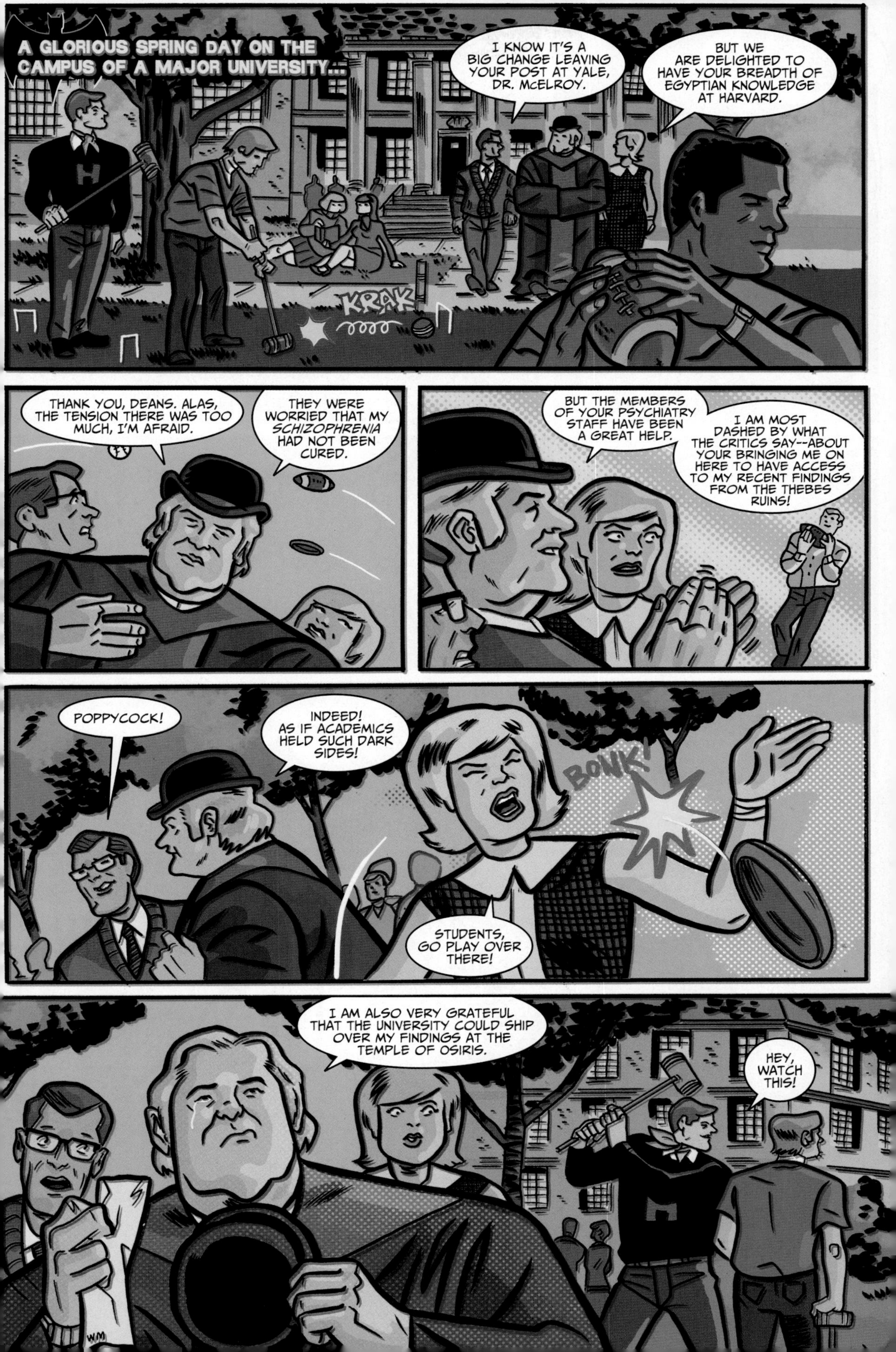
A GLORIOUS SPRING DAY ON THE CAMPUS OF A MAJOR UNIVERSITY...
I KNOW IT'S A BIG CHANGE LEAVING YOUR POST AT YALE, DR. McELROY.
BUT WE ARE DELIGHTED TO HAVE YOUR BREADTH OF EGYPTIAN KNOWLEDGE AT HARVARD.
KRAK
THANK YOU, DEANS. ALAS, THE TENSION THERE WAS TOO MUCH, I'M AFRAID.
THEY WERE WORRIED THAT MY *SCHIZOPHRENIA* HAD NOT BEEN CURED.
BUT THE MEMBERS OF YOUR PSYCHIATRY STAFF HAVE BEEN A GREAT HELP.
I AM MOST DASHED BY WHAT THE CRITICS SAY--ABOUT YOUR BRINGING ME ON HERE TO HAVE ACCESS TO MY RECENT FINDINGS FROM THE THEBES RUINS!
POPPYCOCK!
INDEED! AS IF ACADEMICS HELD SUCH DARK SIDES!
BONK!
STUDENTS, GO PLAY OVER THERE!
I AM ALSO VERY GRATEFUL THAT THE UNIVERSITY COULD SHIP OVER MY FINDINGS AT THE TEMPLE OF OSIRIS.
HEY, WATCH THIS!

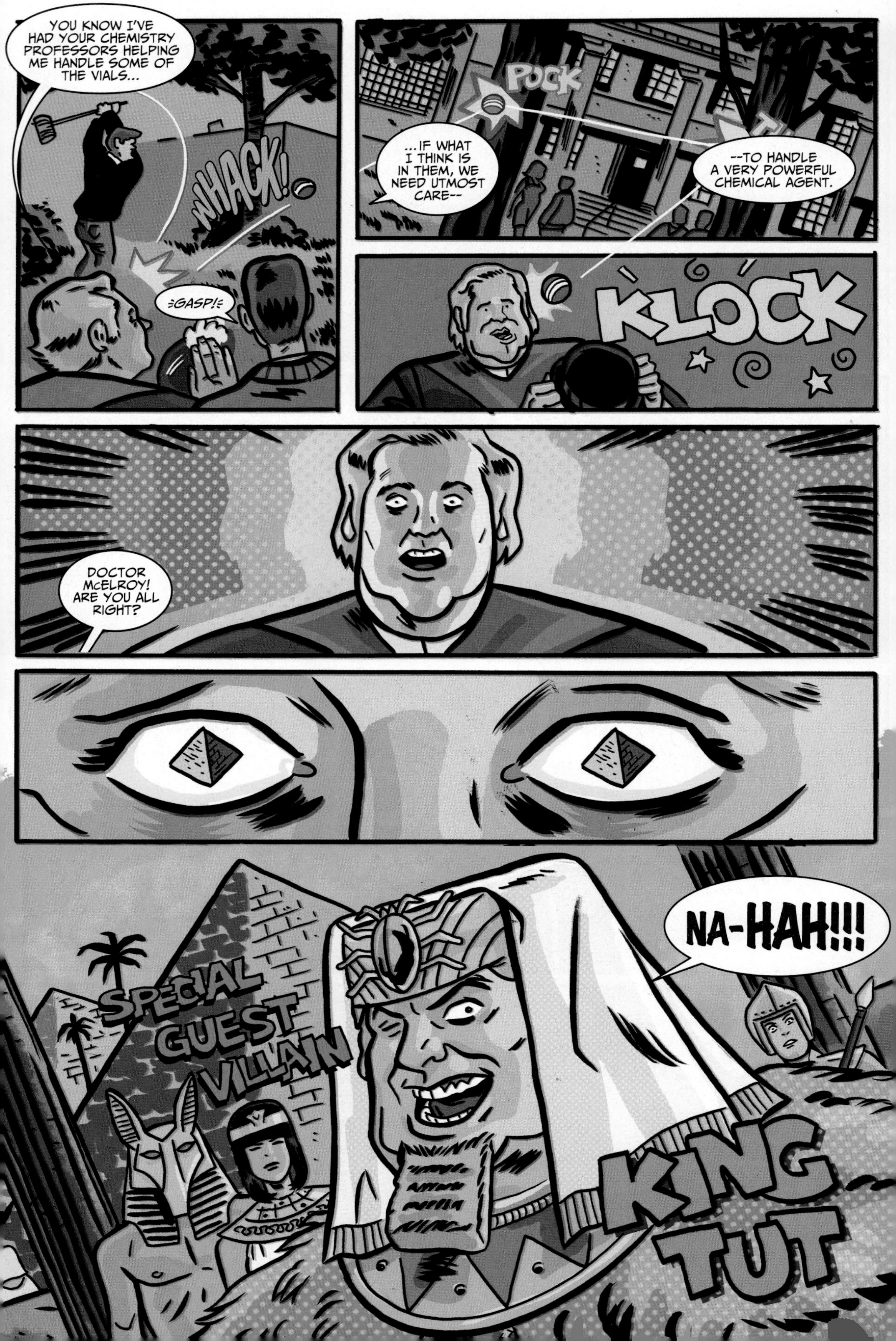
YOU KNOW I'VE HAD YOUR CHEMISTRY PROFESSORS HELPING ME HANDLE SOME OF THE VIALS...
WHACK!
GASP!
PUCK
...IF WHAT I THINK IS IN THEM, WE NEED UTMOST CARE--
--TO HANDLE A VERY POWERFUL CHEMICAL AGENT.
KLOCK
DOCTOR McELROY! ARE YOU ALL RIGHT?
NA-HAH!!!
SPECIAL GUEST VILLAIN
KING TUT

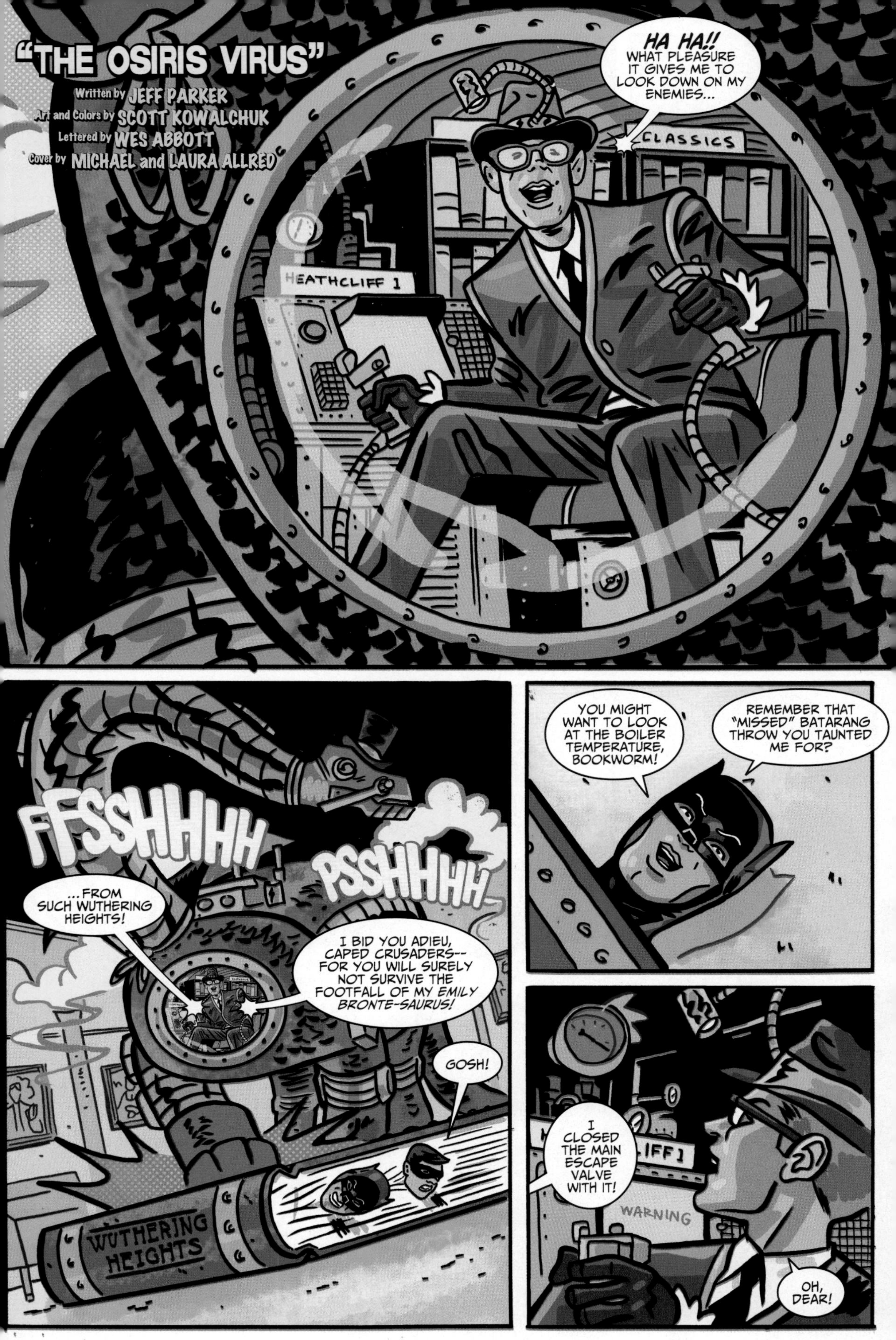
"THE OSIRIS VIRUS"
Written by JEFF PARKER
Art and Colors by SCOTT KOWALCHUK
Lettered by WES ABBOTT
Cover by MICHAEL and LAURA ALLRED
HA HA!! WHAT PLEASURE IT GIVES ME TO LOOK DOWN ON MY ENEMIES...
CLASSICS
HEATHCLIFF 1
FFSSHHHH
PSSHHHH
...FROM SUCH WUTHERING HEIGHTS!
I BID YOU ADIEU, CAPED CRUSADERS-- FOR YOU WILL SURELY NOT SURVIVE THE FOOTFALL OF MY *EMILY BRONTE-SAURUS!*
GOSH!
WUTHERING HEIGHTS
YOU MIGHT WANT TO LOOK AT THE BOILER TEMPERATURE, BOOKWORM!
REMEMBER THAT "MISSED" BATARANG THROW YOU TAUNTED ME FOR?
I CLOSED THE MAIN ESCAPE VALVE WITH IT!
WARNING
OH, DEAR!

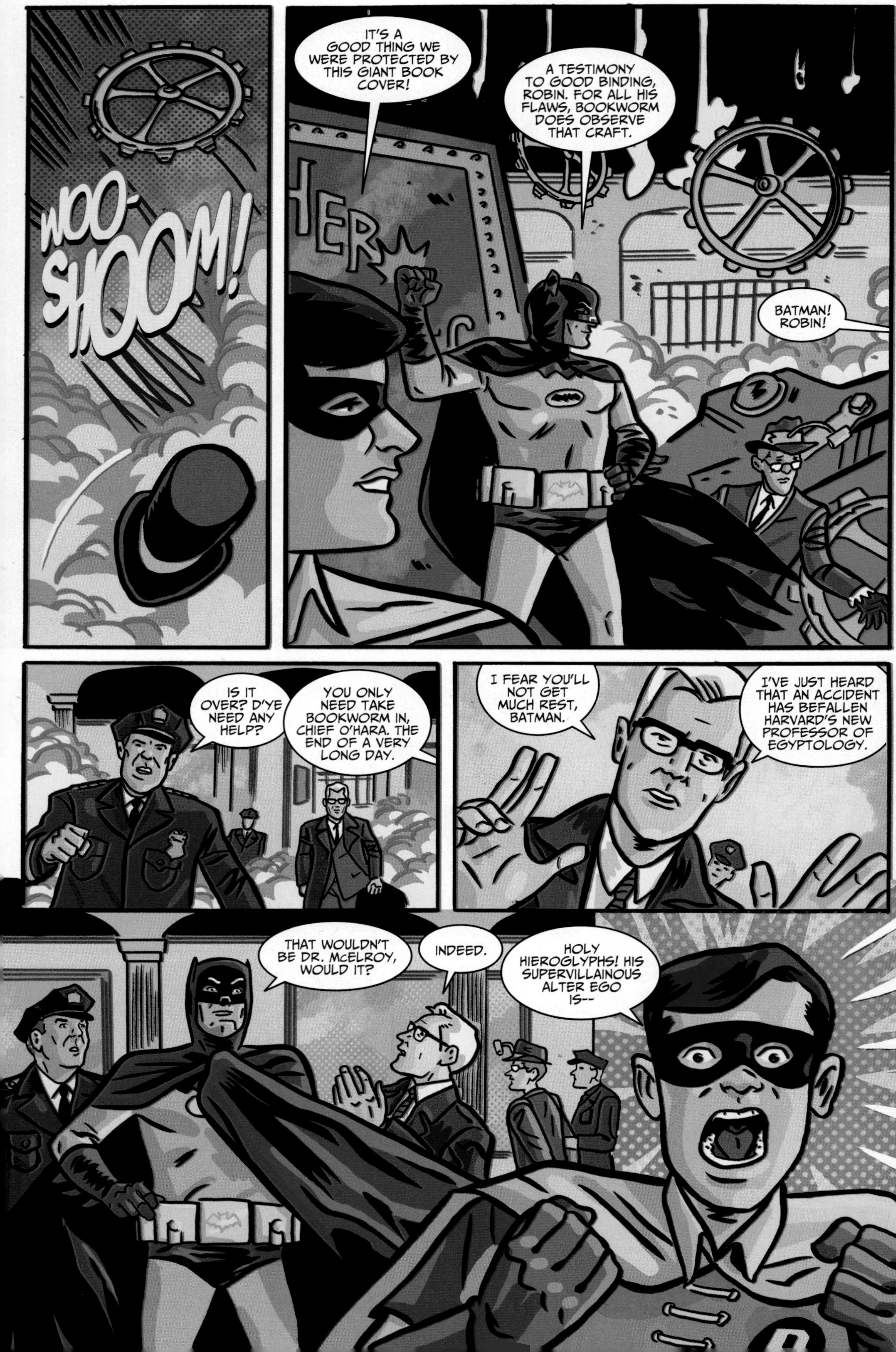
WOO-SHOOM!
IT'S A GOOD THING WE WERE PROTECTED BY THIS GIANT BOOK COVER!
A TESTIMONY TO GOOD BINDING, ROBIN. FOR ALL HIS FLAWS, BOOKWORM DOES OBSERVE THAT CRAFT.
BATMAN! ROBIN!
IS IT OVER? D'YE NEED ANY HELP?
YOU ONLY NEED TAKE BOOKWORM IN, CHIEF O'HARA. THE END OF A VERY LONG DAY.
I FEAR YOU'LL NOT GET MUCH REST, BATMAN.
I'VE JUST HEARD THAT AN ACCIDENT HAS BEFALLEN HARVARD'S NEW PROFESSOR OF EGYPTOLOGY.
THAT WOULDN'T BE DR. McELROY, WOULD IT?
INDEED.
HOLY HIEROGLYPHS! HIS SUPERVILLAINOUS ALTER EGO IS--

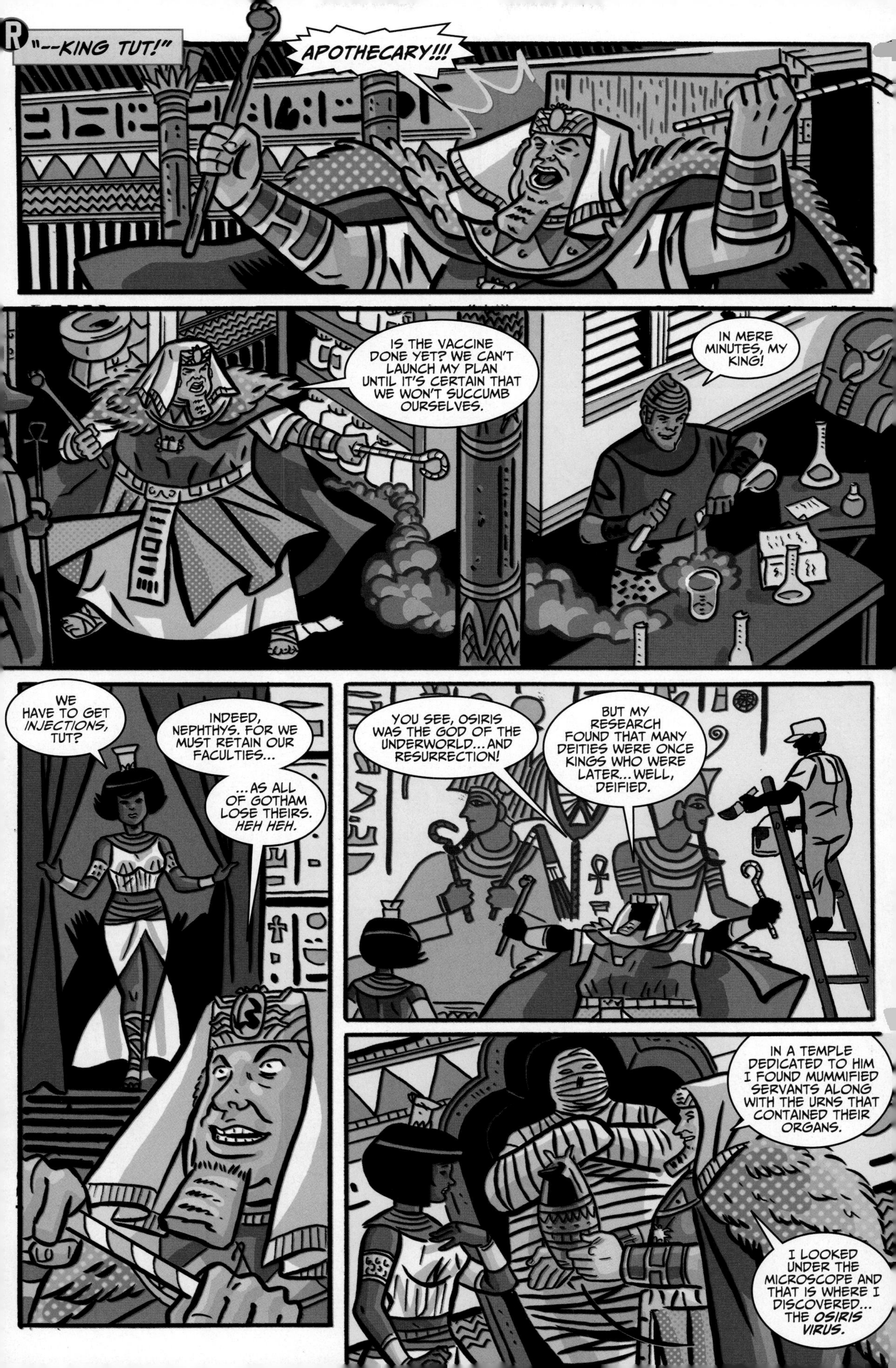
"--KING TUT!"
APOTHECARY!!!
IS THE VACCINE DONE YET? WE CAN'T LAUNCH MY PLAN UNTIL IT'S CERTAIN THAT WE WON'T SUCCUMB OURSELVES.
IN MERE MINUTES, MY KING!
WE HAVE TO GET *INJECTIONS,* TUT?
INDEED, NEPHTHYS. FOR WE MUST RETAIN OUR FACULTIES...
...AS ALL OF GOTHAM LOSE THEIRS. *HEH HEH.*
YOU SEE, OSIRIS WAS THE GOD OF THE UNDERWORLD...AND RESURRECTION!
BUT MY RESEARCH FOUND THAT MANY DEITIES WERE ONCE KINGS WHO WERE LATER...WELL, DEIFIED.
IN A TEMPLE DEDICATED TO HIM I FOUND MUMMIFIED SERVANTS ALONG WITH THE URNS THAT CONTAINED THEIR ORGANS.
I LOOKED UNDER THE MICROSCOPE AND THAT IS WHERE I DISCOVERED... THE *OSIRIS VIRUS.*

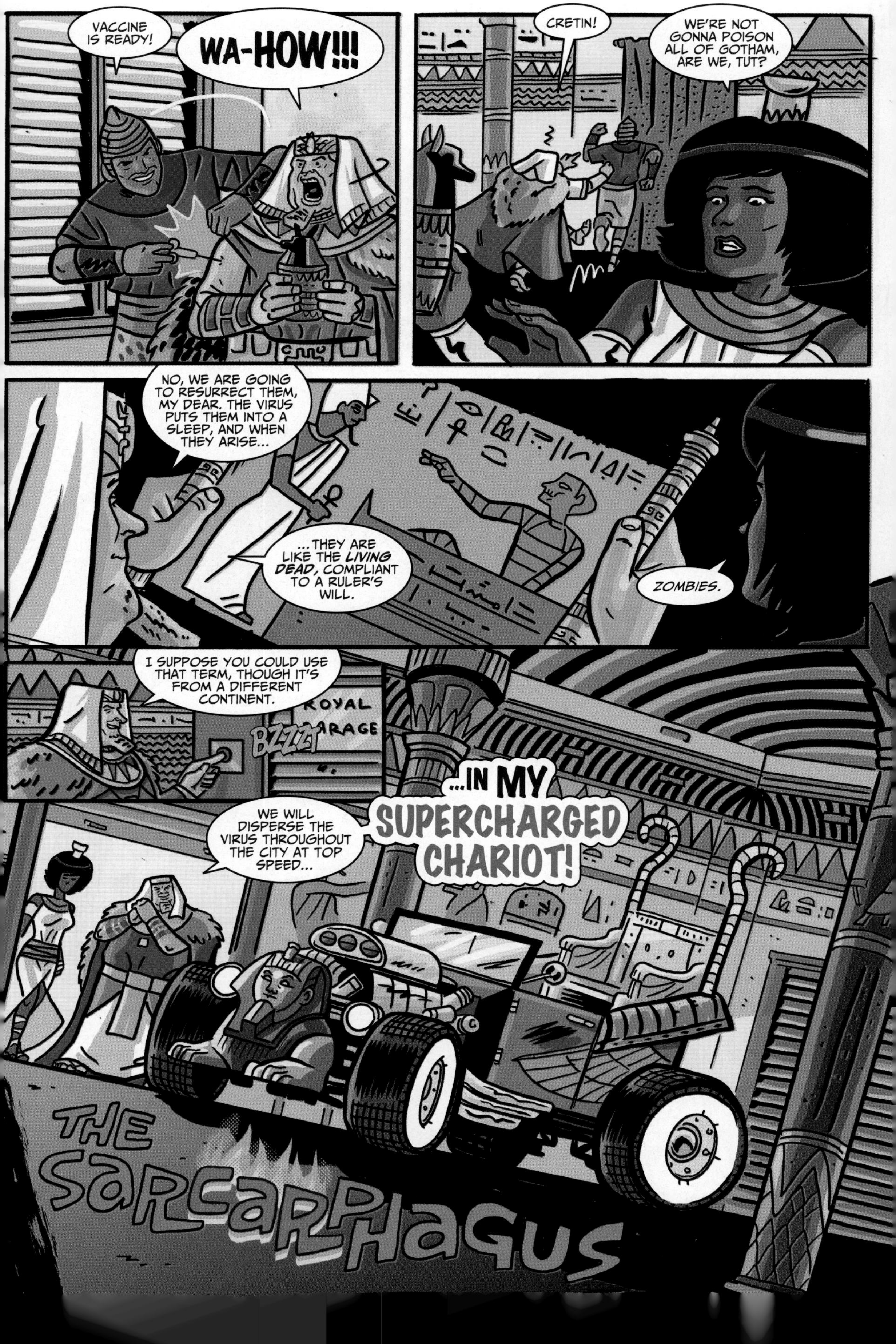
VACCINE IS READY!
WA-HOW!!!
CRETIN!
WE'RE NOT GONNA POISON ALL OF GOTHAM, ARE WE, TUT?
NO, WE ARE GOING TO RESURRECT THEM, MY DEAR. THE VIRUS PUTS THEM INTO A SLEEP, AND WHEN THEY ARISE...
...THEY ARE LIKE THE *LIVING DEAD*, COMPLIANT TO A RULER'S WILL.
ZOMBIES.
I SUPPOSE YOU COULD USE THAT TERM, THOUGH IT'S FROM A DIFFERENT CONTINENT.
ROYAL GARAGE
BZZZT
WE WILL DISPERSE THE VIRUS THROUGHOUT THE CITY AT TOP SPEED...
...IN MY SUPERCHARGED CHARIOT!
THE SARCARPHAGUS

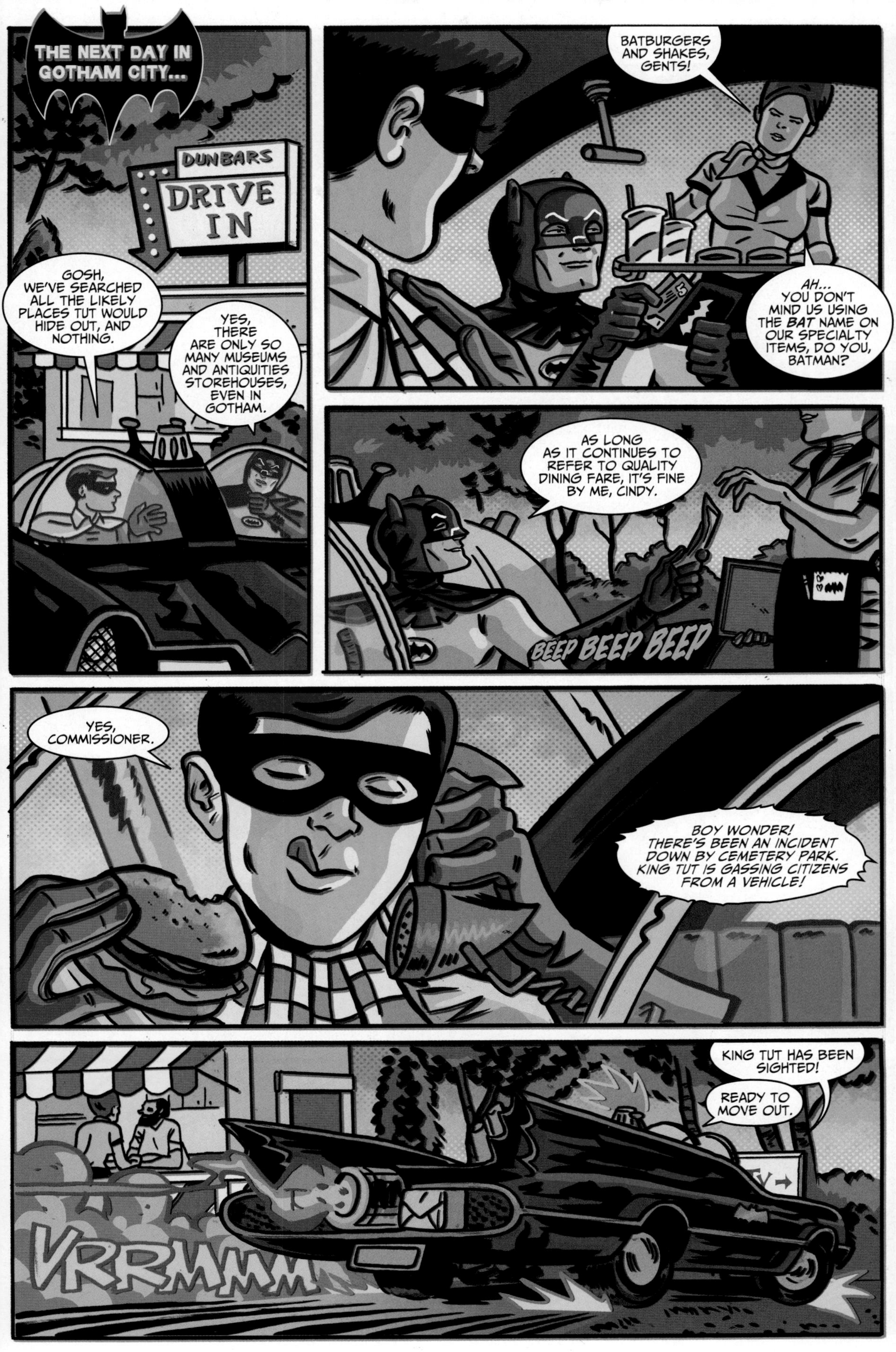
THE NEXT DAY IN GOTHAM CITY...
DUNBARS
DRIVE IN
GOSH, WE'VE SEARCHED ALL THE LIKELY PLACES TUT WOULD HIDE OUT, AND NOTHING.
YES, THERE ARE ONLY SO MANY MUSEUMS AND ANTIQUITIES STOREHOUSES, EVEN IN GOTHAM.
BATBURGERS AND SHAKES, GENTS!
AH... YOU DON'T MIND US USING THE BAT NAME ON OUR SPECIALTY ITEMS, DO YOU, BATMAN?
AS LONG AS IT CONTINUES TO REFER TO QUALITY DINING FARE, IT'S FINE BY ME, CINDY.
BEEP BEEP BEEP
YES, COMMISSIONER.
BOY WONDER! THERE'S BEEN AN INCIDENT DOWN BY CEMETERY PARK. KING TUT IS GASSING CITIZENS FROM A VEHICLE!
KING TUT HAS BEEN SIGHTED!
READY TO MOVE OUT.
VRRMMM

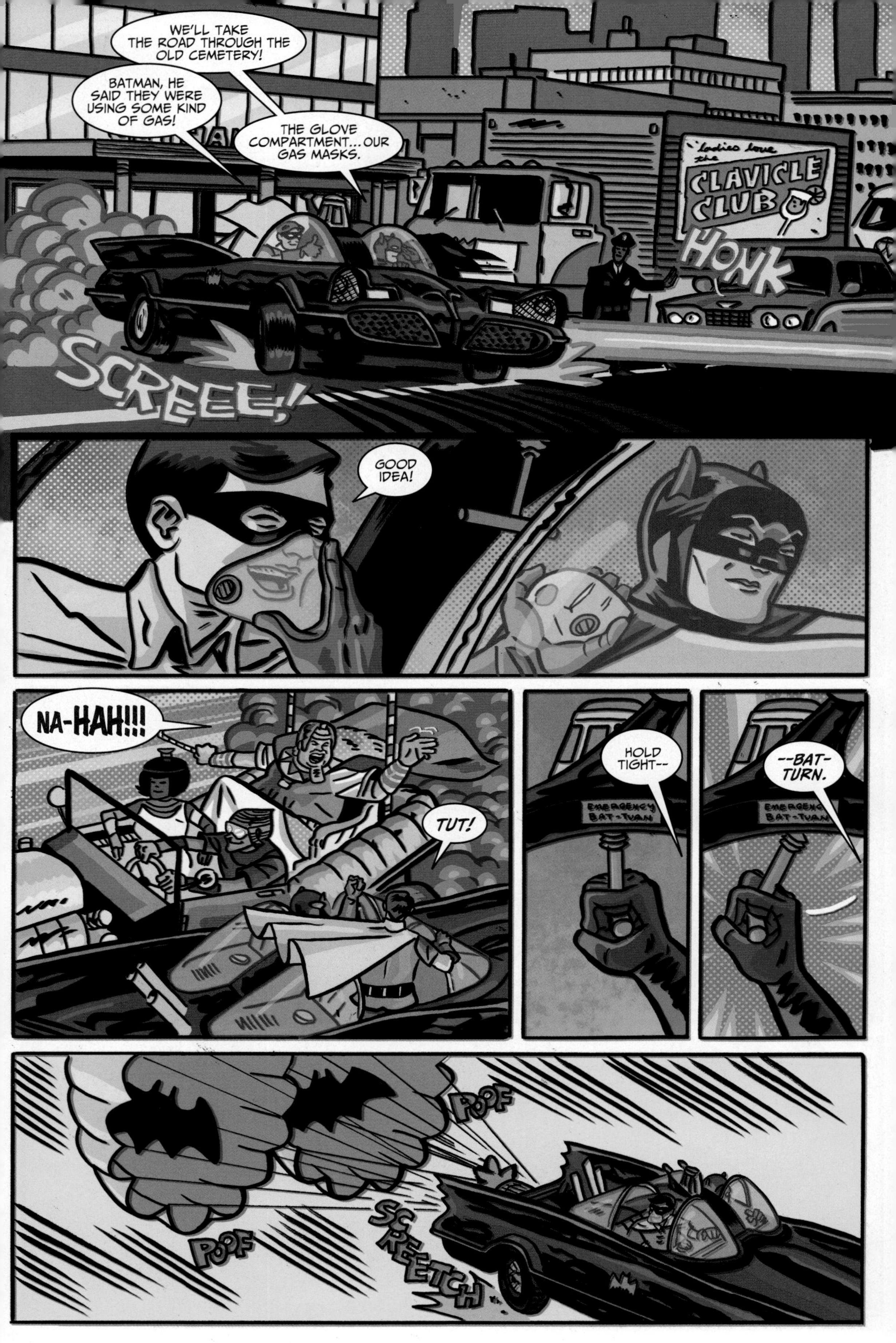
WE'LL TAKE THE ROAD THROUGH THE OLD CEMETERY!
BATMAN, HE SAID THEY WERE USING SOME KIND OF GAS!
THE GLOVE COMPARTMENT... OUR GAS MASKS.
ladies love the CLAVICLE CLUB
HONK
SCREEE!
GOOD IDEA!
NA-HAH!!!
TUT!
HOLD TIGHT--
EMERGENCY BAT-TURN
--BAT-TURN.
POOF
SCREETCH
POOF

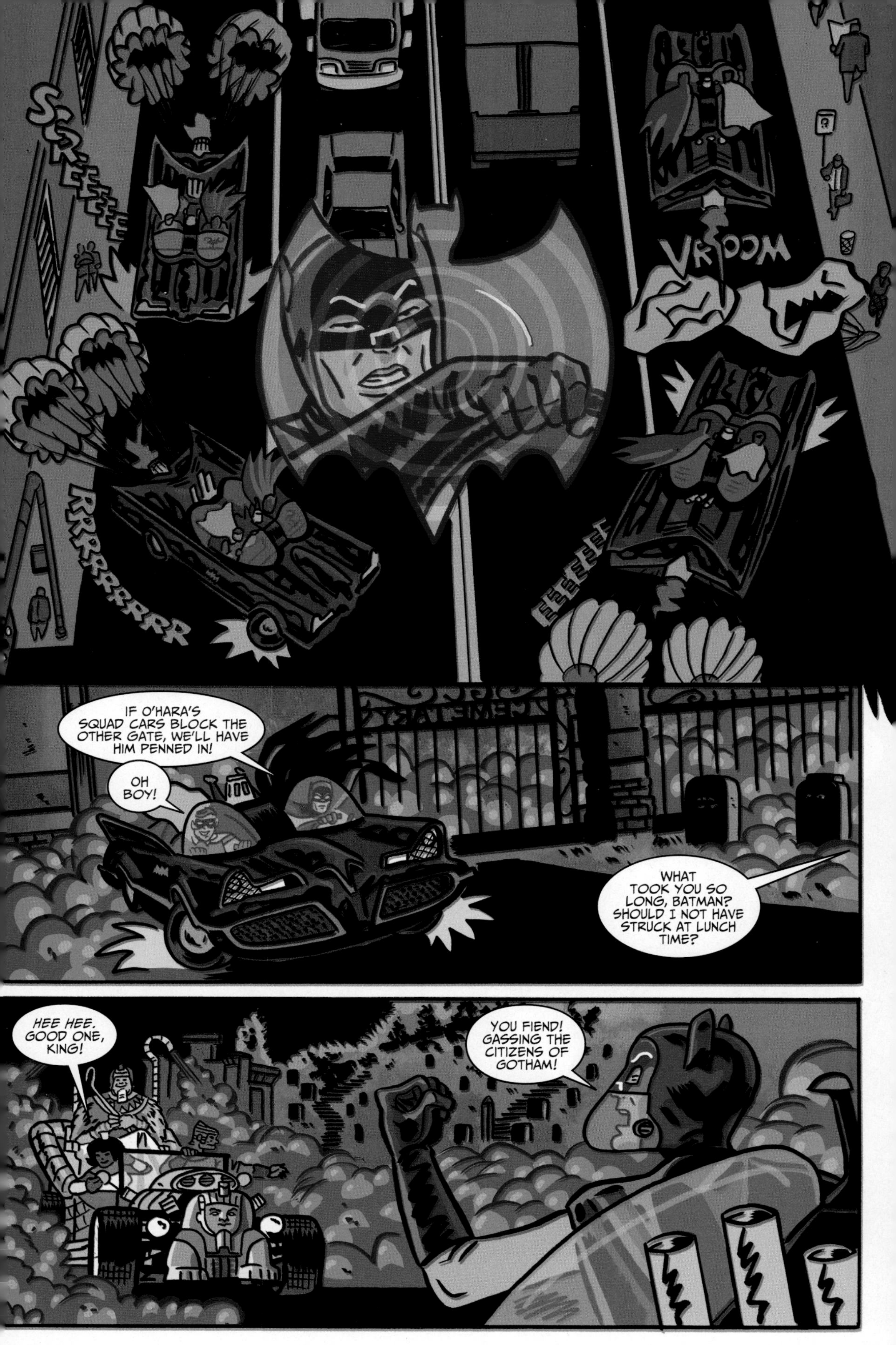
SCREEEEE
VROOM
IF O'HARA'S SQUAD CARS BLOCK THE OTHER GATE, WE'LL HAVE HIM PENNED IN!
OH BOY!
CEMETARY
WHAT TOOK YOU SO LONG, BATMAN? SHOULD I NOT HAVE STRUCK AT LUNCH TIME?
HEE HEE. GOOD ONE, KING!
YOU FIEND! GASSING THE CITIZENS OF GOTHAM!

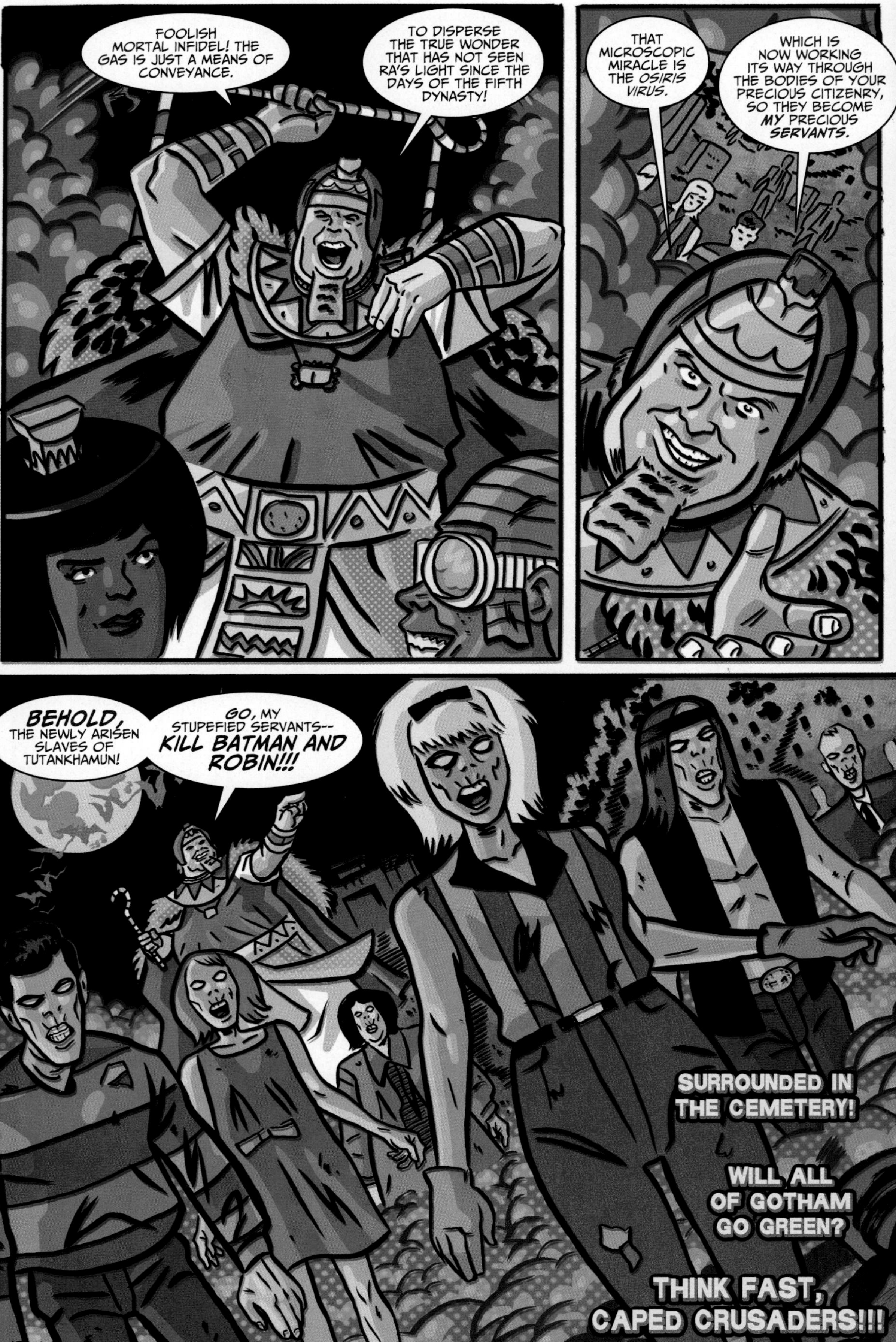
FOOLISH MORTAL INFIDEL! THE GAS IS JUST A MEANS OF CONVEYANCE.
TO DISPERSE THE TRUE WONDER THAT HAS NOT SEEN RA'S LIGHT SINCE THE DAYS OF THE FIFTH DYNASTY!
THAT MICROSCOPIC MIRACLE IS THE OSIRIS VIRUS.
WHICH IS NOW WORKING ITS WAY THROUGH THE BODIES OF YOUR PRECIOUS CITIZENRY, SO THEY BECOME MY PRECIOUS SERVANTS.
BEHOLD, THE NEWLY ARISEN SLAVES OF TUTANKHAMUN!
GO, MY STUPEFIED SERVANTS-- KILL BATMAN AND ROBIN!!!
SURROUNDED IN THE CEMETERY!
WILL ALL OF GOTHAM GO GREEN?
THINK FAST, CAPED CRUSADERS!!!

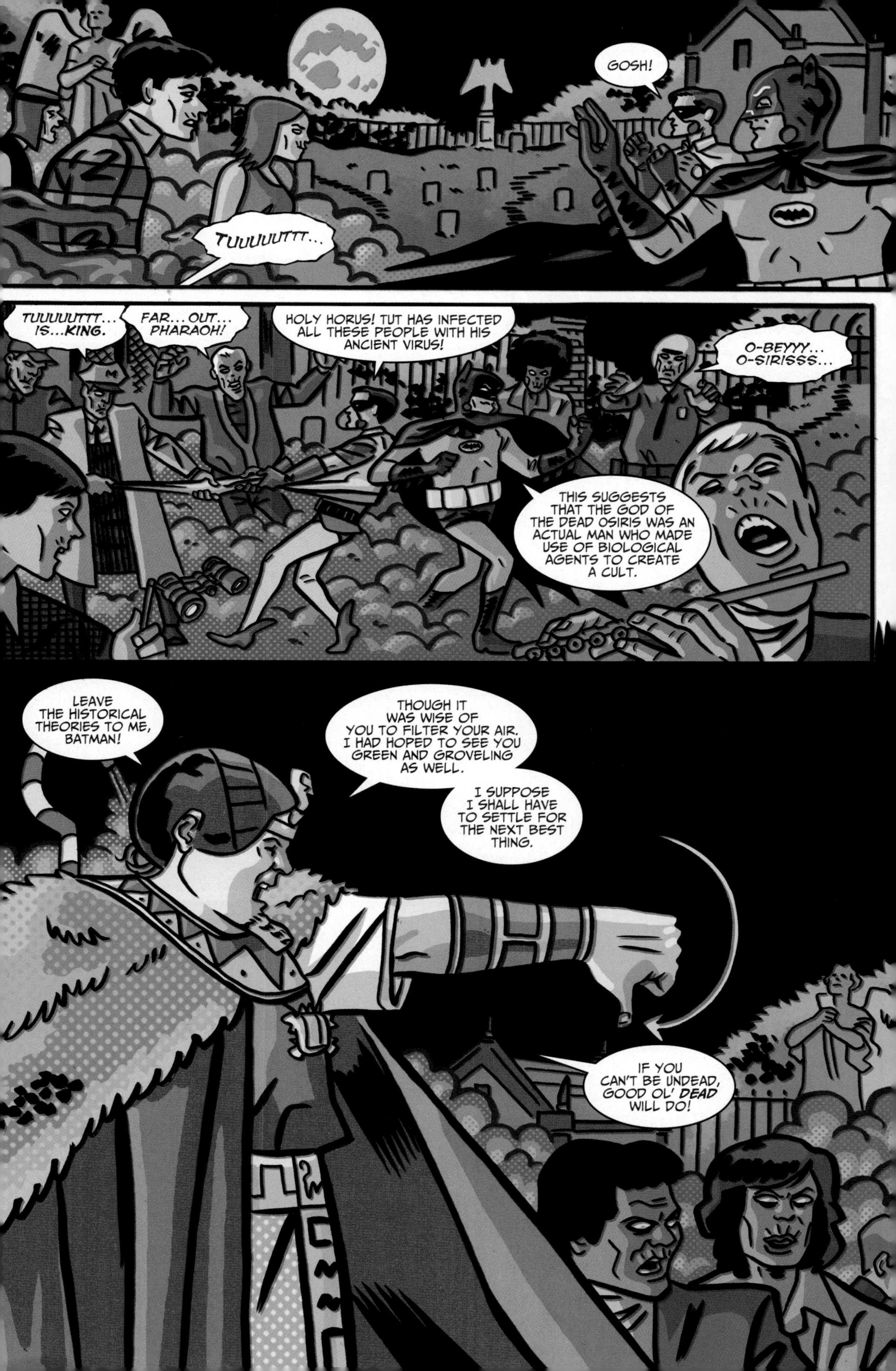
GOSH!
TUUUUUTTT...
TUUUUUTTT... IS...KING.
FAR...OUT... PHARAOH!
HOLY HORUS! TUT HAS INFECTED ALL THESE PEOPLE WITH HIS ANCIENT VIRUS!
O-BEYYY... O-SIRISSS...
THIS SUGGESTS THAT THE GOD OF THE DEAD OSIRIS WAS AN ACTUAL MAN WHO MADE USE OF BIOLOGICAL AGENTS TO CREATE A CULT.
LEAVE THE HISTORICAL THEORIES TO ME, BATMAN!
THOUGH IT WAS WISE OF YOU TO FILTER YOUR AIR. I HAD HOPED TO SEE YOU GREEN AND GROVELING AS WELL.
I SUPPOSE I SHALL HAVE TO SETTLE FOR THE NEXT BEST THING.
IF YOU CAN'T BE UNDEAD, GOOD OL' DEAD WILL DO!

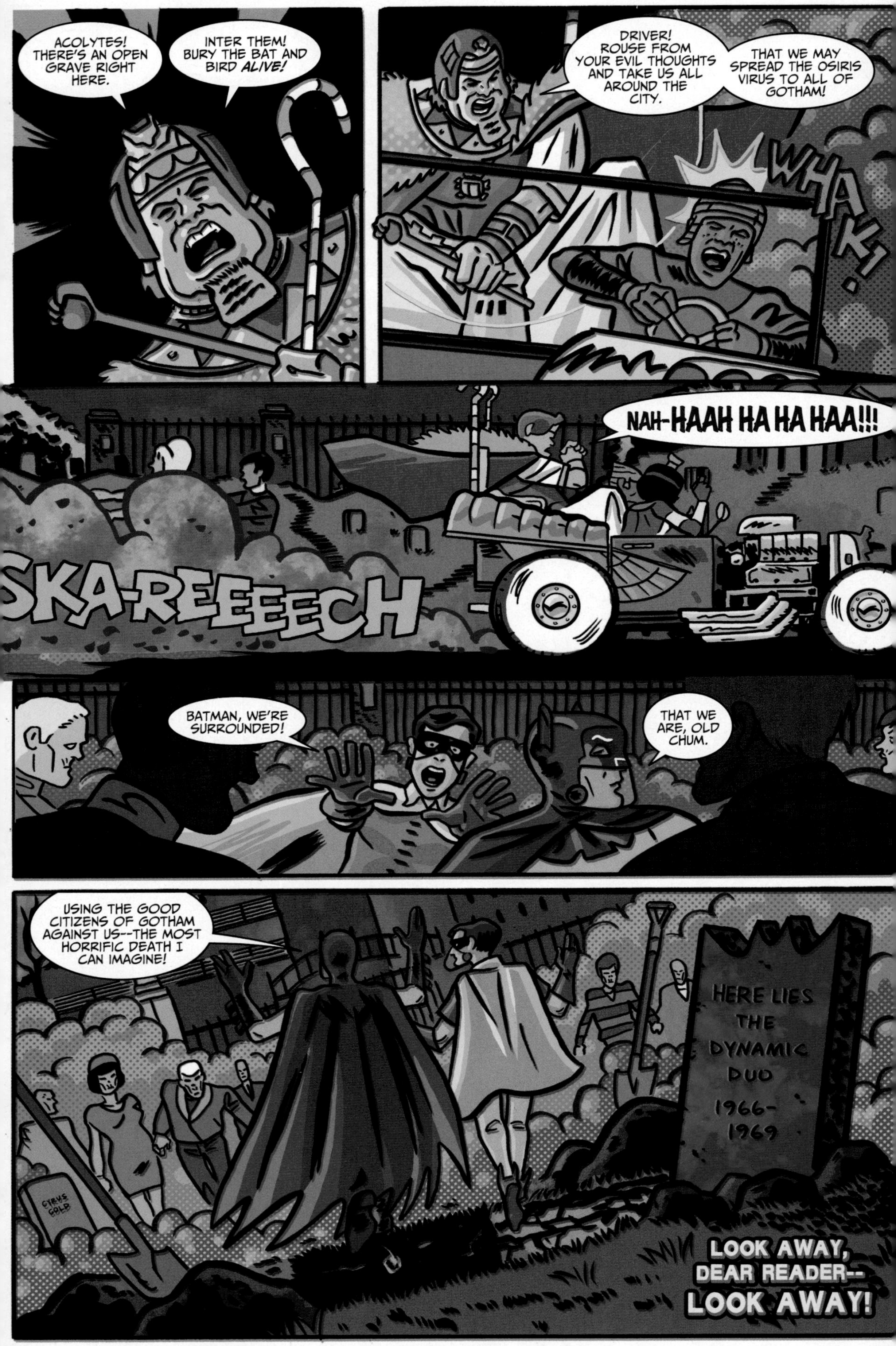
ACOLYTES! THERE'S AN OPEN GRAVE RIGHT HERE.
INTER THEM! BURY THE BAT AND BIRD *ALIVE!*
DRIVER! ROUSE FROM YOUR EVIL THOUGHTS AND TAKE US ALL AROUND THE CITY.
THAT WE MAY SPREAD THE OSIRIS VIRUS TO ALL OF GOTHAM!
WHAK!
NAH-HAAH HA HA HAA!!!
SKA-REEEECH
BATMAN, WE'RE SURROUNDED!
THAT WE ARE, OLD CHUM.
USING THE GOOD CITIZENS OF GOTHAM AGAINST US--THE MOST HORRIFIC DEATH I CAN IMAGINE!
CYRUS GOLD
HERE LIES THE DYNAMIC DUO 1966-1969
LOOK AWAY, DEAR READER-- LOOK AWAY!

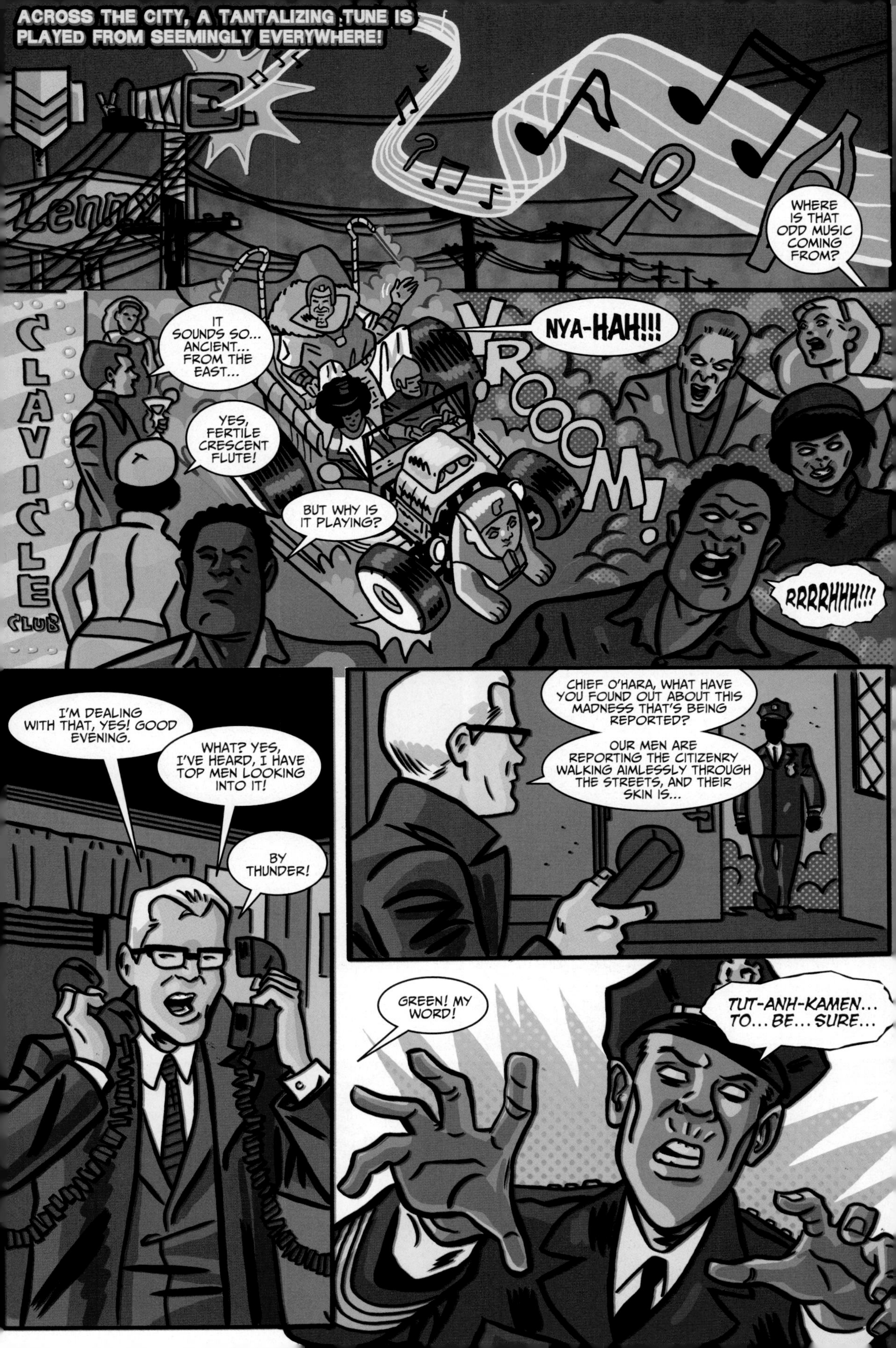
ACROSS THE CITY, A TANTALIZING TUNE IS PLAYED FROM SEEMINGLY EVERYWHERE!
Lenn
WHERE IS THAT ODD MUSIC COMING FROM?
CLAVICLE CLUB
IT SOUNDS SO... ANCIENT... FROM THE EAST...
YES, FERTILE CRESCENT FLUTE!
BUT WHY IS IT PLAYING?
VROOOM!
NYA-HAH!!!
RRRRHHH!!!
I'M DEALING WITH THAT, YES! GOOD EVENING.
WHAT? YES, I'VE HEARD, I HAVE TOP MEN LOOKING INTO IT!
BY THUNDER!
CHIEF O'HARA, WHAT HAVE YOU FOUND OUT ABOUT THIS MADNESS THAT'S BEING REPORTED?
OUR MEN ARE REPORTING THE CITIZENRY WALKING AIMLESSLY THROUGH THE STREETS, AND THEIR SKIN IS...
GREEN! MY WORD!
TUT-ANH-KAMEN... TO... BE... SURE...

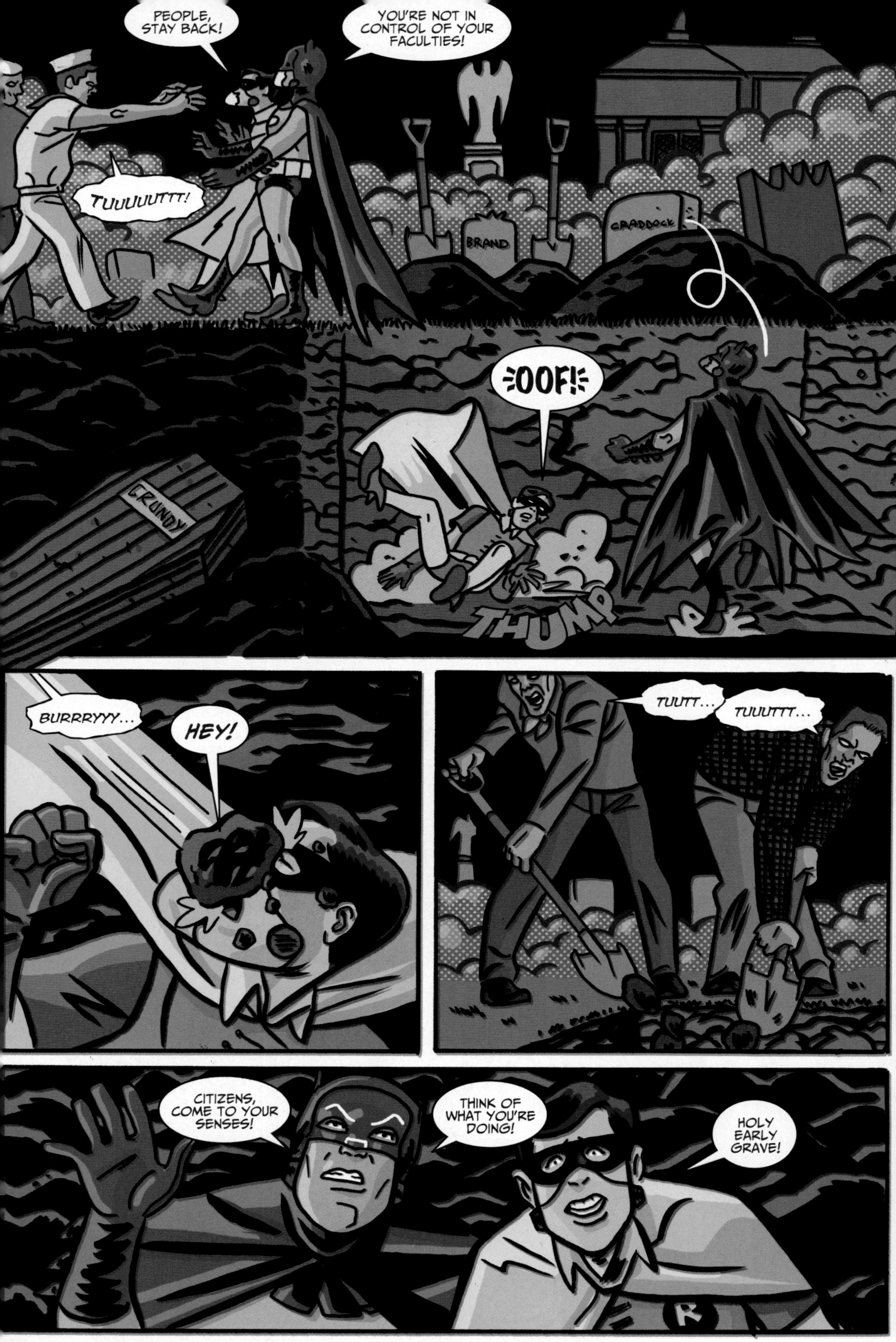

PEOPLE, STAY BACK!
YOU'RE NOT IN CONTROL OF YOUR FACULTIES!
TUUUUUTTT!
BRAND
CRADDOCK
GRUNDY
OOF!
THUMP
BURRRYYY...
HEY!
TUUTT...
TUUUTTT...
CITIZENS, COME TO YOUR SENSES!
THINK OF WHAT YOU'RE DOING!
HOLY EARLY GRAVE!

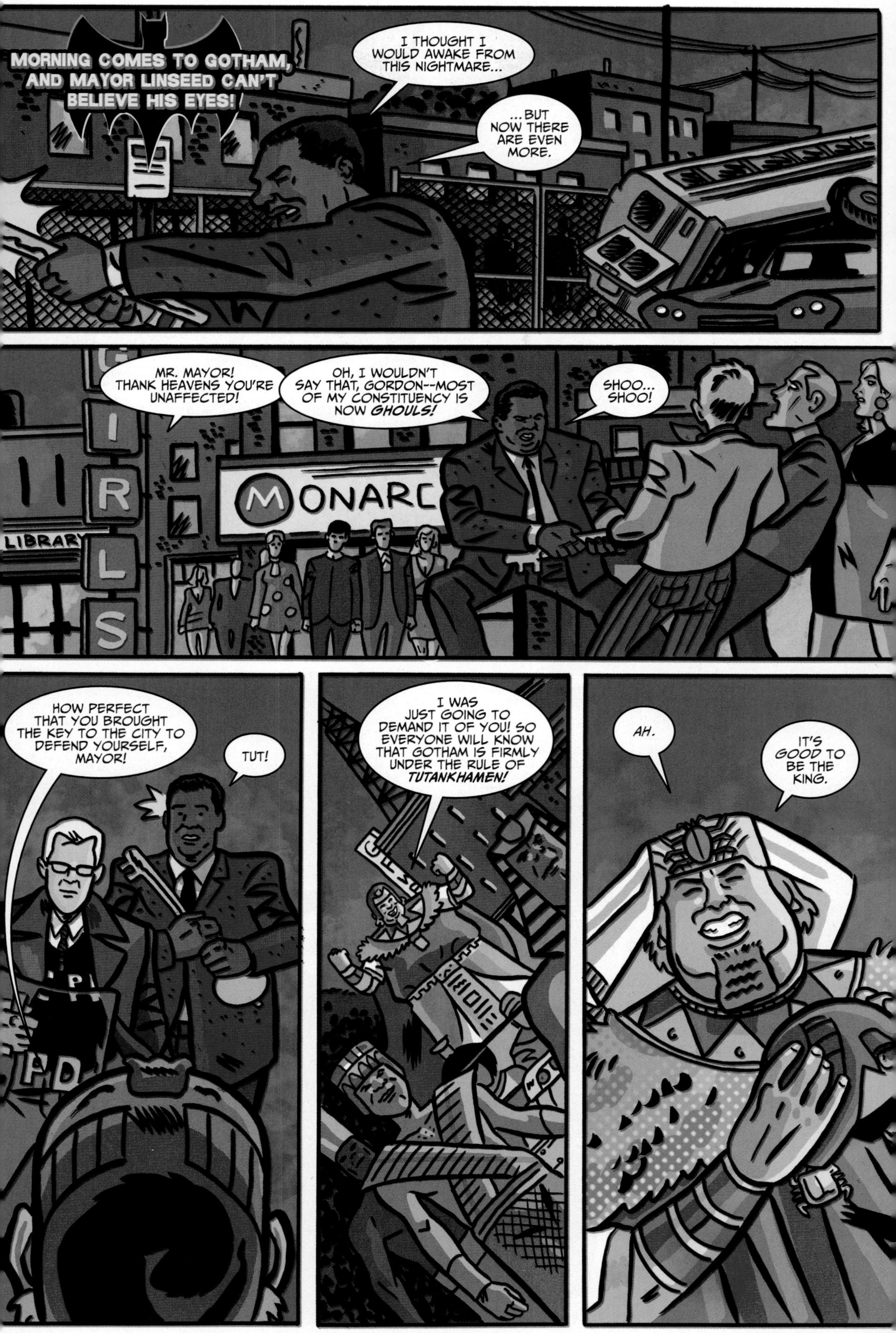
MORNING COMES TO GOTHAM, AND MAYOR LINSEED CAN'T BELIEVE HIS EYES!
I THOUGHT I WOULD AWAKE FROM THIS NIGHTMARE...
...BUT NOW THERE ARE EVEN MORE.
MR. MAYOR! THANK HEAVENS YOU'RE UNAFFECTED!
OH, I WOULDN'T SAY THAT, GORDON--MOST OF MY CONSTITUENCY IS NOW GHOULS!
SHOO... SHOO!
MONARC
LIBRARY
GIRLS
HOW PERFECT THAT YOU BROUGHT THE KEY TO THE CITY TO DEFEND YOURSELF, MAYOR!
TUT!
I WAS JUST GOING TO DEMAND IT OF YOU! SO EVERYONE WILL KNOW THAT GOTHAM IS FIRMLY UNDER THE RULE OF TUTANKHAMEN!
AH.
IT'S GOOD TO BE THE KING.

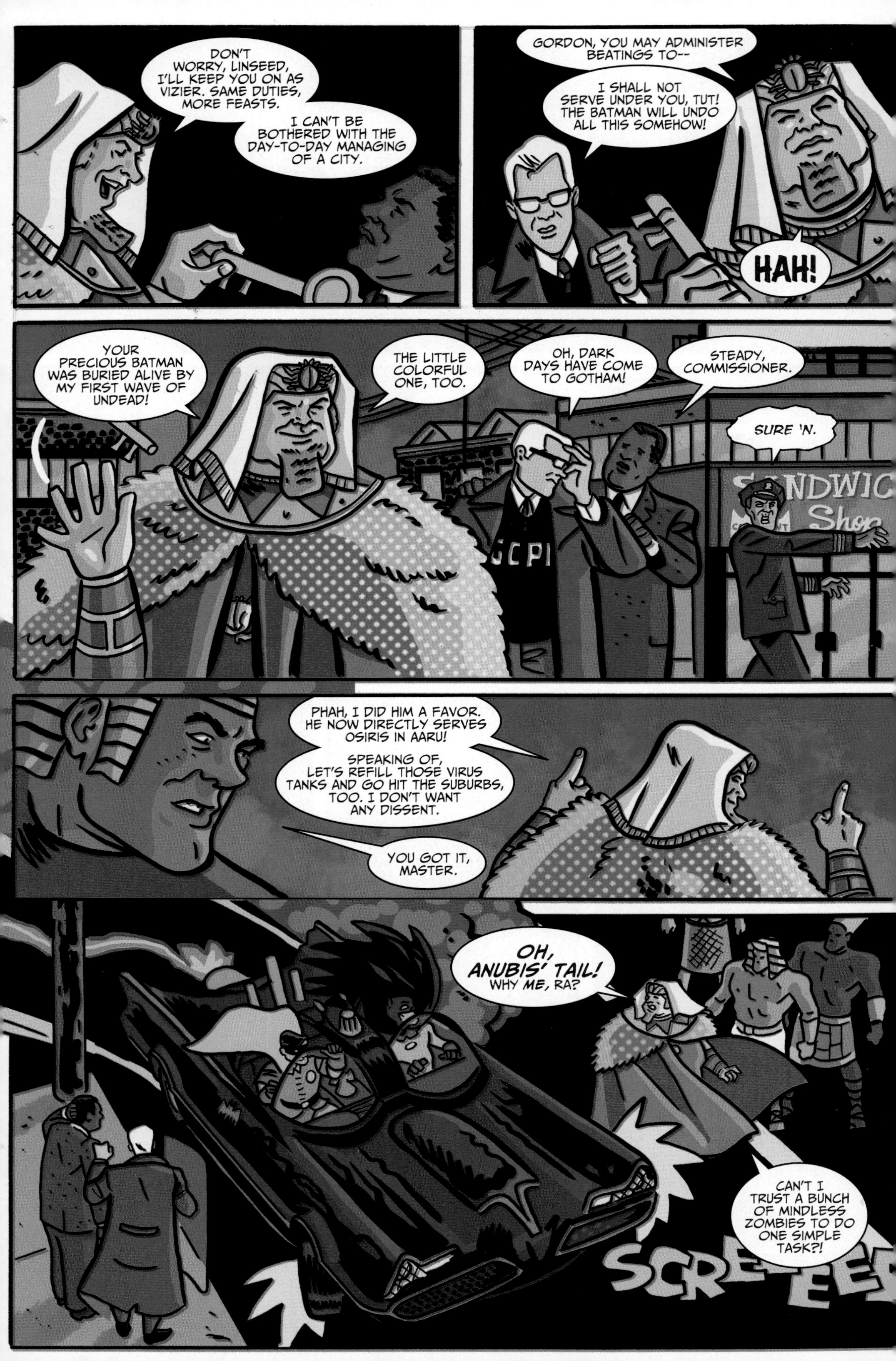
DON'T WORRY, LINSEED, I'LL KEEP YOU ON AS VIZIER. SAME DUTIES, MORE FEASTS.
I CAN'T BE BOTHERED WITH THE DAY-TO-DAY MANAGING OF A CITY.
GORDON, YOU MAY ADMINISTER BEATINGS TO--
I SHALL NOT SERVE UNDER YOU, TUT! THE BATMAN WILL UNDO ALL THIS SOMEHOW!
HAH!
YOUR PRECIOUS BATMAN WAS BURIED ALIVE BY MY FIRST WAVE OF UNDEAD!
THE LITTLE COLORFUL ONE, TOO.
OH, DARK DAYS HAVE COME TO GOTHAM!
STEADY, COMMISSIONER.
SURE 'N.
GCPD
PHAH, I DID HIM A FAVOR. HE NOW DIRECTLY SERVES OSIRIS IN AARU!
SPEAKING OF, LET'S REFILL THOSE VIRUS TANKS AND GO HIT THE SUBURBS, TOO. I DON'T WANT ANY DISSENT.
YOU GOT IT, MASTER.
OH, ANUBIS' TAIL! WHY ME, RA?
CAN'T I TRUST A BUNCH OF MINDLESS ZOMBIES TO DO ONE SIMPLE TASK?!
SCREEEEE

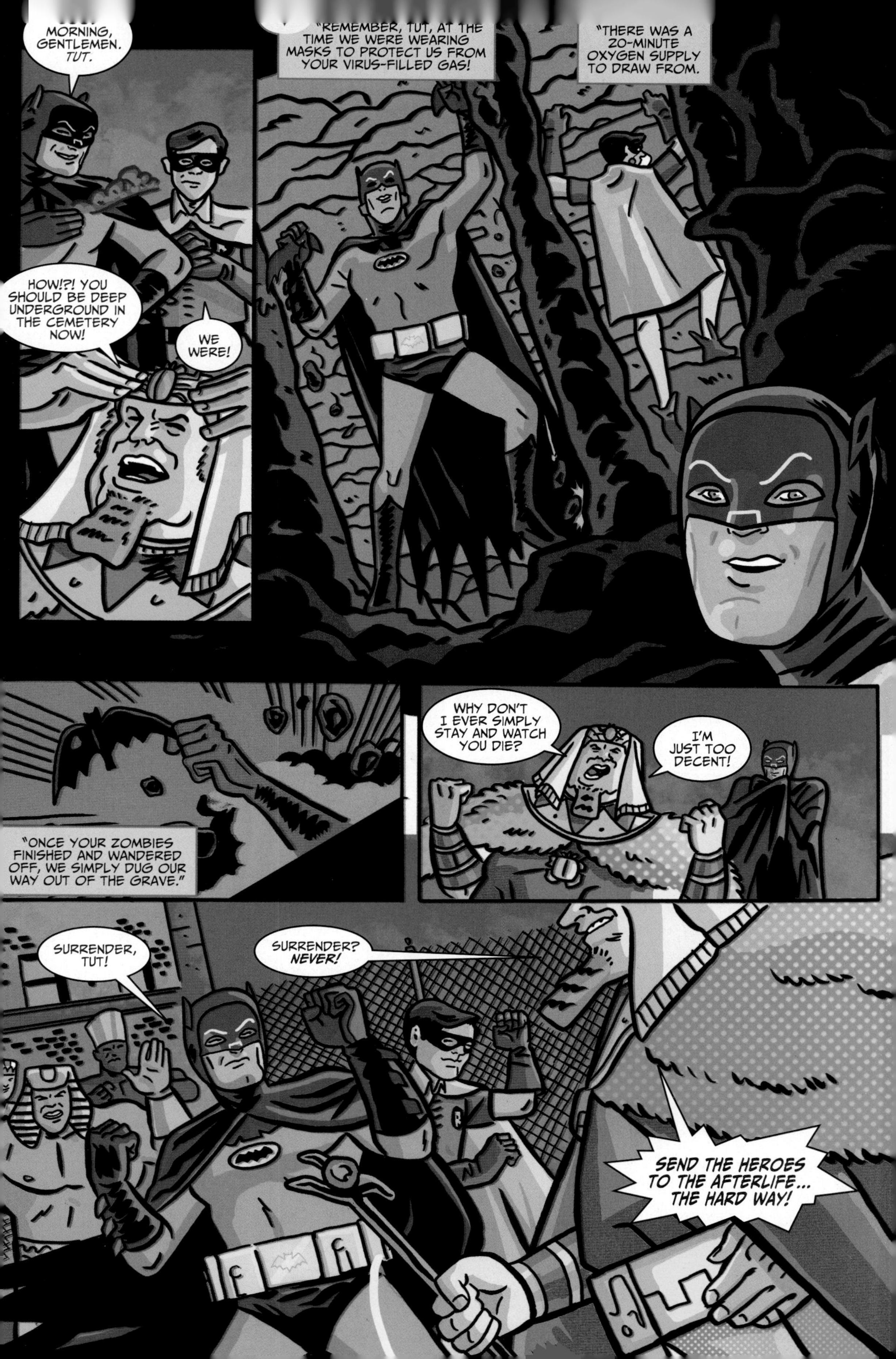
MORNING, GENTLEMEN. TUT.
"REMEMBER, TUT, AT THE TIME WE WERE WEARING MASKS TO PROTECT US FROM YOUR VIRUS-FILLED GAS!
"THERE WAS A 20-MINUTE OXYGEN SUPPLY TO DRAW FROM.
HOW!?! YOU SHOULD BE DEEP UNDERGROUND IN THE CEMETERY NOW!
WE WERE!
"ONCE YOUR ZOMBIES FINISHED AND WANDERED OFF, WE SIMPLY DUG OUR WAY OUT OF THE GRAVE."
WHY DON'T I EVER SIMPLY STAY AND WATCH YOU DIE?
I'M JUST TOO DECENT!
SURRENDER, TUT!
SURRENDER? NEVER!
SEND THE HEROES TO THE AFTERLIFE... THE HARD WAY!

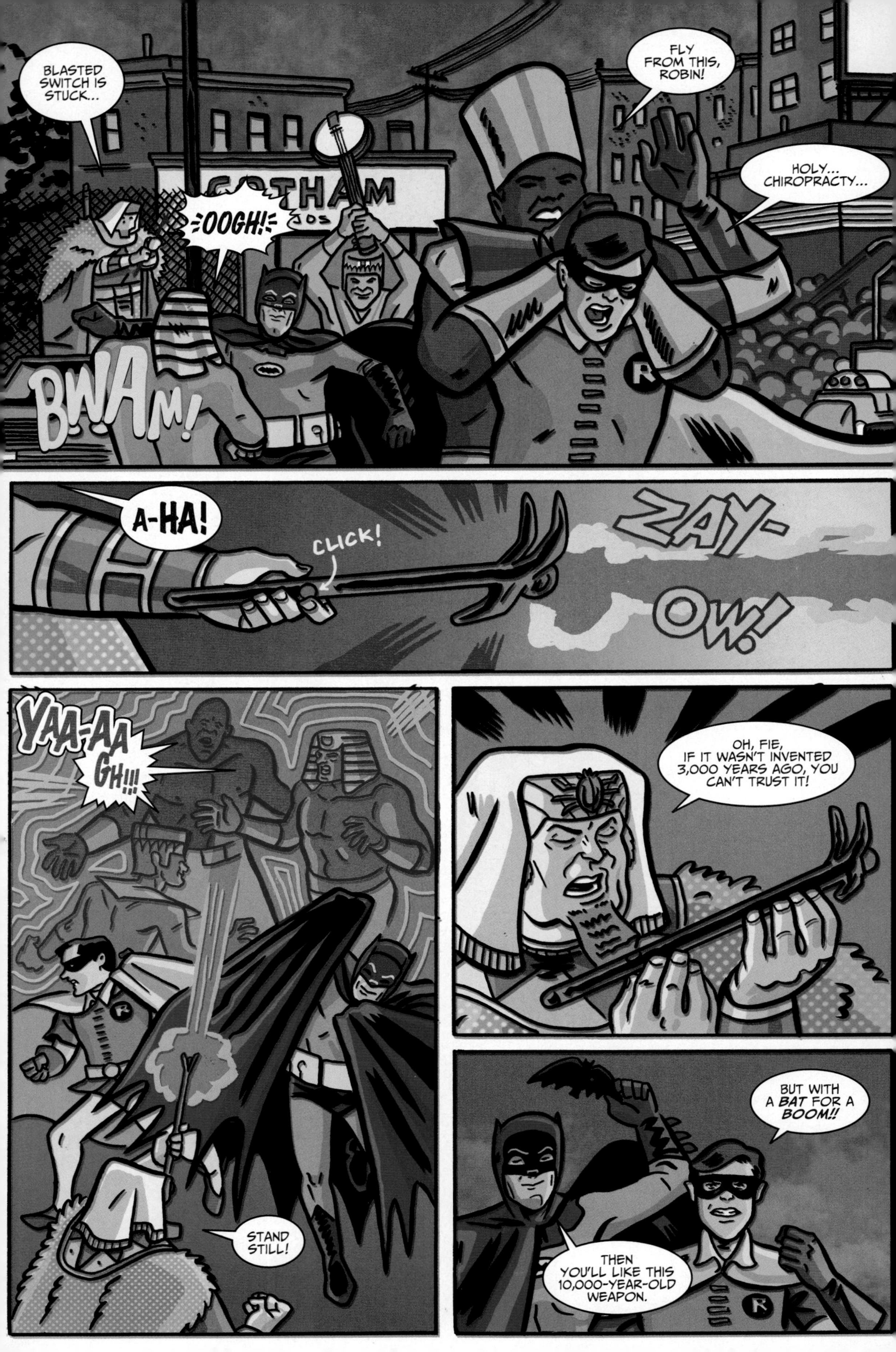
BLASTED SWITCH IS STUCK...
OOGH!
FLY FROM THIS, ROBIN!
HOLY... CHIROPRACTY...
BWAM!
A-HA!
CLICK!
ZAY-OW!
YAA-AAGH!!!
STAND STILL!
OH, FIE, IF IT WASN'T INVENTED 3,000 YEARS AGO, YOU CAN'T TRUST IT!
THEN YOU'LL LIKE THIS 10,000-YEAR-OLD WEAPON.
BUT WITH A *BAT* FOR A *BOOM!!*

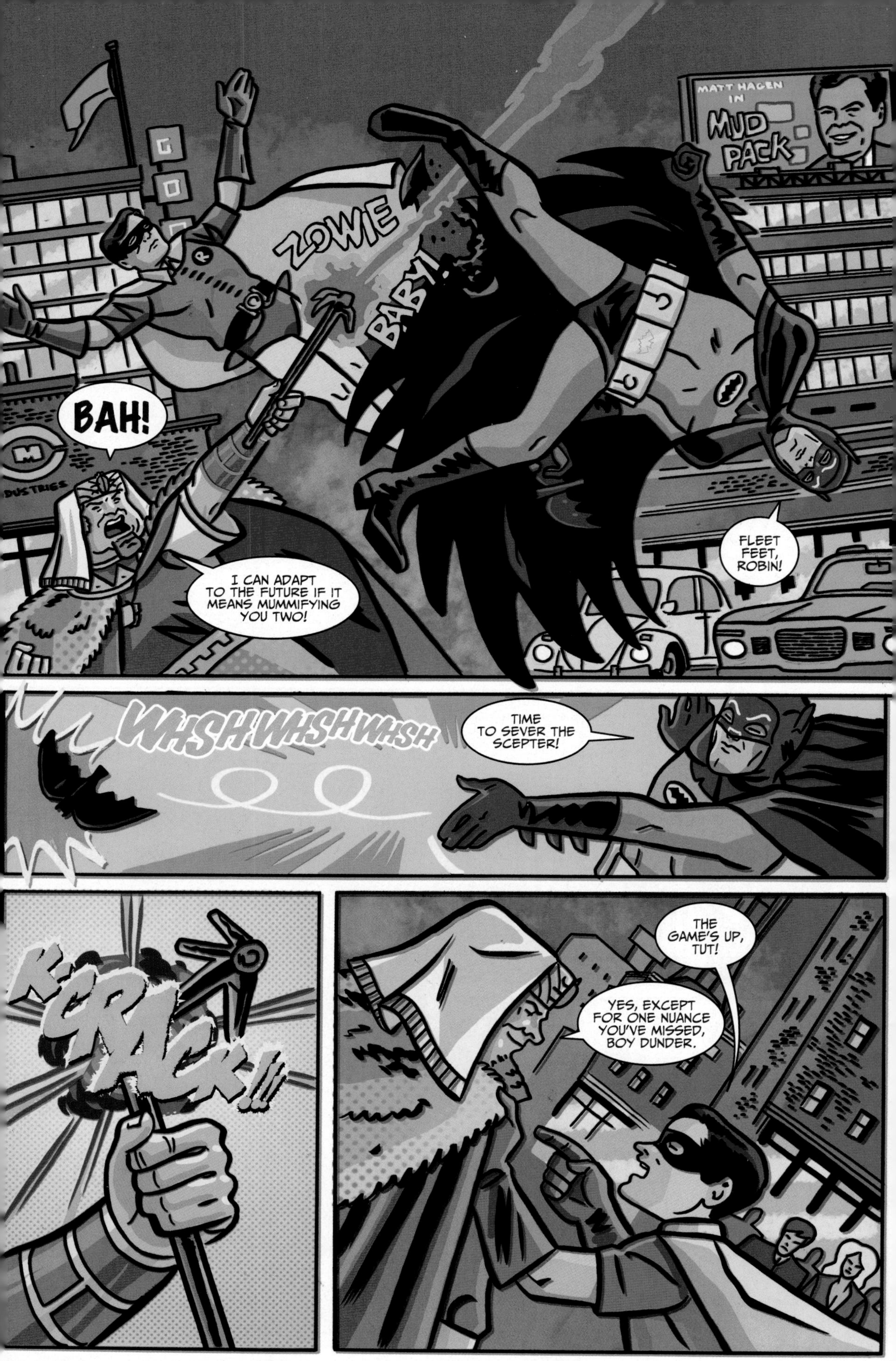
MATT HAGEN IN MUD PACK
ZOWIE BABY!
BAH!
I CAN ADAPT TO THE FUTURE IF IT MEANS MUMMIFYING YOU TWO!
FLEET FEET, ROBIN!
WHSH WHSH WHSH
TIME TO SEVER THE SCEPTER!
K-CRACK!!!
THE GAME'S UP, TUT!
YES, EXCEPT FOR ONE NUANCE YOU'VE MISSED, BOY DUNDER.

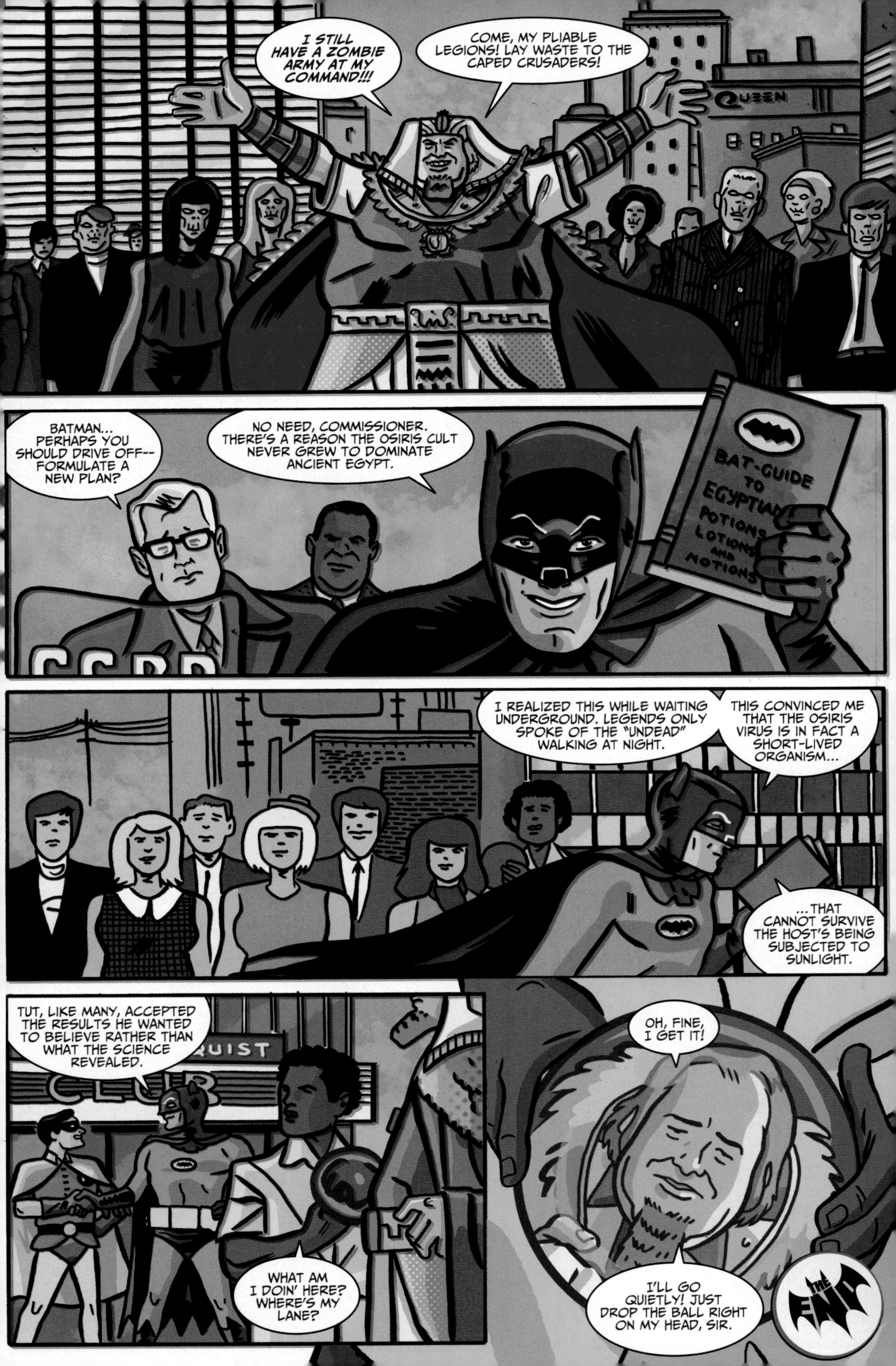
I STILL HAVE A ZOMBIE ARMY AT MY COMMAND!!!
COME, MY PLIABLE LEGIONS! LAY WASTE TO THE CAPED CRUSADERS!
QUEEN
BATMAN... PERHAPS YOU SHOULD DRIVE OFF-- FORMULATE A NEW PLAN?
NO NEED, COMMISSIONER. THERE'S A REASON THE OSIRIS CULT NEVER GREW TO DOMINATE ANCIENT EGYPT.
BAT-GUIDE TO EGYPTIAN POTIONS LOTIONS AND NOTIONS
I REALIZED THIS WHILE WAITING UNDERGROUND. LEGENDS ONLY SPOKE OF THE "UNDEAD" WALKING AT NIGHT.
THIS CONVINCED ME THAT THE OSIRIS VIRUS IS IN FACT A SHORT-LIVED ORGANISM...
...THAT CANNOT SURVIVE THE HOST'S BEING SUBJECTED TO SUNLIGHT.
TUT, LIKE MANY, ACCEPTED THE RESULTS HE WANTED TO BELIEVE RATHER THAN WHAT THE SCIENCE REVEALED.
QUIST
CLUB
WHAT AM I DOIN' HERE? WHERE'S MY LANE?
OH, FINE, I GET IT!
I'LL GO QUIETLY! JUST DROP THE BALL RIGHT ON MY HEAD, SIR.
THE END

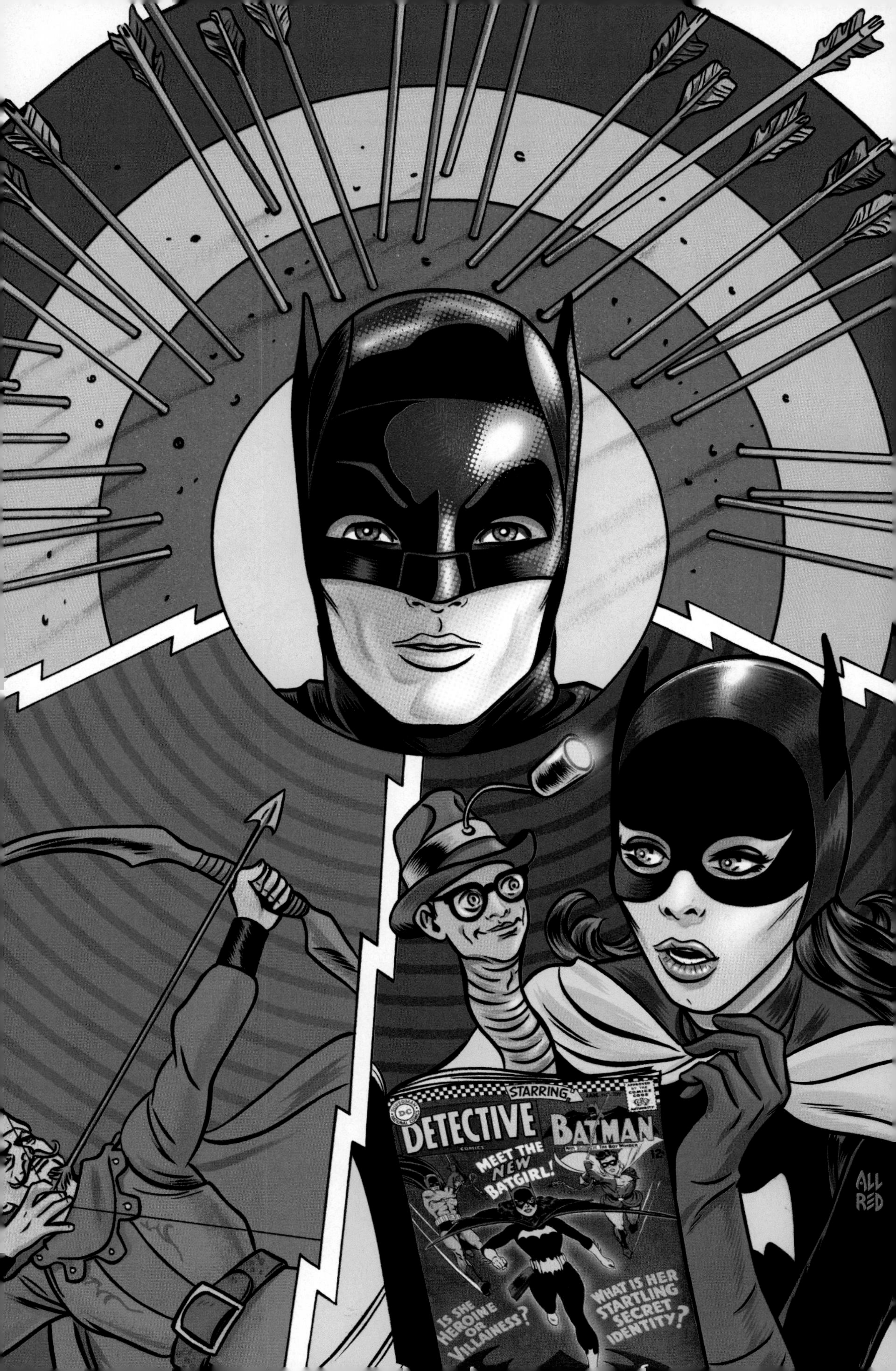
STARRING
DETECTIVE COMICS
BATMAN
MEET THE NEW BATGIRL!
IS SHE HEROINE OR VILLAINESS?
WHAT IS HER STARTLING SECRET IDENTITY?
ALL RED

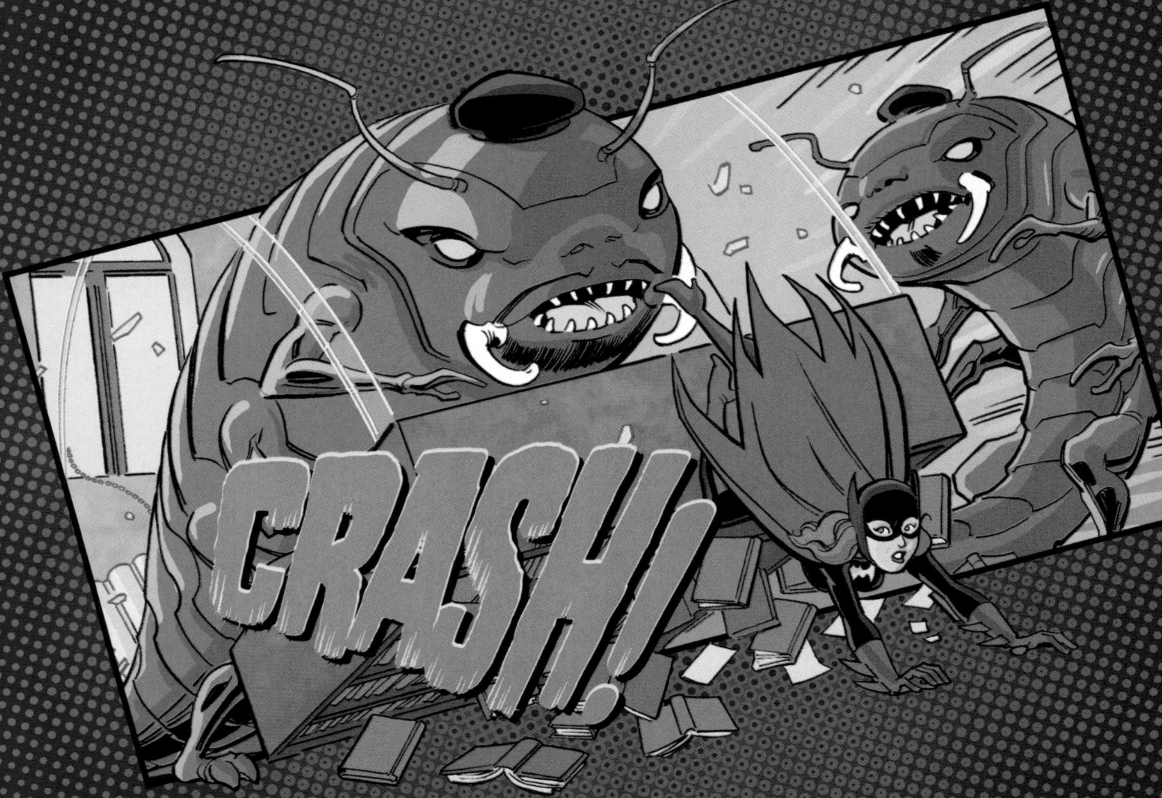
CRASH!

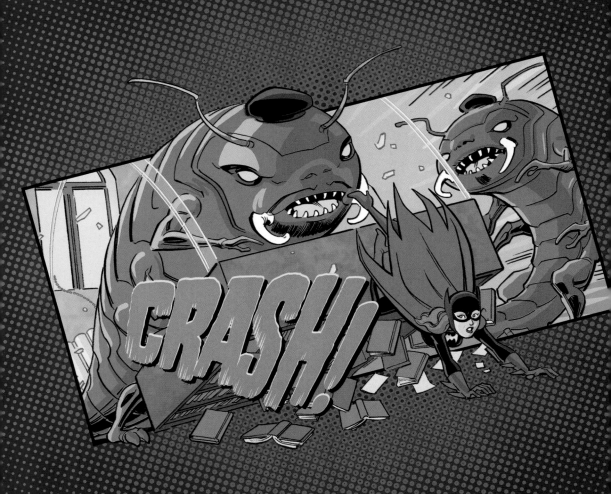

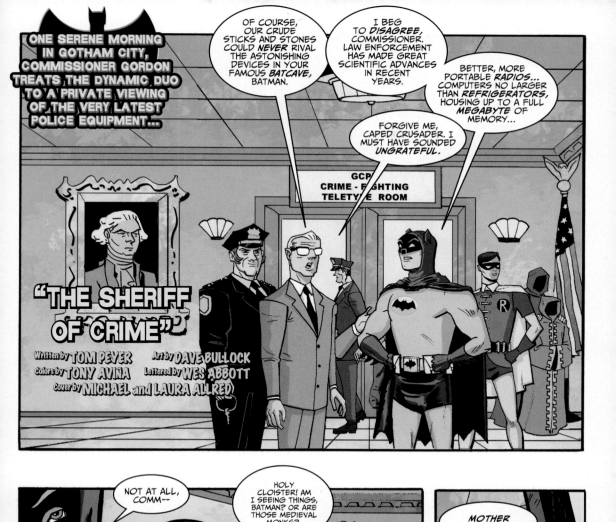

ONE SERENE MORNING IN GOTHAM CITY, COMMISSIONER GORDON TREATS THE DYNAMIC DUO TO A PRIVATE VIEWING OF THE VERY LATEST POLICE EQUIPMENT...

OF COURSE, OUR CRUDE STICKS AND STONES COULD *NEVER* RIVAL THE ASTONISHING DEVICES IN YOUR FAMOUS *BATCAVE*, BATMAN.

I BEG TO *DISAGREE*, COMMISSIONER. LAW ENFORCEMENT HAS MADE GREAT SCIENTIFIC ADVANCES IN RECENT YEARS.

BETTER, MORE PORTABLE *RADIOS*... COMPUTERS NO LARGER THAN *REFRIGERATORS*, HOUSING UP TO A FULL *MEGABYTE* OF MEMORY...

FORGIVE ME, CAPED CRUSADER. I MUST HAVE SOUNDED *UNGRATEFUL*.

GCPD CRIME-FIGHTING TELETYPE ROOM

"THE SHERIFF OF CRIME"

Written by TOM PEYER   Art by DAVE BULLOCK
Colors by TONY AVINA   Lettered by WES ABBOTT
Cover by MICHAEL and LAURA ALLRED

NOT AT ALL, COMM--

HOLY CLOISTER! AM I SEEING THINGS, BATMAN? OR ARE THOSE MEDIEVAL MONKS?

CLOSE, ROBIN. THEIR DISTINCTIVE ROBES PLACE THEM IN THE CATHAR SECT, WHICH HAD ITS HEYDAY IN 13TH CENTURY FRANCE.

HOW LUCKY WE ARE TO LIVE IN A CITY THAT PROVIDES SAFE HARBOR FOR *ALL* FAITHS.

GREAT SLITHERING SNAKES!

MOTHER McGILLICUTTY!

O'HARA! WHAT *IS* IT? WHAT'S *WRONG*?

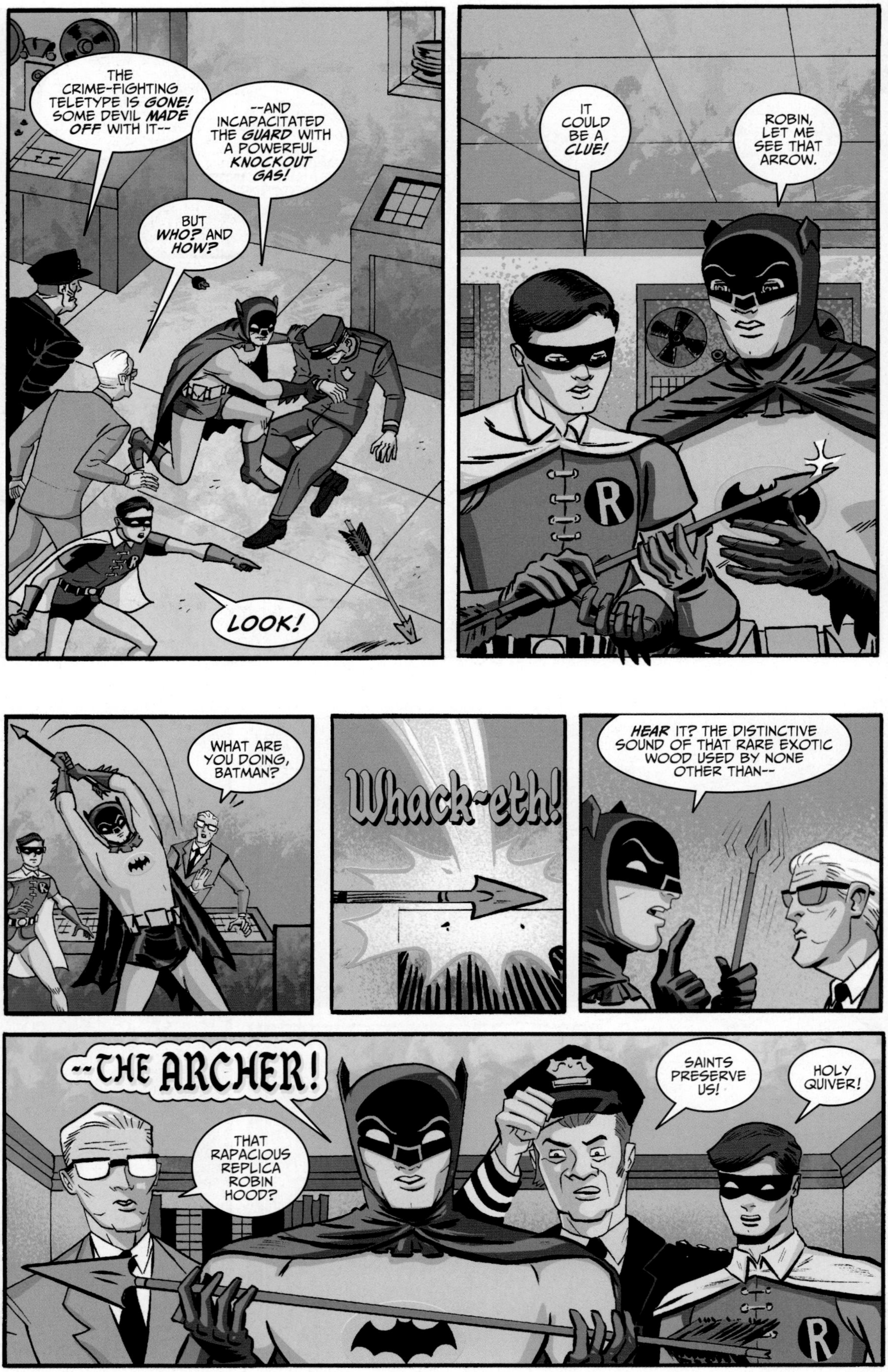
THE CRIME-FIGHTING TELETYPE IS GONE! SOME DEVIL MADE OFF WITH IT--
--AND INCAPACITATED THE GUARD WITH A POWERFUL KNOCKOUT GAS!
BUT WHO? AND HOW?
LOOK!
IT COULD BE A CLUE!
ROBIN, LET ME SEE THAT ARROW.
WHAT ARE YOU DOING, BATMAN?
Whack-eth!
HEAR IT? THE DISTINCTIVE SOUND OF THAT RARE EXOTIC WOOD USED BY NONE OTHER THAN--
--THE ARCHER!
THAT RAPACIOUS REPLICA ROBIN HOOD?
SAINTS PRESERVE US!
HOLY QUIVER!

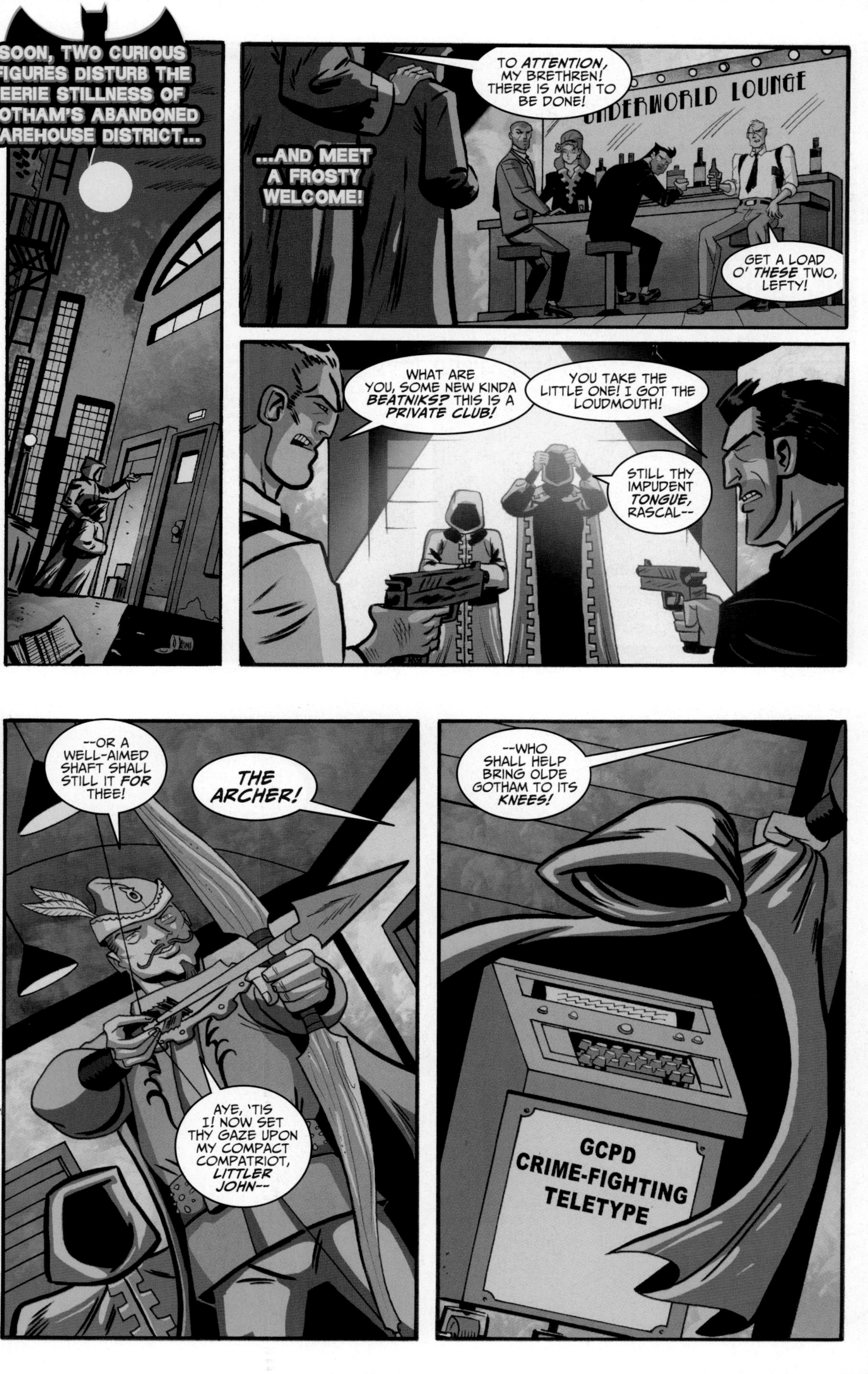
SOON, TWO CURIOUS FIGURES DISTURB THE EERIE STILLNESS OF GOTHAM'S ABANDONED WAREHOUSE DISTRICT...
TO ATTENTION, MY BRETHREN! THERE IS MUCH TO BE DONE!
...AND MEET A FROSTY WELCOME!
UNDERWORLD LOUNGE
GET A LOAD O' THESE TWO, LEFTY!
WHAT ARE YOU, SOME NEW KINDA BEATNIKS? THIS IS A PRIVATE CLUB!
YOU TAKE THE LITTLE ONE! I GOT THE LOUDMOUTH!
STILL THY IMPUDENT TONGUE, RASCAL--
--OR A WELL-AIMED SHAFT SHALL STILL IT FOR THEE!
THE ARCHER!
AYE, 'TIS I! NOW SET THY GAZE UPON MY COMPACT COMPATRIOT, LITTLER JOHN--
--WHO SHALL HELP BRING OLDE GOTHAM TO ITS KNEES!
GCPD CRIME-FIGHTING TELETYPE

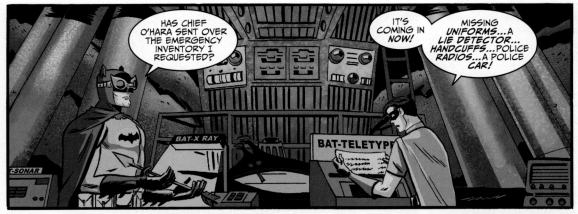

HAS CHIEF O'HARA SENT OVER THE EMERGENCY INVENTORY I REQUESTED?

IT'S COMING IN NOW!

MISSING UNIFORMS...A LIE DETECTOR... HANDCUFFS...POLICE RADIOS...A POLICE CAR!

BAT-X RAY

BAT-TELETYPE

T-SONAR

HOLY SCOTLAND YARD! IT'S ENOUGH LOOT TO START A PRECINCT!

BUT WHY? ARCHER PRESENTS HIMSELF AS A REBEL WHO TAKES FROM THE RICH AND GIVES TO THE POOR.

WOULDN'T THESE TRAPPINGS OF AUTHORITY UNDERMINE THE ILLUSION?

MAYBE HE HAD TO CHANGE THE ILLUSION! LAST TIME, HE STOLE FROM RICH AND POOR! WHO'D EVER TRUST HIM AGAIN?

EXCELLENT, ROBIN! SO IF WE SUBTRACT HIS OLD METHOD OF OPERATION, WHAT'S LEFT?

THAT'S A STUMPER, BATMAN!

FILL IN THE BLANK! TAKE FROM THE POLICE AND GIVE...TO...THE...

OH, NO!

TAKE FROM THE POLICE--AND GIVE TO THE CROOKS!

I FEAR YOU HIT THE BULLS-EYE, BOY WONDER! AND IF EVILDOERS CONTROL THE VERY LATEST IN CRIME-FIGHTING EQUIPMENT--

--IT COULD SPELL THE END OF LAW AND ORDER IN GOTHAM CITY!

A FORECAST OF CHAOS FROM THE CAPED CRUSADER--

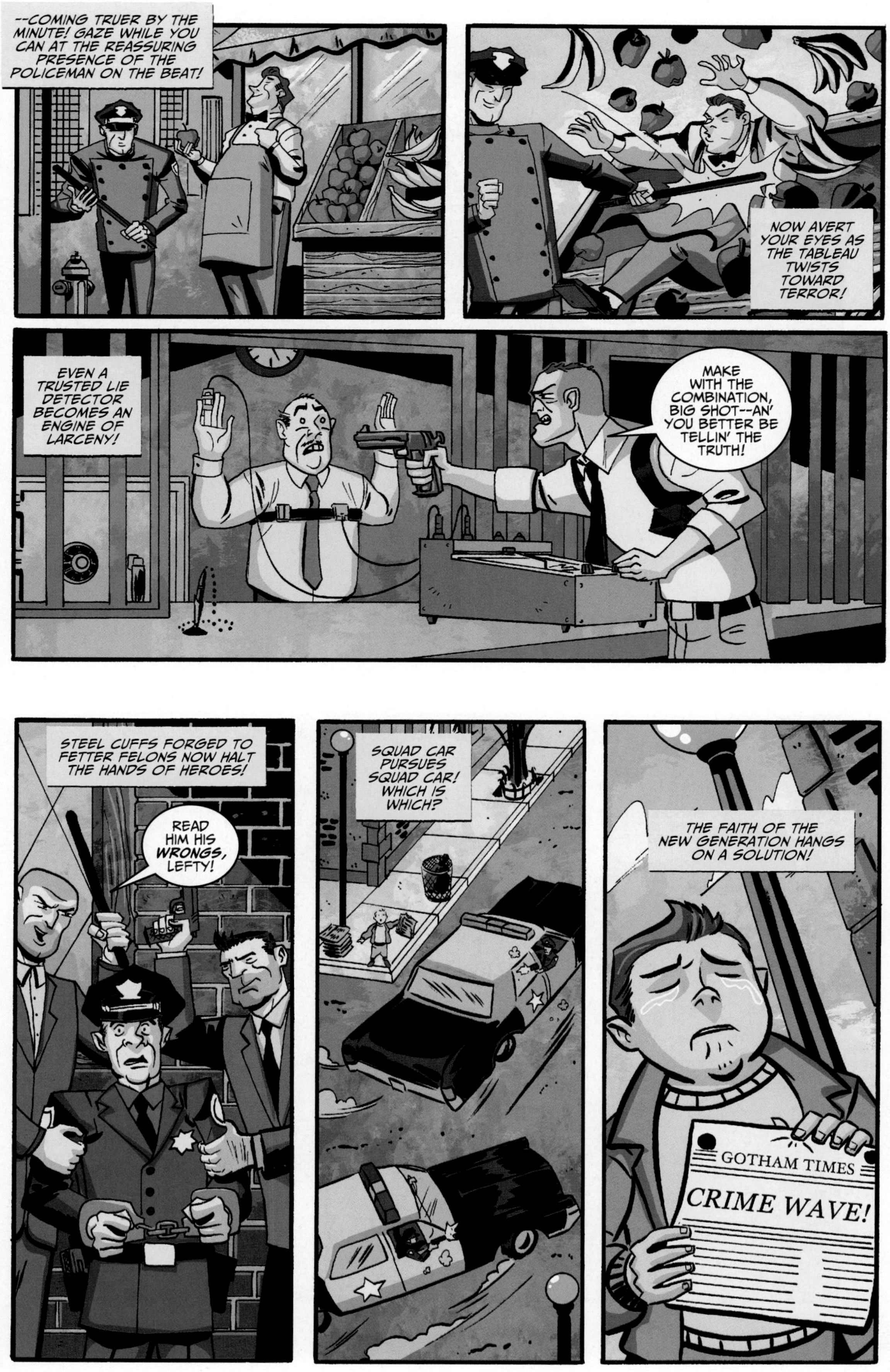
--COMING TRUER BY THE MINUTE! GAZE WHILE YOU CAN AT THE REASSURING PRESENCE OF THE POLICEMAN ON THE BEAT!
NOW AVERT YOUR EYES AS THE TABLEAU TWISTS TOWARD TERROR!
EVEN A TRUSTED LIE DETECTOR BECOMES AN ENGINE OF LARCENY!
MAKE WITH THE COMBINATION, BIG SHOT--AN' YOU BETTER BE TELLIN' THE TRUTH!
STEEL CUFFS FORGED TO FETTER FELONS NOW HALT THE HANDS OF HEROES!
READ HIM HIS WRONGS, LEFTY!
SQUAD CAR PURSUES SQUAD CAR! WHICH IS WHICH?
THE FAITH OF THE NEW GENERATION HANGS ON A SOLUTION!
GOTHAM TIMES
CRIME WAVE!

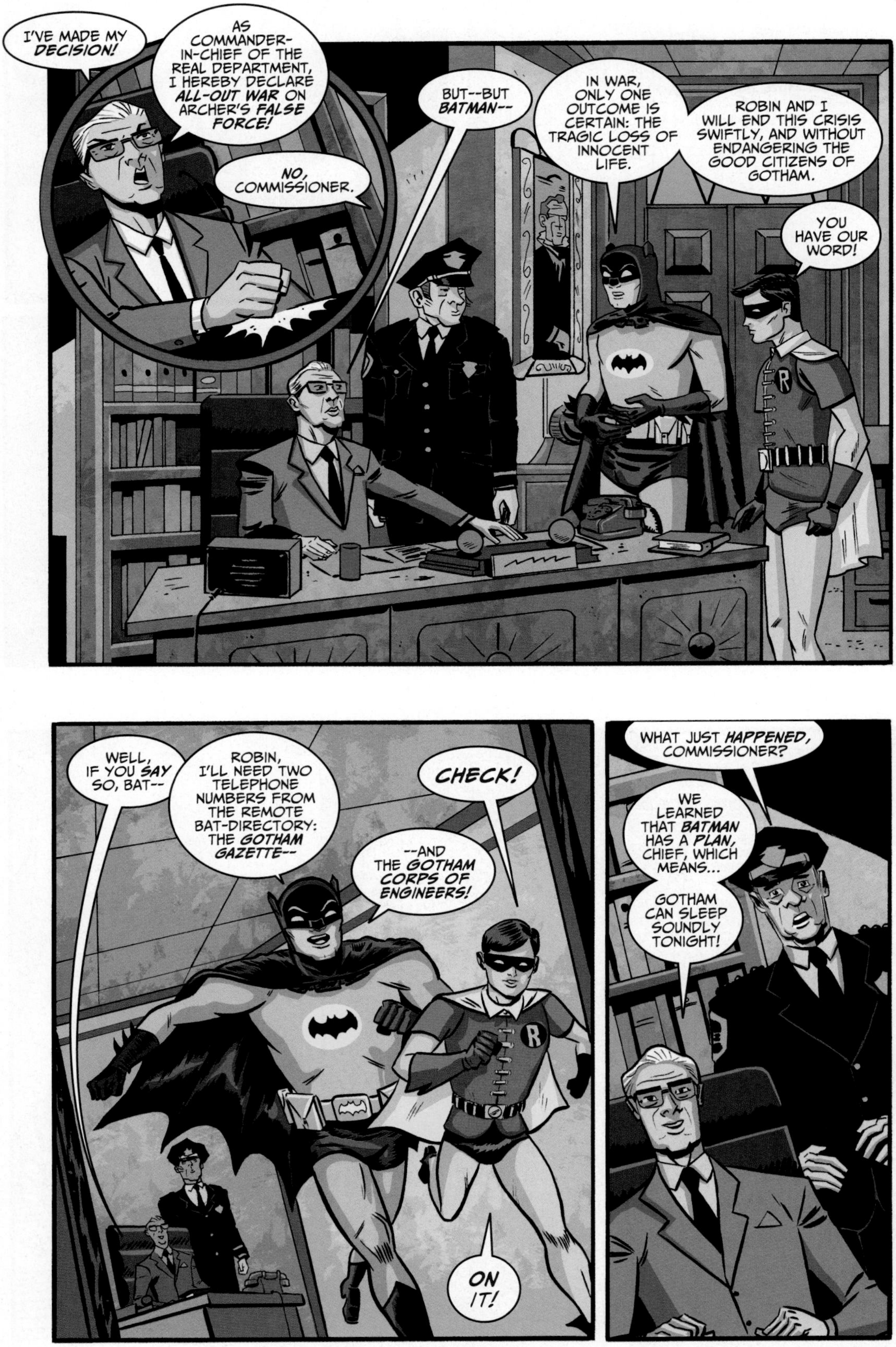
I'VE MADE MY DECISION!
AS COMMANDER-IN-CHIEF OF THE REAL DEPARTMENT, I HEREBY DECLARE ALL-OUT WAR ON ARCHER'S FALSE FORCE!
NO, COMMISSIONER.
BUT--BUT BATMAN--
IN WAR, ONLY ONE OUTCOME IS CERTAIN: THE TRAGIC LOSS OF INNOCENT LIFE.
ROBIN AND I WILL END THIS CRISIS SWIFTLY, AND WITHOUT ENDANGERING THE GOOD CITIZENS OF GOTHAM.
YOU HAVE OUR WORD!
WELL, IF YOU SAY SO, BAT--
ROBIN, I'LL NEED TWO TELEPHONE NUMBERS FROM THE REMOTE BAT-DIRECTORY: THE GOTHAM GAZETTE--
CHECK!
--AND THE GOTHAM CORPS OF ENGINEERS!
ON IT!
WHAT JUST HAPPENED, COMMISSIONER?
WE LEARNED THAT BATMAN HAS A PLAN, CHIEF, WHICH MEANS...
GOTHAM CAN SLEEP SOUNDLY TONIGHT!

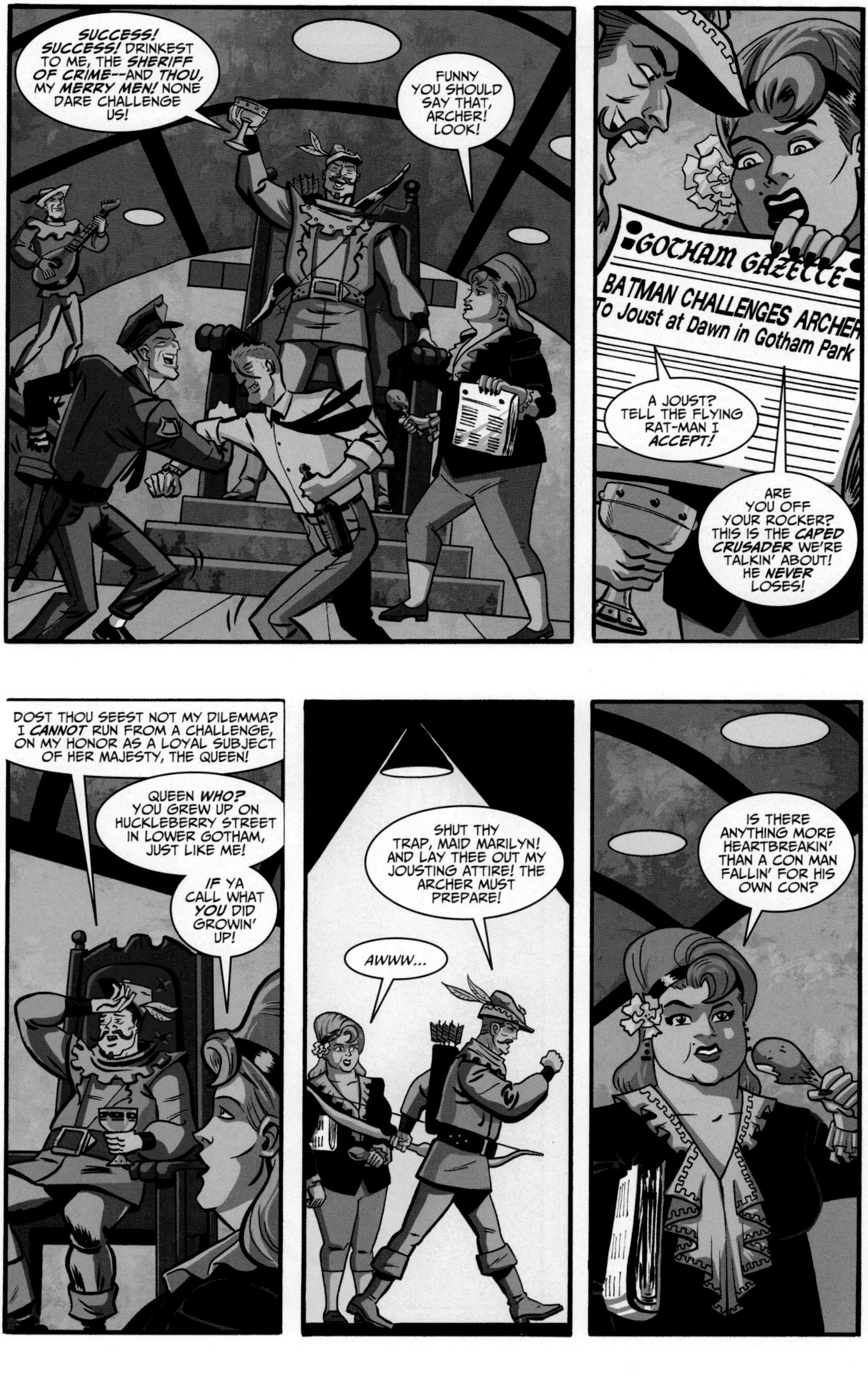
SUCCESS! SUCCESS! DRINKEST TO ME, THE SHERIFF OF CRIME--AND THOU, MY MERRY MEN! NONE DARE CHALLENGE US!
FUNNY YOU SHOULD SAY THAT, ARCHER! LOOK!
GOTHAM GAZETTE
BATMAN CHALLENGES ARCHER
To Joust at Dawn in Gotham Park
A JOUST? TELL THE FLYING RAT-MAN I ACCEPT!
ARE YOU OFF YOUR ROCKER? THIS IS THE CAPED CRUSADER WE'RE TALKIN' ABOUT! HE NEVER LOSES!
DOST THOU SEEST NOT MY DILEMMA? I CANNOT RUN FROM A CHALLENGE, ON MY HONOR AS A LOYAL SUBJECT OF HER MAJESTY, THE QUEEN!
QUEEN WHO? YOU GREW UP ON HUCKLEBERRY STREET IN LOWER GOTHAM, JUST LIKE ME!
IF YA CALL WHAT YOU DID GROWIN' UP!
SHUT THY TRAP, MAID MARILYN! AND LAY THEE OUT MY JOUSTING ATTIRE! THE ARCHER MUST PREPARE!
AWWW...
IS THERE ANYTHING MORE HEARTBREAKIN' THAN A CON MAN FALLIN' FOR HIS OWN CON?

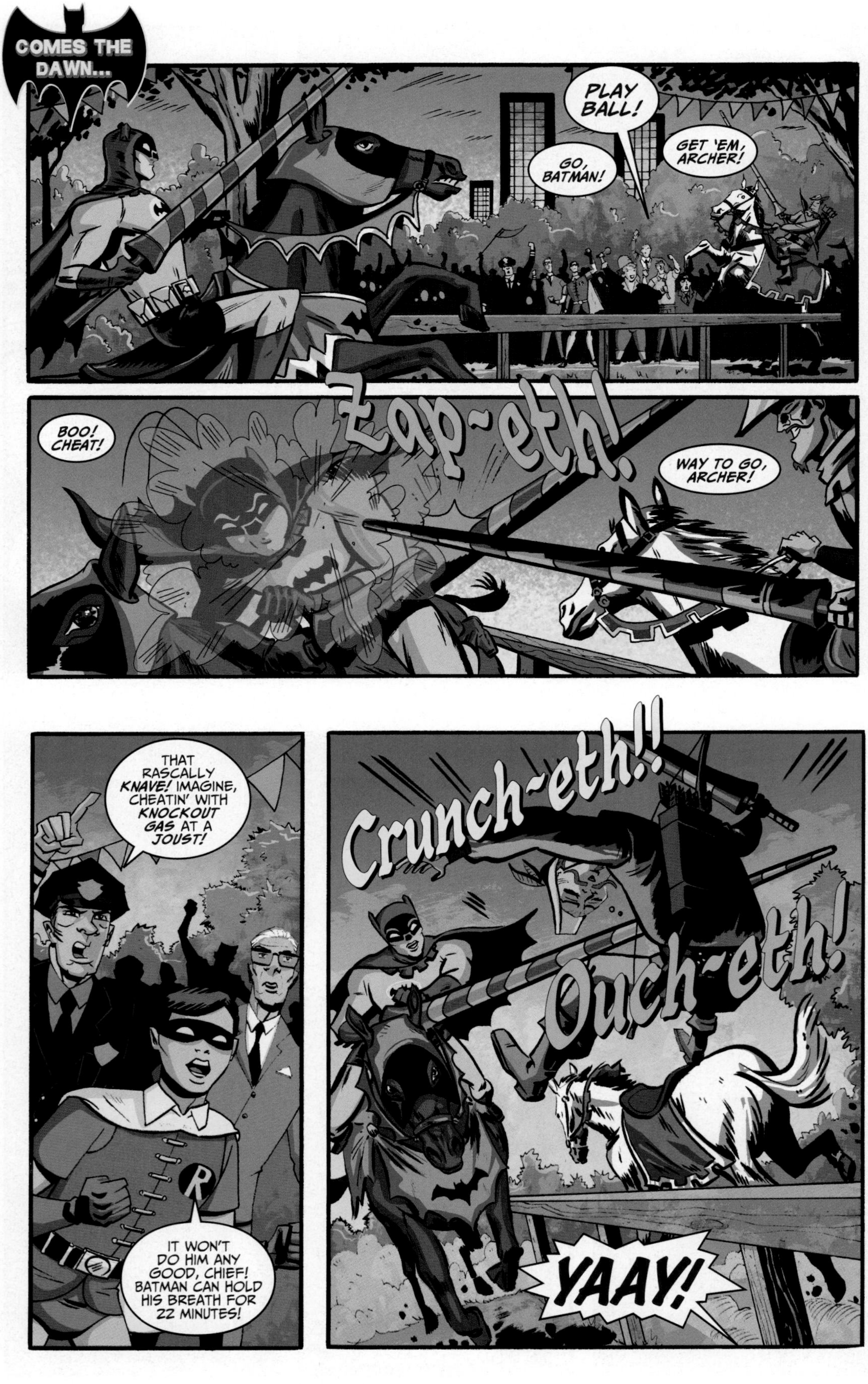
COMES THE DAWN...
PLAY BALL!
GO, BATMAN!
GET 'EM, ARCHER!
Zap-eth!
BOO! CHEAT!
WAY TO GO, ARCHER!
THAT RASCALLY KNAVE! IMAGINE, CHEATIN' WITH KNOCKOUT GAS AT A JOUST!
IT WON'T DO HIM ANY GOOD, CHIEF! BATMAN CAN HOLD HIS BREATH FOR 22 MINUTES!
Crunch-eth!!
Ouch-eth!
YAAY!

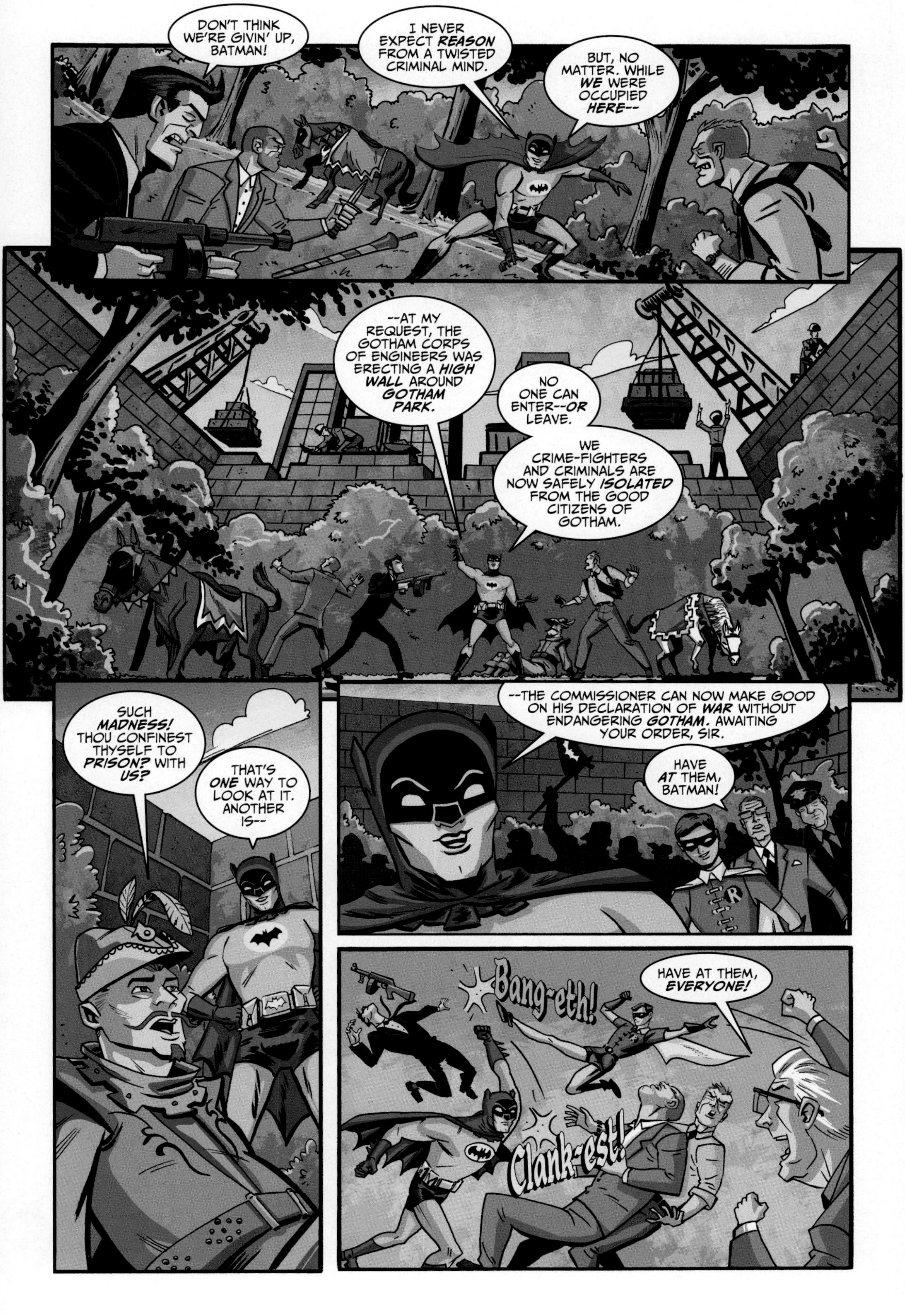
DON'T THINK WE'RE GIVIN' UP, BATMAN!
I NEVER EXPECT REASON FROM A TWISTED CRIMINAL MIND.
BUT, NO MATTER. WHILE WE WERE OCCUPIED HERE--
--AT MY REQUEST, THE GOTHAM CORPS OF ENGINEERS WAS ERECTING A HIGH WALL AROUND GOTHAM PARK.
NO ONE CAN ENTER--OR LEAVE.
WE CRIME-FIGHTERS AND CRIMINALS ARE NOW SAFELY ISOLATED FROM THE GOOD CITIZENS OF GOTHAM.
SUCH MADNESS! THOU CONFINEST THYSELF TO PRISON? WITH US?
THAT'S ONE WAY TO LOOK AT IT. ANOTHER IS--
--THE COMMISSIONER CAN NOW MAKE GOOD ON HIS DECLARATION OF WAR WITHOUT ENDANGERING GOTHAM. AWAITING YOUR ORDER, SIR.
HAVE AT THEM, BATMAN!
Bang-eth!
HAVE AT THEM, EVERYONE!
Clank-est!

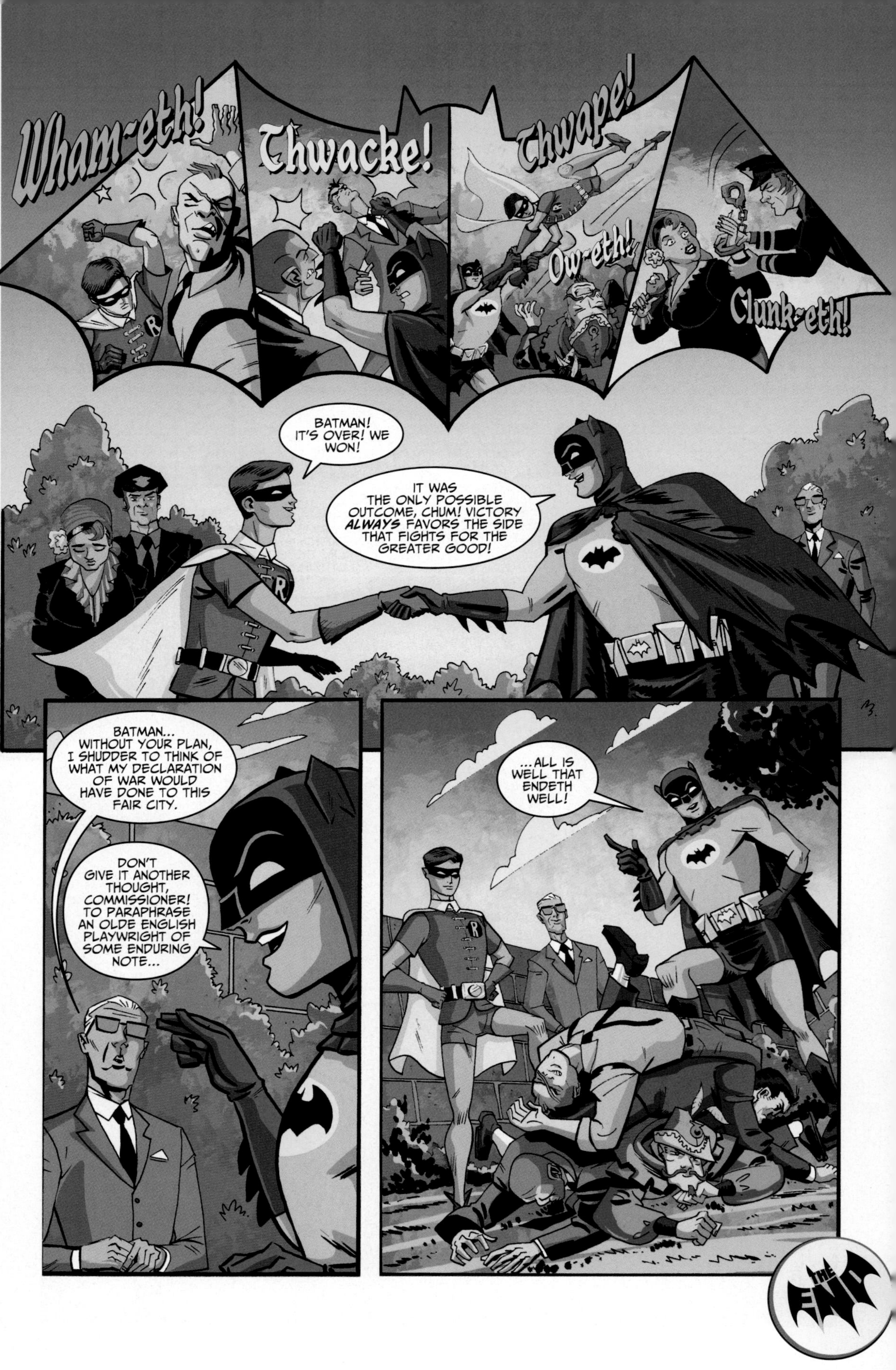
Wham-eth!
Thwacke!
Thwape!
Ow-eth!
Clunk-eth!
BATMAN! IT'S OVER! WE WON!
IT WAS THE ONLY POSSIBLE OUTCOME, CHUM! VICTORY *ALWAYS* FAVORS THE SIDE THAT FIGHTS FOR THE GREATER GOOD!
BATMAN... WITHOUT YOUR PLAN, I SHUDDER TO THINK OF WHAT MY DECLARATION OF WAR WOULD HAVE DONE TO THIS FAIR CITY.
DON'T GIVE IT ANOTHER THOUGHT, COMMISSIONER! TO PARAPHRASE AN OLDE ENGLISH PLAYWRIGHT OF SOME ENDURING NOTE...
...ALL IS WELL THAT ENDETH WELL!
THE END

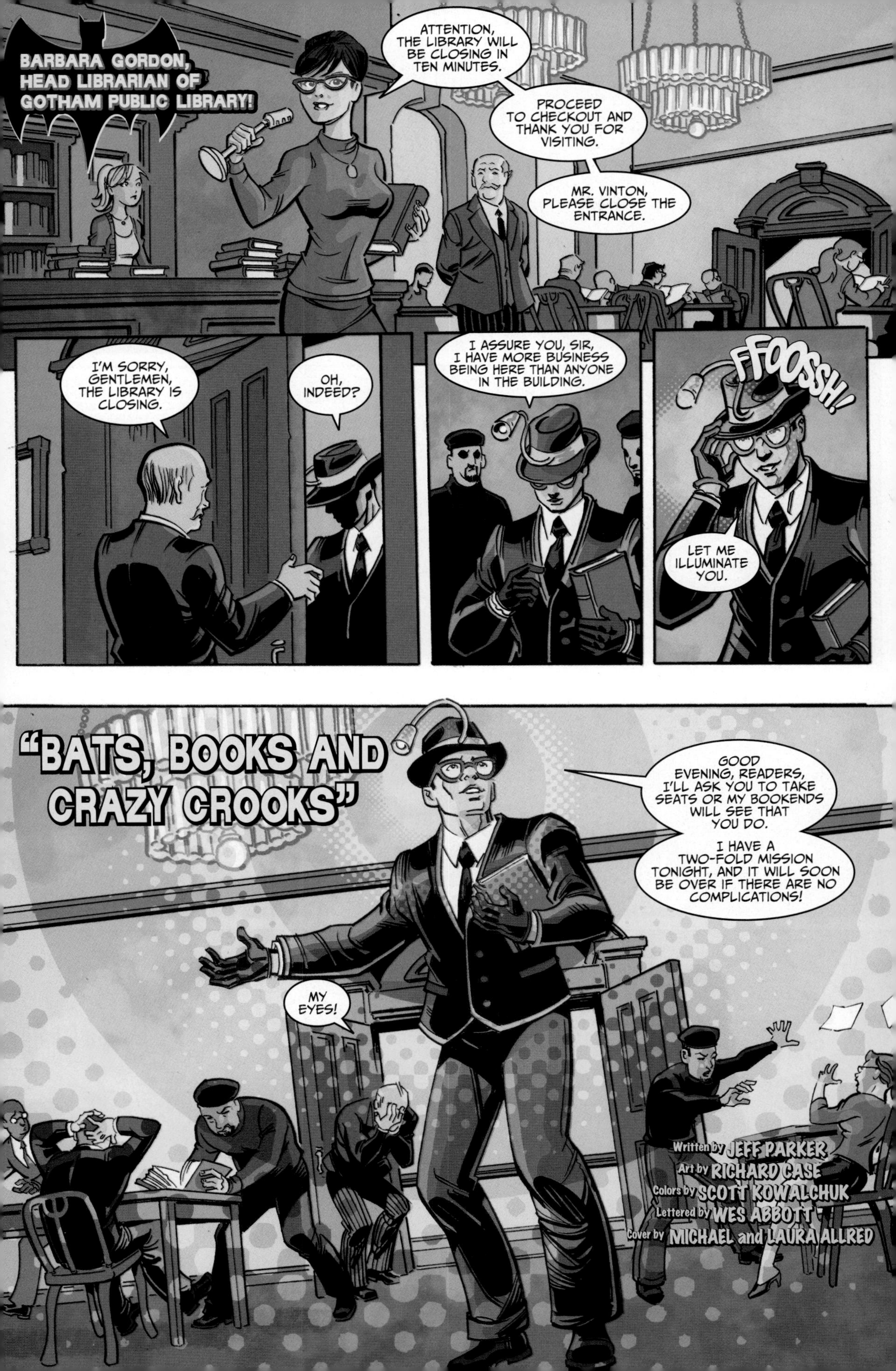
BARBARA GORDON, HEAD LIBRARIAN OF GOTHAM PUBLIC LIBRARY!
ATTENTION, THE LIBRARY WILL BE CLOSING IN TEN MINUTES.
PROCEED TO CHECKOUT AND THANK YOU FOR VISITING.
MR. VINTON, PLEASE CLOSE THE ENTRANCE.
I'M SORRY, GENTLEMEN, THE LIBRARY IS CLOSING.
OH, INDEED?
I ASSURE YOU, SIR, I HAVE MORE BUSINESS BEING HERE THAN ANYONE IN THE BUILDING.
FFOOSSH!
LET ME ILLUMINATE YOU.
"BATS, BOOKS AND CRAZY CROOKS"
GOOD EVENING, READERS, I'LL ASK YOU TO TAKE SEATS OR MY BOOKENDS WILL SEE THAT YOU DO.
I HAVE A TWO-FOLD MISSION TONIGHT, AND IT WILL SOON BE OVER IF THERE ARE NO COMPLICATIONS!
MY EYES!
Written by JEFF PARKER
Art by RICHARD CASE
Colors by SCOTT KOWALCHUK
Lettered by WES ABBOTT
Cover by MICHAEL and LAURA ALLRED

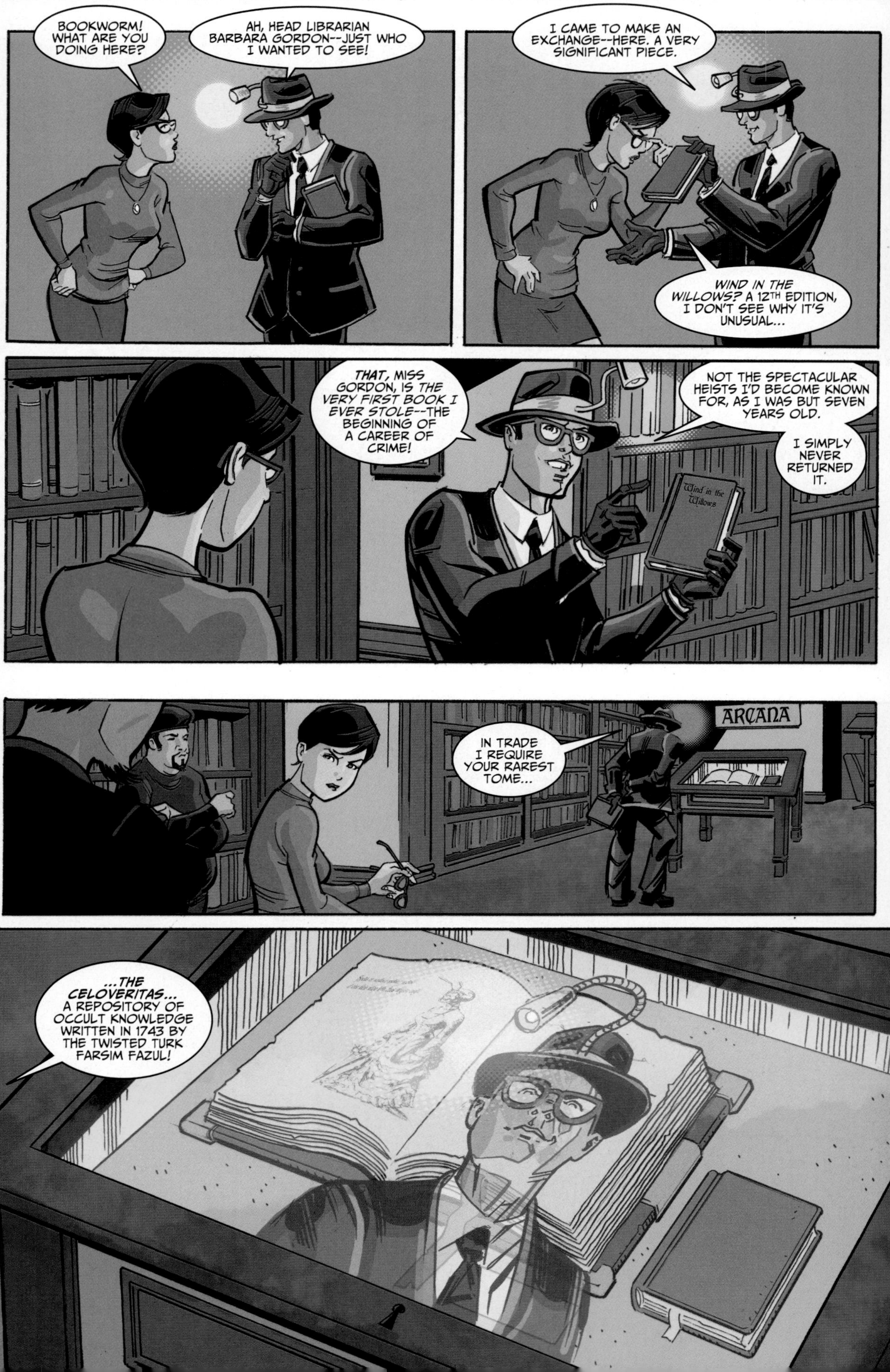
BOOKWORM! WHAT ARE YOU DOING HERE?
AH, HEAD LIBRARIAN BARBARA GORDON--JUST WHO I WANTED TO SEE!
I CAME TO MAKE AN EXCHANGE--HERE. A VERY SIGNIFICANT PIECE.
WIND IN THE WILLOWS? A 12TH EDITION, I DON'T SEE WHY IT'S UNUSUAL...
THAT, MISS GORDON, IS *THE VERY FIRST BOOK I EVER STOLE*--THE BEGINNING OF A CAREER OF CRIME!
Wind in the Willows
NOT THE SPECTACULAR HEISTS I'D BECOME KNOWN FOR, AS I WAS BUT SEVEN YEARS OLD.
I SIMPLY NEVER RETURNED IT.
ARCANA
IN TRADE I REQUIRE YOUR RAREST TOME...
...THE CELOVERITAS... A REPOSITORY OF OCCULT KNOWLEDGE WRITTEN IN 1743 BY THE TWISTED TURK FARSIM FAZUL!

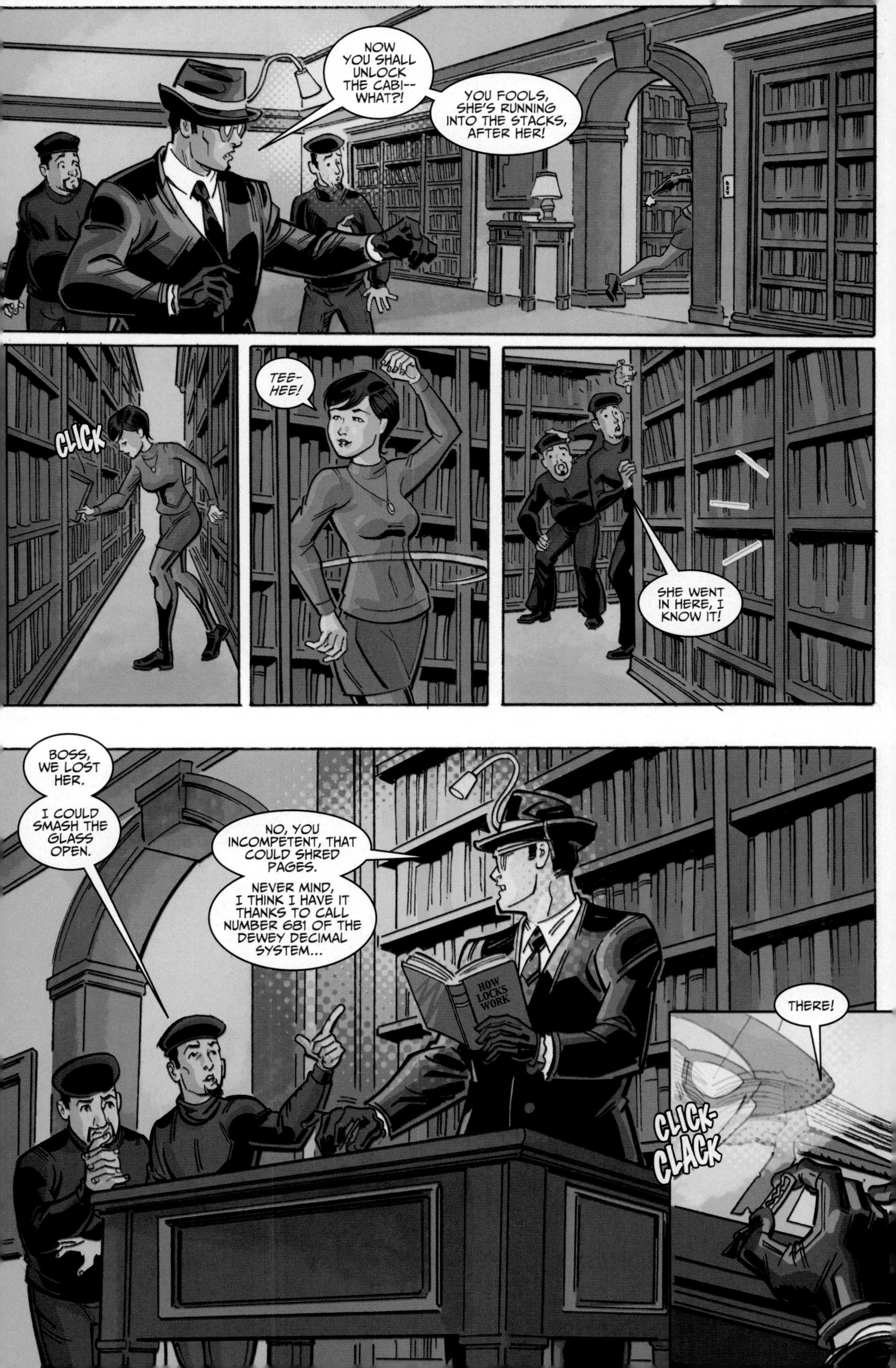
NOW YOU SHALL UNLOCK THE CABI-- WHAT?!
YOU FOOLS, SHE'S RUNNING INTO THE STACKS, AFTER HER!
CLICK
TEE-HEE!
SHE WENT IN HERE, I KNOW IT!
BOSS, WE LOST HER.
I COULD SMASH THE GLASS OPEN.
NO, YOU INCOMPETENT, THAT COULD SHRED PAGES.
NEVER MIND, I THINK I HAVE IT THANKS TO CALL NUMBER 681 OF THE DEWEY DECIMAL SYSTEM...
HOW LOCKS WORK
THERE!
CLICK-CLACK

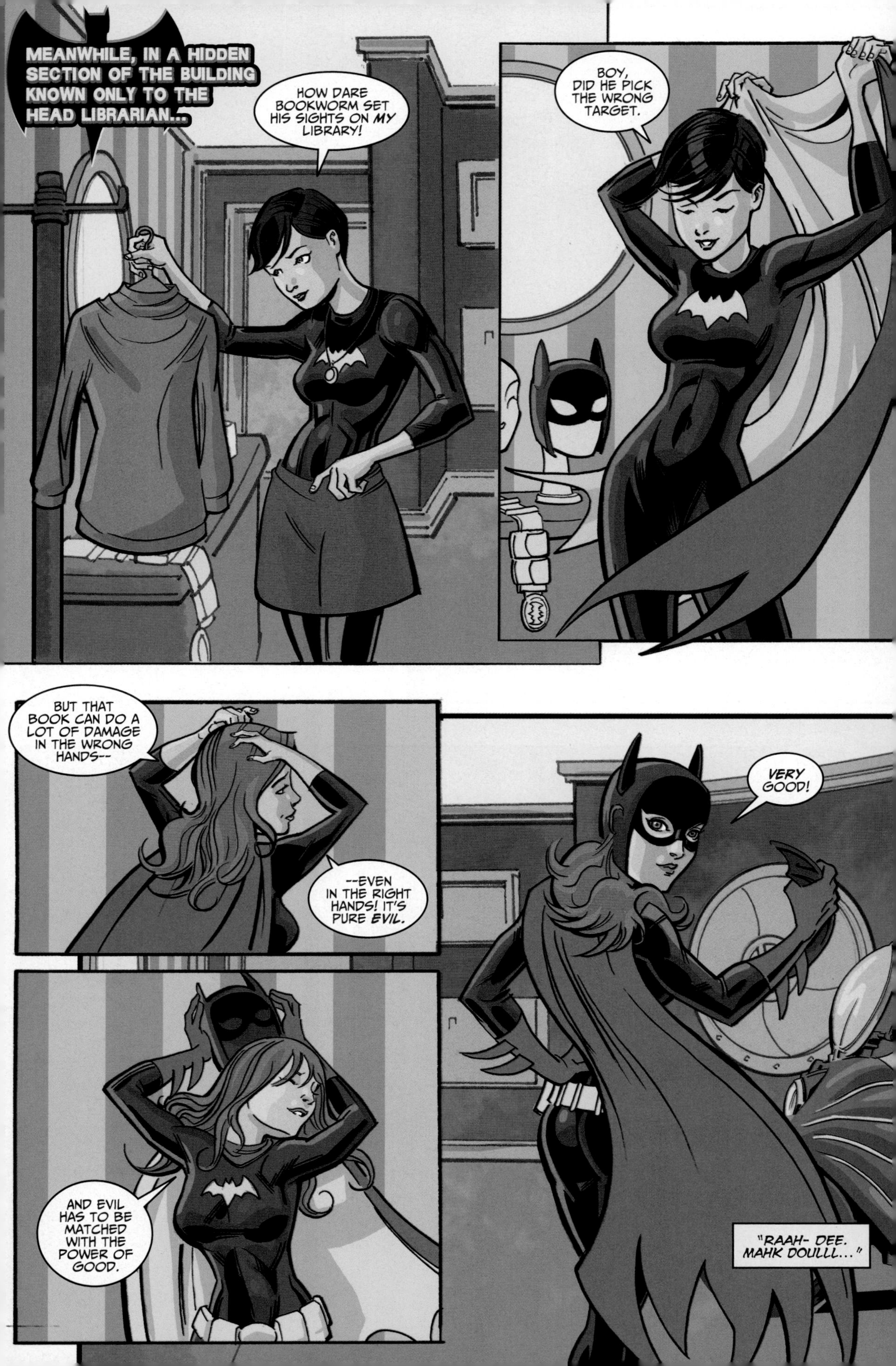
MEANWHILE, IN A HIDDEN SECTION OF THE BUILDING KNOWN ONLY TO THE HEAD LIBRARIAN...
HOW DARE BOOKWORM SET HIS SIGHTS ON MY LIBRARY!
BOY, DID HE PICK THE WRONG TARGET.
BUT THAT BOOK CAN DO A LOT OF DAMAGE IN THE WRONG HANDS--
--EVEN IN THE RIGHT HANDS! IT'S PURE EVIL.
AND EVIL HAS TO BE MATCHED WITH THE POWER OF GOOD.
VERY GOOD!
"RAAH- DEE. MAHK DOULLL..."

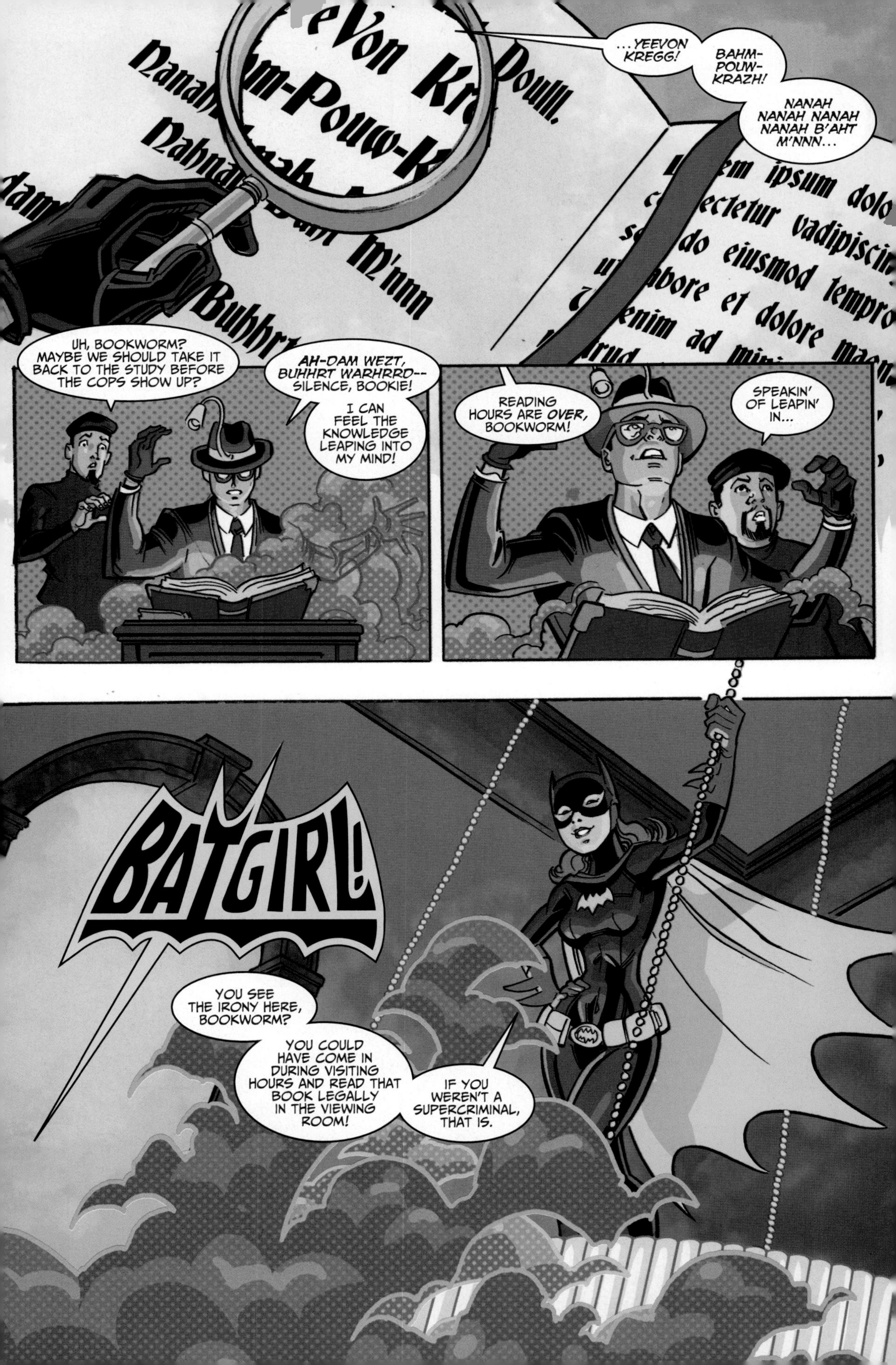

...YEEVON KREGG!
BAHM-POUW-KRAZH!
NANAH NANAH NANAH NANAH B'AHT M'NNN...
UH, BOOKWORM? MAYBE WE SHOULD TAKE IT BACK TO THE STUDY BEFORE THE COPS SHOW UP?
AH-DAM WEZT, BUHHRT WARHRRD-- SILENCE, BOOKIE!
I CAN FEEL THE KNOWLEDGE LEAPING INTO MY MIND!
READING HOURS ARE OVER, BOOKWORM!
SPEAKIN' OF LEAPIN' IN...
BATGIRL!
YOU SEE THE IRONY HERE, BOOKWORM?
YOU COULD HAVE COME IN DURING VISITING HOURS AND READ THAT BOOK LEGALLY IN THE VIEWING ROOM!
IF YOU WEREN'T A SUPERCRIMINAL, THAT IS.

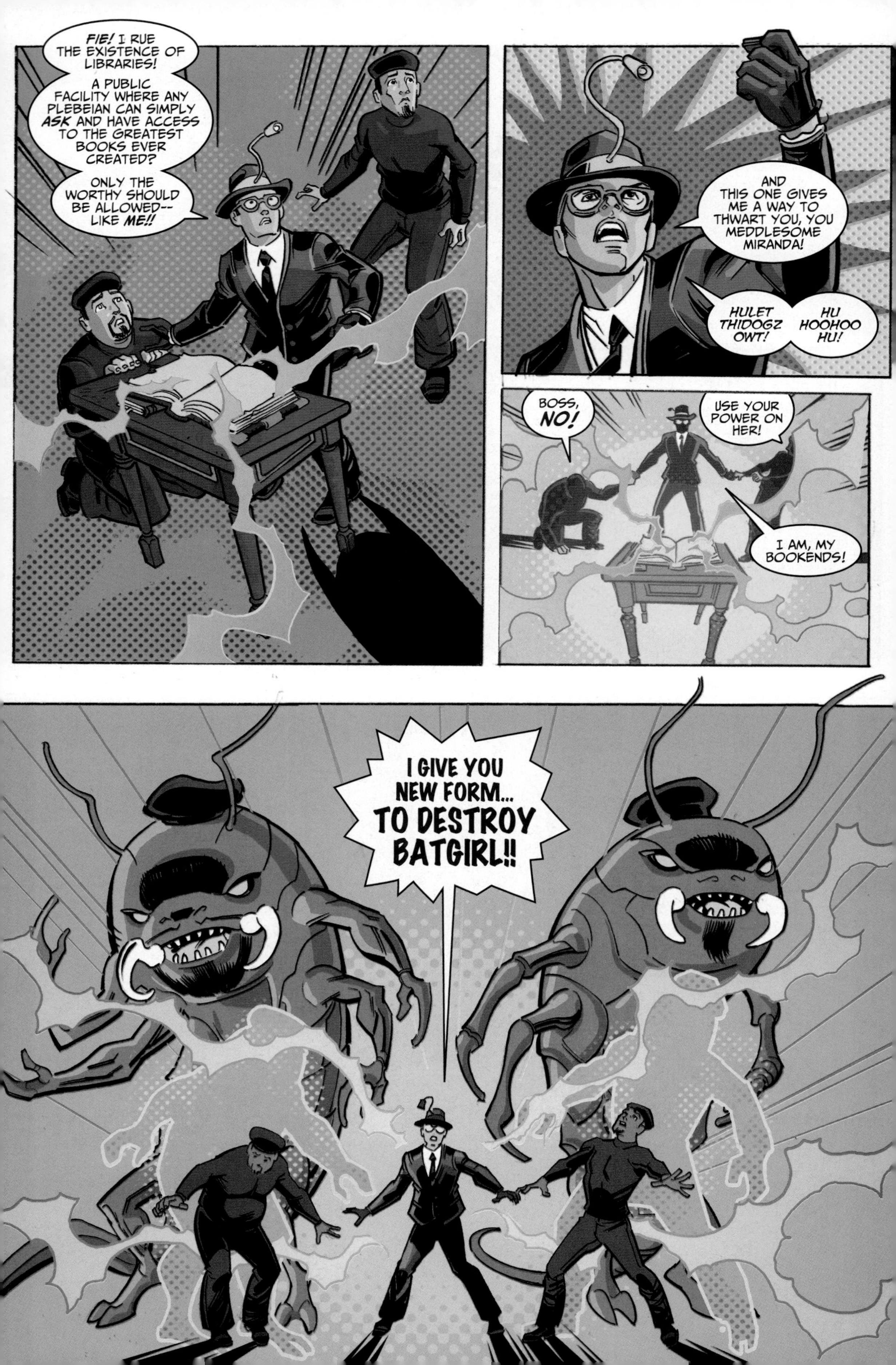
FIE! I RUE THE EXISTENCE OF LIBRARIES!
A PUBLIC FACILITY WHERE ANY PLEBEIAN CAN SIMPLY ASK AND HAVE ACCESS TO THE GREATEST BOOKS EVER CREATED?
ONLY THE WORTHY SHOULD BE ALLOWED-- LIKE ME!!
AND THIS ONE GIVES ME A WAY TO THWART YOU, YOU MEDDLESOME MIRANDA!
HULET THIDOGZ OWT!
HU HOOHOO HU!
BOSS, NO!
USE YOUR POWER ON HER!
I AM, MY BOOKENDS!
I GIVE YOU NEW FORM... TO DESTROY BATGIRL!!

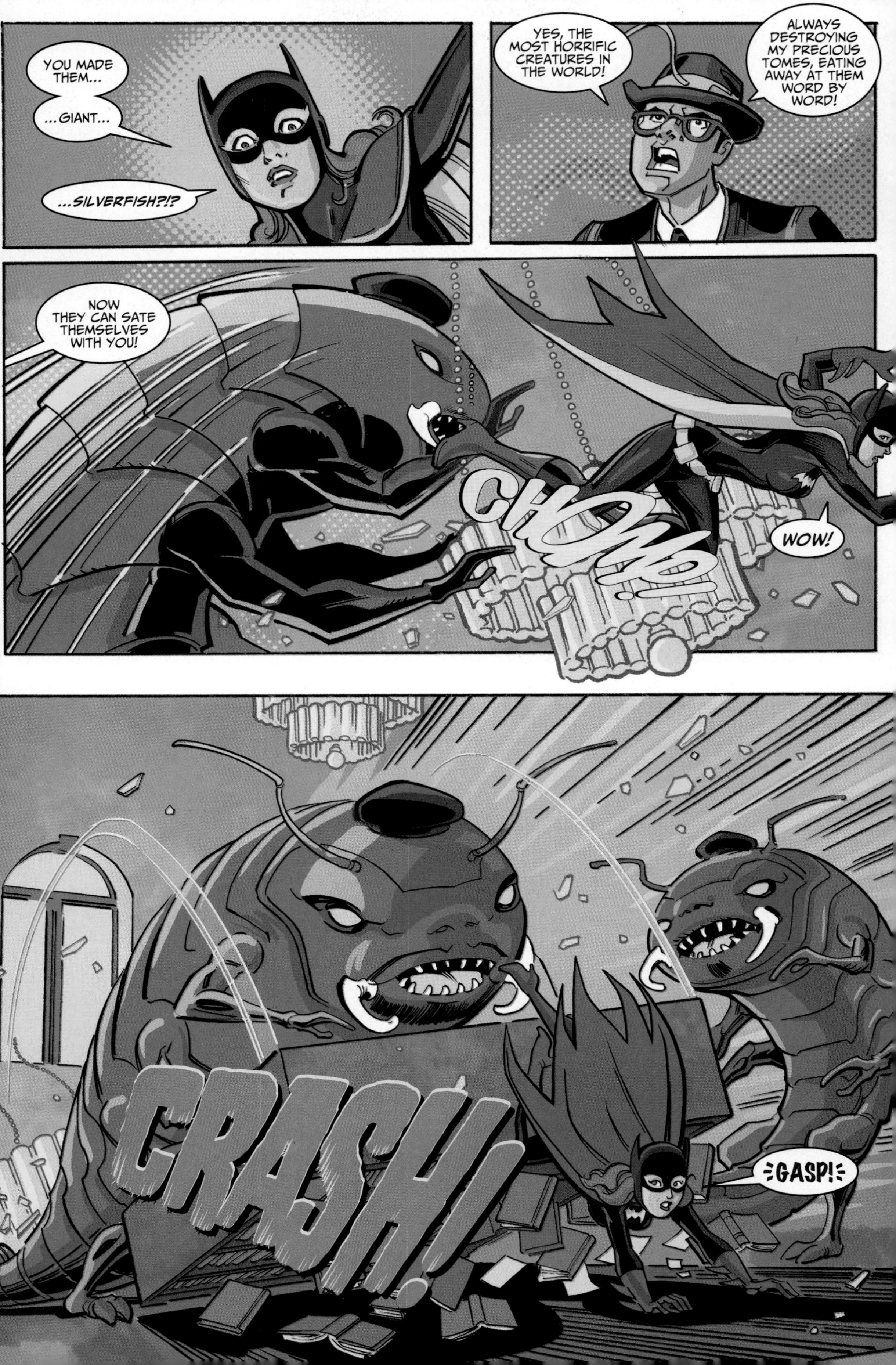

YOU MADE THEM...
...GIANT...
...SILVERFISH?!?
YES, THE MOST HORRIFIC CREATURES IN THE WORLD!
ALWAYS DESTROYING MY PRECIOUS TOMES, EATING AWAY AT THEM WORD BY WORD!
NOW THEY CAN SATE THEMSELVES WITH YOU!
CHOMP!
WOW!
CRASH!
GASP!

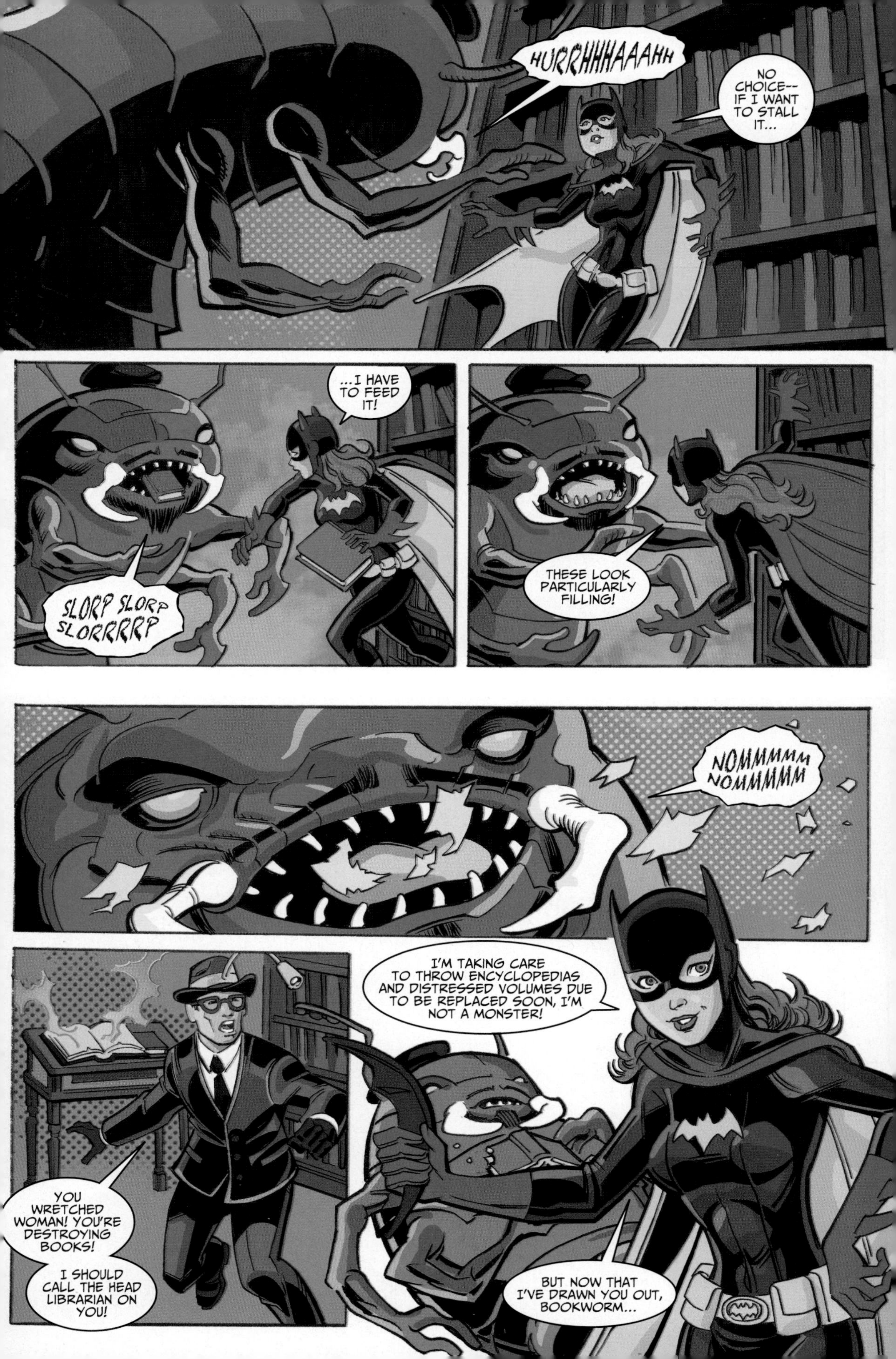
HURRHHHAAAHH
NO CHOICE-- IF I WANT TO STALL IT...
...I HAVE TO FEED IT!
SLORP SLORP SLORRRRP
THESE LOOK PARTICULARLY FILLING!
NOMMMMM NOMMMMM
I'M TAKING CARE TO THROW ENCYCLOPEDIAS AND DISTRESSED VOLUMES DUE TO BE REPLACED SOON, I'M NOT A MONSTER!
YOU WRETCHED WOMAN! YOU'RE DESTROYING BOOKS!
I SHOULD CALL THE HEAD LIBRARIAN ON YOU!
BUT NOW THAT I'VE DRAWN YOU OUT, BOOKWORM...

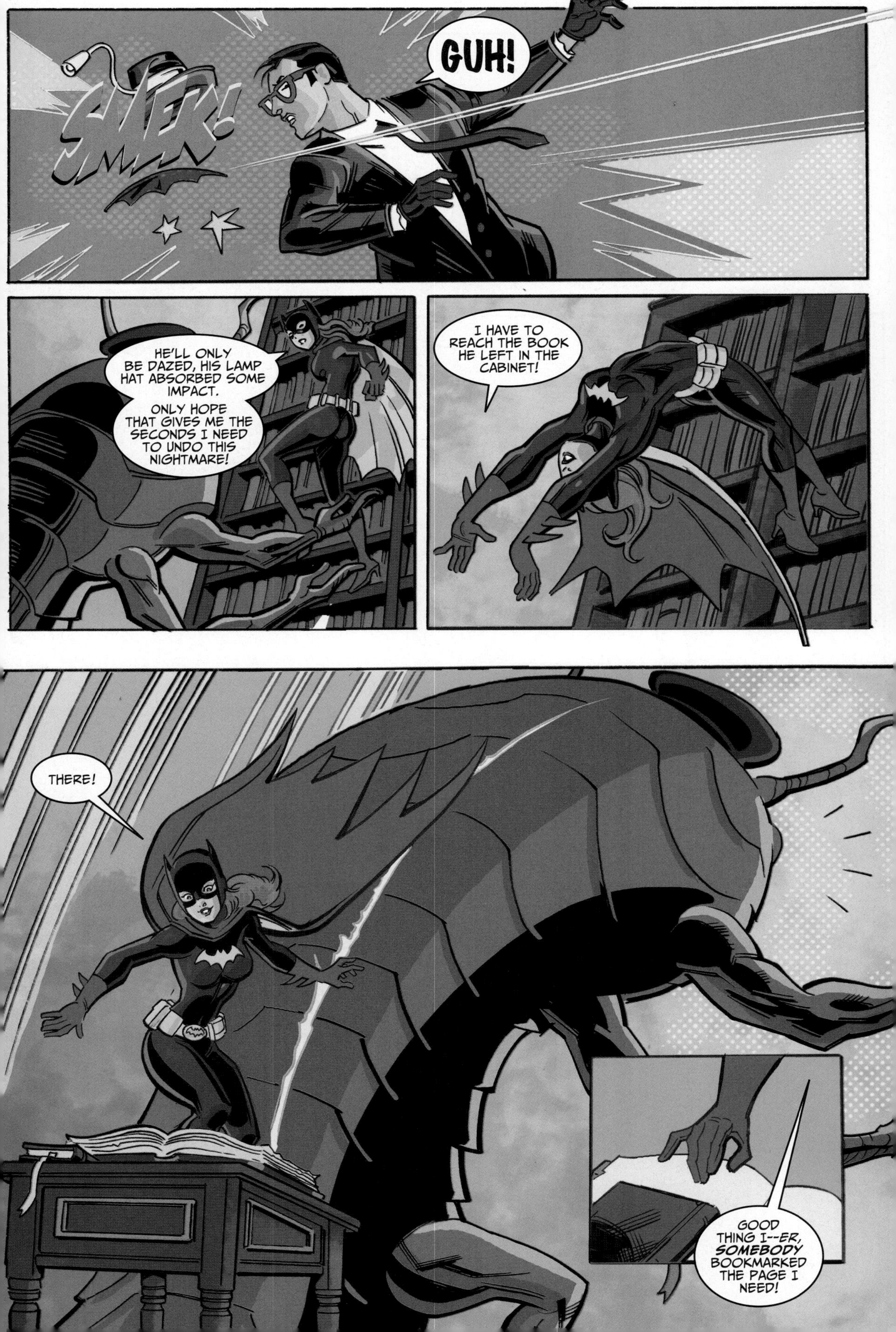
SMEK!
GUH!
HE'LL ONLY BE DAZED, HIS LAMP HAT ABSORBED SOME IMPACT.
ONLY HOPE THAT GIVES ME THE SECONDS I NEED TO UNDO THIS NIGHTMARE!
I HAVE TO REACH THE BOOK HE LEFT IN THE CABINET!
THERE!
GOOD THING I--ER, SOMEBODY BOOKMARKED THE PAGE I NEED!

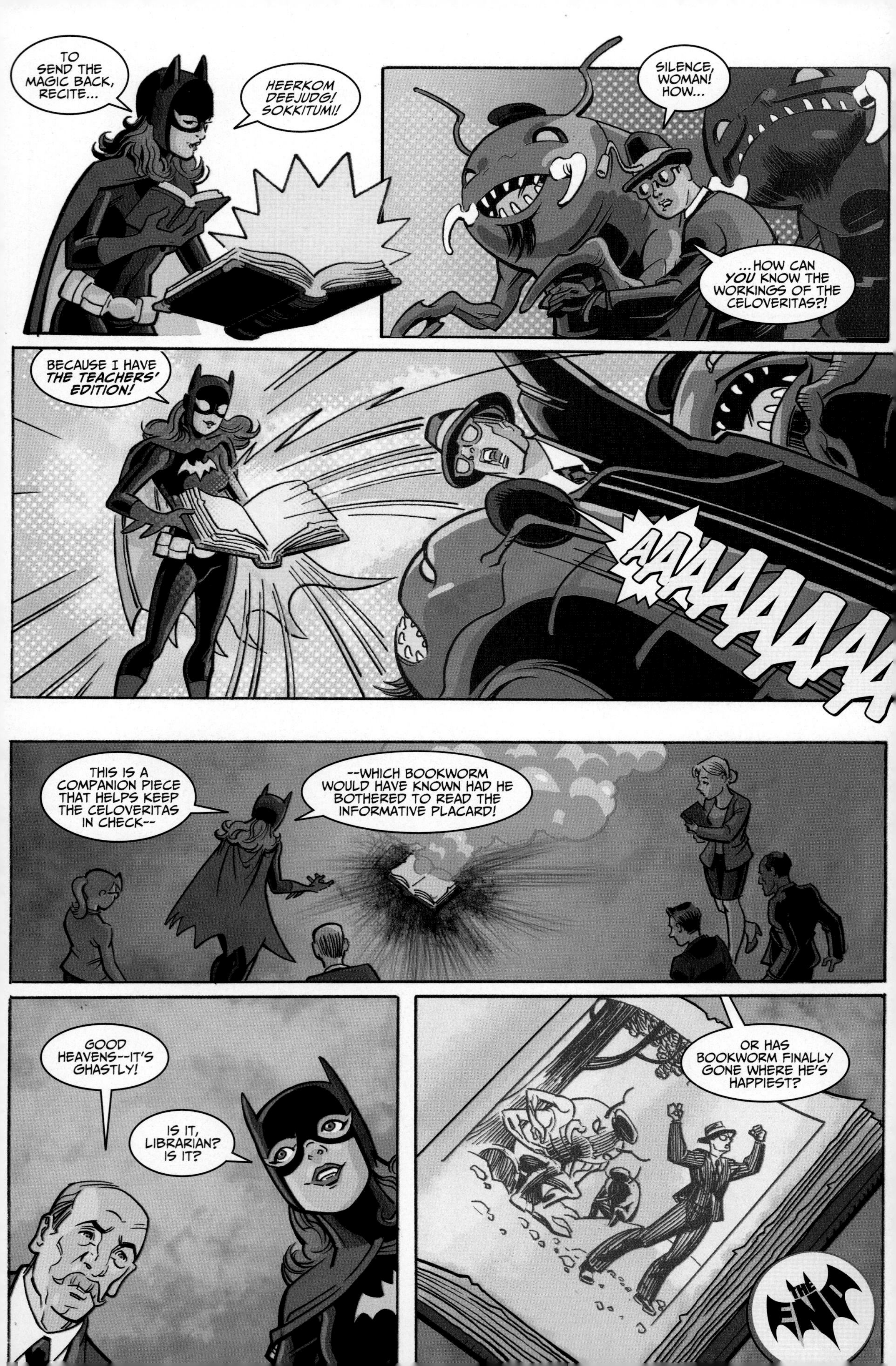

TO SEND THE MAGIC BACK, RECITE...
HEERKOM DEEJUDG! SOKKITUMI!
SILENCE, WOMAN! HOW...
...HOW CAN YOU KNOW THE WORKINGS OF THE CELOVERITAS?!
BECAUSE I HAVE THE TEACHERS' EDITION!
AAAAAAAAAAAA
THIS IS A COMPANION PIECE THAT HELPS KEEP THE CELOVERITAS IN CHECK--
--WHICH BOOKWORM WOULD HAVE KNOWN HAD HE BOTHERED TO READ THE INFORMATIVE PLACARD!
GOOD HEAVENS--IT'S GHASTLY!
IS IT, LIBRARIAN? IS IT?
OR HAS BOOKWORM FINALLY GONE WHERE HE'S HAPPIEST?
THE END

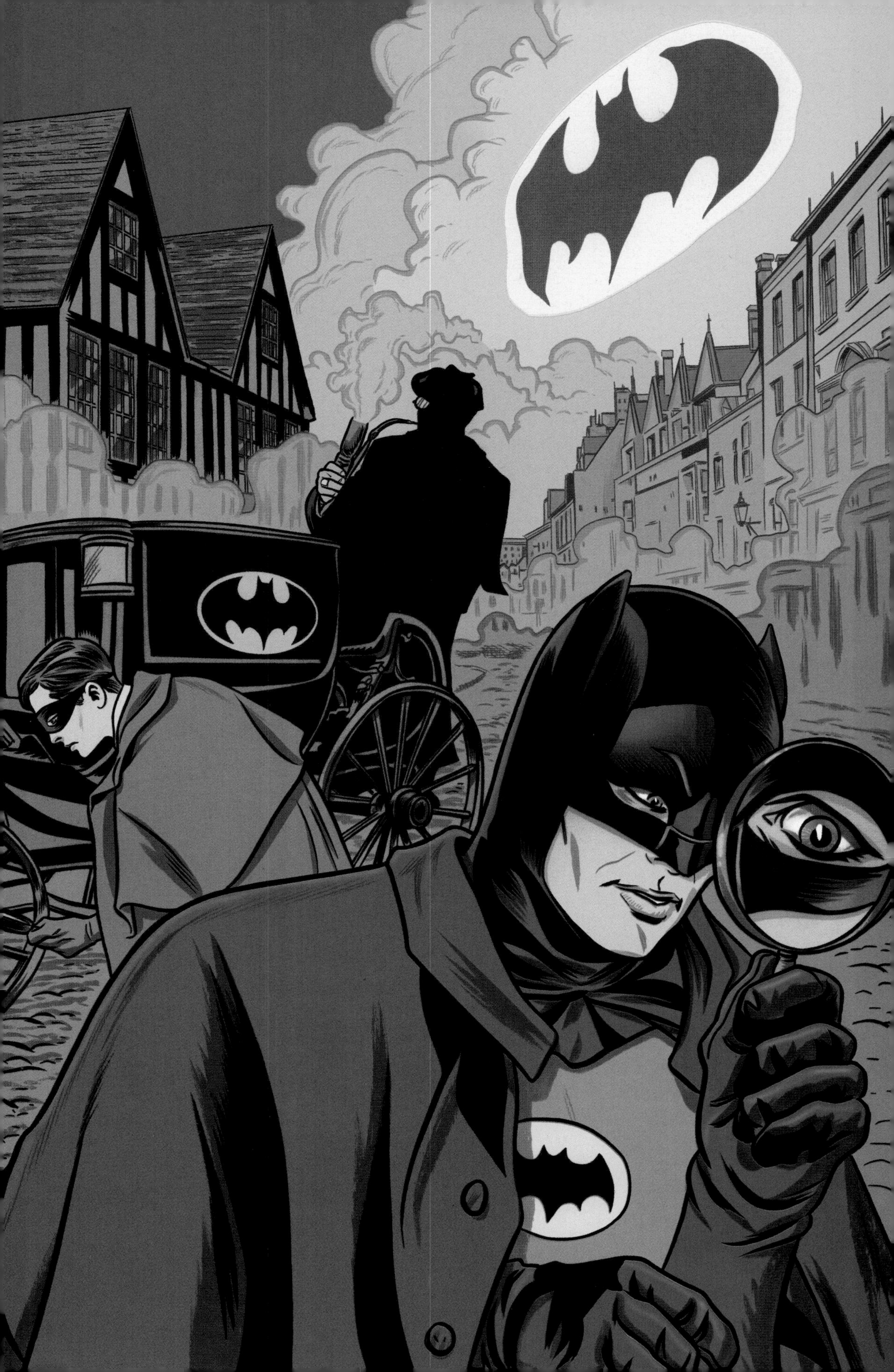

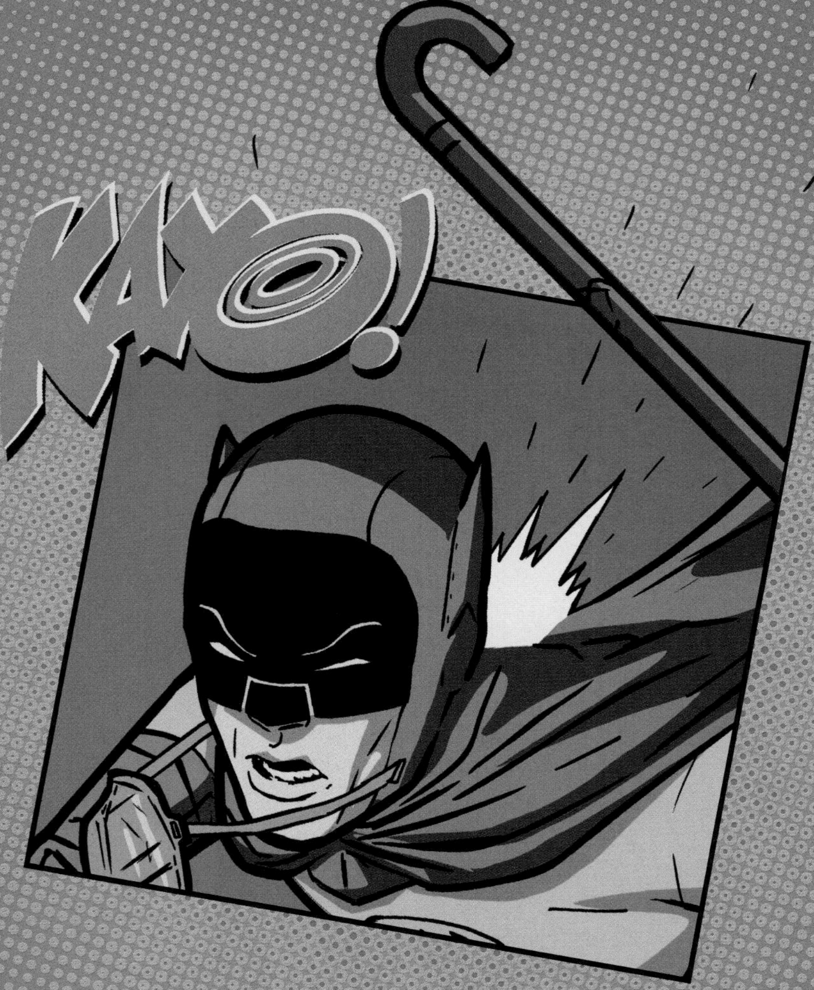
KAPOW!

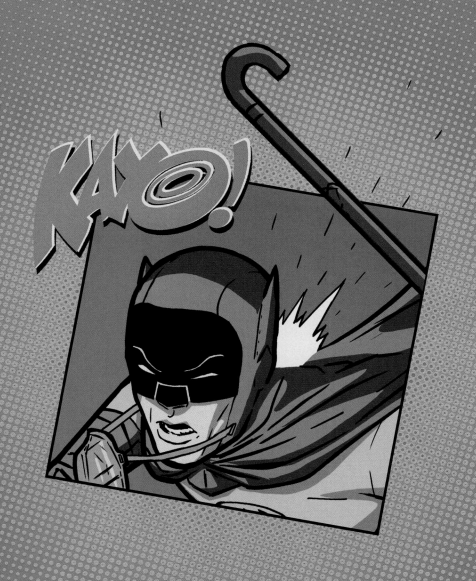

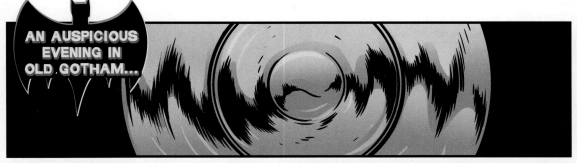

AN AUSPICIOUS EVENING IN OLD GOTHAM...

...AS BRUCE WAYNE AND HIS YOUTHFUL WARD ATTEND A LOCAL NEIGHBORHOOD FESTIVAL!

AH, THIS SECTION OF TOWN ALWAYS MAKES ME A BIT HOMESICK FOR LONDON.

GOSH, IS IT TRUE THE LAMP LIGHTS ARE GAS?

INDEED, DICK. THE WAYNE FOUNDATION DONATED TO THE RESTORATION OF THIS, GOTHAM'S FIRST BOROUGH, YOU KNOW.

I SHALL RETURN AT THE END OF YOUR EVENT, MASTER BRUCE.

WOW, EVERYONE IS WEARING PERIOD CLOTHES, BRUCE.

NOW I FEEL A LITTLE OUT OF PLACE.

NO TIME TO CHANGE FROM OUR EARLIER FUNCTION, BUT...

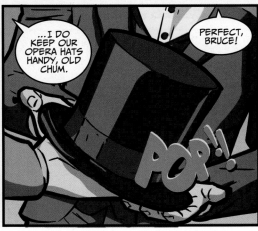

...I DO KEEP OUR OPERA HATS HANDY, OLD CHUM.

PERFECT, BRUCE!

POP!!

DONG

DONGG

OH HEAR YE, CITIZENS O' FAIR GOTHAM!

THE MAYOR IS NOW IN THE OLDE TOWN SQUARE TO MAKE THE TOAST!

TUPPENCE, SIRS? TUPPENCE A BAG!

WE'D BETTER HURRY--MAYOR LINSEED WILL NOTICE IF WE AREN'T IN THE FRONT ROW AND MAKE AUNT HARRIET CHIDE US.

BAGS OF SEEDS

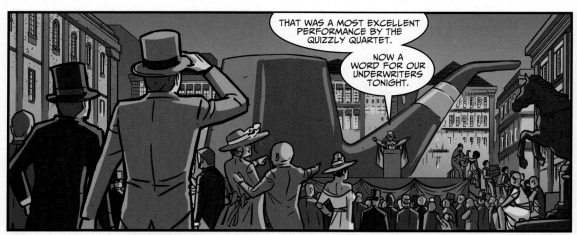

THAT WAS A MOST EXCELLENT PERFORMANCE BY THE QUIZZLY QUARTET.

NOW A WORD FOR OUR UNDERWRITERS TONIGHT.

I'D LIKE TO THANK DUKE'S FINE PIPES FOR SPONSORING THIS YEAR'S OLDE GOTHAM FESTIVAL.

"DUKE'S. SMOKE 'EM IF YOU GOT 'EM!"

AHEH.

AND NOW JOIN ME IN WELCOMING OUR NEXT PRESENTATION...

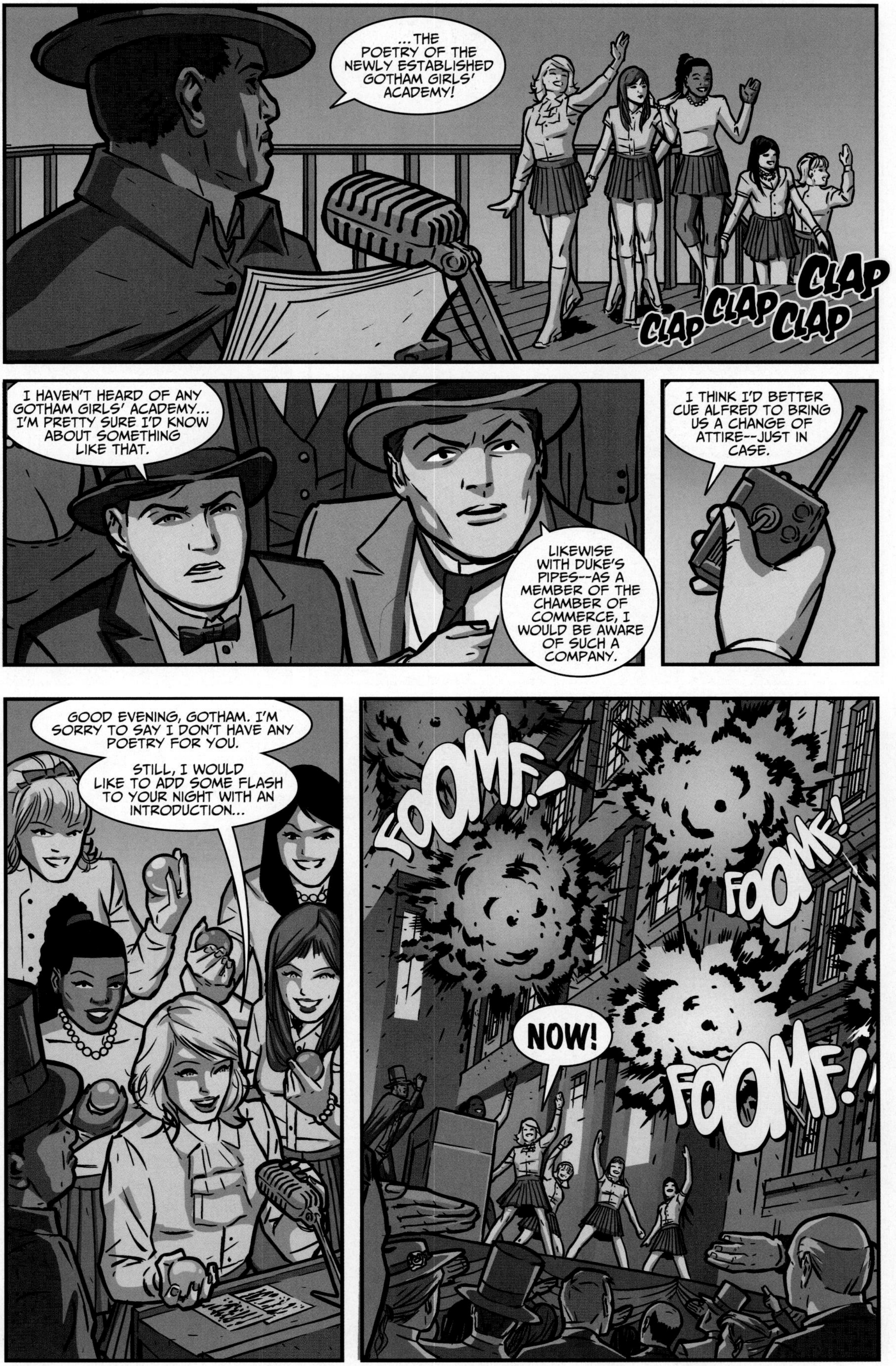
...THE POETRY OF THE NEWLY ESTABLISHED GOTHAM GIRLS' ACADEMY!
CLAP CLAP CLAP CLAP
I HAVEN'T HEARD OF ANY GOTHAM GIRLS' ACADEMY... I'M PRETTY SURE I'D KNOW ABOUT SOMETHING LIKE THAT.
LIKEWISE WITH DUKE'S PIPES--AS A MEMBER OF THE CHAMBER OF COMMERCE, I WOULD BE AWARE OF SUCH A COMPANY.
I THINK I'D BETTER CUE ALFRED TO BRING US A CHANGE OF ATTIRE--JUST IN CASE.
GOOD EVENING, GOTHAM. I'M SORRY TO SAY I DON'T HAVE ANY POETRY FOR YOU.
STILL, I WOULD LIKE TO ADD SOME FLASH TO YOUR NIGHT WITH AN INTRODUCTION...
FOOMF!
FOOMF!
NOW!
FOOMF!!

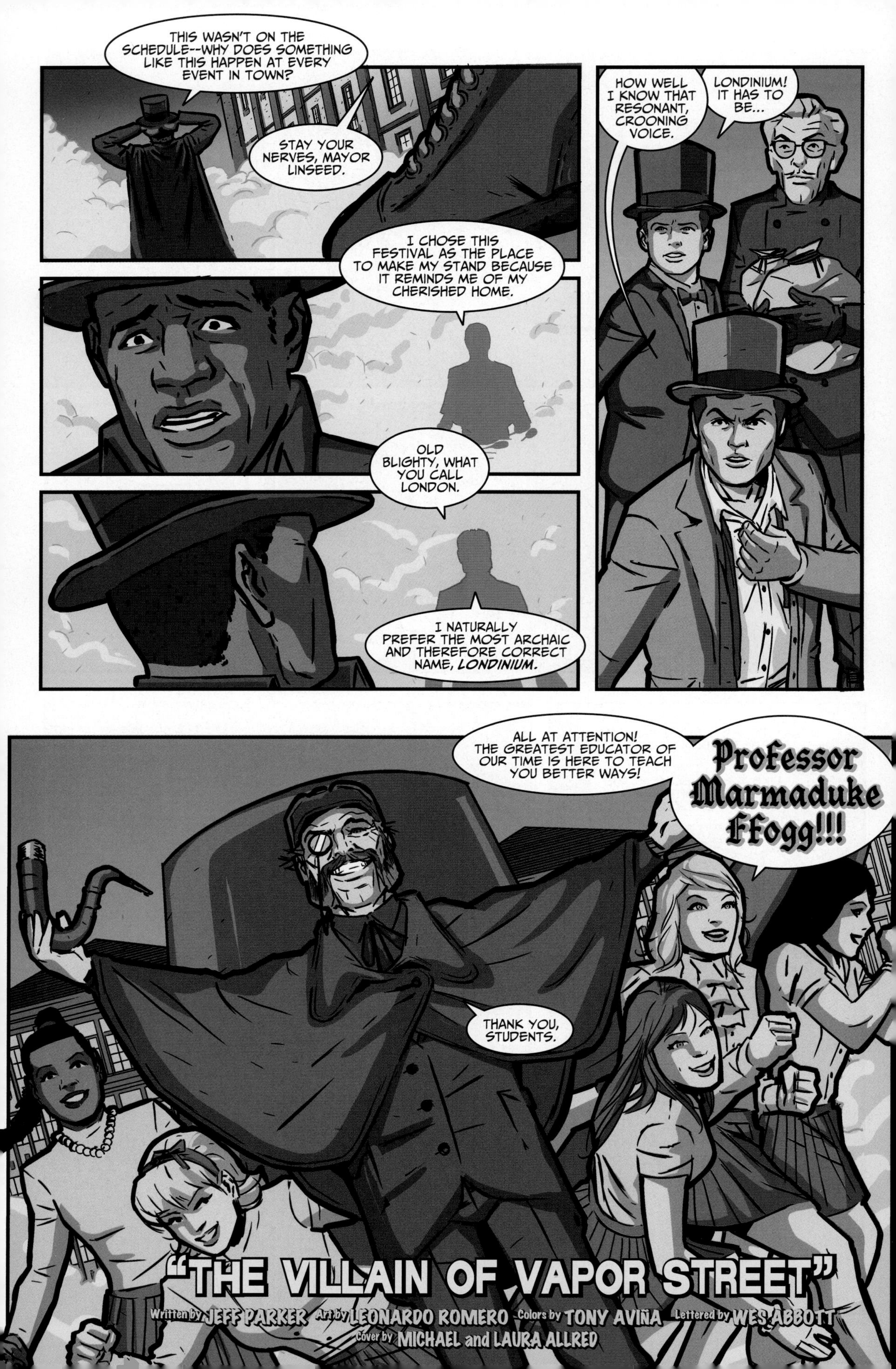
THIS WASN'T ON THE SCHEDULE--WHY DOES SOMETHING LIKE THIS HAPPEN AT EVERY EVENT IN TOWN?
STAY YOUR NERVES, MAYOR LINSEED.
I CHOSE THIS FESTIVAL AS THE PLACE TO MAKE MY STAND BECAUSE IT REMINDS ME OF MY CHERISHED HOME.
OLD BLIGHTY, WHAT YOU CALL LONDON.
I NATURALLY PREFER THE MOST ARCHAIC AND THEREFORE CORRECT NAME, *LONDINIUM.*
HOW WELL I KNOW THAT RESONANT, CROONING VOICE.
LONDINIUM! IT HAS TO BE...
ALL AT ATTENTION! THE GREATEST EDUCATOR OF OUR TIME IS HERE TO TEACH YOU BETTER WAYS!
Professor Marmaduke Ffogg!!!
THANK YOU, STUDENTS.
"THE VILLAIN OF VAPOR STREET"
Written by JEFF PARKER Art by LEONARDO ROMERO Colors by TONY AVIÑA Lettered by WES ABBOTT
Cover by MICHAEL and LAURA ALLRED

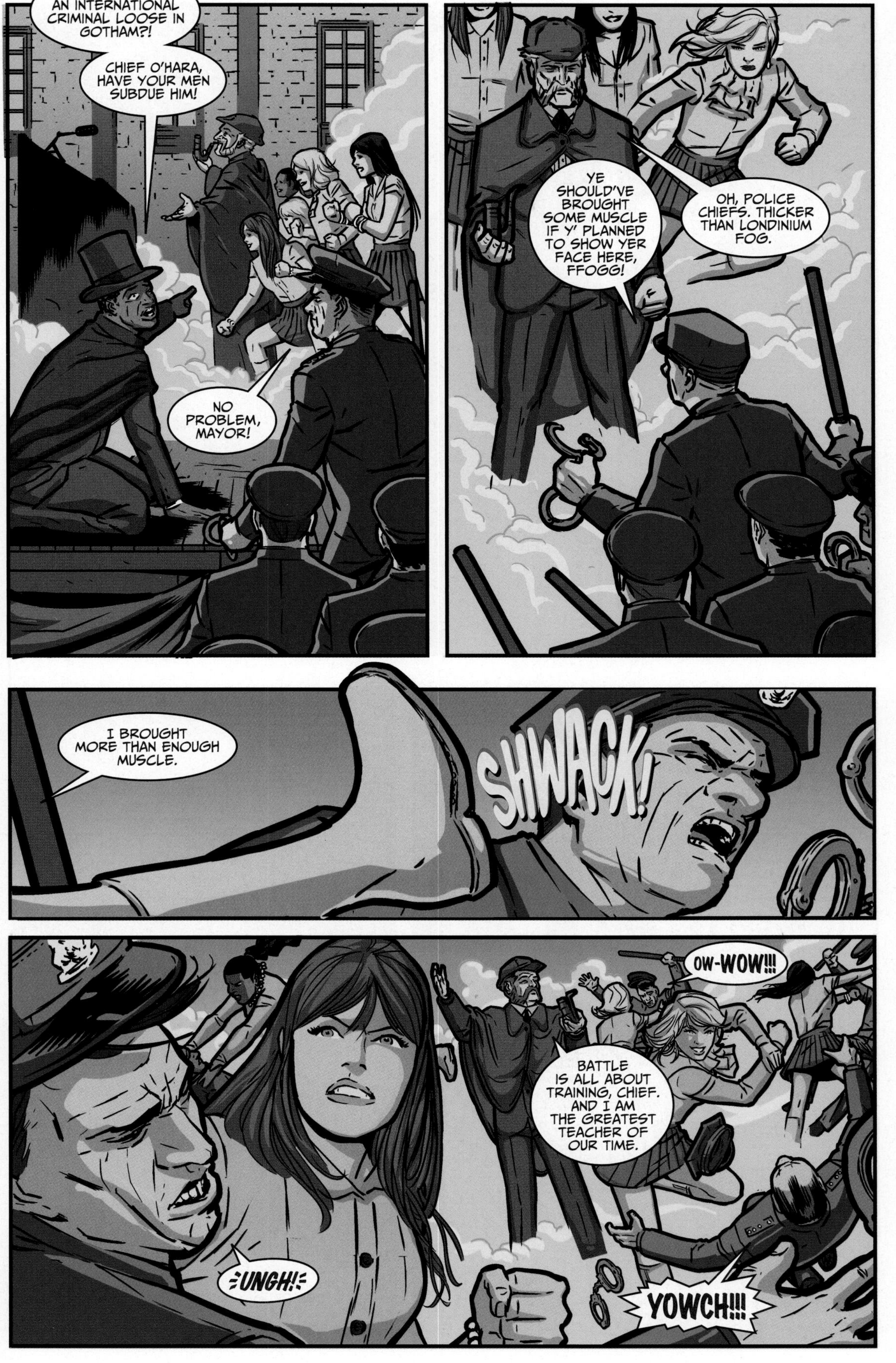
FFOGG, AN INTERNATIONAL CRIMINAL LOOSE IN GOTHAM?!
CHIEF O'HARA, HAVE YOUR MEN SUBDUE HIM!
NO PROBLEM, MAYOR!
YE SHOULD'VE BROUGHT SOME MUSCLE IF Y' PLANNED TO SHOW YER FACE HERE, FFOGG!
OH, POLICE CHIEFS. THICKER THAN LONDINIUM FOG.
I BROUGHT MORE THAN ENOUGH MUSCLE.
SHWACK!
OW-WOW!!!
BATTLE IS ALL ABOUT TRAINING, CHIEF. AND I AM THE GREATEST TEACHER OF OUR TIME.
UNGH!
YOWCH!!!

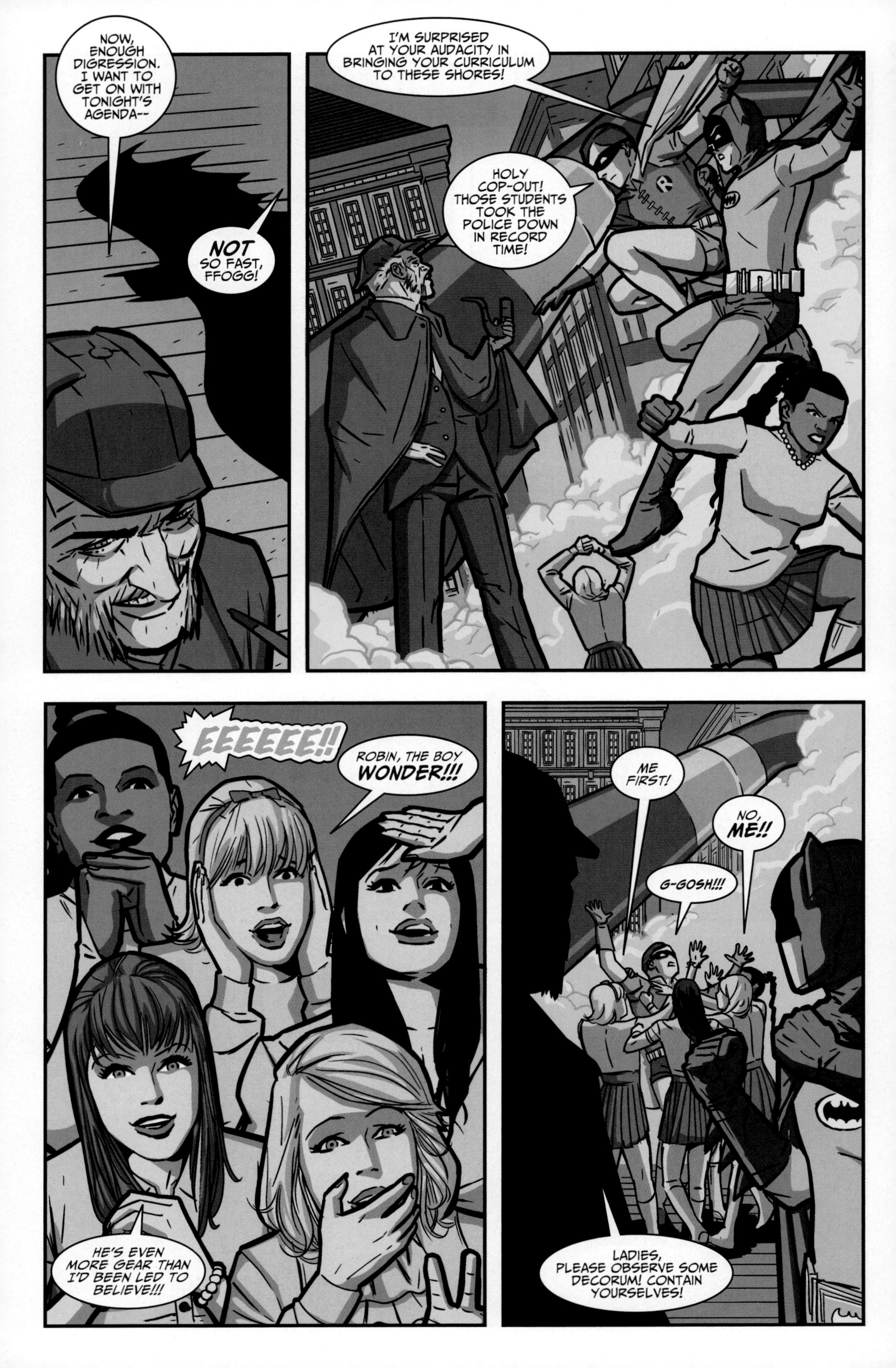
NOW, ENOUGH DIGRESSION. I WANT TO GET ON WITH TONIGHT'S AGENDA--
NOT SO FAST, FFOGG!
I'M SURPRISED AT YOUR AUDACITY IN BRINGING YOUR CURRICULUM TO THESE SHORES!
HOLY COP-OUT! THOSE STUDENTS TOOK THE POLICE DOWN IN RECORD TIME!
EEEEEE!!
ROBIN, THE BOY WONDER!!!
HE'S EVEN MORE GEAR THAN I'D BEEN LED TO BELIEVE!!!
ME FIRST!
NO, ME!!
G-GOSH!!!
LADIES, PLEASE OBSERVE SOME DECORUM! CONTAIN YOURSELVES!

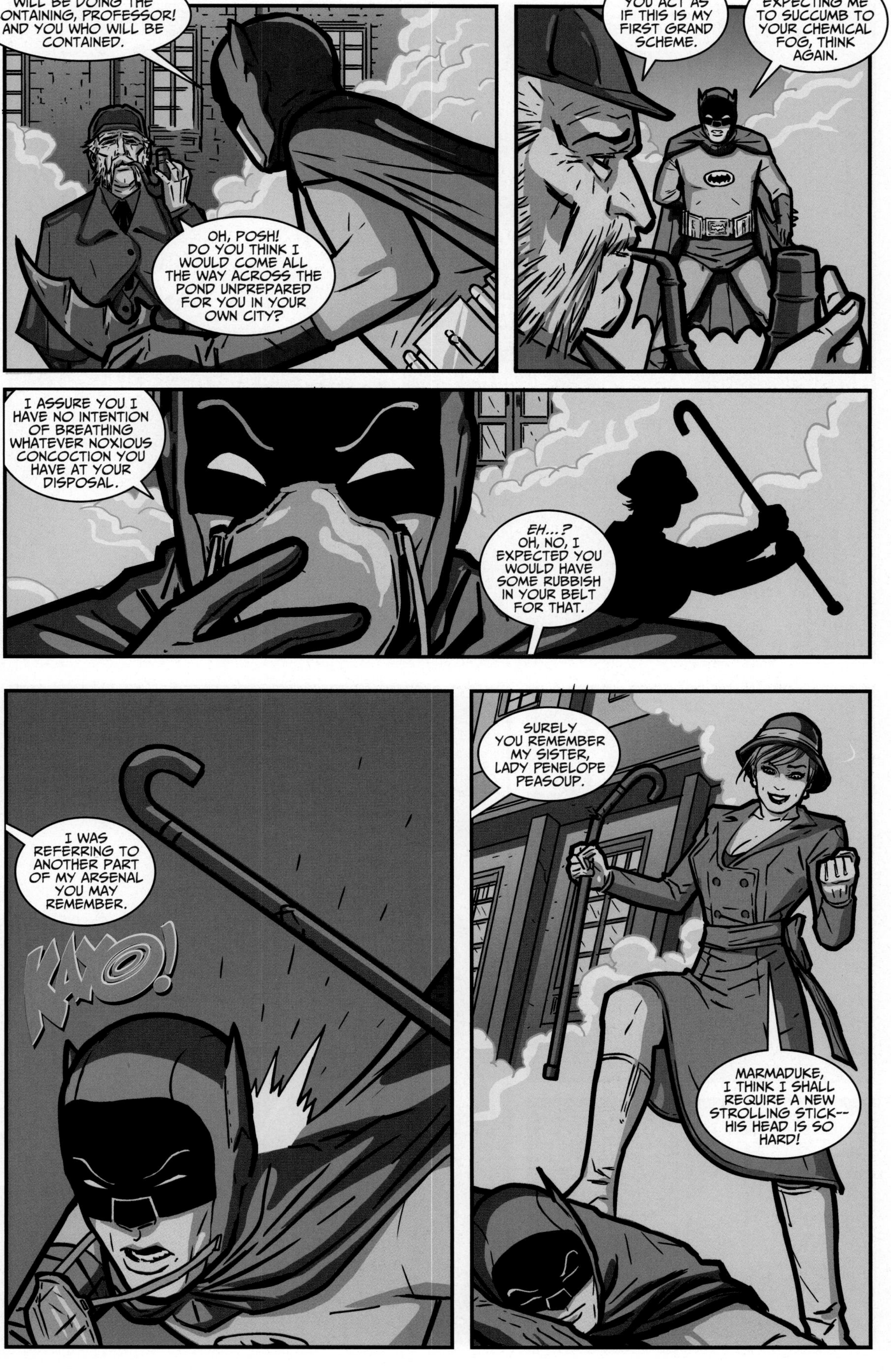
IT IS I WHO WILL BE DOING THE CONTAINING, PROFESSOR! AND YOU WHO WILL BE CONTAINED.
OH, POSH! DO YOU THINK I WOULD COME ALL THE WAY ACROSS THE POND UNPREPARED FOR YOU IN YOUR OWN CITY?
HONESTLY, YOU ACT AS IF THIS IS MY FIRST GRAND SCHEME.
IF YOU'RE EXPECTING ME TO SUCCUMB TO YOUR CHEMICAL FOG, THINK AGAIN.
I ASSURE YOU I HAVE NO INTENTION OF BREATHING WHATEVER NOXIOUS CONCOCTION YOU HAVE AT YOUR DISPOSAL.
EH...? OH, NO, I EXPECTED YOU WOULD HAVE SOME RUBBISH IN YOUR BELT FOR THAT.
I WAS REFERRING TO ANOTHER PART OF MY ARSENAL YOU MAY REMEMBER.
KAYO!
SURELY YOU REMEMBER MY SISTER, LADY PENELOPE PEASOUP.
MARMADUKE, I THINK I SHALL REQUIRE A NEW STROLLING STICK-- HIS HEAD IS SO HARD!

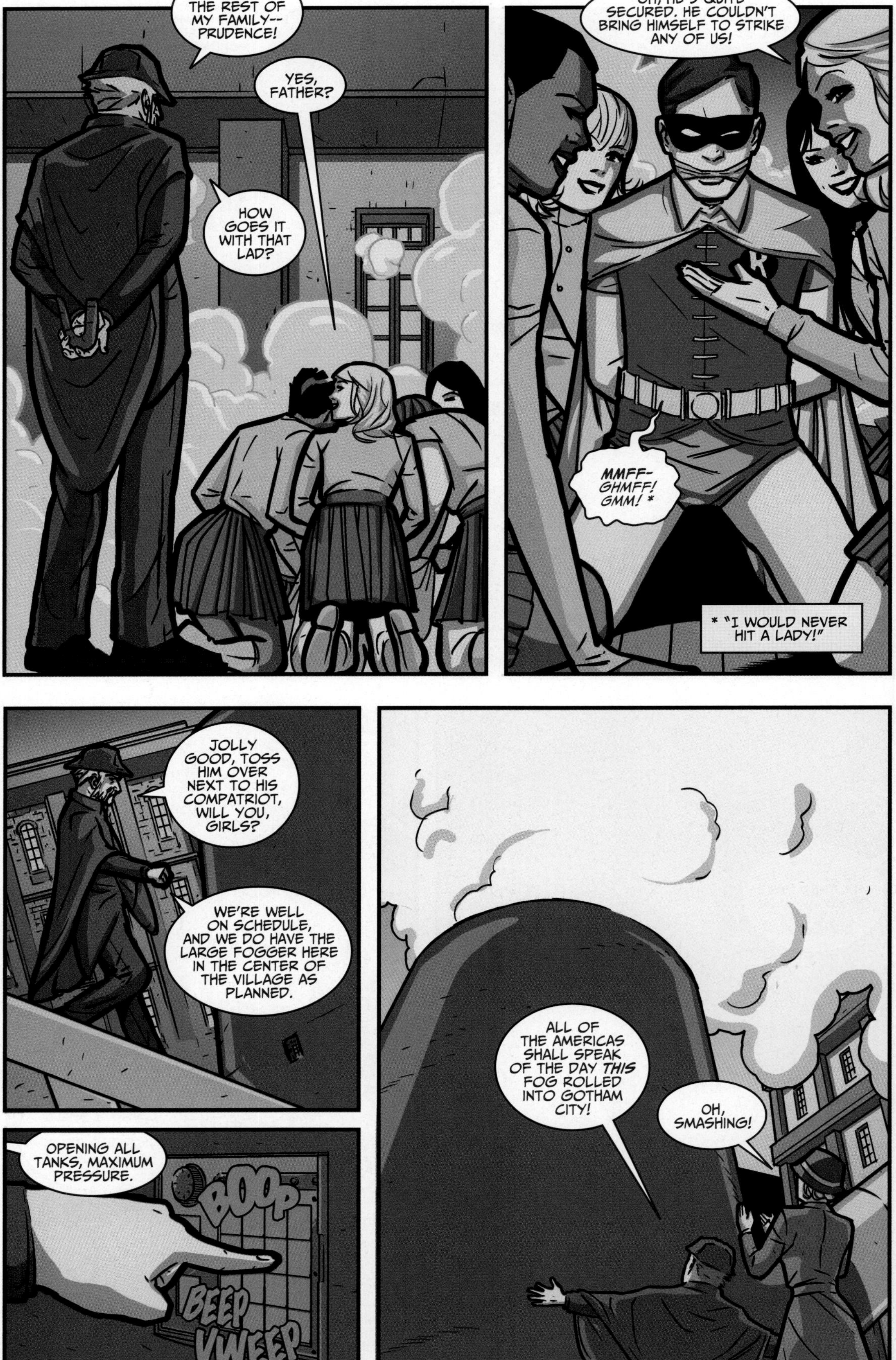
NOW TO THE REST OF MY FAMILY-- PRUDENCE!
YES, FATHER?
HOW GOES IT WITH THAT LAD?
OH, HE'S QUITE SECURED. HE COULDN'T BRING HIMSELF TO STRIKE ANY OF US!
MMFF-GHMFF! GMM! *
* "I WOULD NEVER HIT A LADY!"
JOLLY GOOD, TOSS HIM OVER NEXT TO HIS COMPATRIOT, WILL YOU, GIRLS?
WE'RE WELL ON SCHEDULE, AND WE DO HAVE THE LARGE FOGGER HERE IN THE CENTER OF THE VILLAGE AS PLANNED.
OPENING ALL TANKS, MAXIMUM PRESSURE.
BOOP
BEEP
VWEEP
ALL OF THE AMERICAS SHALL SPEAK OF THE DAY THIS FOG ROLLED INTO GOTHAM CITY!
OH, SMASHING!

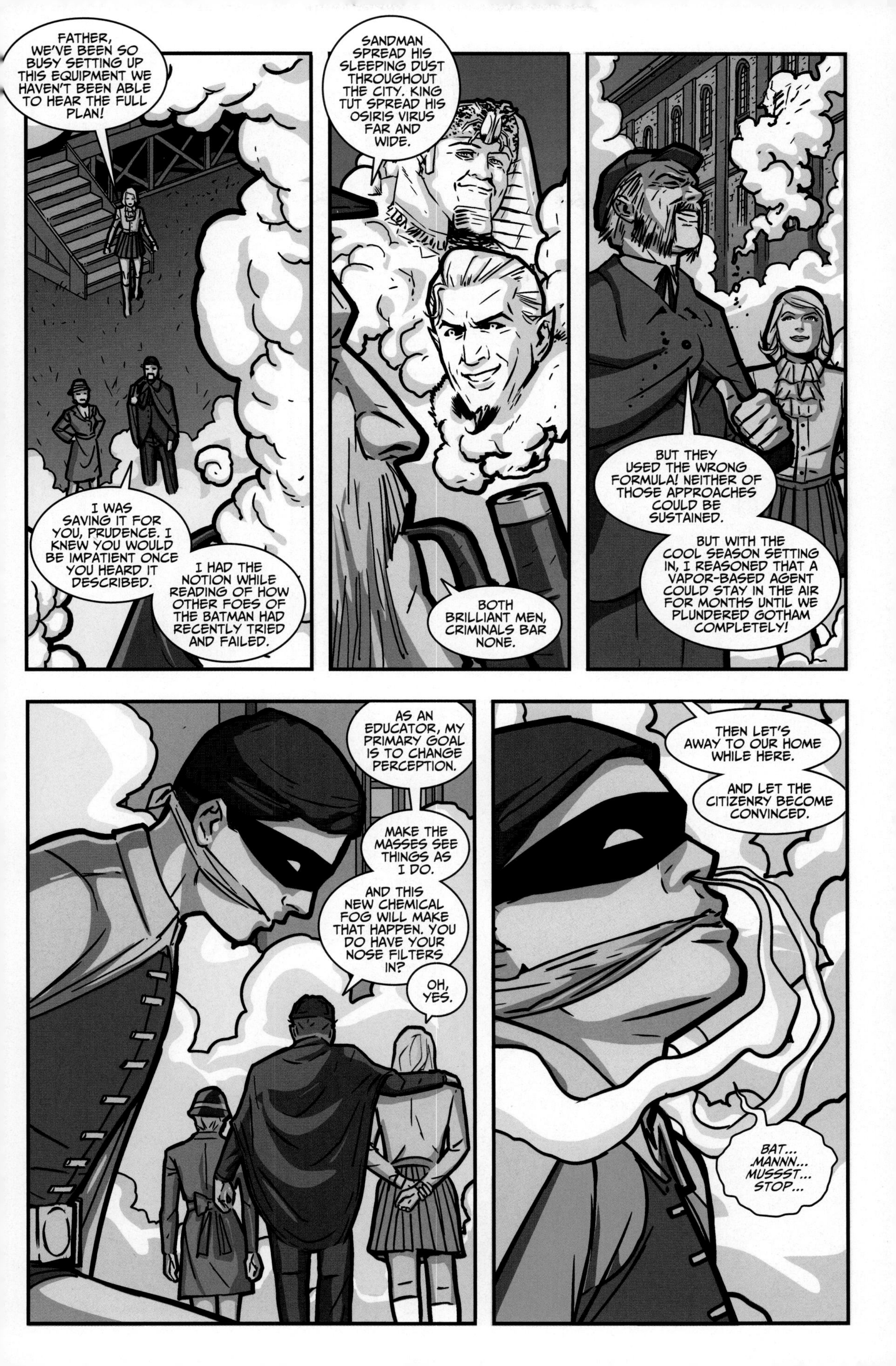
FATHER, WE'VE BEEN SO BUSY SETTING UP THIS EQUIPMENT WE HAVEN'T BEEN ABLE TO HEAR THE FULL PLAN!
I WAS SAVING IT FOR YOU, PRUDENCE. I KNEW YOU WOULD BE IMPATIENT ONCE YOU HEARD IT DESCRIBED.
I HAD THE NOTION WHILE READING OF HOW OTHER FOES OF THE BATMAN HAD RECENTLY TRIED AND FAILED.
SANDMAN SPREAD HIS SLEEPING DUST THROUGHOUT THE CITY. KING TUT SPREAD HIS OSIRIS VIRUS FAR AND WIDE.
BOTH BRILLIANT MEN, CRIMINALS BAR NONE.
BUT THEY USED THE WRONG FORMULA! NEITHER OF THOSE APPROACHES COULD BE SUSTAINED.
BUT WITH THE COOL SEASON SETTING IN, I REASONED THAT A VAPOR-BASED AGENT COULD STAY IN THE AIR FOR MONTHS UNTIL WE PLUNDERED GOTHAM COMPLETELY!
AS AN EDUCATOR, MY PRIMARY GOAL IS TO CHANGE PERCEPTION.
MAKE THE MASSES SEE THINGS AS I DO.
AND THIS NEW CHEMICAL FOG WILL MAKE THAT HAPPEN. YOU DO HAVE YOUR NOSE FILTERS IN?
OH, YES.
THEN LET'S AWAY TO OUR HOME WHILE HERE.
AND LET THE CITIZENRY BECOME CONVINCED.
BAT... .MANNN... MUSSST... STOP...

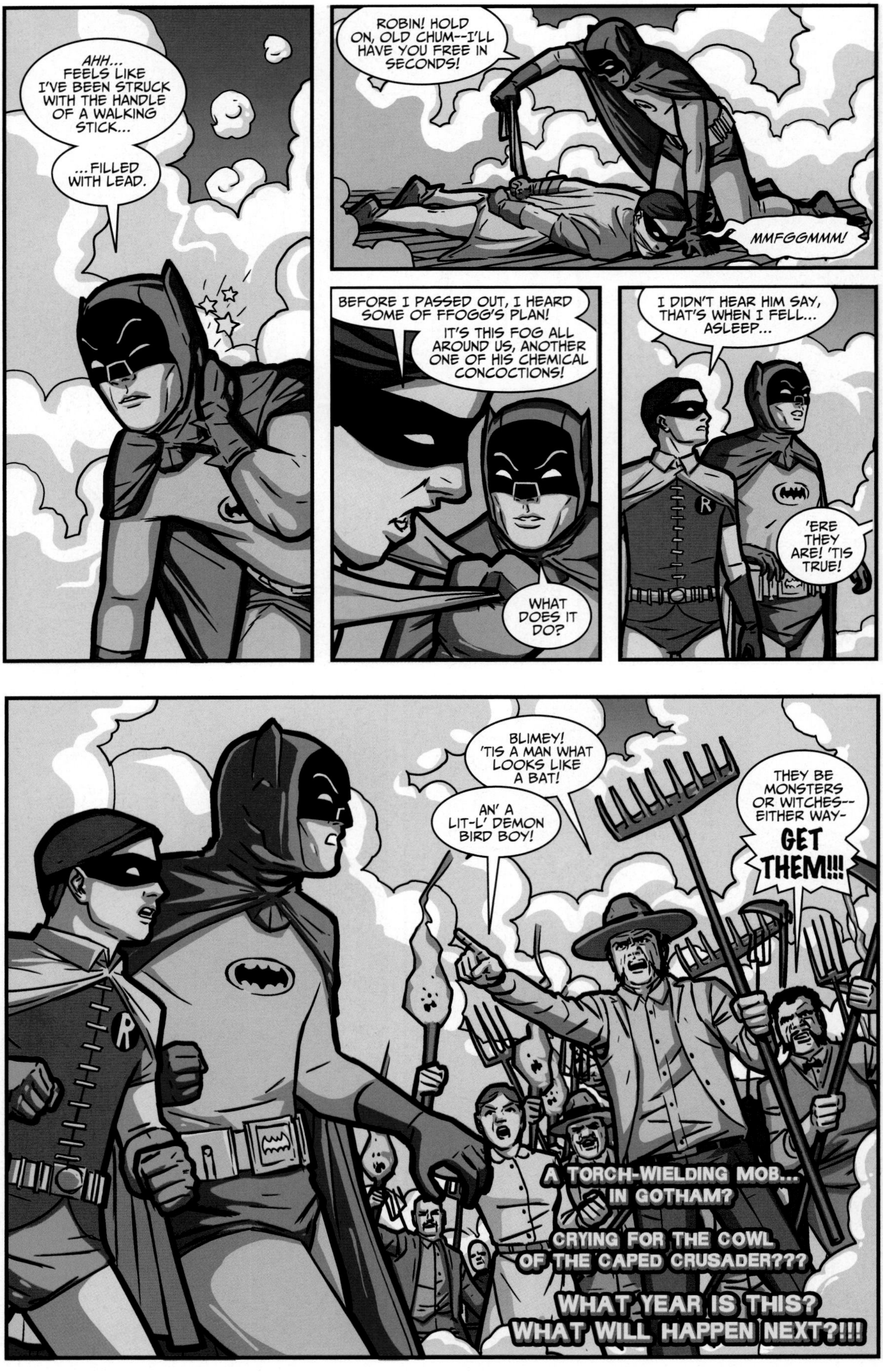

AHH... FEELS LIKE I'VE BEEN STRUCK WITH THE HANDLE OF A WALKING STICK...
...FILLED WITH LEAD.
ROBIN! HOLD ON, OLD CHUM--I'LL HAVE YOU FREE IN SECONDS!
MMFGGMMM!
BEFORE I PASSED OUT, I HEARD SOME OF FFOGG'S PLAN!
IT'S THIS FOG ALL AROUND US, ANOTHER ONE OF HIS CHEMICAL CONCOCTIONS!
WHAT DOES IT DO?
I DIDN'T HEAR HIM SAY, THAT'S WHEN I FELL... ASLEEP...
'ERE THEY ARE! 'TIS TRUE!
BLIMEY! 'TIS A MAN WHAT LOOKS LIKE A BAT!
AN' A LIT-L' DEMON BIRD BOY!
THEY BE MONSTERS OR WITCHES--EITHER WAY- GET THEM!!!
A TORCH-WIELDING MOB... IN GOTHAM?
CRYING FOR THE COWL OF THE CAPED CRUSADER???
WHAT YEAR IS THIS? WHAT WILL HAPPEN NEXT?!!!

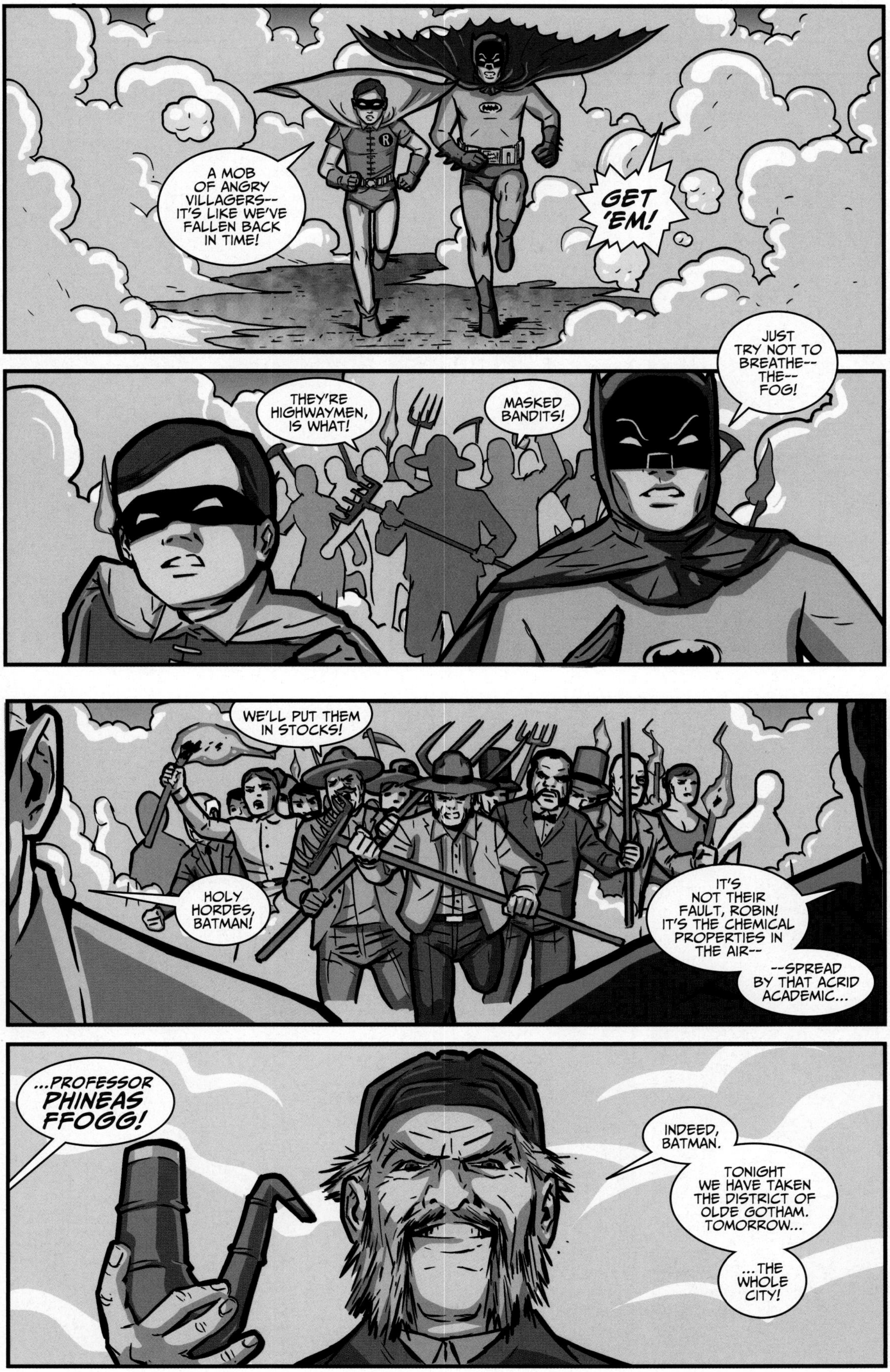

A MOB OF ANGRY VILLAGERS-- IT'S LIKE WE'VE FALLEN BACK IN TIME!
GET 'EM!
JUST TRY NOT TO BREATHE-- THE-- FOG!
THEY'RE HIGHWAYMEN, IS WHAT!
MASKED BANDITS!
WE'LL PUT THEM IN STOCKS!
HOLY HORDES, BATMAN!
IT'S NOT THEIR FAULT, ROBIN! IT'S THE CHEMICAL PROPERTIES IN THE AIR--
--SPREAD BY THAT ACRID ACADEMIC...
...PROFESSOR PHINEAS FFOGG!
INDEED, BATMAN.
TONIGHT WE HAVE TAKEN THE DISTRICT OF OLDE GOTHAM. TOMORROW...
...THE WHOLE CITY!

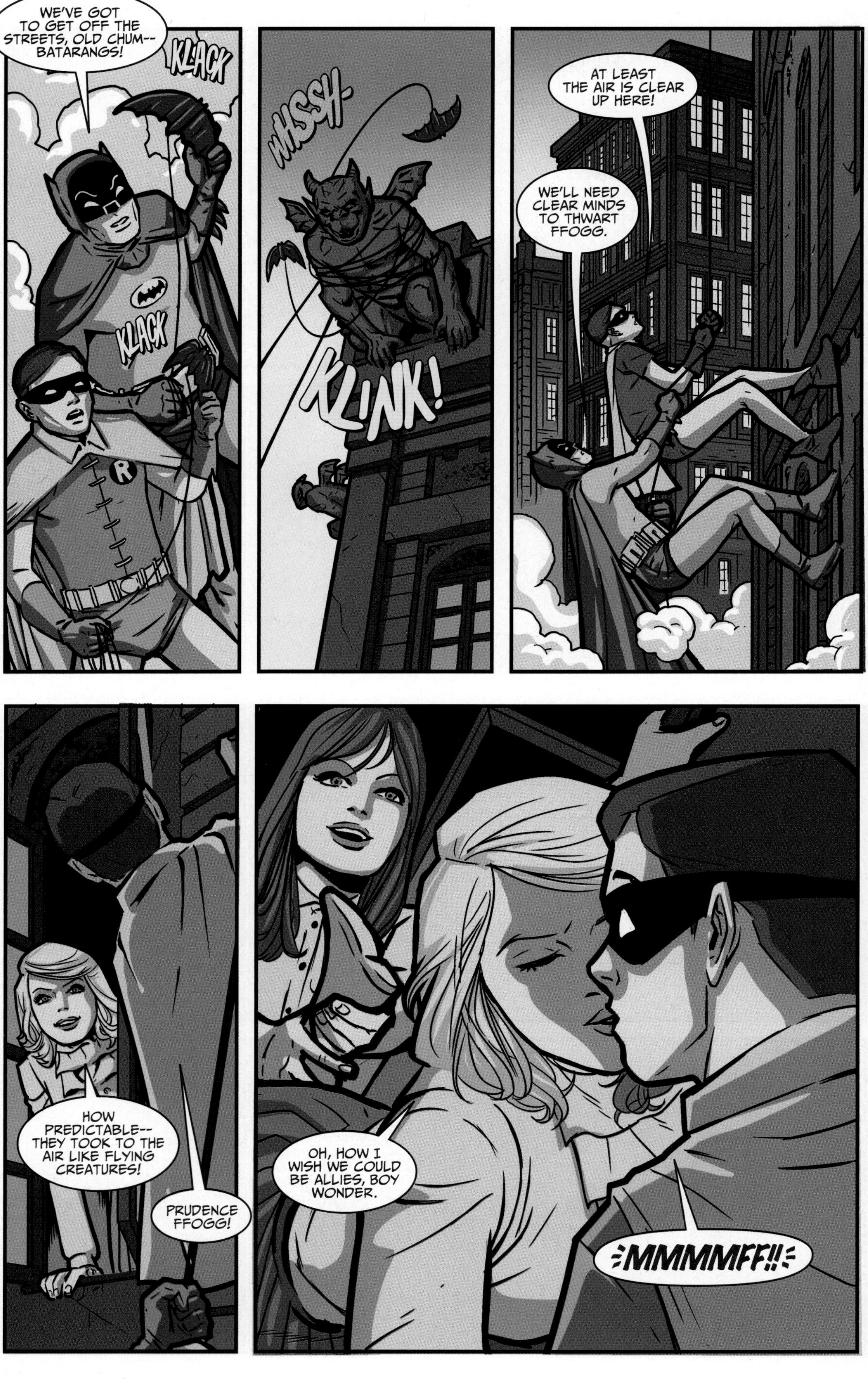

WE'VE GOT TO GET OFF THE STREETS, OLD CHUM-- BATARANGS!
KLACK
KLACK
WHSSH-
KLINK!
AT LEAST THE AIR IS CLEAR UP HERE!
WE'LL NEED CLEAR MINDS TO THWART FFOGG.
HOW PREDICTABLE-- THEY TOOK TO THE AIR LIKE FLYING CREATURES!
PRUDENCE FFOGG!
OH, HOW I WISH WE COULD BE ALLIES, BOY WONDER.
MMMMMFF!!

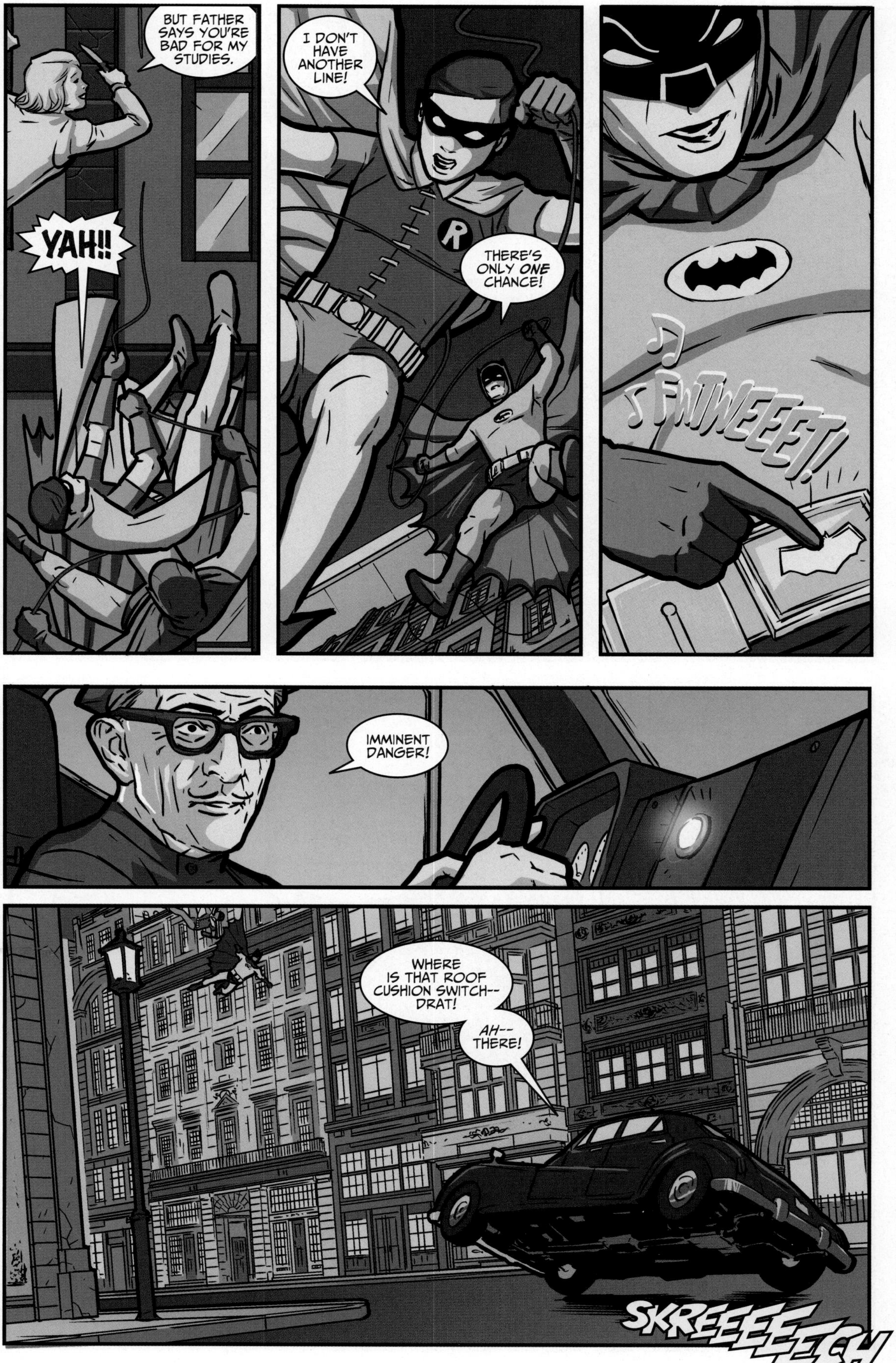
BUT FATHER SAYS YOU'RE BAD FOR MY STUDIES.
YAH!!
I DON'T HAVE ANOTHER LINE!
THERE'S ONLY ONE CHANCE!
FWTWEEET!
IMMINENT DANGER!
WHERE IS THAT ROOF CUSHION SWITCH-- DRAT!
AH-- THERE!
SKREEEEECH

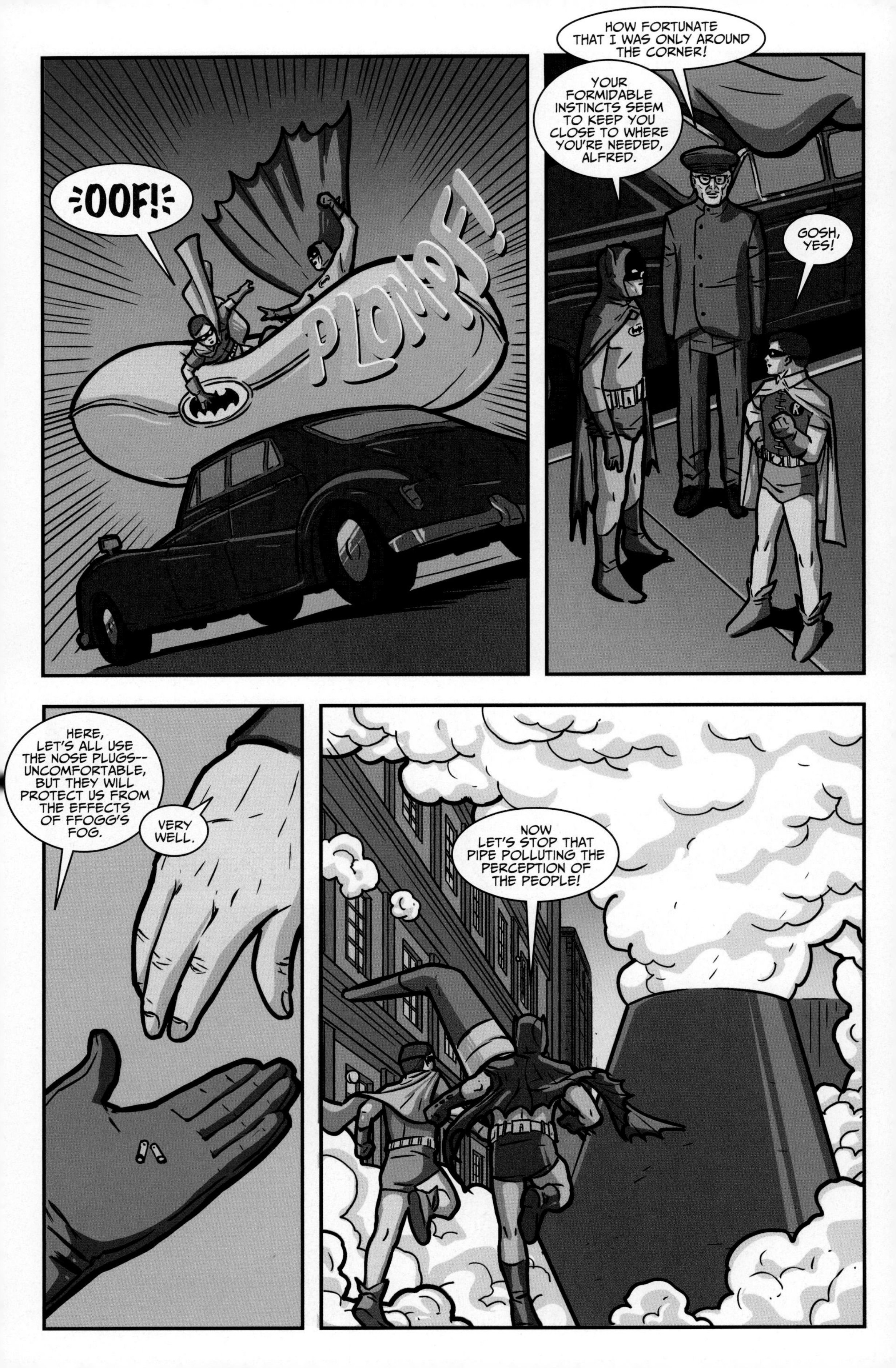

OOF!
PLOMPF!
HOW FORTUNATE THAT I WAS ONLY AROUND THE CORNER!
YOUR FORMIDABLE INSTINCTS SEEM TO KEEP YOU CLOSE TO WHERE YOU'RE NEEDED, ALFRED.
GOSH, YES!
HERE, LET'S ALL USE THE NOSE PLUGS-- UNCOMFORTABLE, BUT THEY WILL PROTECT US FROM THE EFFECTS OF FFOGG'S FOG.
VERY WELL.
NOW LET'S STOP THAT PIPE POLLUTING THE PERCEPTION OF THE PEOPLE!

I DON'T SEE ANY DOOR TO A CONTROL CABINET--I COULD CLIMB IN THROUGH THE TOP...

NO, IT'S TOO MUCH FOR YOUR FILTERS TO BLOCK. HERE.

WE NEED ONLY LOOK FOR THE MOST FINGERPRINTS.

FFOGG IS METICULOUS WITH HIS WORK, HE WOULD NEVER MAKE IT EASY TO FIND...

...AHA!

THIS AREA... HAS BEEN TOUCHED MULTIPLE TIMES BY VARIOUS MEMBERS OF THEIR CRIME SCHOOL.

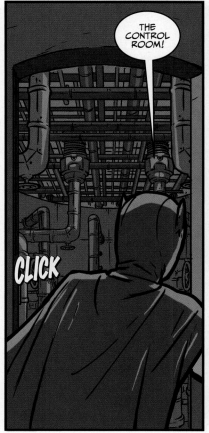

THE CONTROL ROOM!

CLICK

THIS IS IT!

FFOGG HAD ENOUGH CHEMICAL HERE TO DRUG THE AREA FOR A WEEK. SHUT EVERY VALVE OFF TIGHT!

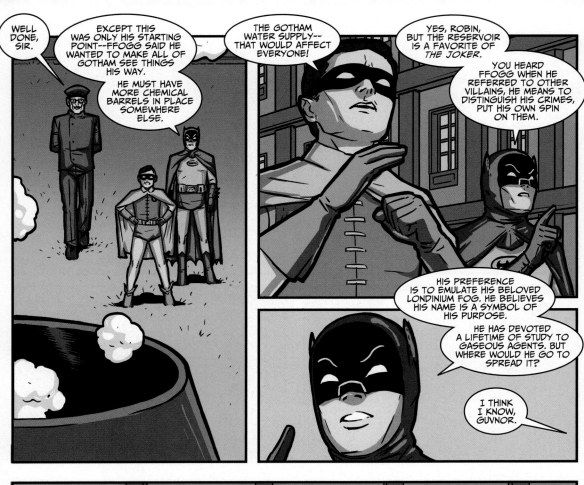

WELL DONE, SIR.

EXCEPT THIS WAS ONLY HIS STARTING POINT--FFOGG SAID HE WANTED TO MAKE ALL OF GOTHAM SEE THINGS HIS WAY.

HE MUST HAVE MORE CHEMICAL BARRELS IN PLACE SOMEWHERE ELSE.

THE GOTHAM WATER SUPPLY-- THAT WOULD AFFECT EVERYONE!

YES, ROBIN, BUT THE RESERVOIR IS A FAVORITE OF *THE JOKER.*

YOU HEARD FFOGG WHEN HE REFERRED TO OTHER VILLAINS, HE MEANS TO DISTINGUISH HIS CRIMES, PUT HIS OWN SPIN ON THEM.

HIS PREFERENCE IS TO EMULATE HIS BELOVED LONDINIUM FOG. HE BELIEVES HIS NAME IS A SYMBOL OF HIS PURPOSE.

HE HAS DEVOTED A LIFETIME OF STUDY TO GASEOUS AGENTS. BUT WHERE WOULD HE GO TO SPREAD IT?

I THINK I KNOW, GUVNOR.

I 'EARD HIS GIRLS TALKIN' ABOUT WHERE THEY 'AD TO SET UP FOR THE "BIG" JOB. RIGHT IN FRONTA ME, THEY DID!

YOU'RE NOT AFRAID OF OUR... APPEARANCE, MA'AM?

I ONLY KNOW THE VOICES OF THE GENTS KIND ENOUGH TO FEED THE PIGEONS.

OF COURSE. *THE BLIND* OFTEN HAVE WELL-TRAINED EARS.

WHERE CAN WE FIND PROFESSOR FFOGG AND HIS ACCOMPLICES?

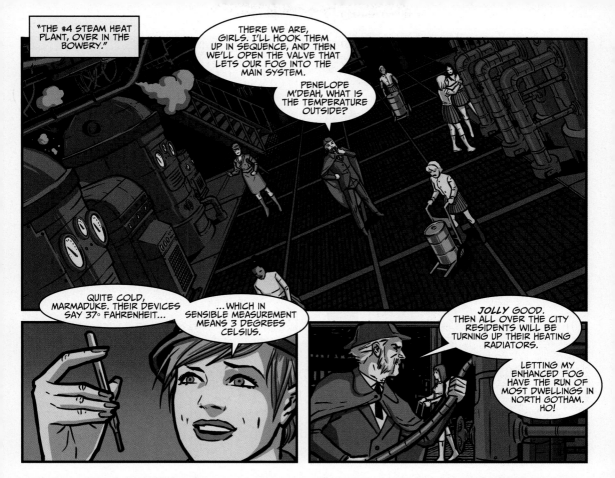

"THE #4 STEAM HEAT PLANT, OVER IN THE BOWERY."

THERE WE ARE, GIRLS. I'LL HOOK THEM UP IN SEQUENCE, AND THEN WE'LL OPEN THE VALVE THAT LETS OUR FOG INTO THE MAIN SYSTEM.

PENELOPE M'DEAH, WHAT IS THE TEMPERATURE OUTSIDE?

QUITE COLD, MARMADUKE. THEIR DEVICES SAY 37° FAHRENHEIT...

...WHICH IN SENSIBLE MEASUREMENT MEANS 3 DEGREES CELSIUS.

JOLLY GOOD. THEN ALL OVER THE CITY RESIDENTS WILL BE TURNING UP THEIR HEATING RADIATORS.

LETTING MY ENHANCED FOG HAVE THE RUN OF MOST DWELLINGS IN NORTH GOTHAM. HO!

TAMPERING WITH CITY MUNICIPALITIES CARRIES A HEAVY SENTENCE, PROFESSOR.

EH?!

YOUR AMERICAN VISA IS REVOKED, FFOGG.

BUT YOU CAN STAY IN ONE OF OUR PRISONS!

ONE OF YOU GIRLS MUST HAVE MENTIONED WE'D BE HERE, SO YOU DEAL WITH THOSE RUFFIANS!

WE SAID NOTHING, AUNTIE!

BUT WE'LL FINISH 'EM.

GOSH, BATMAN, HOW ARE WE GOING TO FIGHT A BUNCH OF WOMEN?!

THEY ARE INDEED FORMIDABLE, ROBIN...

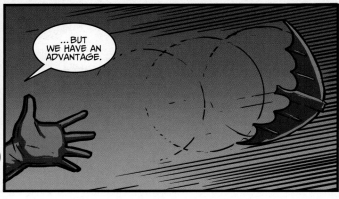

...BUT WE HAVE AN ADVANTAGE.

FFOOSSHH

CLANNG!

THEY'RE TRYIN' TO HIDE!

HIT EVERYTHING THAT MOVES!

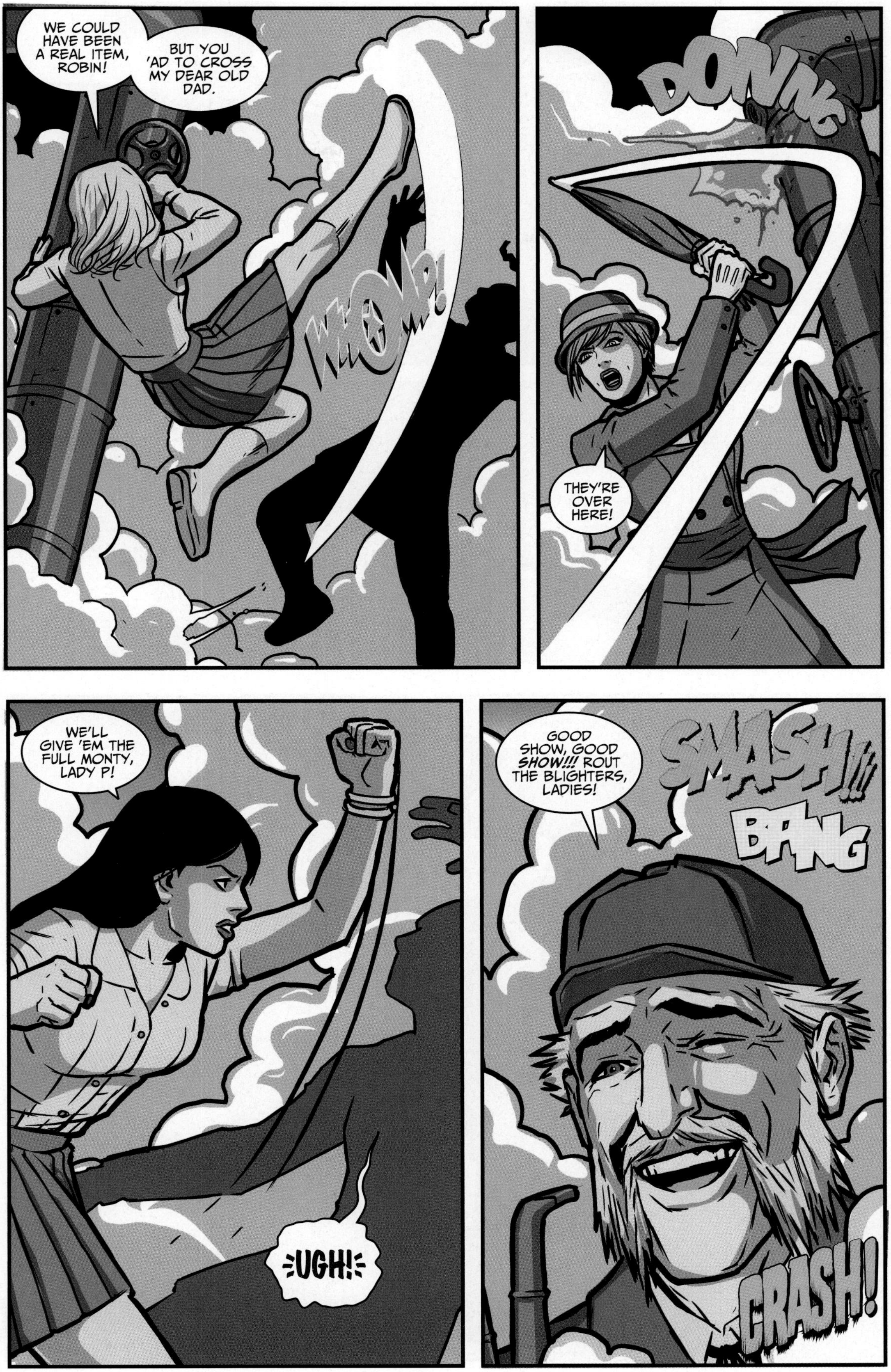
WE COULD HAVE BEEN A REAL ITEM, ROBIN!
BUT YOU 'AD TO CROSS MY DEAR OLD DAD.
WHOMP!
DOING
THEY'RE OVER HERE!
WE'LL GIVE 'EM THE FULL MONTY, LADY P!
UGH!
GOOD SHOW, GOOD SHOW!!! ROUT THE BLIGHTERS, LADIES!
SMASH!!!
BANG
CRASH!

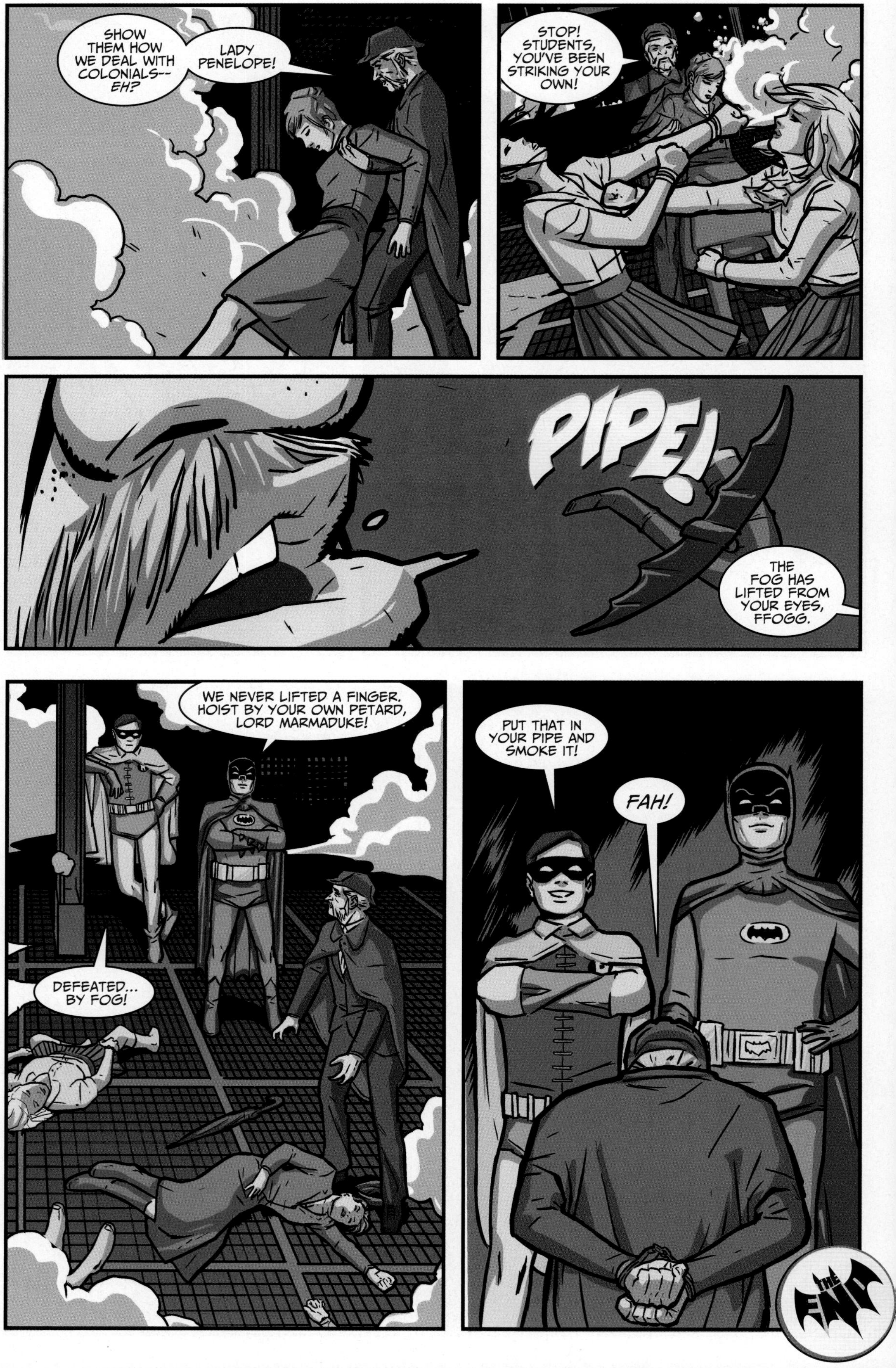
SHOW THEM HOW WE DEAL WITH COLONIALS-- EH?
LADY PENELOPE!
STOP! STUDENTS, YOU'VE BEEN STRIKING YOUR OWN!
PIPE!
THE FOG HAS LIFTED FROM YOUR EYES, FFOGG.
WE NEVER LIFTED A FINGER. HOIST BY YOUR OWN PETARD, LORD MARMADUKE!
DEFEATED... BY FOG!
PUT THAT IN YOUR PIPE AND SMOKE IT!
FAH!
THE END

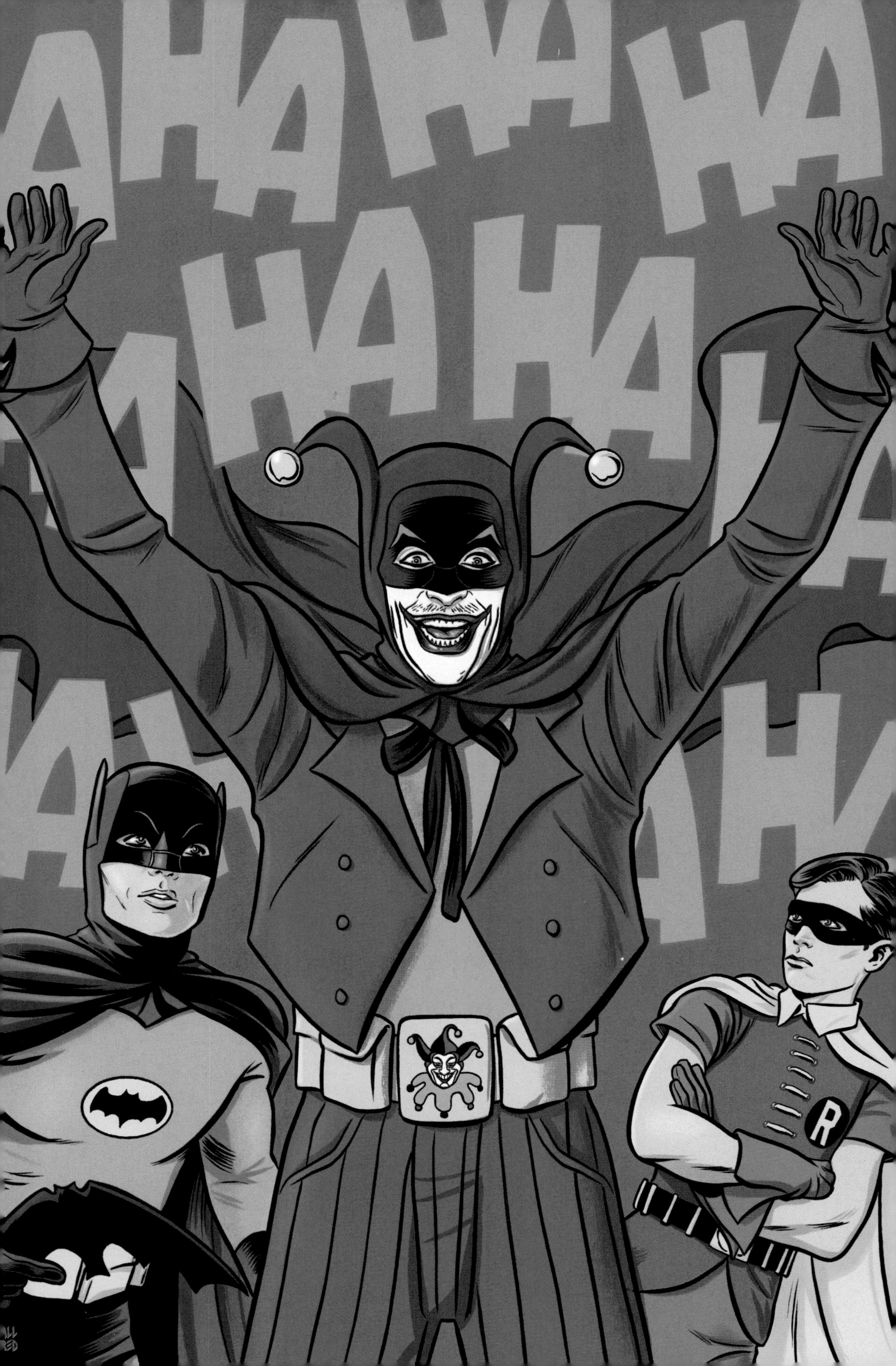
HAHAHA
HAHAHA
HAHAHA
HAHA
R

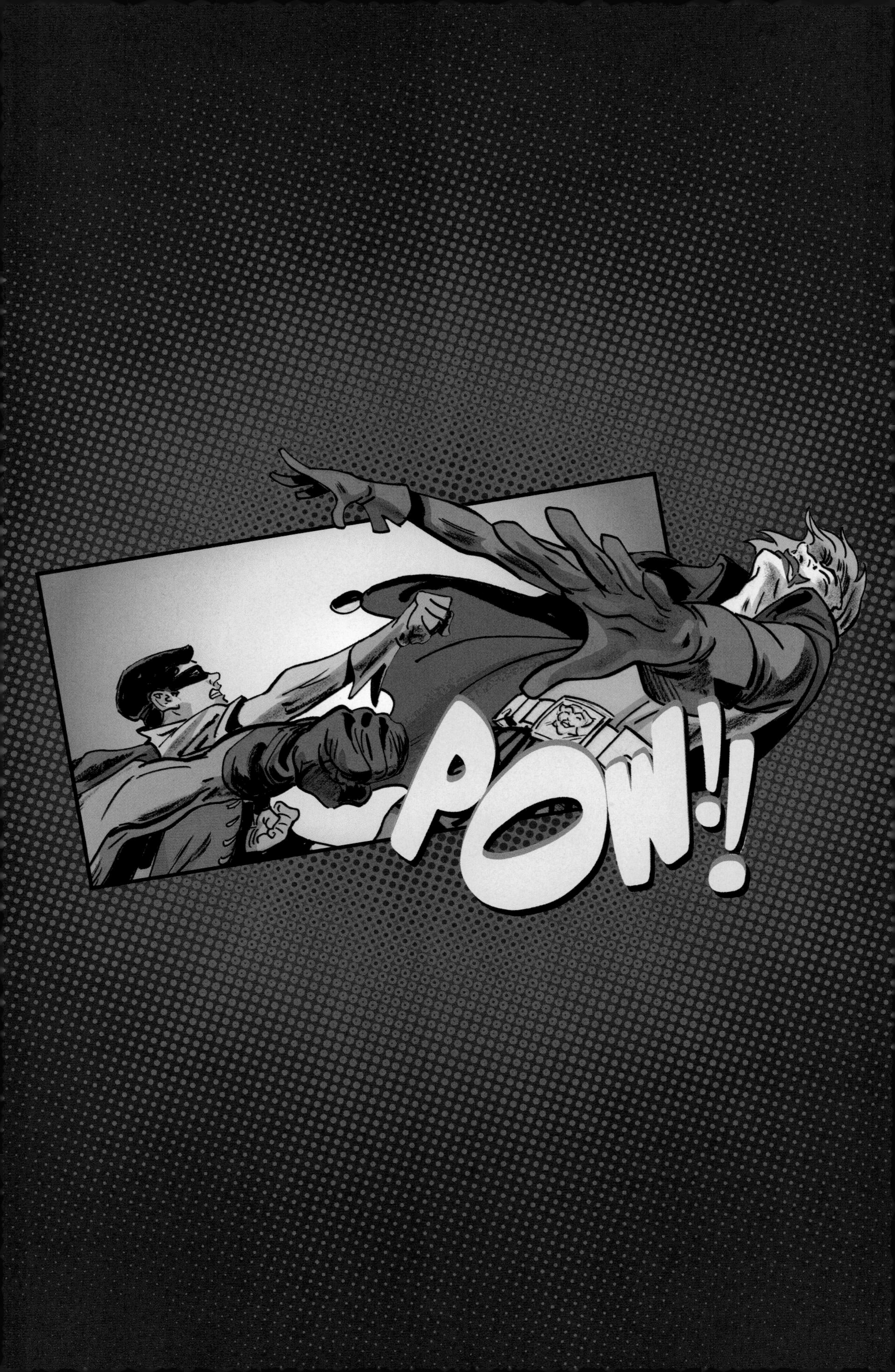
POW!!

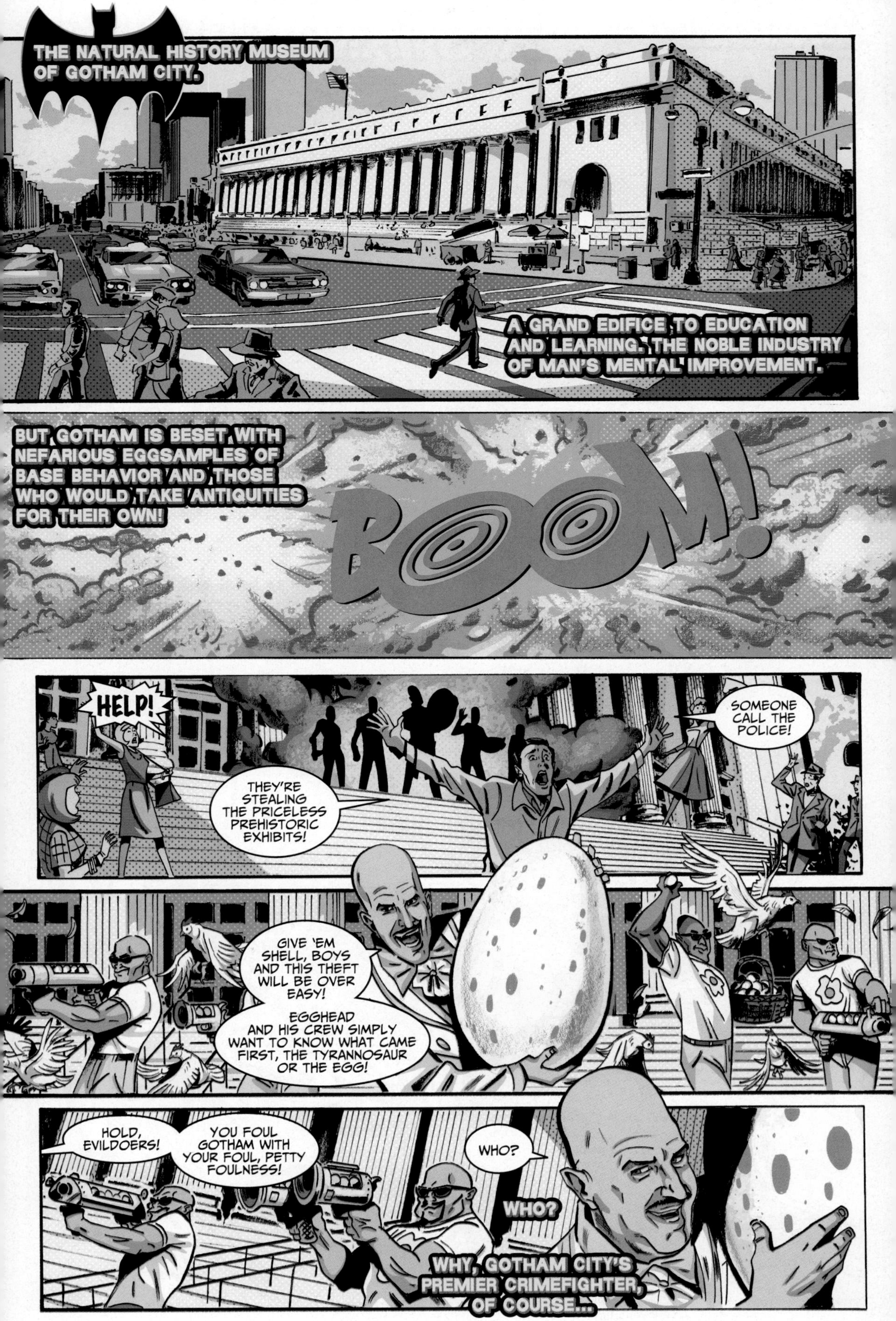
THE NATURAL HISTORY MUSEUM OF GOTHAM CITY.
A GRAND EDIFICE TO EDUCATION AND LEARNING. THE NOBLE INDUSTRY OF MAN'S MENTAL IMPROVEMENT.
BUT GOTHAM IS BESET WITH NEFARIOUS EGGSAMPLES OF BASE BEHAVIOR AND THOSE WHO WOULD TAKE ANTIQUITIES FOR THEIR OWN!
BOOM!
HELP!
SOMEONE CALL THE POLICE!
THEY'RE STEALING THE PRICELESS PREHISTORIC EXHIBITS!
GIVE 'EM SHELL, BOYS AND THIS THEFT WILL BE OVER EASY!
EGGHEAD AND HIS CREW SIMPLY WANT TO KNOW WHAT CAME FIRST, THE TYRANNOSAUR OR THE EGG!
HOLD, EVILDOERS!
YOU FOUL GOTHAM WITH YOUR FOUL, PETTY FOULNESS!
WHO?
WHO?
WHY, GOTHAM CITY'S PREMIER CRIMEFIGHTER, OF COURSE...

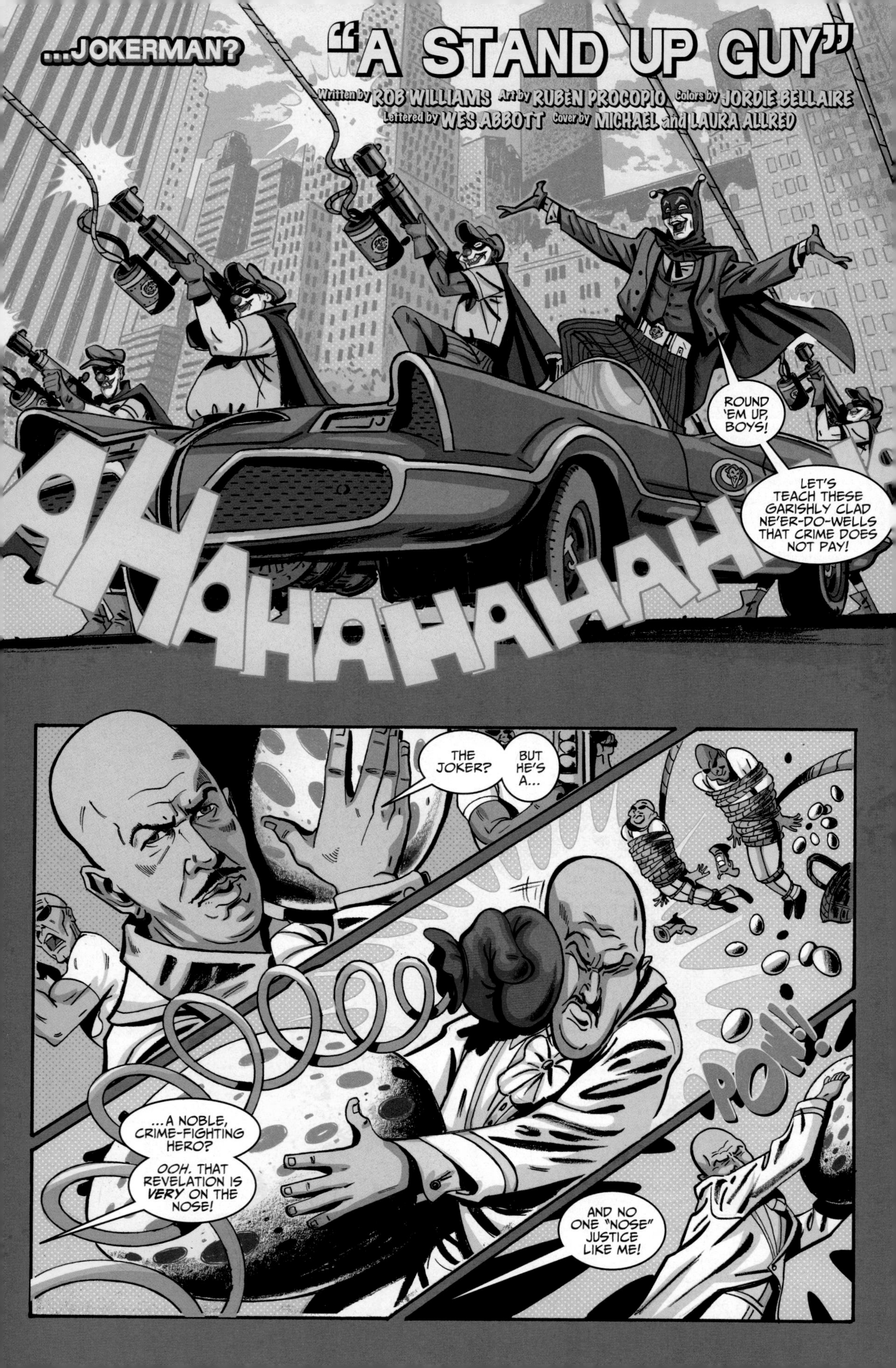

...JOKERMAN?
"A STAND UP GUY"
Written by ROB WILLIAMS Art by RUBEN PROCOPIO Colors by JORDIE BELLAIRE
Lettered by WES ABBOTT Cover by MICHAEL and LAURA ALLRED
ROUND 'EM UP, BOYS!
LET'S TEACH THESE GARISHLY CLAD NE'ER-DO-WELLS THAT CRIME DOES NOT PAY!
HAHAHAHAHAHAH
THE JOKER?
BUT HE'S A...
...A NOBLE, CRIME-FIGHTING HERO?
OOH. THAT REVELATION IS VERY ON THE NOSE!
POW!!
AND NO ONE "NOSE" JUSTICE LIKE ME!

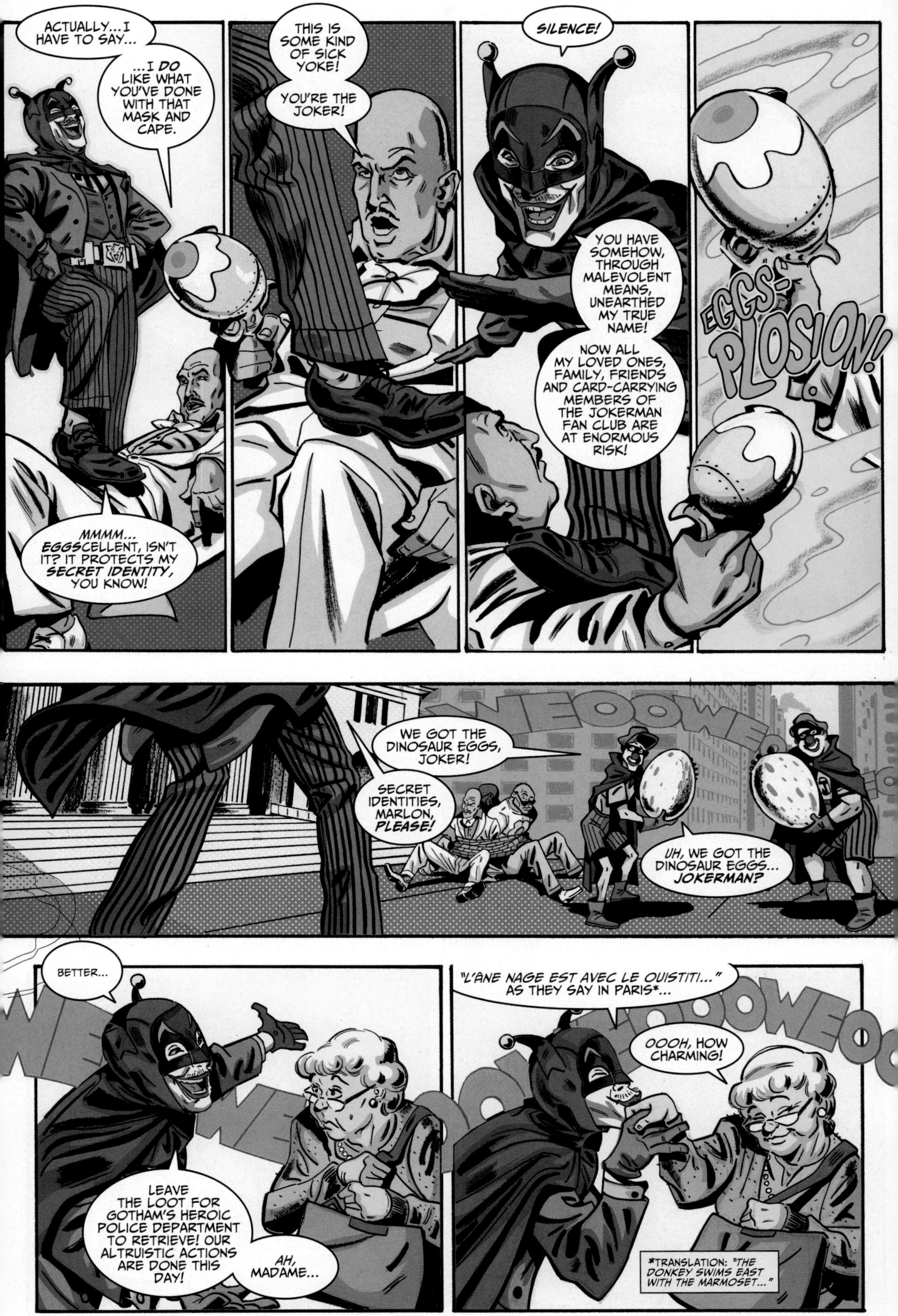
ACTUALLY...I HAVE TO SAY...
...I DO LIKE WHAT YOU'VE DONE WITH THAT MASK AND CAPE.
MMMM... EGGSCELLENT, ISN'T IT? IT PROTECTS MY SECRET IDENTITY, YOU KNOW!
THIS IS SOME KIND OF SICK YOKE!
YOU'RE THE JOKER!
SILENCE!
YOU HAVE SOMEHOW, THROUGH MALEVOLENT MEANS, UNEARTHED MY TRUE NAME!
NOW ALL MY LOVED ONES, FAMILY, FRIENDS AND CARD-CARRYING MEMBERS OF THE JOKERMAN FAN CLUB ARE AT ENORMOUS RISK!
EGGS-PLOSION!
WE GOT THE DINOSAUR EGGS, JOKER!
SECRET IDENTITIES, MARLON, PLEASE!
UH, WE GOT THE DINOSAUR EGGS... JOKERMAN?
BETTER...
LEAVE THE LOOT FOR GOTHAM'S HEROIC POLICE DEPARTMENT TO RETRIEVE! OUR ALTRUISTIC ACTIONS ARE DONE THIS DAY!
AH, MADAME...
"L'ÂNE NAGE EST AVEC LE OUISTITI..." AS THEY SAY IN PARIS*...
OOOH, HOW CHARMING!
*TRANSLATION: "THE DONKEY SWIMS EAST WITH THE MARMOSET..."

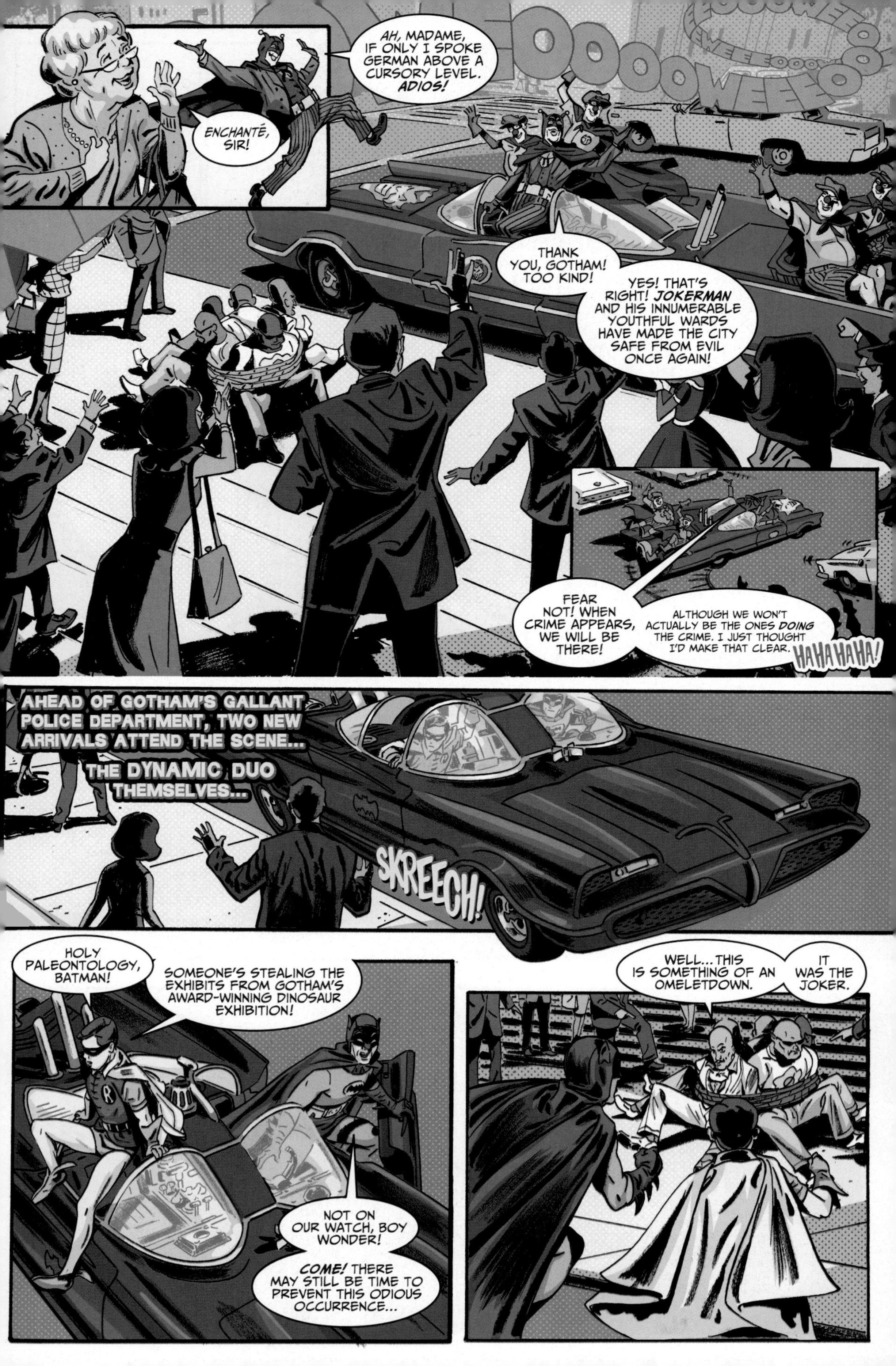
OOOOWEEEOOOWEEEOOOWEEEOOO
AH, MADAME, IF ONLY I SPOKE GERMAN ABOVE A CURSORY LEVEL. ADIOS!
ENCHANTÉ, SIR!
THANK YOU, GOTHAM! TOO KIND!
YES! THAT'S RIGHT! JOKERMAN AND HIS INNUMERABLE YOUTHFUL WARDS HAVE MADE THE CITY SAFE FROM EVIL ONCE AGAIN!
FEAR NOT! WHEN CRIME APPEARS, WE WILL BE THERE!
ALTHOUGH WE WON'T ACTUALLY BE THE ONES DOING THE CRIME. I JUST THOUGHT I'D MAKE THAT CLEAR.
HAHAHAHA!
AHEAD OF GOTHAM'S GALLANT POLICE DEPARTMENT, TWO NEW ARRIVALS ATTEND THE SCENE...
THE DYNAMIC DUO THEMSELVES...
SKREECH!
HOLY PALEONTOLOGY, BATMAN!
SOMEONE'S STEALING THE EXHIBITS FROM GOTHAM'S AWARD-WINNING DINOSAUR EXHIBITION!
NOT ON OUR WATCH, BOY WONDER!
COME! THERE MAY STILL BE TIME TO PREVENT THIS ODIOUS OCCURRENCE...
WELL... THIS IS SOMETHING OF AN OMELETDOWN.
IT WAS THE JOKER.

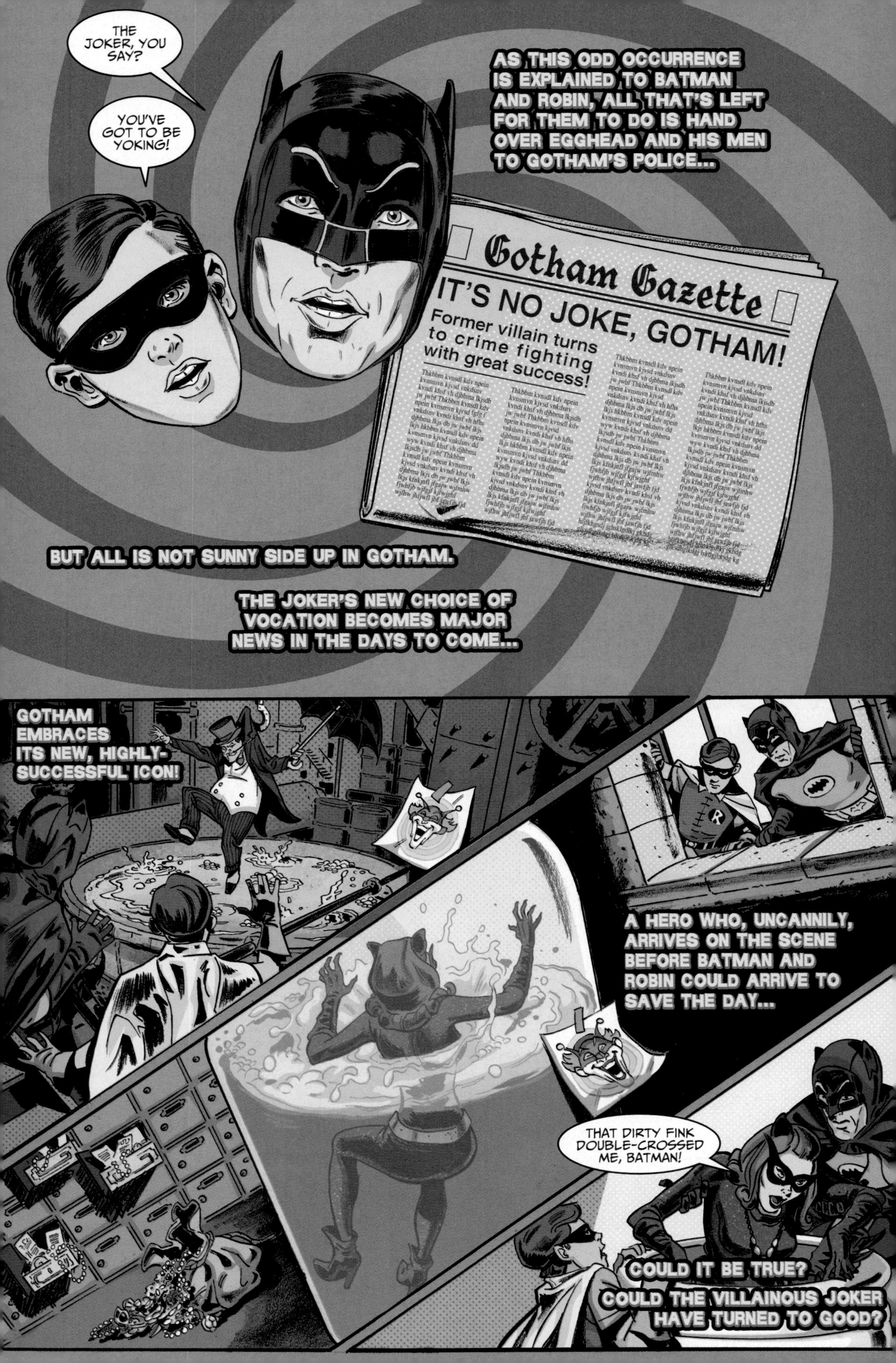
THE JOKER, YOU SAY?
YOU'VE GOT TO BE YOKING!
AS THIS ODD OCCURRENCE IS EXPLAINED TO BATMAN AND ROBIN, ALL THAT'S LEFT FOR THEM TO DO IS HAND OVER EGGHEAD AND HIS MEN TO GOTHAM'S POLICE...
Gotham Gazette
IT'S NO JOKE, GOTHAM!
Former villain turns to crime fighting with great success!
BUT ALL IS NOT SUNNY SIDE UP IN GOTHAM.
THE JOKER'S NEW CHOICE OF VOCATION BECOMES MAJOR NEWS IN THE DAYS TO COME...
GOTHAM EMBRACES ITS NEW, HIGHLY-SUCCESSFUL ICON!
A HERO WHO, UNCANNILY, ARRIVES ON THE SCENE BEFORE BATMAN AND ROBIN COULD ARRIVE TO SAVE THE DAY...
THAT DIRTY FINK DOUBLE-CROSSED ME, BATMAN!
COULD IT BE TRUE?
COULD THE VILLAINOUS JOKER HAVE TURNED TO GOOD?

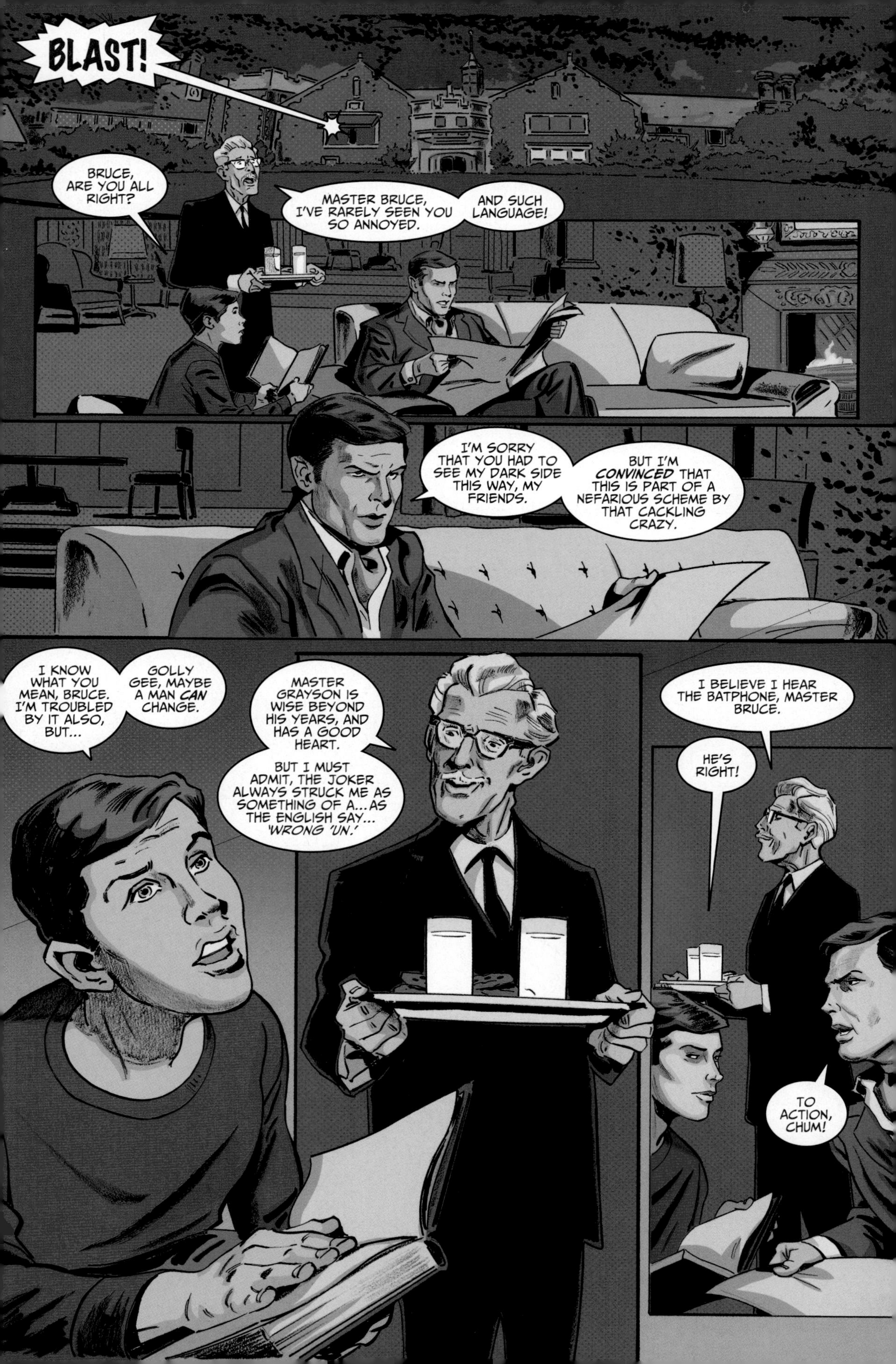
BLAST!
BRUCE, ARE YOU ALL RIGHT?
MASTER BRUCE, I'VE RARELY SEEN YOU SO ANNOYED.
AND SUCH LANGUAGE!
I'M SORRY THAT YOU HAD TO SEE MY DARK SIDE THIS WAY, MY FRIENDS.
BUT I'M *CONVINCED* THAT THIS IS PART OF A NEFARIOUS SCHEME BY THAT CACKLING CRAZY.
I KNOW WHAT YOU MEAN, BRUCE. I'M TROUBLED BY IT ALSO, BUT...
GOLLY GEE, MAYBE A MAN *CAN* CHANGE.
MASTER GRAYSON IS WISE BEYOND HIS YEARS, AND HAS A GOOD HEART.
BUT I MUST ADMIT, THE JOKER ALWAYS STRUCK ME AS SOMETHING OF A... AS THE ENGLISH SAY... *'WRONG 'UN.'*
I BELIEVE I HEAR THE BATPHONE, MASTER BRUCE.
HE'S RIGHT!
TO ACTION, CHUM!

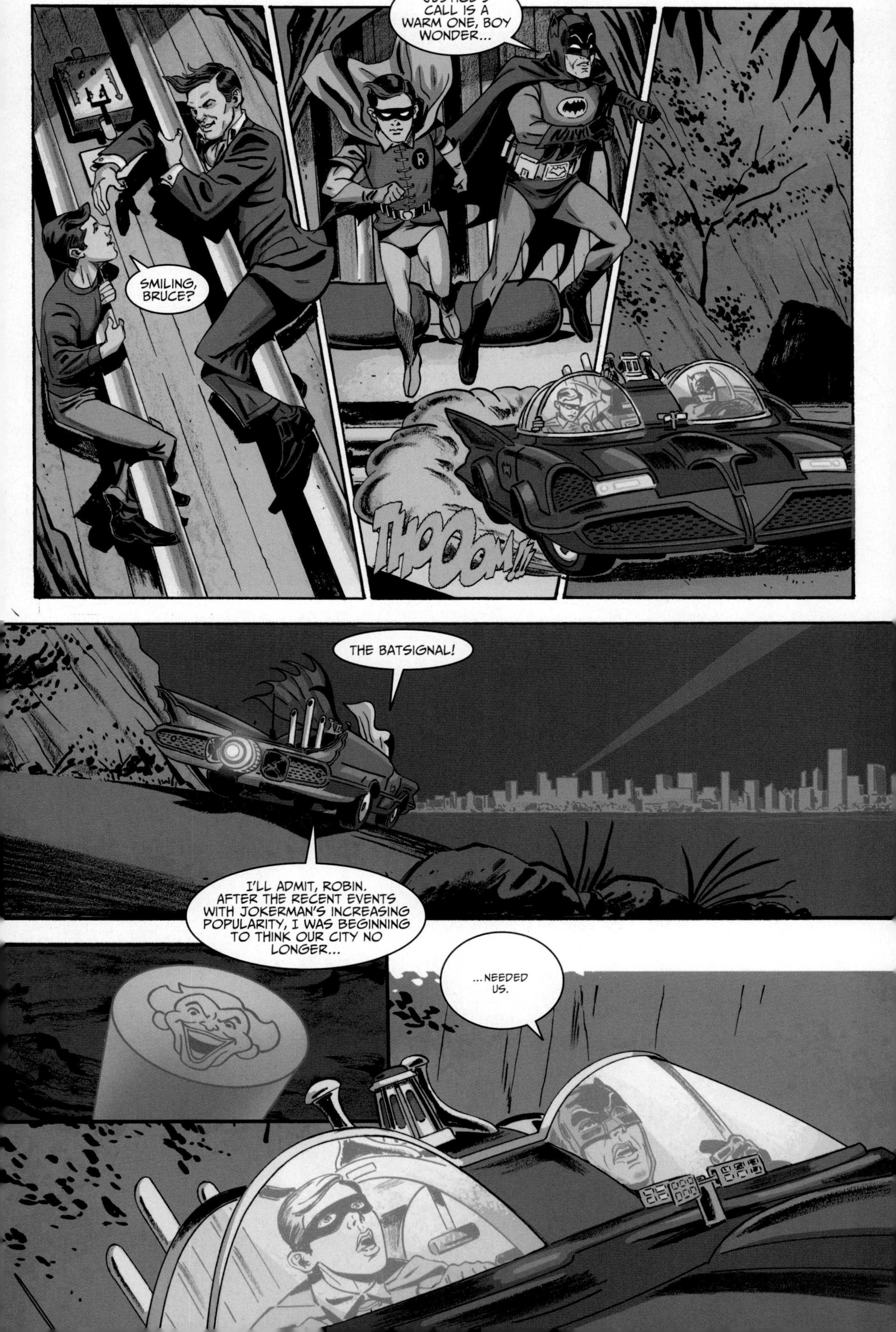
SMILING, BRUCE?
JUSTICE'S CALL IS A WARM ONE, BOY WONDER...
THOOOM!!
THE BATSIGNAL!
I'LL ADMIT, ROBIN. AFTER THE RECENT EVENTS WITH JOKERMAN'S INCREASING POPULARITY, I WAS BEGINNING TO THINK OUR CITY NO LONGER...
...NEEDED US.

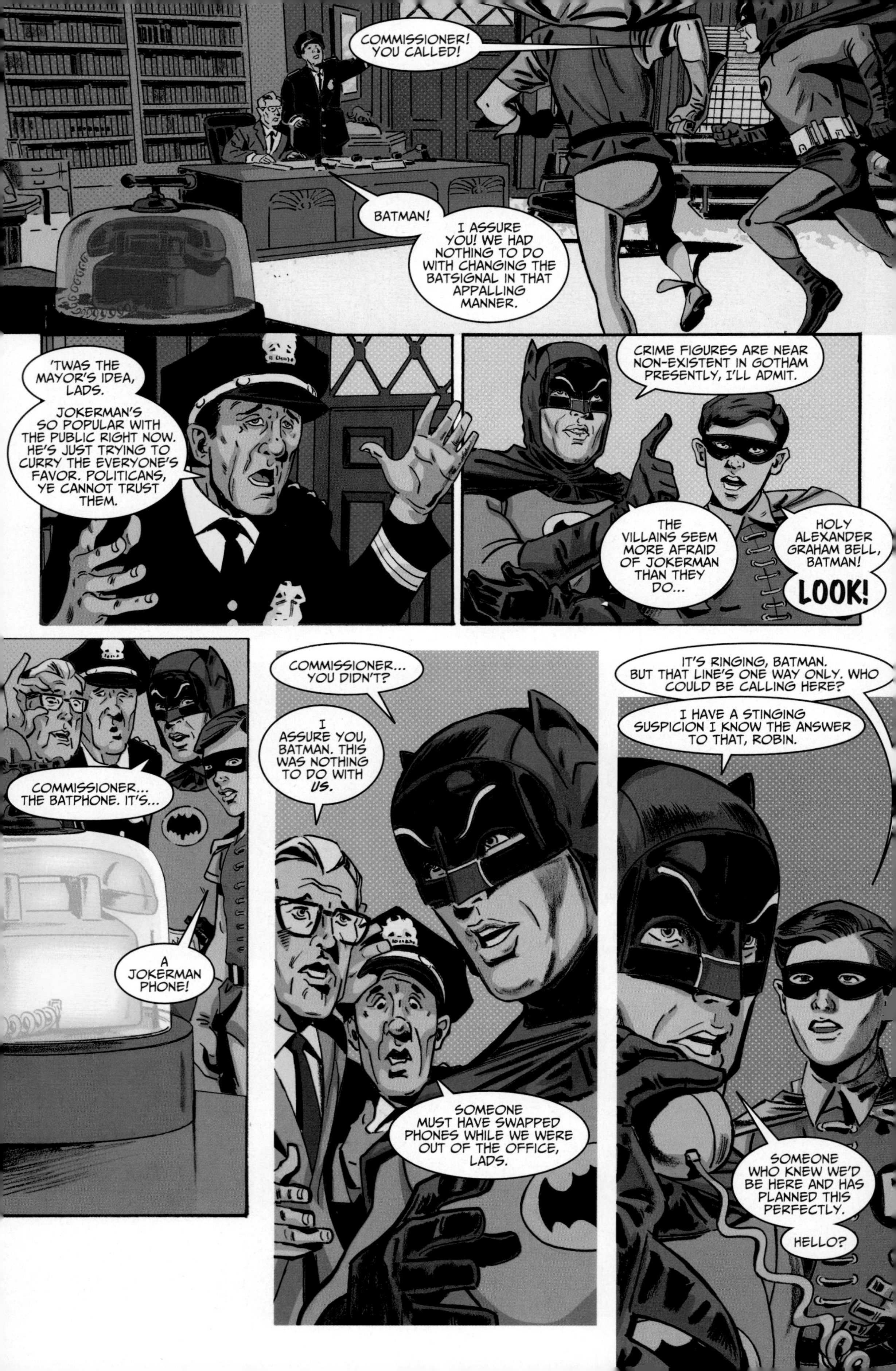
COMMISSIONER! YOU CALLED!
BATMAN!
I ASSURE YOU! WE HAD NOTHING TO DO WITH CHANGING THE BATSIGNAL IN THAT APPALLING MANNER.
'TWAS THE MAYOR'S IDEA, LADS.
JOKERMAN'S SO POPULAR WITH THE PUBLIC RIGHT NOW. HE'S JUST TRYING TO CURRY THE EVERYONE'S FAVOR. POLITICANS, YE CANNOT TRUST THEM.
CRIME FIGURES ARE NEAR NON-EXISTENT IN GOTHAM PRESENTLY, I'LL ADMIT.
THE VILLAINS SEEM MORE AFRAID OF JOKERMAN THAN THEY DO...
HOLY ALEXANDER GRAHAM BELL, BATMAN!
LOOK!
COMMISSIONER... THE BATPHONE. IT'S...
A JOKERMAN PHONE!
COMMISSIONER... YOU DIDN'T?
I ASSURE YOU, BATMAN. THIS WAS NOTHING TO DO WITH US.
SOMEONE MUST HAVE SWAPPED PHONES WHILE WE WERE OUT OF THE OFFICE, LADS.
IT'S RINGING, BATMAN. BUT THAT LINE'S ONE WAY ONLY. WHO COULD BE CALLING HERE?
I HAVE A STINGING SUSPICION I KNOW THE ANSWER TO THAT, ROBIN.
SOMEONE WHO KNEW WE'D BE HERE AND HAS PLANNED THIS PERFECTLY.
HELLO?

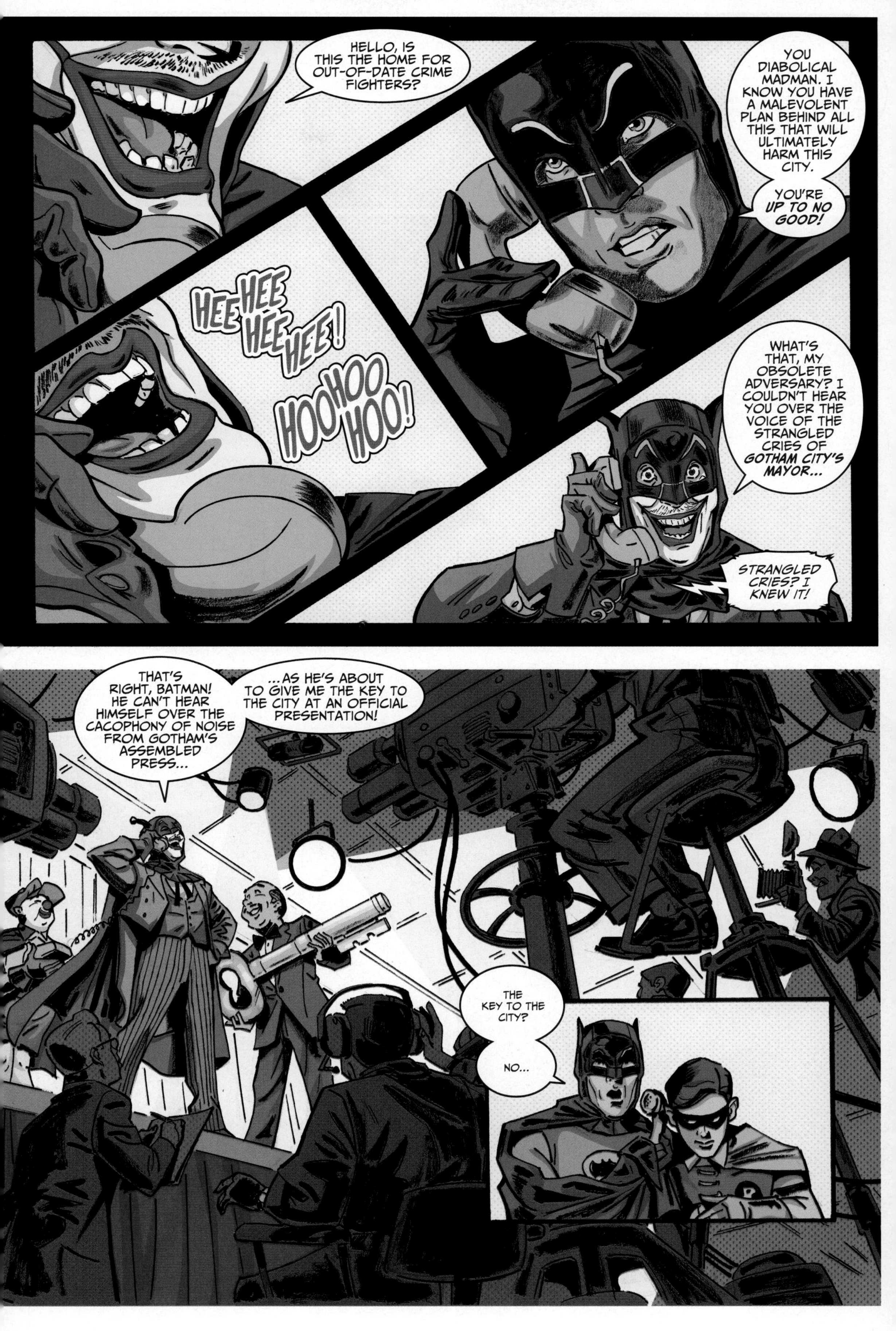
HELLO, IS THIS THE HOME FOR OUT-OF-DATE CRIME FIGHTERS?
YOU DIABOLICAL MADMAN. I KNOW YOU HAVE A MALEVOLENT PLAN BEHIND ALL THIS THAT WILL ULTIMATELY HARM THIS CITY.
YOU'RE UP TO NO GOOD!
HEE HEE HEE HEE!
HOOHOO HOO!
WHAT'S THAT, MY OBSOLETE ADVERSARY? I COULDN'T HEAR YOU OVER THE VOICE OF THE STRANGLED CRIES OF GOTHAM CITY'S MAYOR...
STRANGLED CRIES? I KNEW IT!
THAT'S RIGHT, BATMAN! HE CAN'T HEAR HIMSELF OVER THE CACOPHONY OF NOISE FROM GOTHAM'S ASSEMBLED PRESS...
...AS HE'S ABOUT TO GIVE ME THE KEY TO THE CITY AT AN OFFICIAL PRESENTATION!
THE KEY TO THE CITY?
NO...

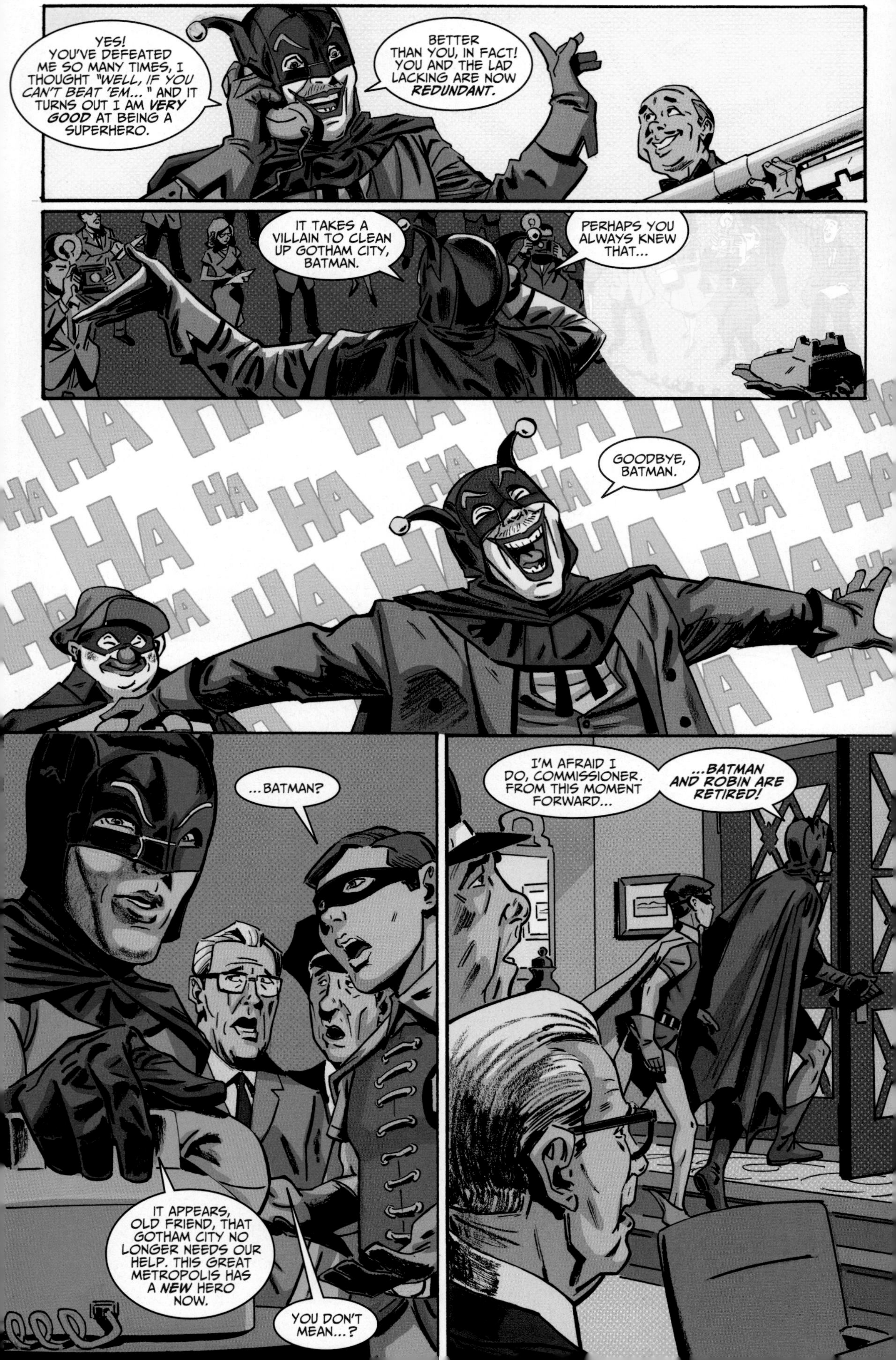
YES! YOU'VE DEFEATED ME SO MANY TIMES, I THOUGHT "WELL, IF YOU CAN'T BEAT 'EM..." AND IT TURNS OUT I AM VERY GOOD AT BEING A SUPERHERO.
BETTER THAN YOU, IN FACT! YOU AND THE LAD LACKING ARE NOW REDUNDANT.
IT TAKES A VILLAIN TO CLEAN UP GOTHAM CITY, BATMAN.
PERHAPS YOU ALWAYS KNEW THAT...
GOODBYE, BATMAN.
HA HA HA HA HA HA HA HA HA HA HA HA HA HA HA HA HA HA HA HA
...BATMAN?
IT APPEARS, OLD FRIEND, THAT GOTHAM CITY NO LONGER NEEDS OUR HELP. THIS GREAT METROPOLIS HAS A NEW HERO NOW.
YOU DON'T MEAN...?
I'M AFRAID I DO, COMMISSIONER. FROM THIS MOMENT FORWARD...
...BATMAN AND ROBIN ARE RETIRED!

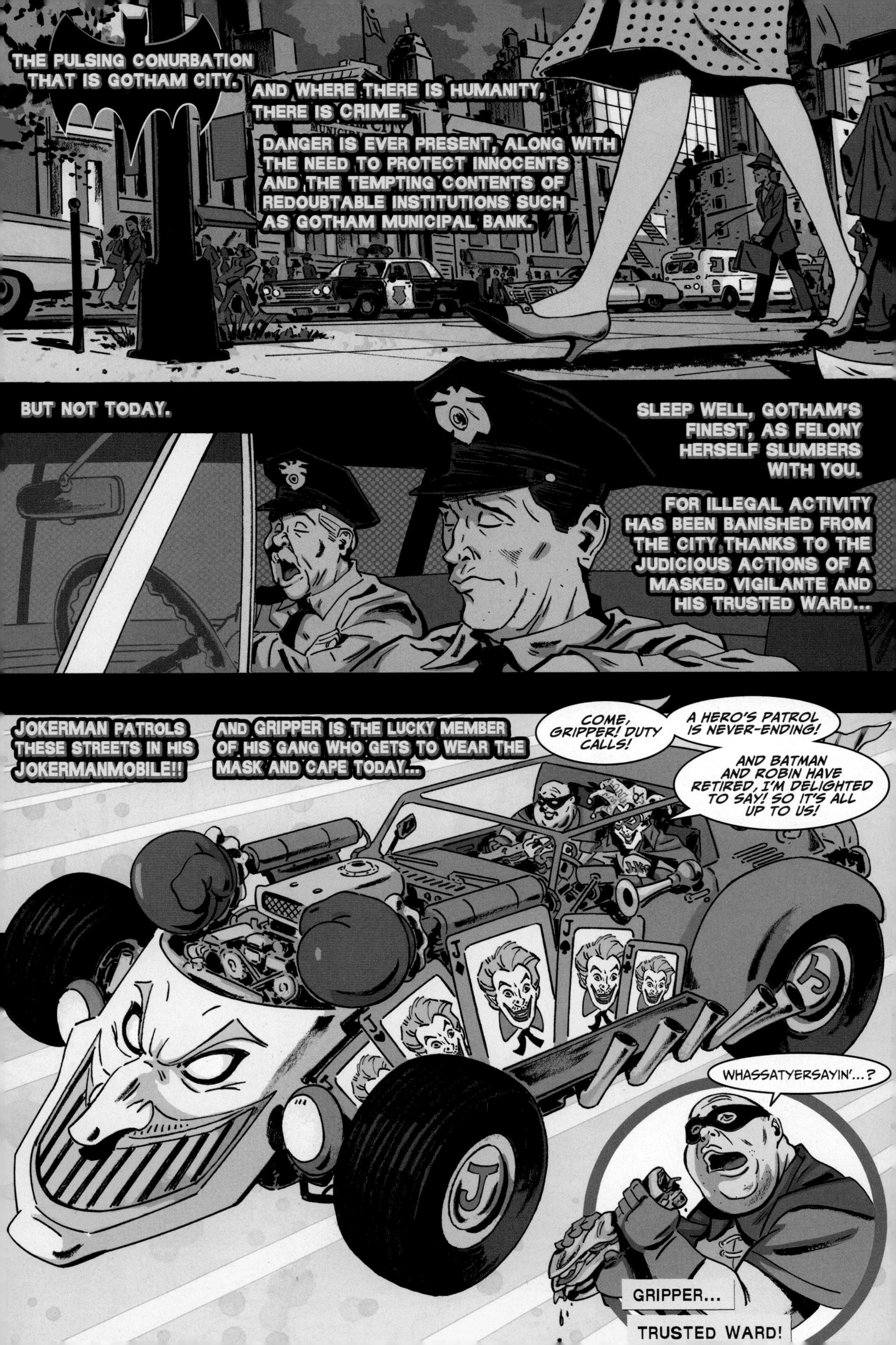

THE PULSING CONURBATION THAT IS GOTHAM CITY.
AND WHERE THERE IS HUMANITY, THERE IS CRIME.
DANGER IS EVER PRESENT, ALONG WITH THE NEED TO PROTECT INNOCENTS AND THE TEMPTING CONTENTS OF REDOUBTABLE INSTITUTIONS SUCH AS GOTHAM MUNICIPAL BANK.
BUT NOT TODAY.
SLEEP WELL, GOTHAM'S FINEST, AS FELONY HERSELF SLUMBERS WITH YOU.
FOR ILLEGAL ACTIVITY HAS BEEN BANISHED FROM THE CITY THANKS TO THE JUDICIOUS ACTIONS OF A MASKED VIGILANTE AND HIS TRUSTED WARD...
JOKERMAN PATROLS THESE STREETS IN HIS JOKERMANMOBILE!!
AND GRIPPER IS THE LUCKY MEMBER OF HIS GANG WHO GETS TO WEAR THE MASK AND CAPE TODAY...
COME, GRIPPER! DUTY CALLS!
A HERO'S PATROL IS NEVER-ENDING!
AND BATMAN AND ROBIN HAVE RETIRED, I'M DELIGHTED TO SAY! SO IT'S ALL UP TO US!
WHASSATYERSAYIN'...?
GRIPPER...
TRUSTED WARD!

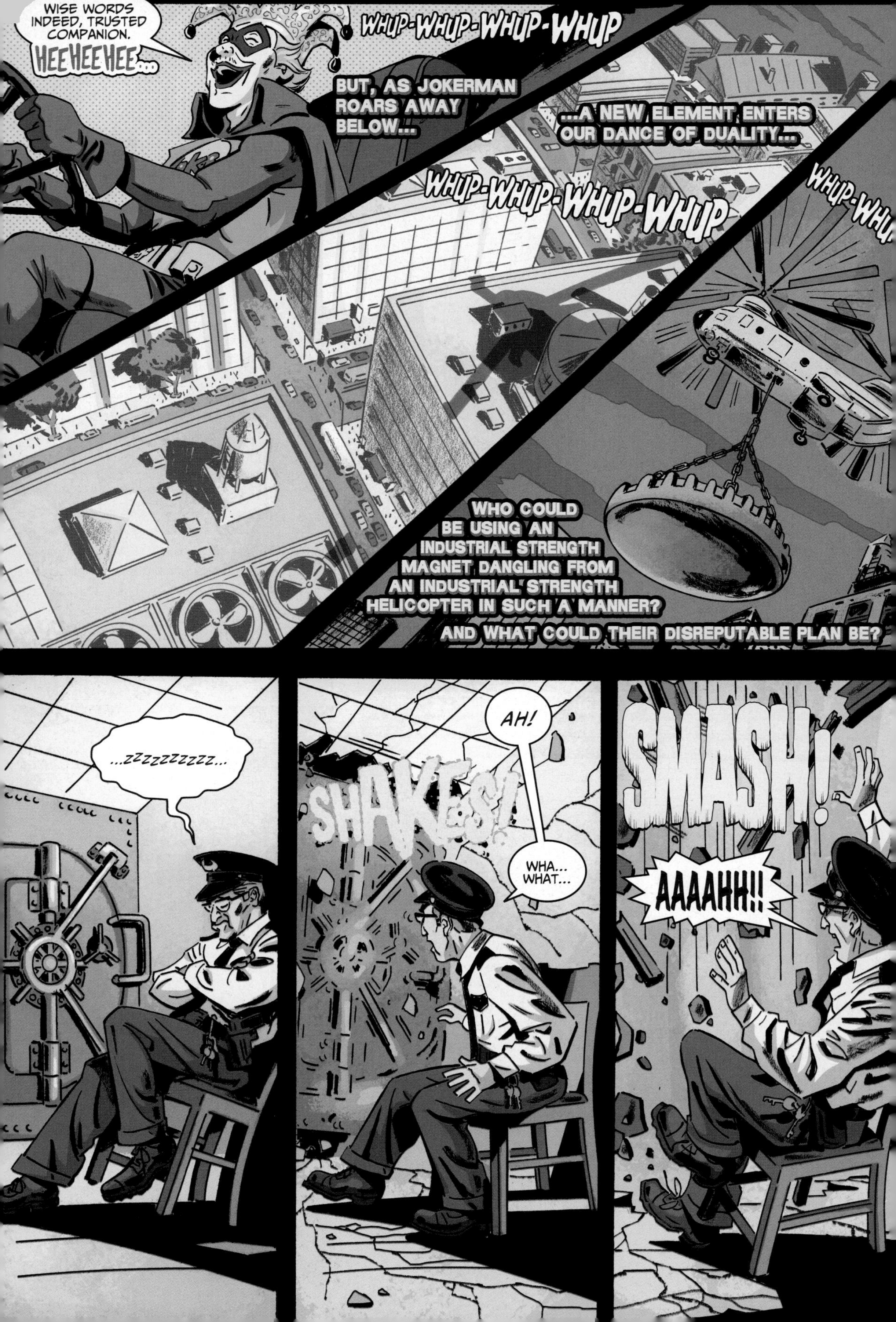

WISE WORDS INDEED, TRUSTED COMPANION.
HEE HEE HEE...
WHUP-WHUP-WHUP-WHUP
BUT, AS JOKERMAN ROARS AWAY BELOW...
...A NEW ELEMENT ENTERS OUR DANCE OF DUALITY...
WHUP-WHUP-WHUP-WHUP
WHUP-WHU
WHO COULD BE USING AN INDUSTRIAL STRENGTH MAGNET DANGLING FROM AN INDUSTRIAL STRENGTH HELICOPTER IN SUCH A MANNER?
AND WHAT COULD THEIR DISREPUTABLE PLAN BE?
...ZZZZZZZZZZ...
SHAKES!
AH!
WHA... WHAT...
SMASH!
AAAAHH!!

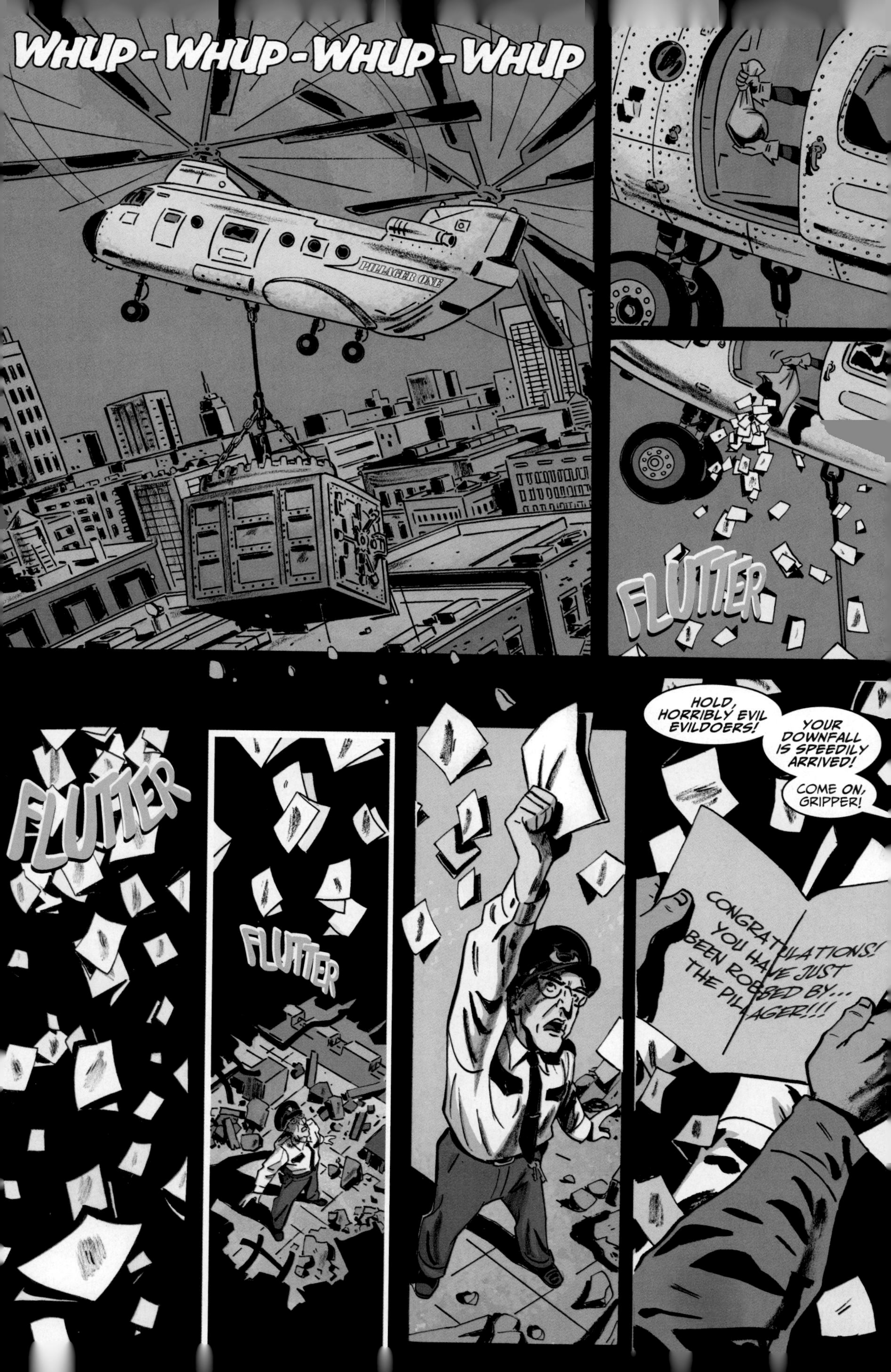
WHUP-WHUP-WHUP-WHUP
PILLAGER ONE
FLUTTER
FLUTTER
FLUTTER
HOLD, HORRIBLY EVIL EVILDOERS!
YOUR DOWNFALL IS SPEEDILY ARRIVED!
COME ON, GRIPPER!
CONGRATULATIONS! YOU HAVE JUST BEEN ROBBED BY... THE PILLAGER!!!

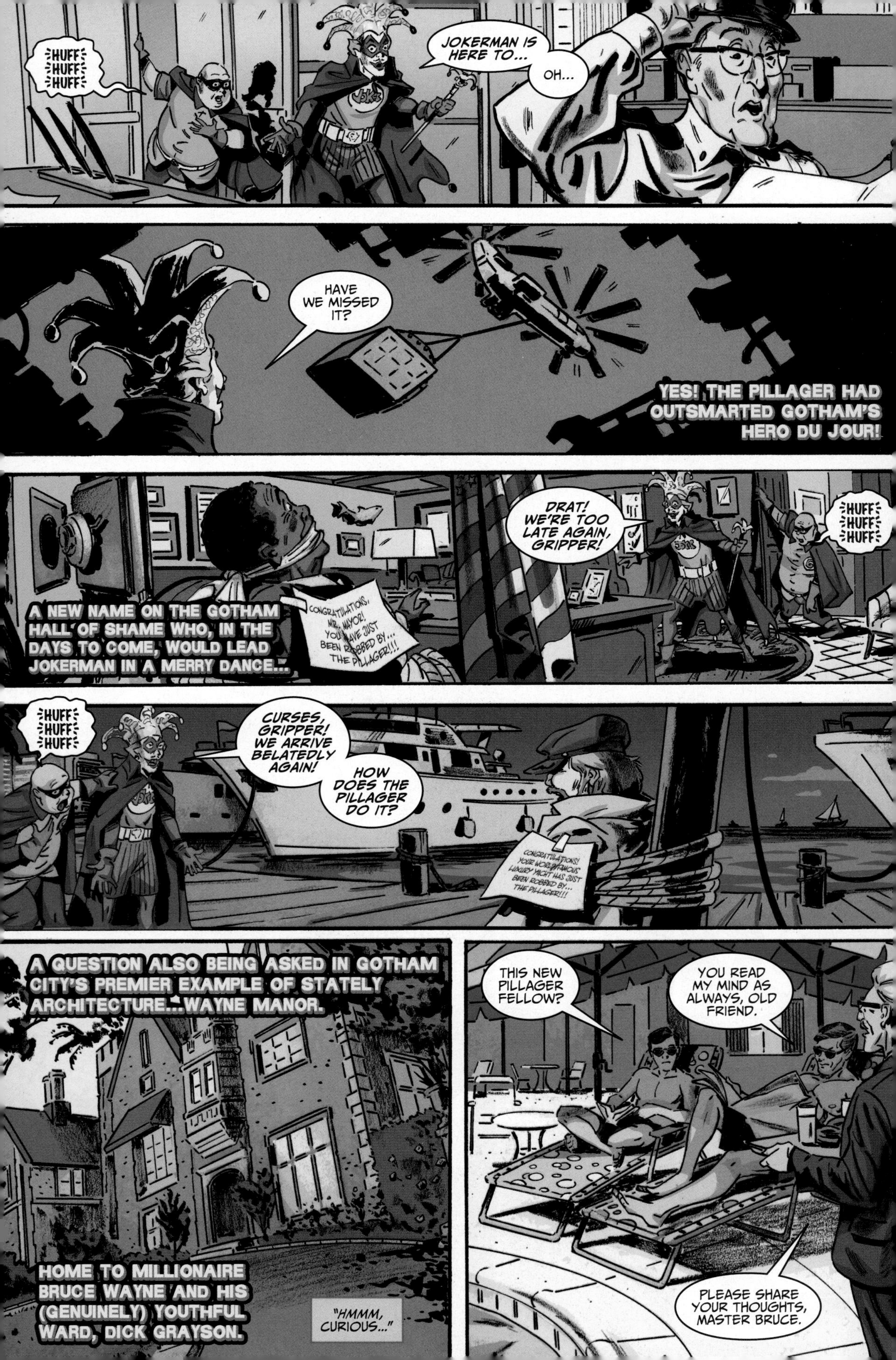

HUFF HUFF HUFF
JOKERMAN IS HERE TO...
OH...
HAVE WE MISSED IT?
YES! THE PILLAGER HAD OUTSMARTED GOTHAM'S HERO DU JOUR!
A NEW NAME ON THE GOTHAM HALL OF SHAME WHO, IN THE DAYS TO COME, WOULD LEAD JOKERMAN IN A MERRY DANCE...
CONGRATULATIONS, MR. MAYOR! YOU HAVE JUST BEEN ROBBED BY... THE PILLAGER!!!
DRAT! WE'RE TOO LATE AGAIN, GRIPPER!
HUFF HUFF HUFF
HUFF HUFF HUFF
CURSES, GRIPPER! WE ARRIVE BELATEDLY AGAIN!
HOW DOES THE PILLAGER DO IT?
CONGRATULATIONS! YOUR WORLD-FAMOUS LUXURY YACHT HAS JUST BEEN ROBBED BY... THE PILLAGER!!!
A QUESTION ALSO BEING ASKED IN GOTHAM CITY'S PREMIER EXAMPLE OF STATELY ARCHITECTURE...WAYNE MANOR.
HOME TO MILLIONAIRE BRUCE WAYNE AND HIS (GENUINELY) YOUTHFUL WARD, DICK GRAYSON.
"HMMM, CURIOUS..."
THIS NEW PILLAGER FELLOW?
YOU READ MY MIND AS ALWAYS, OLD FRIEND.
PLEASE SHARE YOUR THOUGHTS, MASTER BRUCE.

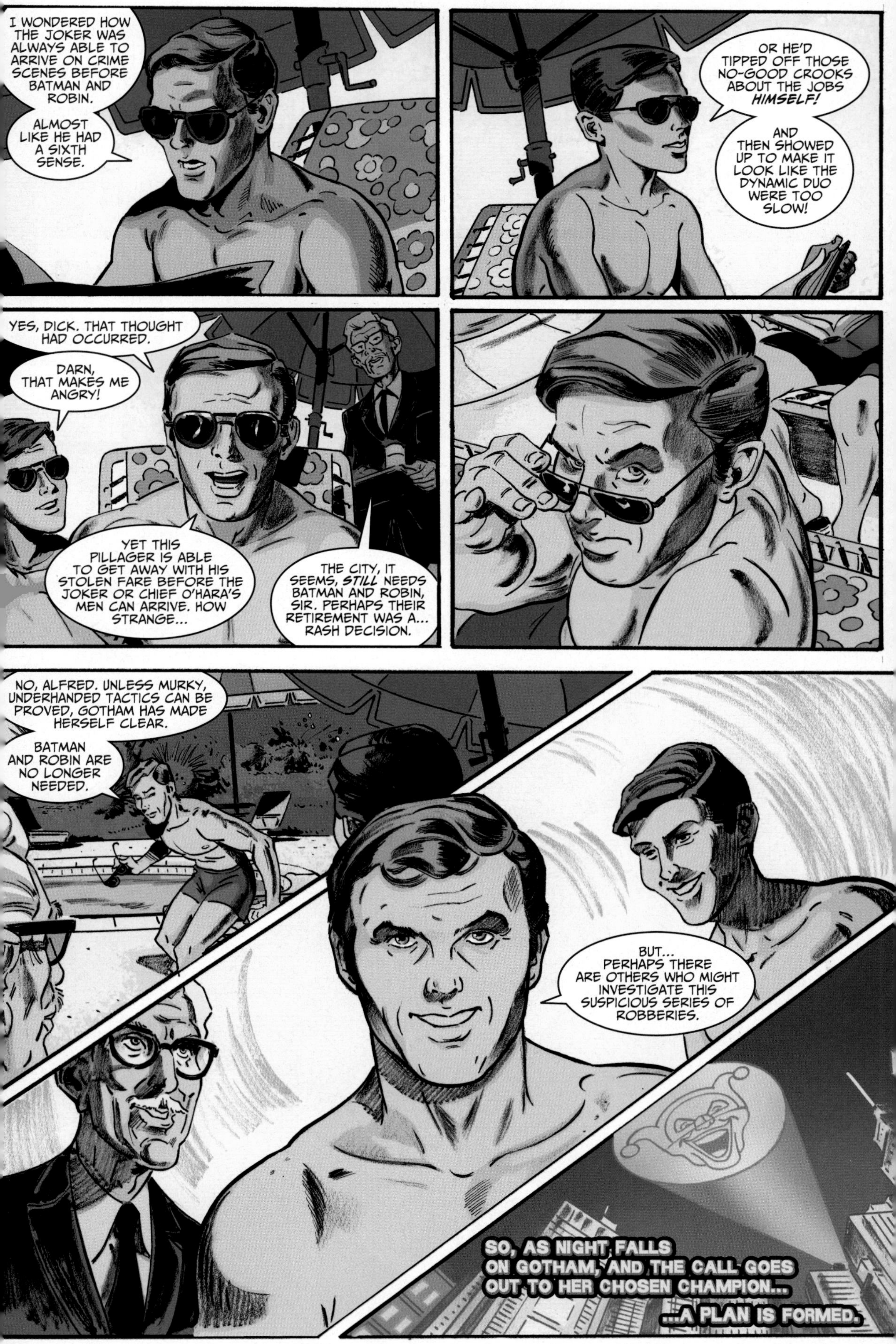

I WONDERED HOW THE JOKER WAS ALWAYS ABLE TO ARRIVE ON CRIME SCENES BEFORE BATMAN AND ROBIN.
ALMOST LIKE HE HAD A SIXTH SENSE.
OR HE'D TIPPED OFF THOSE NO-GOOD CROOKS ABOUT THE JOBS *HIMSELF!*
AND THEN SHOWED UP TO MAKE IT LOOK LIKE THE DYNAMIC DUO WERE TOO SLOW!
YES, DICK. THAT THOUGHT HAD OCCURRED.
DARN, THAT MAKES ME ANGRY!
YET THIS PILLAGER IS ABLE TO GET AWAY WITH HIS STOLEN FARE BEFORE THE JOKER OR CHIEF O'HARA'S MEN CAN ARRIVE. HOW STRANGE...
THE CITY, IT SEEMS, *STILL* NEEDS BATMAN AND ROBIN, SIR. PERHAPS THEIR RETIREMENT WAS A... RASH DECISION.
NO, ALFRED. UNLESS MURKY, UNDERHANDED TACTICS CAN BE PROVED, GOTHAM HAS MADE HERSELF CLEAR.
BATMAN AND ROBIN ARE NO LONGER NEEDED.
BUT... PERHAPS THERE ARE OTHERS WHO MIGHT INVESTIGATE THIS SUSPICIOUS SERIES OF ROBBERIES.
SO, AS NIGHT FALLS ON GOTHAM, AND THE CALL GOES OUT TO HER CHOSEN CHAMPION...
...A PLAN IS FORMED.

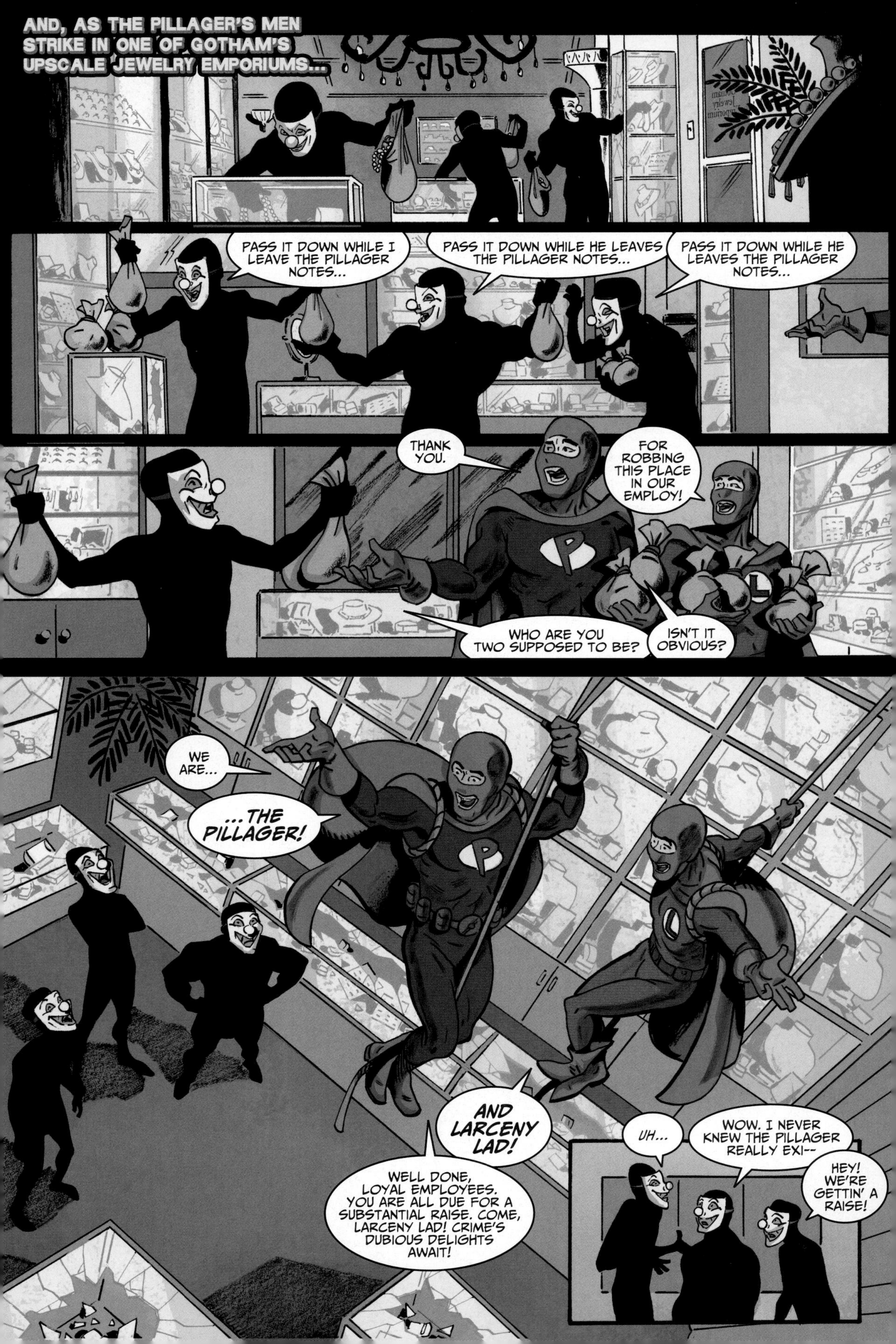
AND, AS THE PILLAGER'S MEN STRIKE IN ONE OF GOTHAM'S UPSCALE JEWELRY EMPORIUMS...
PASS IT DOWN WHILE I LEAVE THE PILLAGER NOTES...
PASS IT DOWN WHILE HE LEAVES THE PILLAGER NOTES...
PASS IT DOWN WHILE HE LEAVES THE PILLAGER NOTES...
THANK YOU.
FOR ROBBING THIS PLACE IN OUR EMPLOY!
WHO ARE YOU TWO SUPPOSED TO BE?
ISN'T IT OBVIOUS?
WE ARE...
...THE PILLAGER!
AND LARCENY LAD!
WELL DONE, LOYAL EMPLOYEES. YOU ARE ALL DUE FOR A SUBSTANTIAL RAISE. COME, LARCENY LAD! CRIME'S DUBIOUS DELIGHTS AWAIT!
UH...
WOW. I NEVER KNEW THE PILLAGER REALLY EXI--
HEY! WE'RE GETTIN' A RAISE!

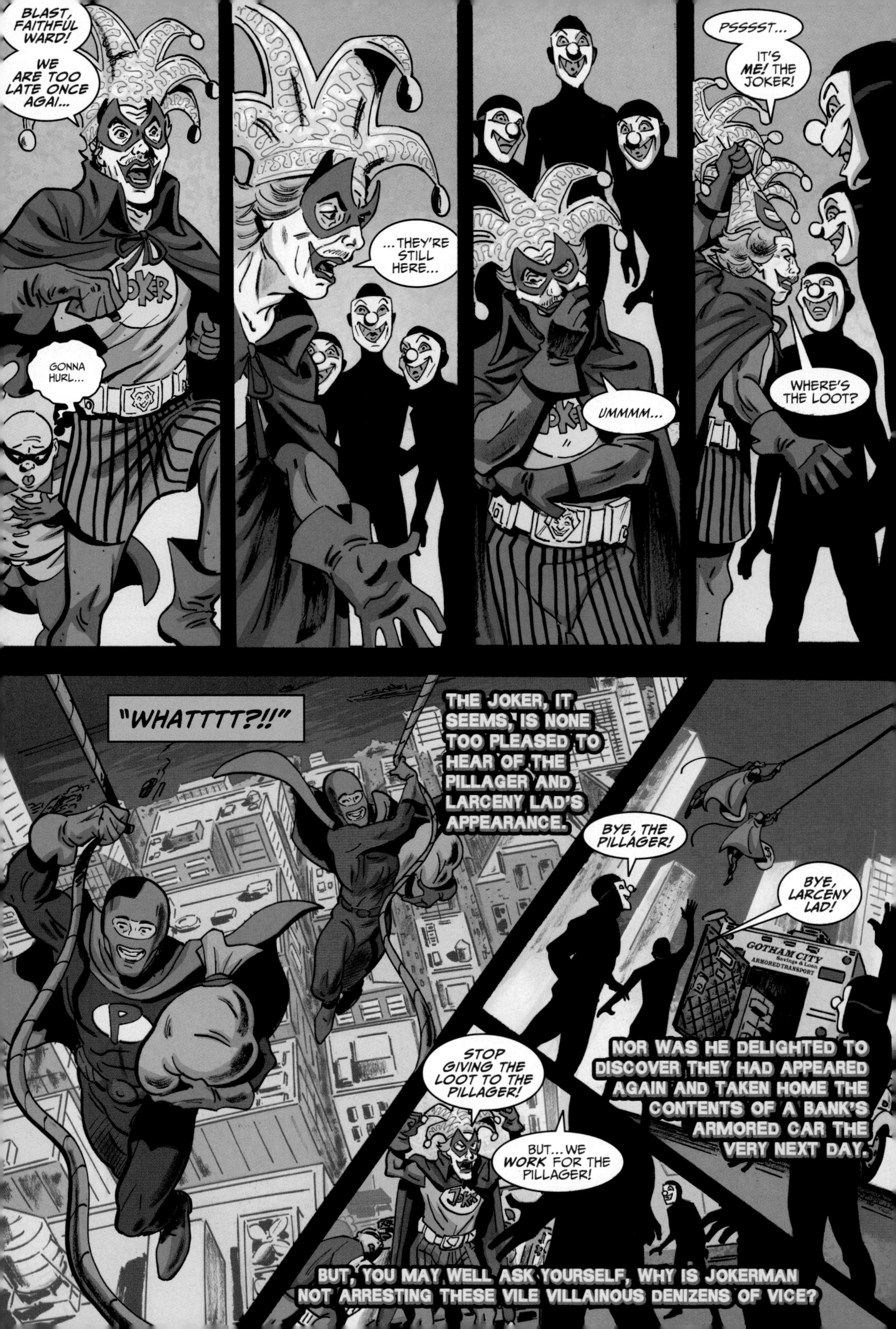
BLAST, FAITHFUL WARD!
WE ARE TOO LATE ONCE AGAI...
GONNA HURL...
...THEY'RE STILL HERE...
UMMMM...
PSSSST...
IT'S ME! THE JOKER!
WHERE'S THE LOOT?
"WHATTTT?!!"
THE JOKER, IT SEEMS, IS NONE TOO PLEASED TO HEAR OF THE PILLAGER AND LARCENY LAD'S APPEARANCE.
BYE, THE PILLAGER!
BYE, LARCENY LAD!
GOTHAM CITY Savings & Loan ARMORED TRANSPORT
NOR WAS HE DELIGHTED TO DISCOVER THEY HAD APPEARED AGAIN AND TAKEN HOME THE CONTENTS OF A BANK'S ARMORED CAR THE VERY NEXT DAY.
STOP GIVING THE LOOT TO THE PILLAGER!
BUT...WE WORK FOR THE PILLAGER!
BUT, YOU MAY WELL ASK YOURSELF, WHY IS JOKERMAN NOT ARRESTING THESE VILE VILLAINOUS DENIZENS OF VICE?

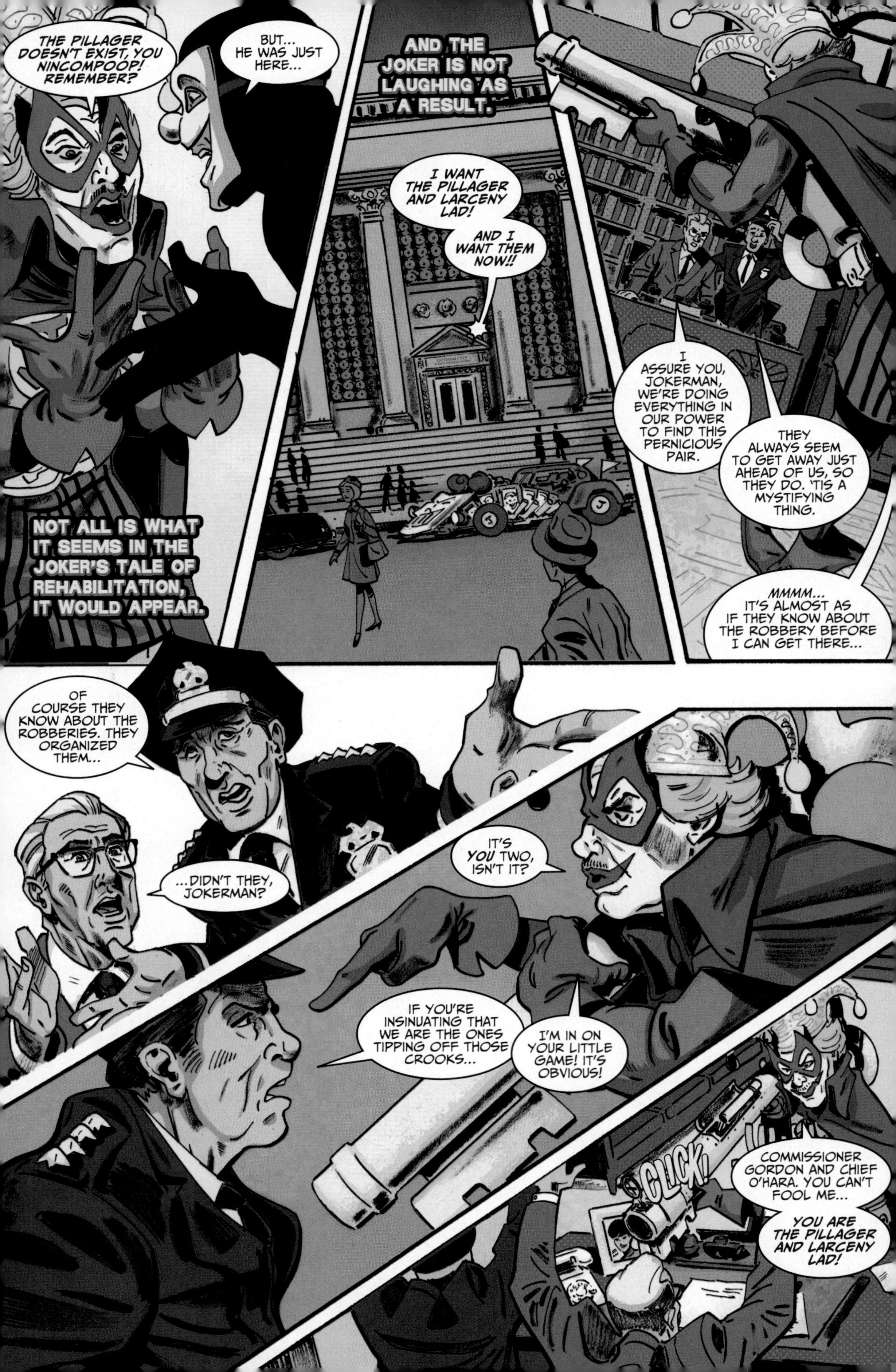
THE PILLAGER DOESN'T EXIST, YOU NINCOMPOOP! REMEMBER?
BUT... HE WAS JUST HERE...
NOT ALL IS WHAT IT SEEMS IN THE JOKER'S TALE OF REHABILITATION, IT WOULD APPEAR.
AND THE JOKER IS NOT LAUGHING AS A RESULT.
I WANT THE PILLAGER AND LARCENY LAD!
AND I WANT THEM NOW!!
GOTHAM CITY POLICE HEADQUARTERS
I ASSURE YOU, JOKERMAN, WE'RE DOING EVERYTHING IN OUR POWER TO FIND THIS PERNICIOUS PAIR.
THEY ALWAYS SEEM TO GET AWAY JUST AHEAD OF US, SO THEY DO. 'TIS A MYSTIFYING THING.
MMMM... IT'S ALMOST AS IF THEY KNOW ABOUT THE ROBBERY BEFORE I CAN GET THERE...
OF COURSE THEY KNOW ABOUT THE ROBBERIES. THEY ORGANIZED THEM...
...DIDN'T THEY, JOKERMAN?
IT'S YOU TWO, ISN'T IT?
IF YOU'RE INSINUATING THAT WE ARE THE ONES TIPPING OFF THOSE CROOKS...
I'M IN ON YOUR LITTLE GAME! IT'S OBVIOUS!
CLICK!
COMMISSIONER GORDON AND CHIEF O'HARA. YOU CAN'T FOOL ME...
YOU ARE THE PILLAGER AND LARCENY LAD!

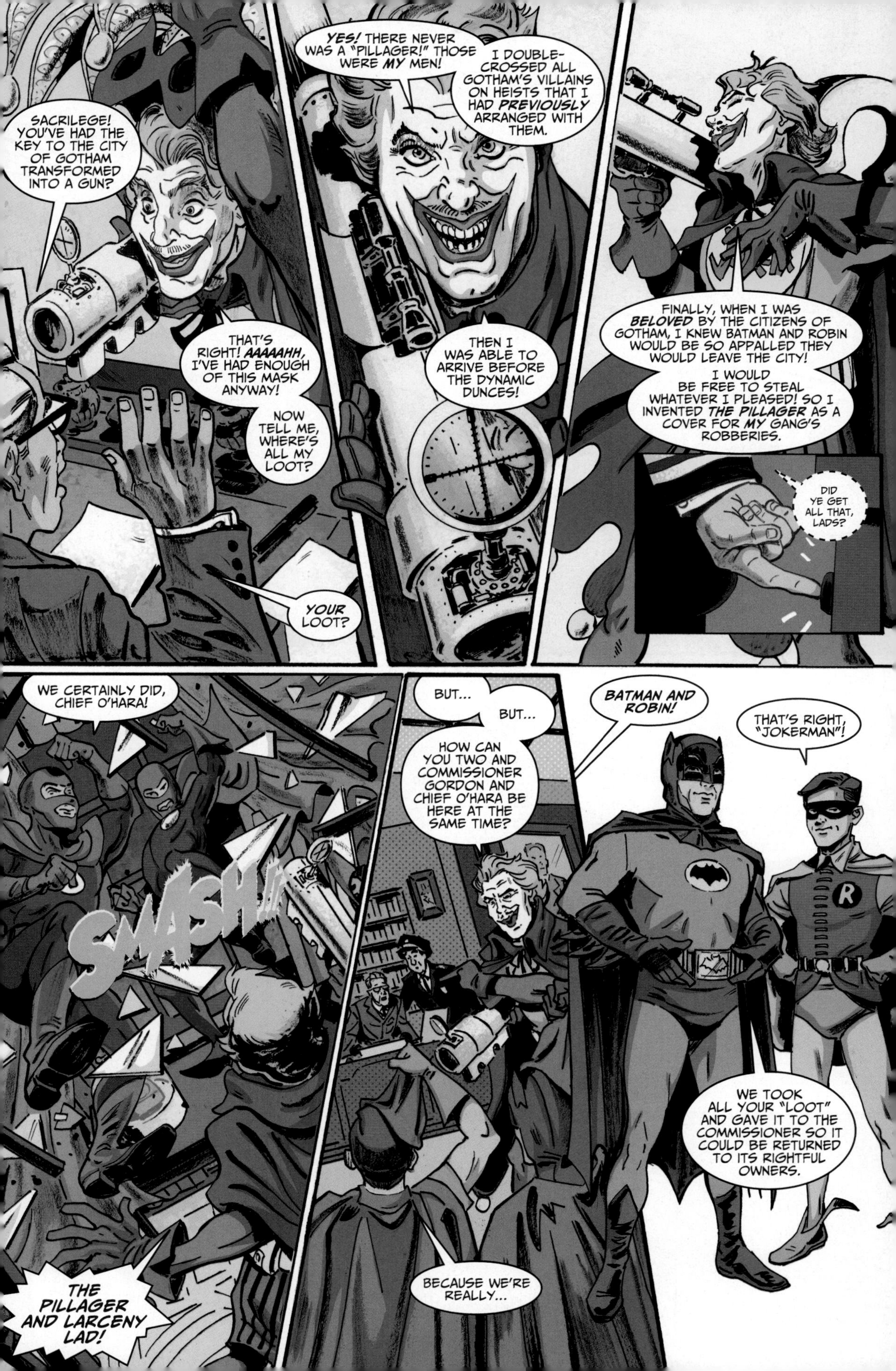
SACRILEGE! YOU'VE HAD THE KEY TO THE CITY OF GOTHAM TRANSFORMED INTO A GUN?
THAT'S RIGHT! AAAAAHH, I'VE HAD ENOUGH OF THIS MASK ANYWAY!
NOW TELL ME, WHERE'S ALL MY LOOT?
YOUR LOOT?
YES! THERE NEVER WAS A "PILLAGER!" THOSE WERE MY MEN!
I DOUBLE-CROSSED ALL GOTHAM'S VILLAINS ON HEISTS THAT I HAD PREVIOUSLY ARRANGED WITH THEM.
THEN I WAS ABLE TO ARRIVE BEFORE THE DYNAMIC DUNCES!
FINALLY, WHEN I WAS BELOVED BY THE CITIZENS OF GOTHAM, I KNEW BATMAN AND ROBIN WOULD BE SO APPALLED THEY WOULD LEAVE THE CITY!
I WOULD BE FREE TO STEAL WHATEVER I PLEASED! SO I INVENTED THE PILLAGER AS A COVER FOR MY GANG'S ROBBERIES.
DID YE GET ALL THAT, LADS?
WE CERTAINLY DID, CHIEF O'HARA!
SMASH!!!
THE PILLAGER AND LARCENY LAD!
BUT...
BUT...
HOW CAN YOU TWO AND COMMISSIONER GORDON AND CHIEF O'HARA BE HERE AT THE SAME TIME?
BECAUSE WE'RE REALLY...
BATMAN AND ROBIN!
THAT'S RIGHT, "JOKERMAN"!
WE TOOK ALL YOUR "LOOT" AND GAVE IT TO THE COMMISSIONER SO IT COULD BE RETURNED TO ITS RIGHTFUL OWNERS.

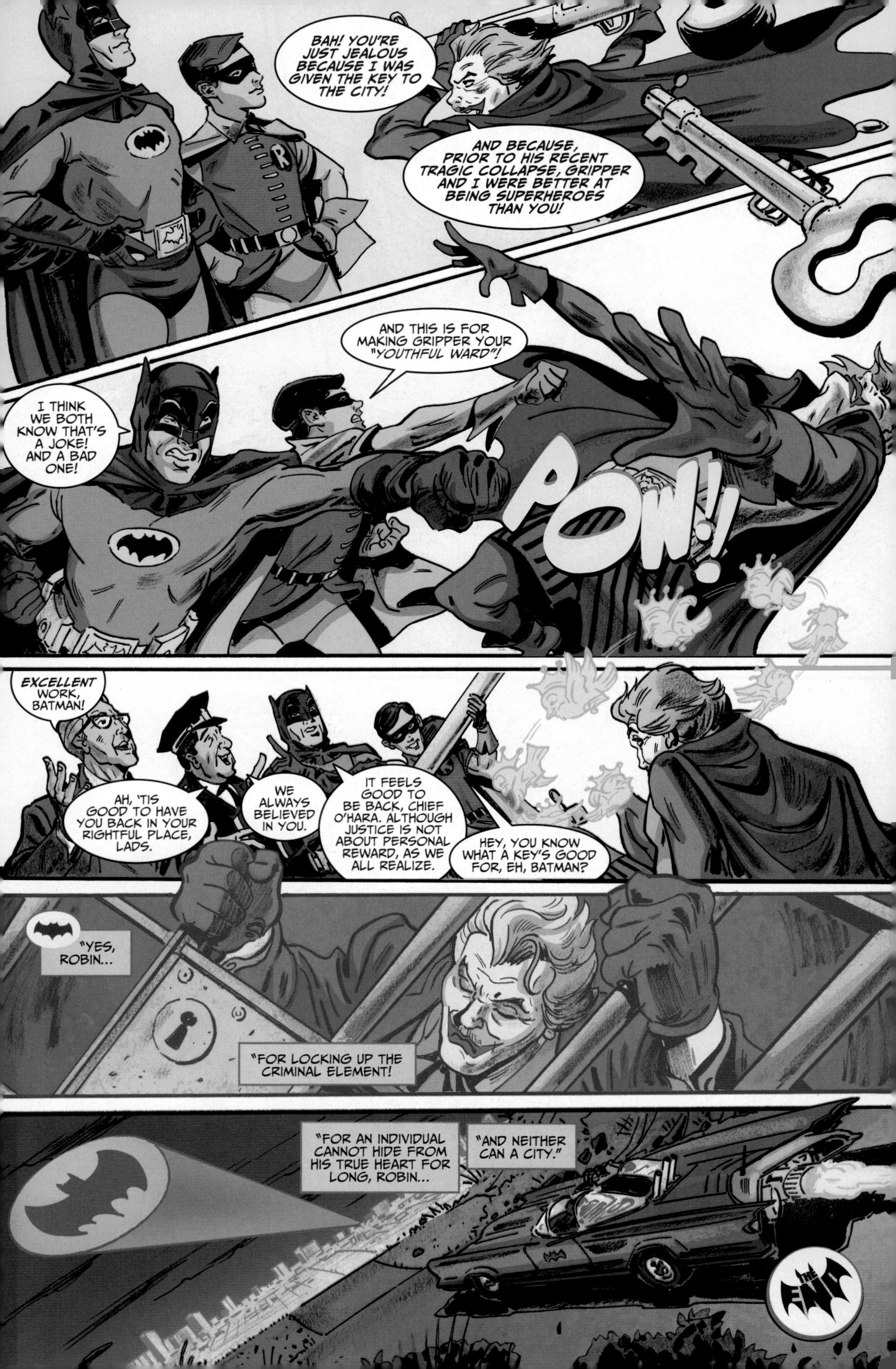
BAH! YOU'RE JUST JEALOUS BECAUSE I WAS GIVEN THE KEY TO THE CITY!
AND BECAUSE, PRIOR TO HIS RECENT TRAGIC COLLAPSE, GRIPPER AND I WERE BETTER AT BEING SUPERHEROES THAN YOU!
I THINK WE BOTH KNOW THAT'S A JOKE! AND A BAD ONE!
AND THIS IS FOR MAKING GRIPPER YOUR "YOUTHFUL WARD"!
POW!!
EXCELLENT WORK, BATMAN!
AH, 'TIS GOOD TO HAVE YOU BACK IN YOUR RIGHTFUL PLACE, LADS.
WE ALWAYS BELIEVED IN YOU.
IT FEELS GOOD TO BE BACK, CHIEF O'HARA. ALTHOUGH JUSTICE IS NOT ABOUT PERSONAL REWARD, AS WE ALL REALIZE.
HEY, YOU KNOW WHAT A KEY'S GOOD FOR, EH, BATMAN?
"YES, ROBIN...
"FOR LOCKING UP THE CRIMINAL ELEMENT!
"FOR AN INDIVIDUAL CANNOT HIDE FROM HIS TRUE HEART FOR LONG, ROBIN...
"AND NEITHER CAN A CITY."
THE END

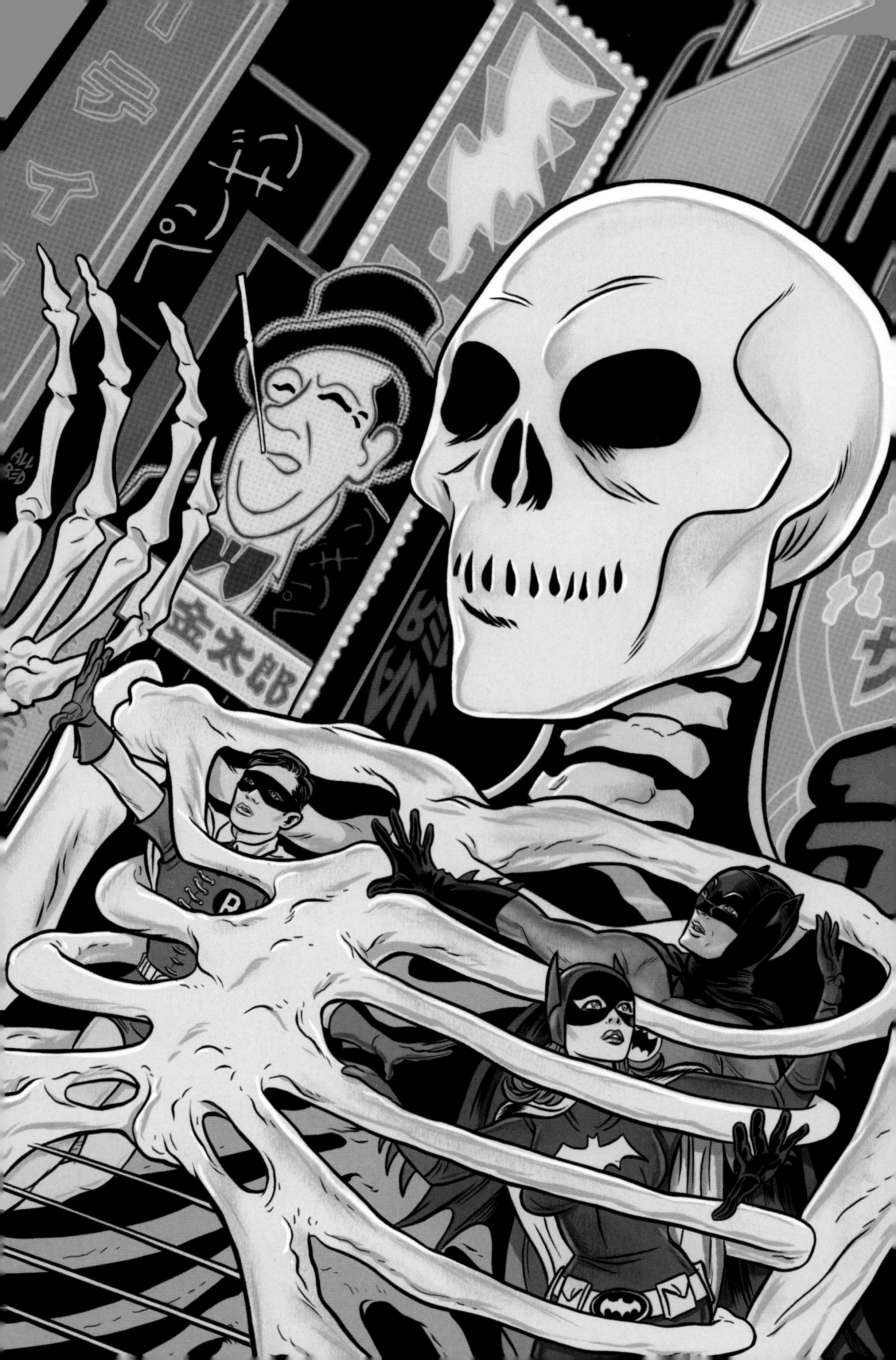
金太郎

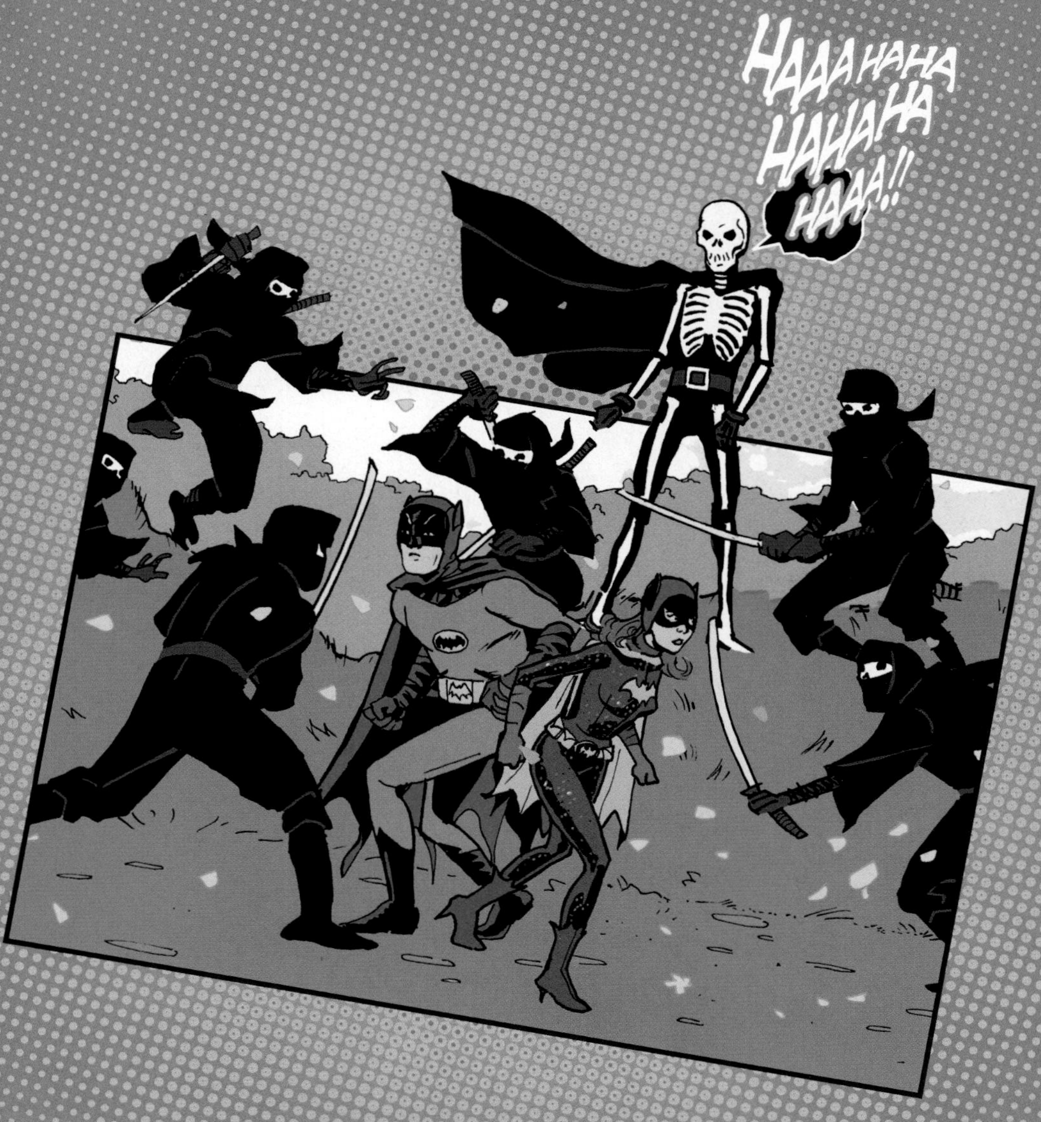
HAAAHAHA HAHAHA HAAA!!

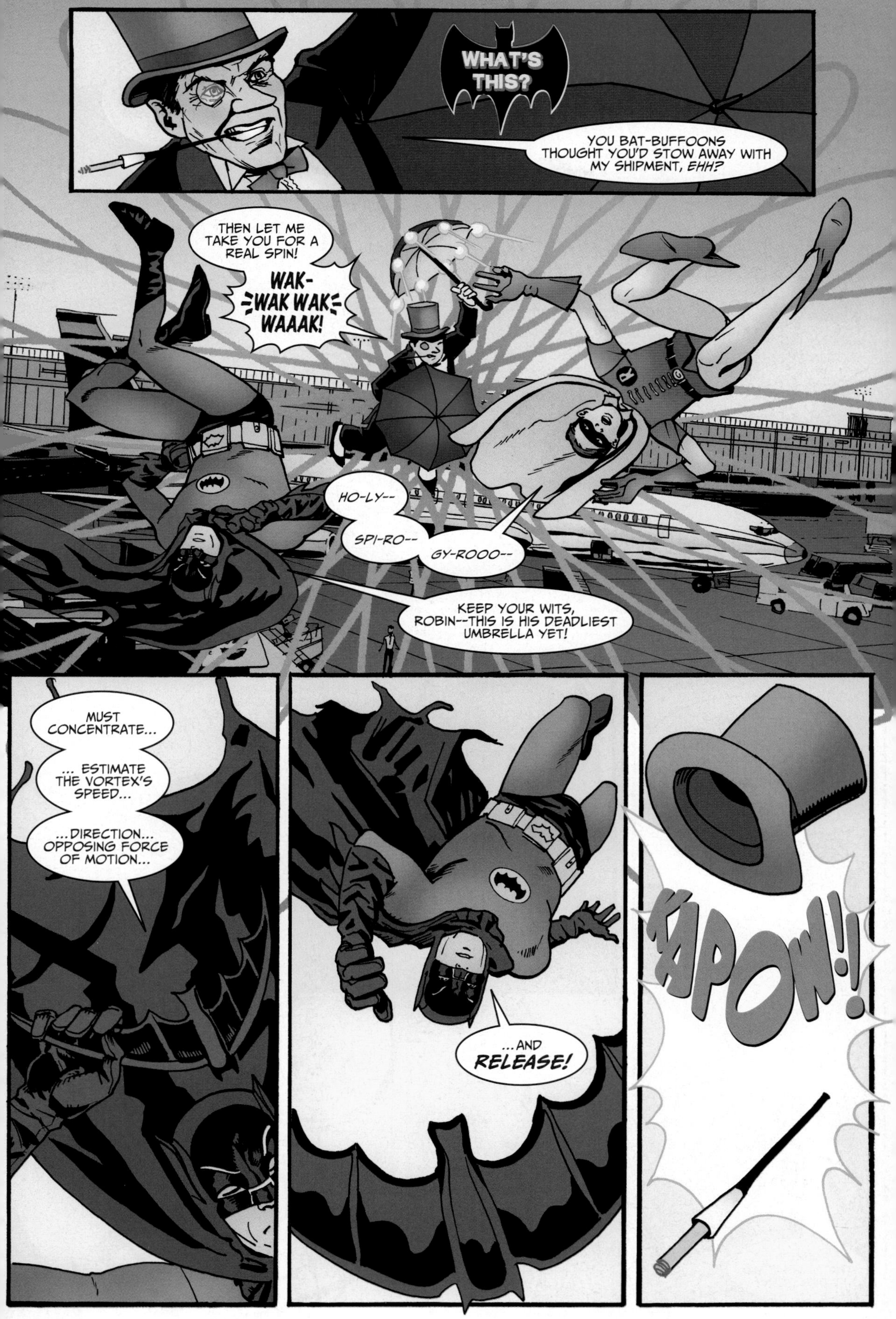
WHAT'S THIS?
YOU BAT-BUFFOONS THOUGHT YOU'D STOW AWAY WITH MY SHIPMENT, *EHH?*
THEN LET ME TAKE YOU FOR A REAL SPIN!
WAK-WAK WAK WAAAK!
HO-LY--
SPI-RO--
GY-ROOO--
KEEP YOUR WITS, ROBIN--THIS IS HIS DEADLIEST UMBRELLA YET!
MUST CONCENTRATE...
... ESTIMATE THE VORTEX'S SPEED...
...DIRECTION... OPPOSING FORCE OF MOTION...
...AND *RELEASE!*
KAPOW!!

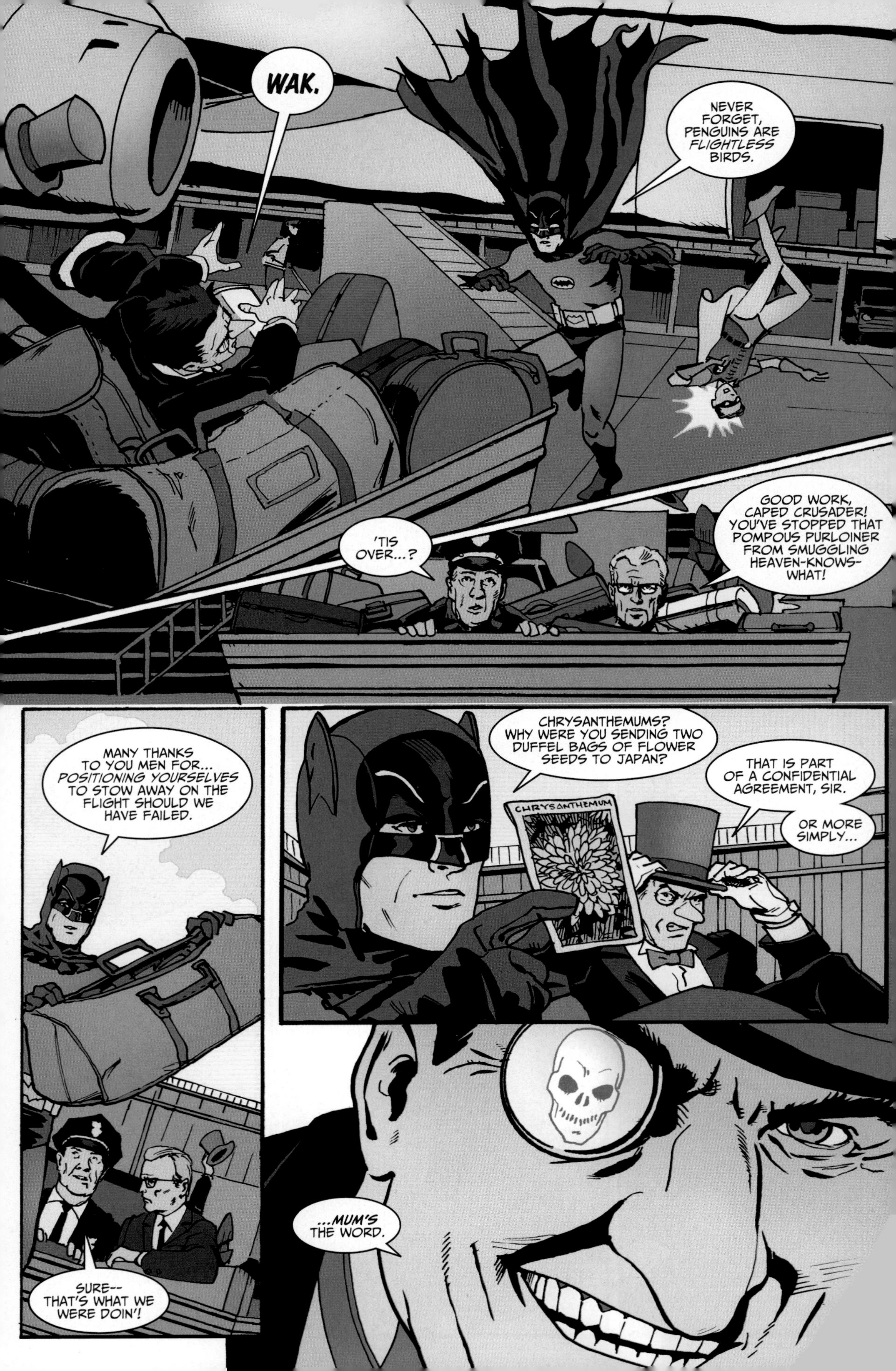

WAK.
NEVER FORGET, PENGUINS ARE *FLIGHTLESS* BIRDS.
GOOD WORK, CAPED CRUSADER! YOU'VE STOPPED THAT POMPOUS PURLOINER FROM SMUGGLING HEAVEN-KNOWS-WHAT!
'TIS OVER...?
MANY THANKS TO YOU MEN FOR... *POSITIONING YOURSELVES* TO STOW AWAY ON THE FLIGHT SHOULD WE HAVE FAILED.
SURE-- THAT'S WHAT WE WERE DOIN'!
CHRYSANTHEMUMS? WHY WERE YOU SENDING TWO DUFFEL BAGS OF FLOWER SEEDS TO JAPAN?
CHRYSANTHEMUM
THAT IS PART OF A CONFIDENTIAL AGREEMENT, SIR.
OR MORE SIMPLY...
...MUM'S THE WORD.

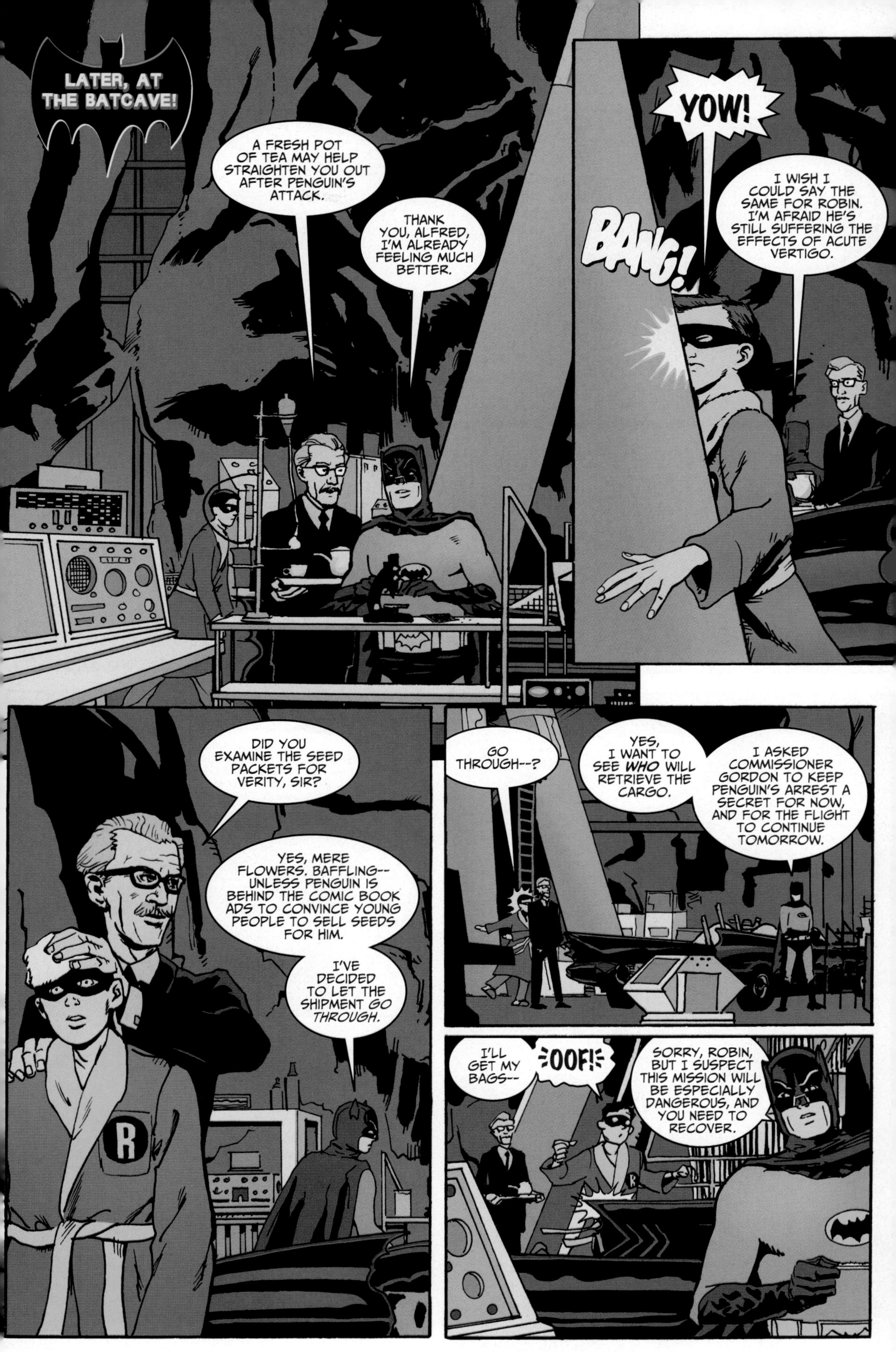

LATER, AT THE BATCAVE!
A FRESH POT OF TEA MAY HELP STRAIGHTEN YOU OUT AFTER PENGUIN'S ATTACK.
THANK YOU, ALFRED, I'M ALREADY FEELING MUCH BETTER.
YOW!
BANG!
I WISH I COULD SAY THE SAME FOR ROBIN. I'M AFRAID HE'S STILL SUFFERING THE EFFECTS OF ACUTE VERTIGO.
DID YOU EXAMINE THE SEED PACKETS FOR VERITY, SIR?
YES, MERE FLOWERS. BAFFLING--UNLESS PENGUIN IS BEHIND THE COMIC BOOK ADS TO CONVINCE YOUNG PEOPLE TO SELL SEEDS FOR HIM.
I'VE DECIDED TO LET THE SHIPMENT GO THROUGH.
GO THROUGH--?
YES, I WANT TO SEE WHO WILL RETRIEVE THE CARGO.
I ASKED COMMISSIONER GORDON TO KEEP PENGUIN'S ARREST A SECRET FOR NOW, AND FOR THE FLIGHT TO CONTINUE TOMORROW.
I'LL GET MY BAGS--
OOF!
SORRY, ROBIN, BUT I SUSPECT THIS MISSION WILL BE ESPECIALLY DANGEROUS, AND YOU NEED TO RECOVER.

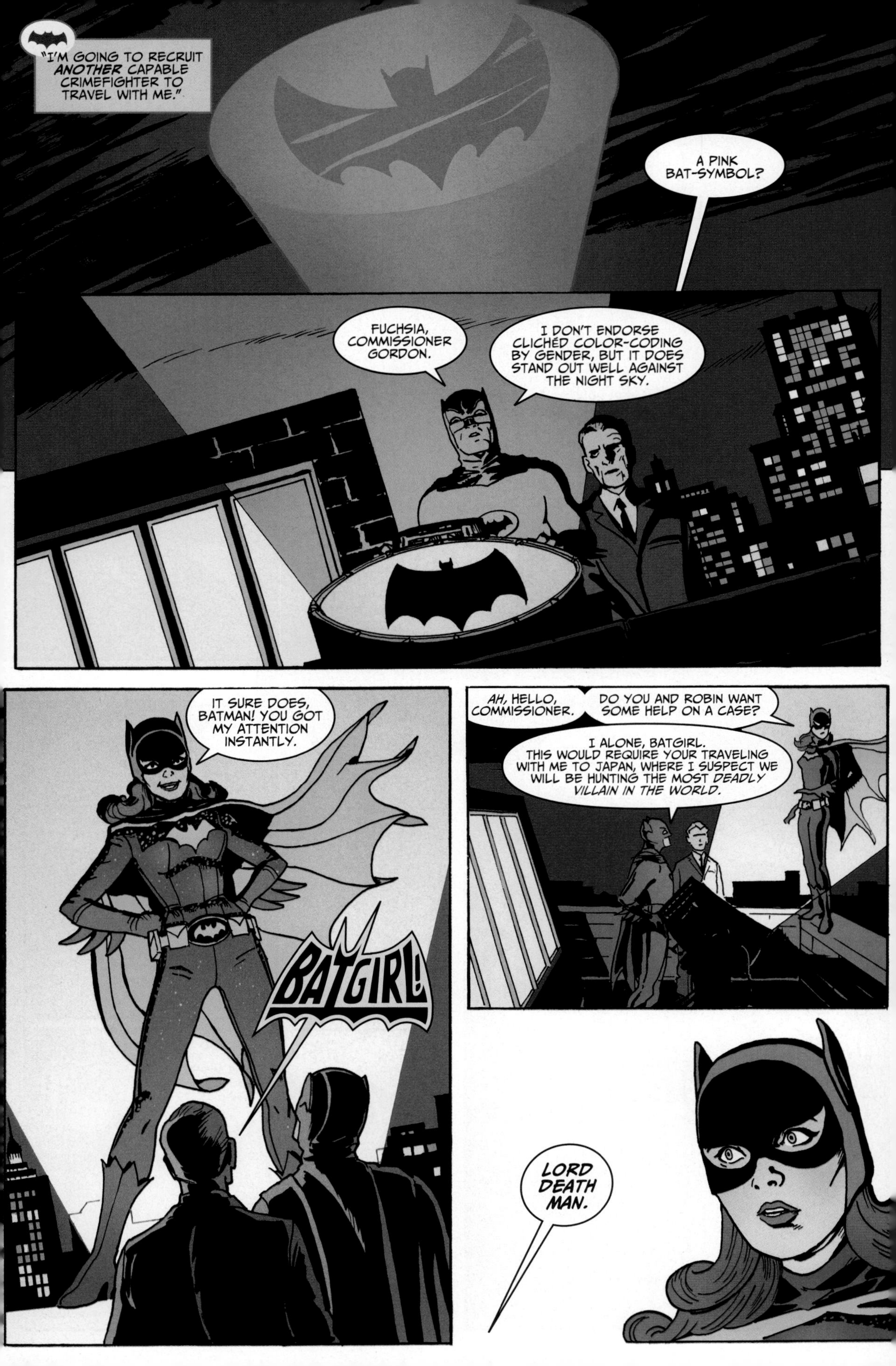
"I'M GOING TO RECRUIT *ANOTHER* CAPABLE CRIMEFIGHTER TO TRAVEL WITH ME."
A PINK BAT-SYMBOL?
FUCHSIA, COMMISSIONER GORDON.
I DON'T ENDORSE CLICHÉD COLOR-CODING BY GENDER, BUT IT DOES STAND OUT WELL AGAINST THE NIGHT SKY.
IT SURE DOES, BATMAN! YOU GOT MY ATTENTION INSTANTLY.
BATGIRL!
AH, HELLO, COMMISSIONER.
DO YOU AND ROBIN WANT SOME HELP ON A CASE?
I ALONE, BATGIRL. THIS WOULD REQUIRE YOUR TRAVELING WITH ME TO JAPAN, WHERE I SUSPECT WE WILL BE HUNTING THE MOST *DEADLY VILLAIN IN THE WORLD.*
LORD DEATH MAN.

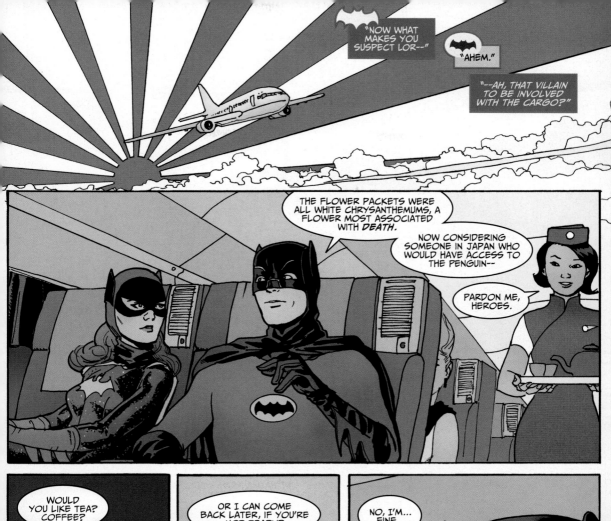

"NOW WHAT MAKES YOU SUSPECT LOR--"

"AHEM."

"--AH, THAT VILLAIN TO BE INVOLVED WITH THE CARGO?"

THE FLOWER PACKETS WERE ALL WHITE CHRYSANTHEMUMS, A FLOWER MOST ASSOCIATED WITH *DEATH.*

NOW CONSIDERING SOMEONE IN JAPAN WHO WOULD HAVE ACCESS TO THE PENGUIN--

PARDON ME, HEROES.

WOULD YOU LIKE TEA? COFFEE?

OR DEATH?

OR I CAN COME BACK LATER, IF YOU'RE NOT READY?

NO, I'M... FINE...

WE'RE HERE--I CAN SEE TOKYO!

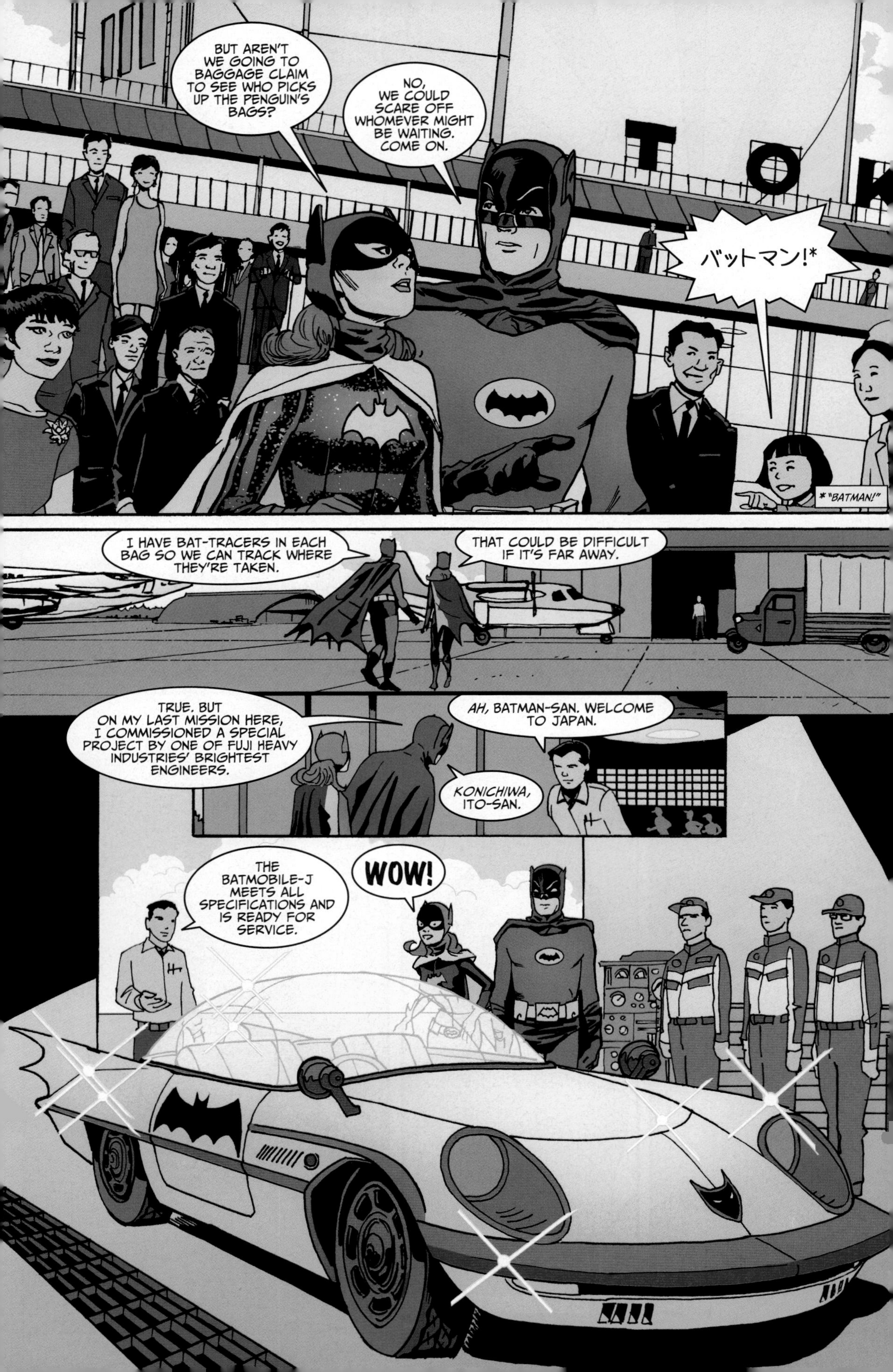
BUT AREN'T WE GOING TO BAGGAGE CLAIM TO SEE WHO PICKS UP THE PENGUIN'S BAGS?
NO, WE COULD SCARE OFF WHOMEVER MIGHT BE WAITING. COME ON.
TOK
バットマン!*
*"BATMAN!"
I HAVE BAT-TRACERS IN EACH BAG SO WE CAN TRACK WHERE THEY'RE TAKEN.
THAT COULD BE DIFFICULT IF IT'S FAR AWAY.
TRUE. BUT ON MY LAST MISSION HERE, I COMMISSIONED A SPECIAL PROJECT BY ONE OF FUJI HEAVY INDUSTRIES' BRIGHTEST ENGINEERS.
AH, BATMAN-SAN. WELCOME TO JAPAN.
KONICHIWA, ITO-SAN.
THE BATMOBILE-J MEETS ALL SPECIFICATIONS AND IS READY FOR SERVICE.
WOW!

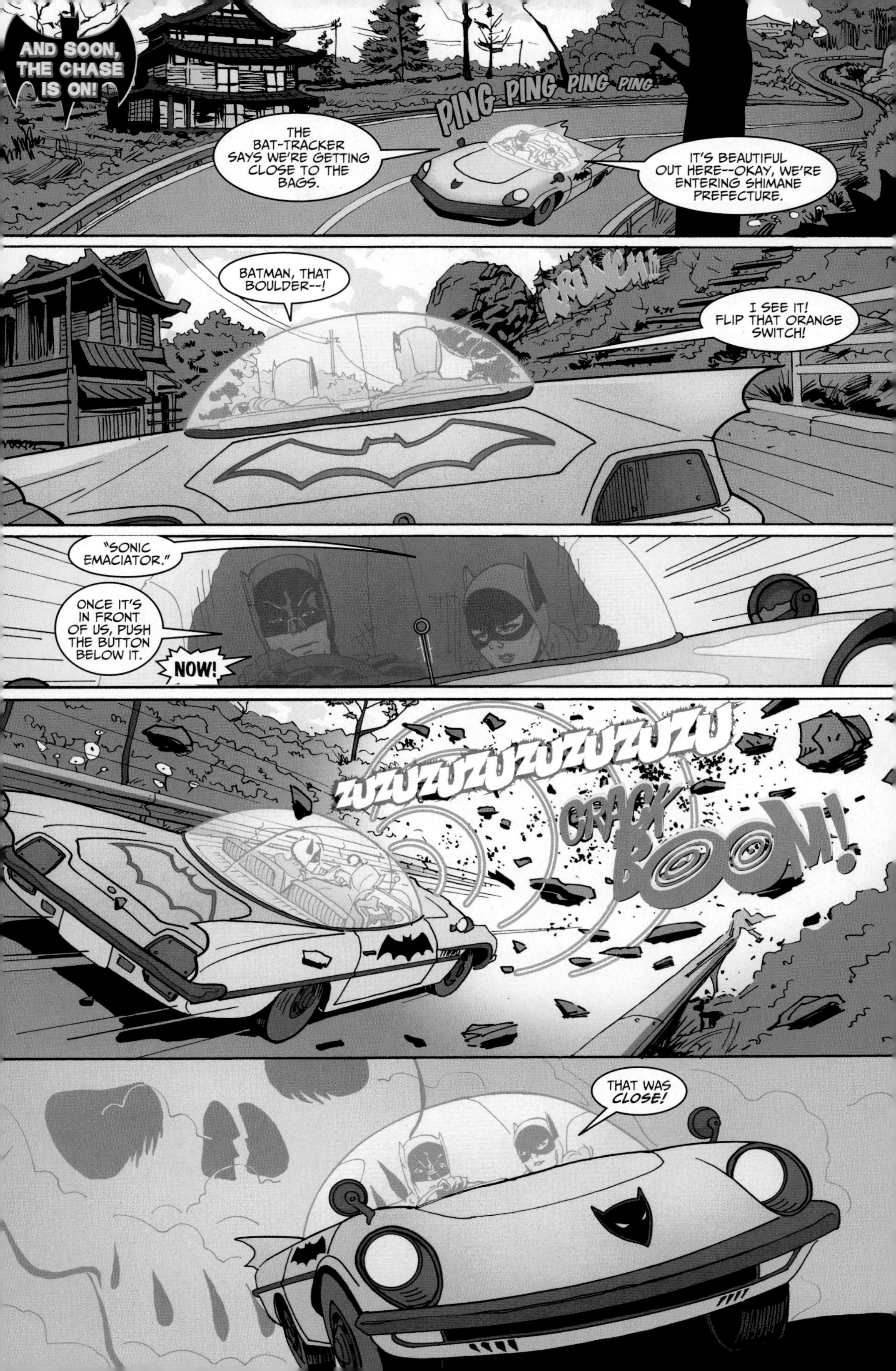
AND SOON, THE CHASE IS ON!
PING PING PING PING
THE BAT-TRACKER SAYS WE'RE GETTING CLOSE TO THE BAGS.
IT'S BEAUTIFUL OUT HERE--OKAY, WE'RE ENTERING SHIMANE PREFECTURE.
BATMAN, THAT BOULDER--!
KRUNCH!!!
I SEE IT! FLIP THAT ORANGE SWITCH!
"SONIC EMACIATOR."
ONCE IT'S IN FRONT OF US, PUSH THE BUTTON BELOW IT.
NOW!
ZUZUZUZUZUZUZUZUZUZU
CRACK
BOOM!
THAT WAS CLOSE!

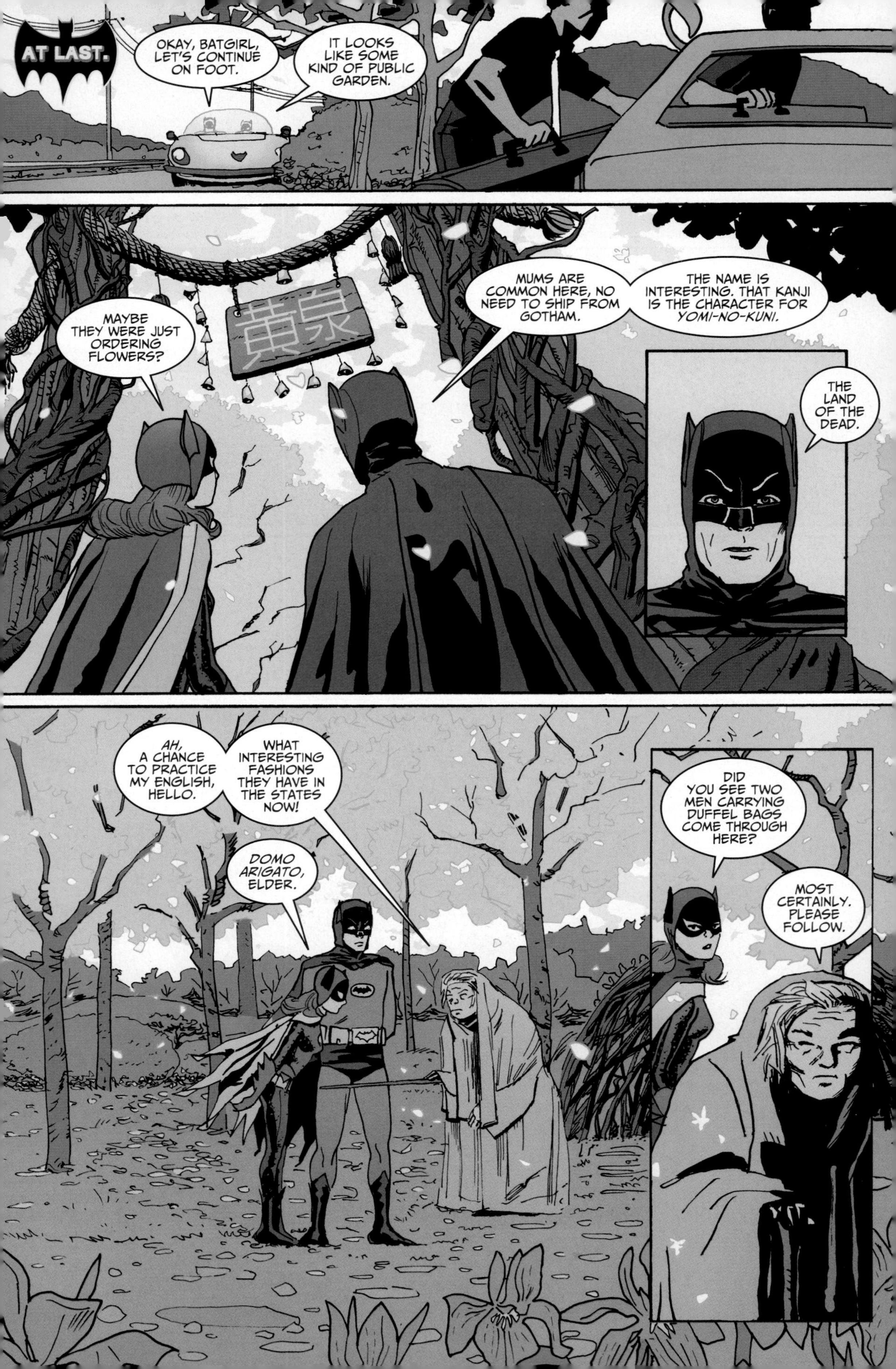
AT LAST.
OKAY, BATGIRL, LET'S CONTINUE ON FOOT.
IT LOOKS LIKE SOME KIND OF PUBLIC GARDEN.
MAYBE THEY WERE JUST ORDERING FLOWERS?
黄泉
MUMS ARE COMMON HERE, NO NEED TO SHIP FROM GOTHAM.
THE NAME IS INTERESTING. THAT KANJI IS THE CHARACTER FOR *YOMI-NO-KUNI*.
THE LAND OF THE DEAD.
AH, A CHANCE TO PRACTICE MY ENGLISH, HELLO.
WHAT INTERESTING FASHIONS THEY HAVE IN THE STATES NOW!
DOMO ARIGATO, ELDER.
DID YOU SEE TWO MEN CARRYING DUFFEL BAGS COME THROUGH HERE?
MOST CERTAINLY. PLEASE FOLLOW.

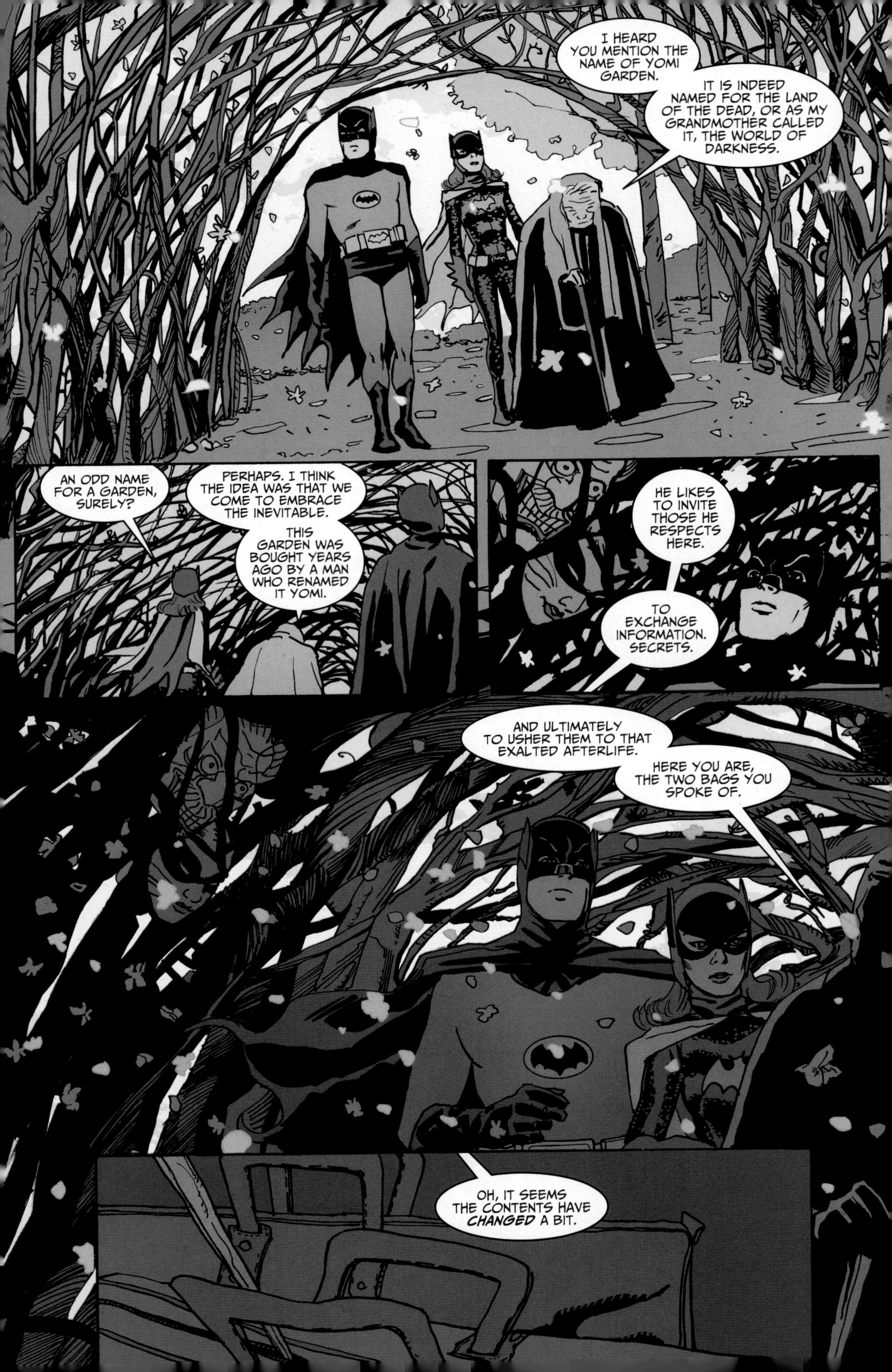
I HEARD YOU MENTION THE NAME OF YOMI GARDEN.
IT IS INDEED NAMED FOR THE LAND OF THE DEAD, OR AS MY GRANDMOTHER CALLED IT, THE WORLD OF DARKNESS.
AN ODD NAME FOR A GARDEN, SURELY?
PERHAPS. I THINK THE IDEA WAS THAT WE COME TO EMBRACE THE INEVITABLE.
THIS GARDEN WAS BOUGHT YEARS AGO BY A MAN WHO RENAMED IT YOMI.
HE LIKES TO INVITE THOSE HE RESPECTS HERE.
TO EXCHANGE INFORMATION. SECRETS.
AND ULTIMATELY TO USHER THEM TO THAT EXALTED AFTERLIFE.
HERE YOU ARE, THE TWO BAGS YOU SPOKE OF.
OH, IT SEEMS THE CONTENTS HAVE *CHANGED* A BIT.

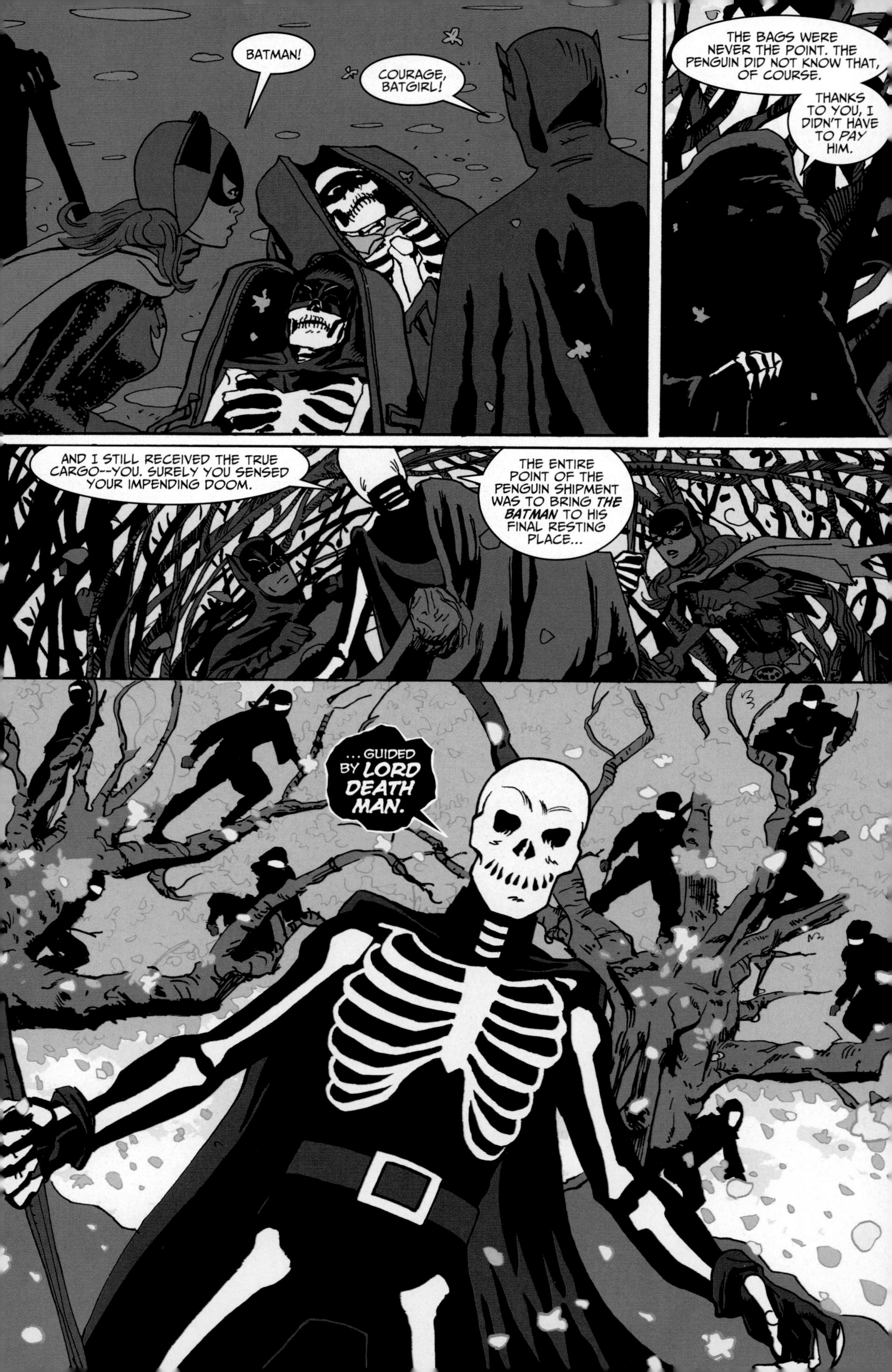
BATMAN!
COURAGE, BATGIRL!
THE BAGS WERE NEVER THE POINT. THE PENGUIN DID NOT KNOW THAT, OF COURSE.
THANKS TO YOU, I DIDN'T HAVE TO PAY HIM.
AND I STILL RECEIVED THE TRUE CARGO--YOU. SURELY YOU SENSED YOUR IMPENDING DOOM.
THE ENTIRE POINT OF THE PENGUIN SHIPMENT WAS TO BRING THE BATMAN TO HIS FINAL RESTING PLACE...
...GUIDED BY LORD DEATH MAN.

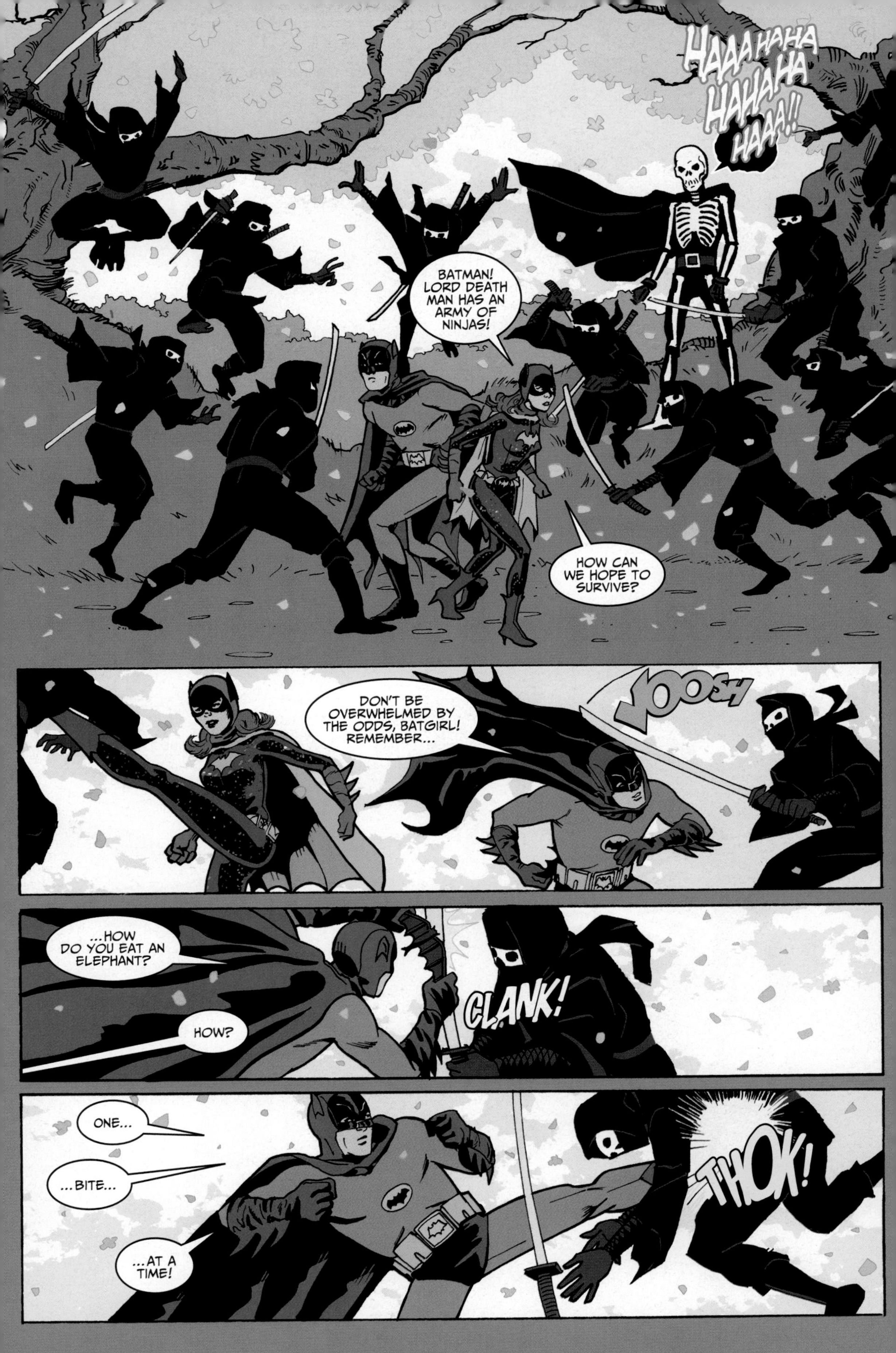
HAAAHAHA HAHAHA HAAA!!
BATMAN! LORD DEATH MAN HAS AN ARMY OF NINJAS!
HOW CAN WE HOPE TO SURVIVE?
DON'T BE OVERWHELMED BY THE ODDS, BATGIRL! REMEMBER...
VOOSH
...HOW DO YOU EAT AN ELEPHANT?
CLANK!
HOW?
ONE...
...BITE...
...AT A TIME!
THOK!

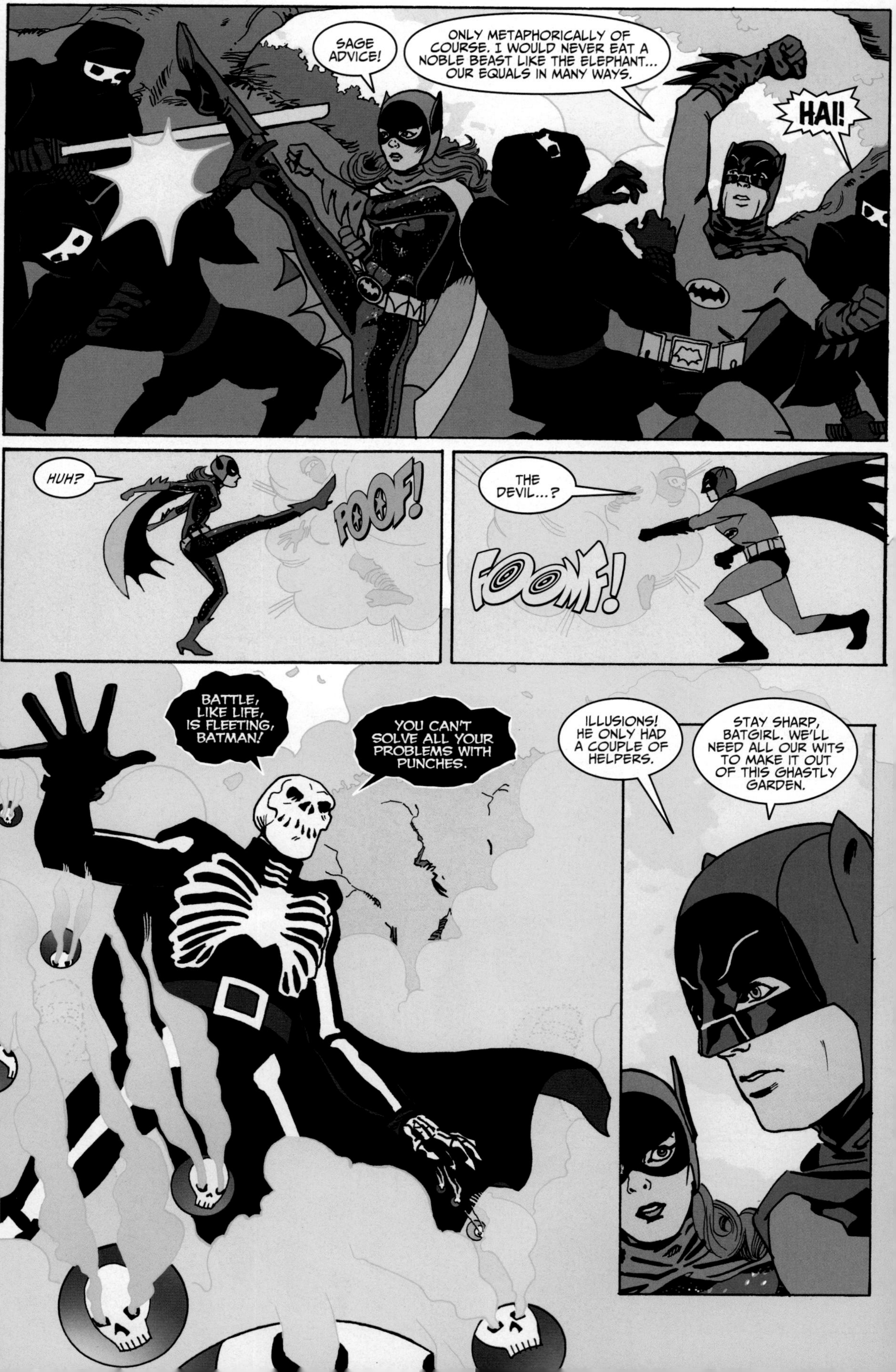
SAGE ADVICE!
ONLY METAPHORICALLY OF COURSE. I WOULD NEVER EAT A NOBLE BEAST LIKE THE ELEPHANT... OUR EQUALS IN MANY WAYS.
HAI!
HUH?
POOF!
THE DEVIL...?
FOOMF!
BATTLE, LIKE LIFE, IS FLEETING, BATMAN!
YOU CAN'T SOLVE ALL YOUR PROBLEMS WITH PUNCHES.
ILLUSIONS! HE ONLY HAD A COUPLE OF HELPERS.
STAY SHARP, BATGIRL. WE'LL NEED ALL OUR WITS TO MAKE IT OUT OF THIS GHASTLY GARDEN.

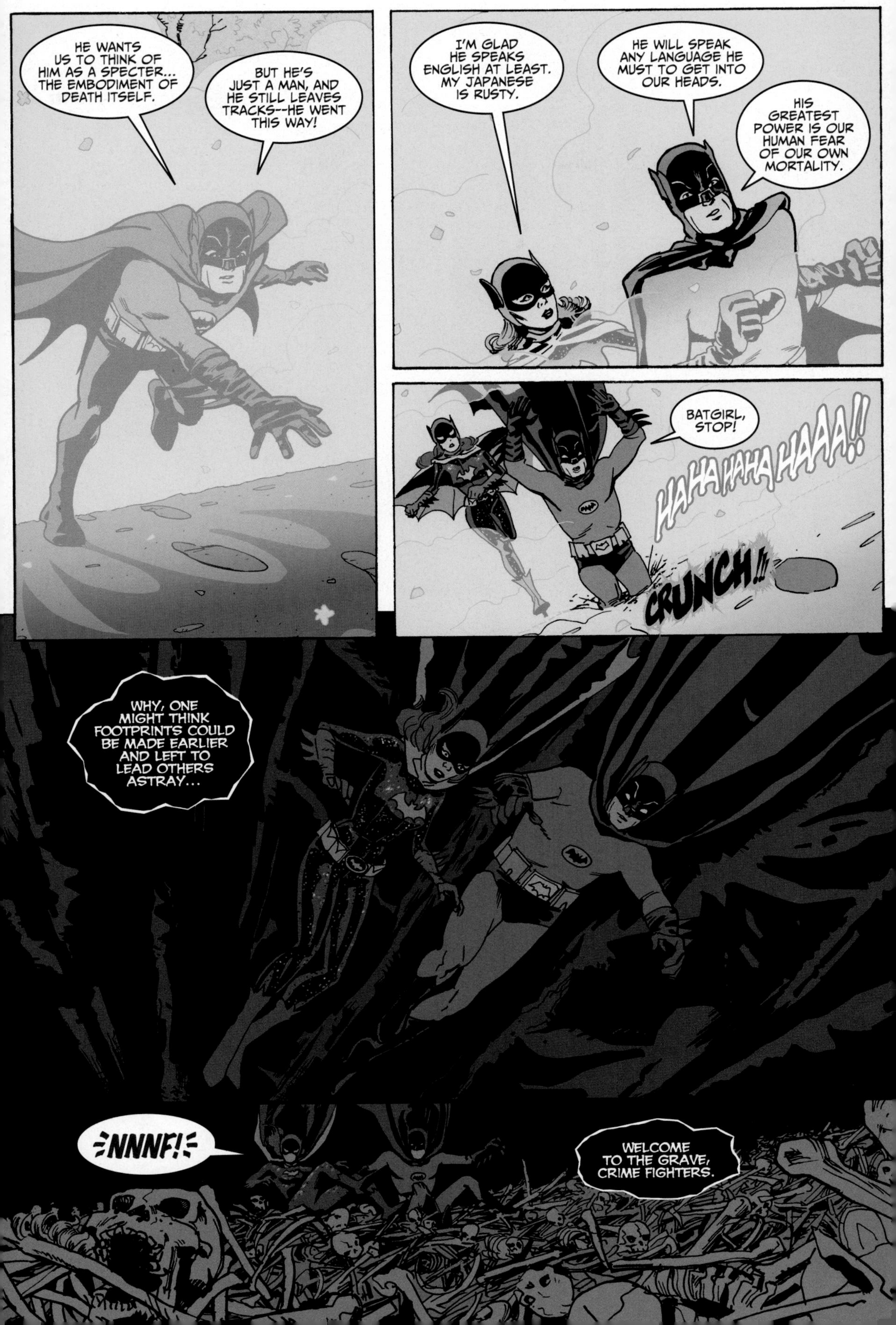
HE WANTS US TO THINK OF HIM AS A SPECTER... THE EMBODIMENT OF DEATH ITSELF.
BUT HE'S JUST A MAN, AND HE STILL LEAVES TRACKS--HE WENT THIS WAY!
I'M GLAD HE SPEAKS ENGLISH AT LEAST. MY JAPANESE IS RUSTY.
HE WILL SPEAK ANY LANGUAGE HE MUST TO GET INTO OUR HEADS.
HIS GREATEST POWER IS OUR HUMAN FEAR OF OUR OWN MORTALITY.
BATGIRL, STOP!
HAHAHAHAHAAA!!
CRUNCH!!
WHY, ONE MIGHT THINK FOOTPRINTS COULD BE MADE EARLIER AND LEFT TO LEAD OTHERS ASTRAY...
NNNF!
WELCOME TO THE GRAVE, CRIME FIGHTERS.

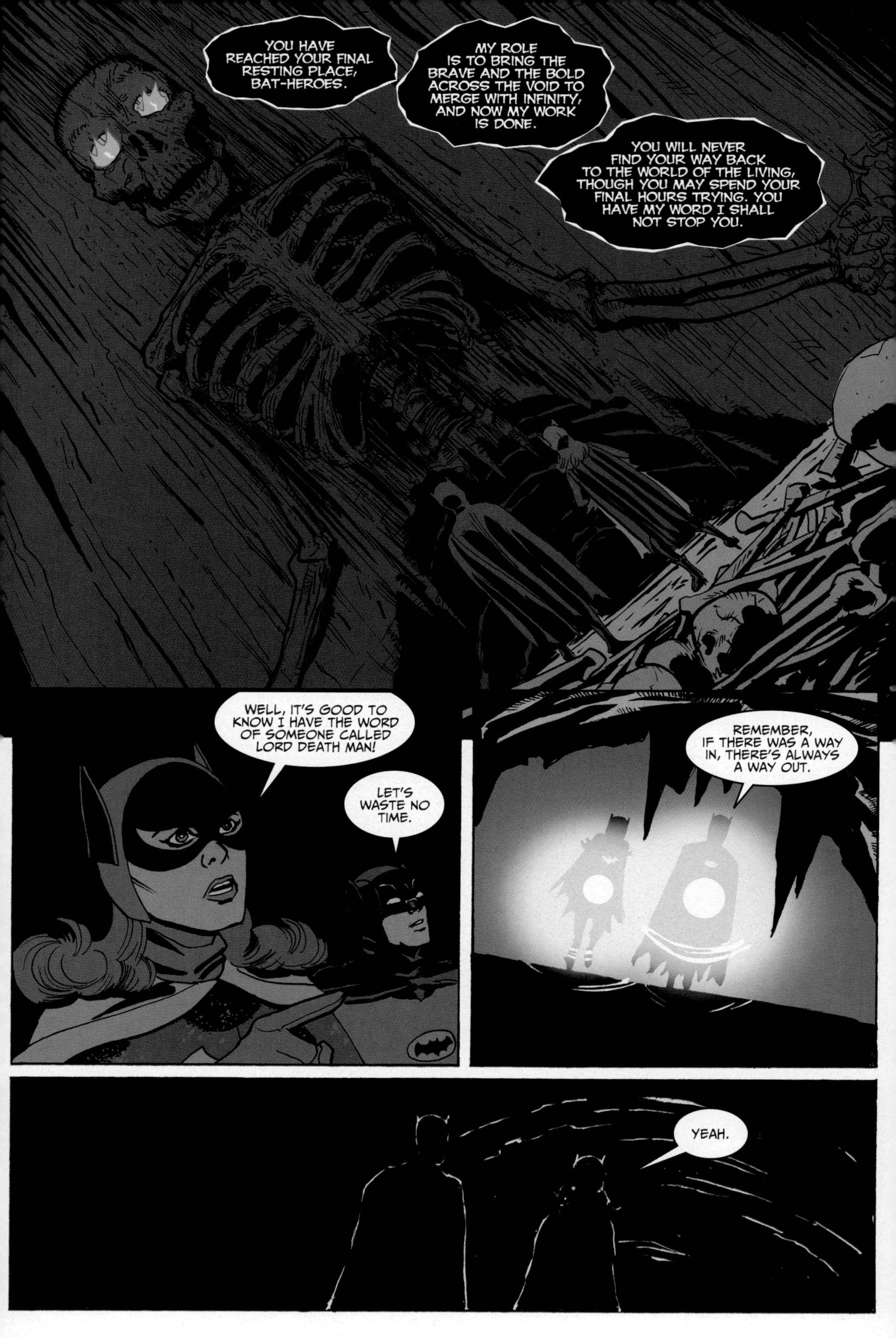
YOU HAVE REACHED YOUR FINAL RESTING PLACE, BAT-HEROES.
MY ROLE IS TO BRING THE BRAVE AND THE BOLD ACROSS THE VOID TO MERGE WITH INFINITY, AND NOW MY WORK IS DONE.
YOU WILL NEVER FIND YOUR WAY BACK TO THE WORLD OF THE LIVING, THOUGH YOU MAY SPEND YOUR FINAL HOURS TRYING. YOU HAVE MY WORD I SHALL NOT STOP YOU.
WELL, IT'S GOOD TO KNOW I HAVE THE WORD OF SOMEONE CALLED LORD DEATH MAN!
LET'S WASTE NO TIME.
REMEMBER, IF THERE WAS A WAY IN, THERE'S ALWAYS A WAY OUT.
YEAH.

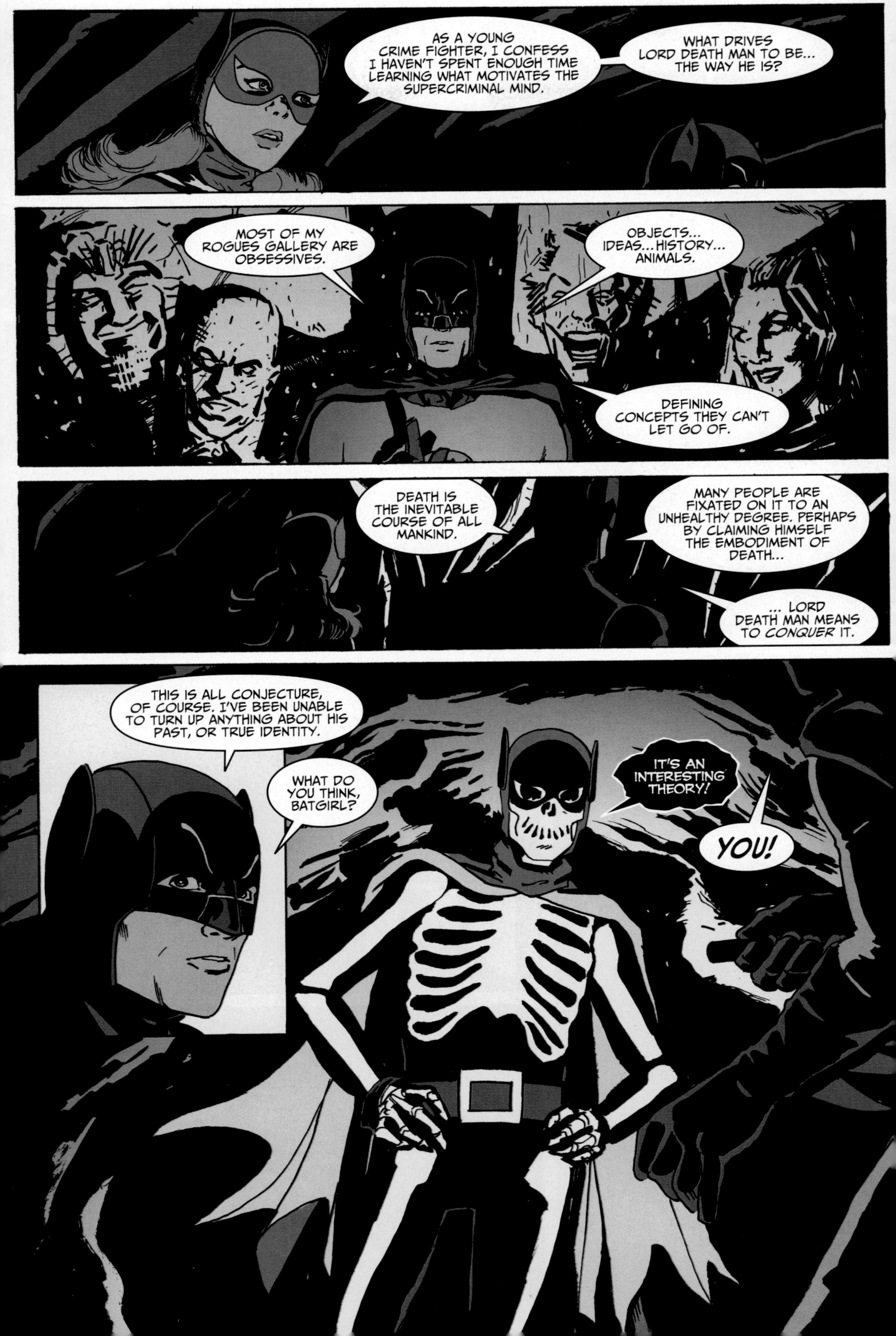
AS A YOUNG CRIME FIGHTER, I CONFESS I HAVEN'T SPENT ENOUGH TIME LEARNING WHAT MOTIVATES THE SUPERCRIMINAL MIND.
WHAT DRIVES LORD DEATH MAN TO BE... THE WAY HE IS?
MOST OF MY ROGUES GALLERY ARE OBSESSIVES.
OBJECTS... IDEAS... HISTORY... ANIMALS.
DEFINING CONCEPTS THEY CAN'T LET GO OF.
DEATH IS THE INEVITABLE COURSE OF ALL MANKIND.
MANY PEOPLE ARE FIXATED ON IT TO AN UNHEALTHY DEGREE. PERHAPS BY CLAIMING HIMSELF THE EMBODIMENT OF DEATH...
... LORD DEATH MAN MEANS TO *CONQUER* IT.
THIS IS ALL CONJECTURE, OF COURSE. I'VE BEEN UNABLE TO TURN UP ANYTHING ABOUT HIS PAST, OR TRUE IDENTITY.
WHAT DO YOU THINK, BATGIRL?
IT'S AN INTERESTING THEORY!
YOU!

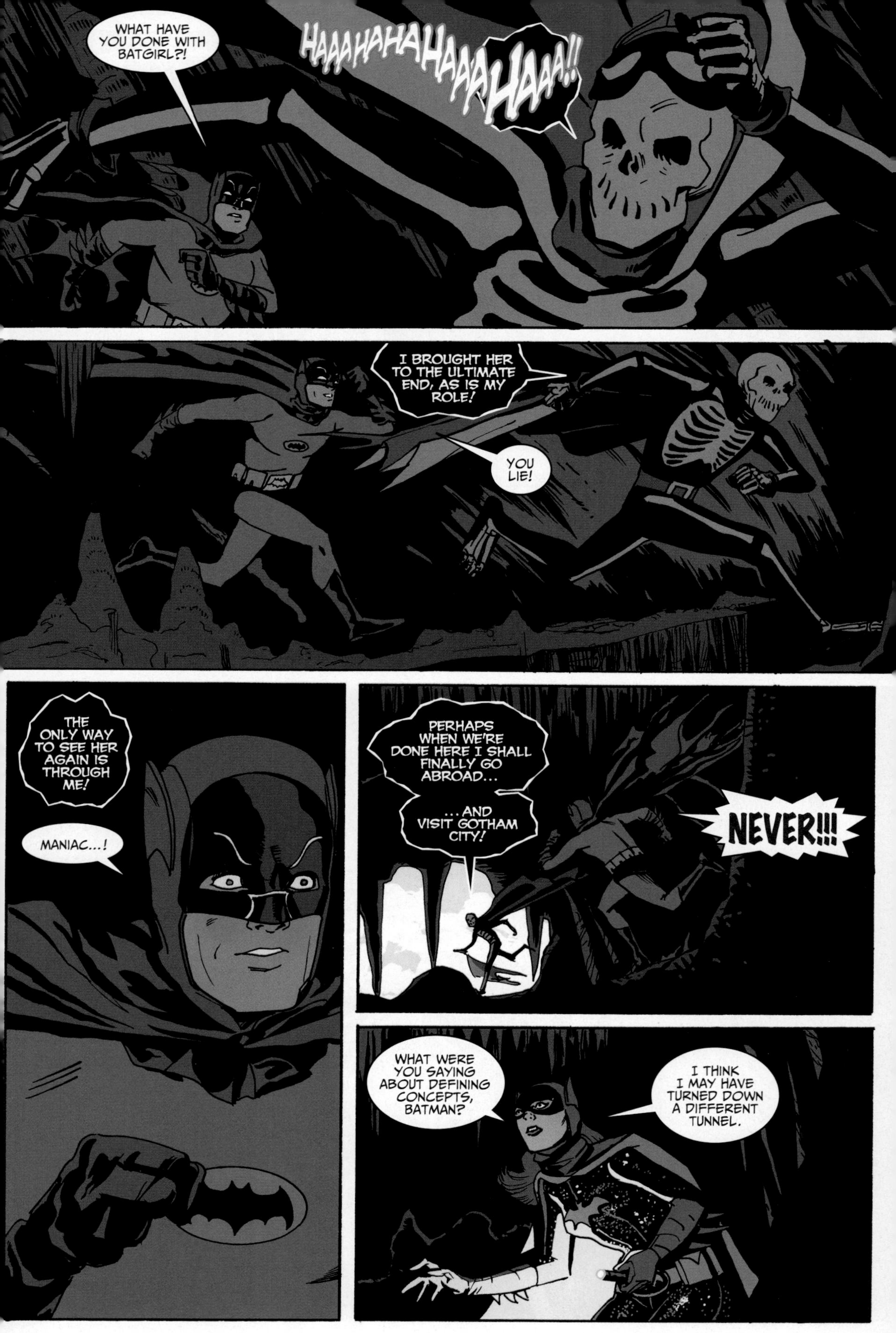
WHAT HAVE YOU DONE WITH BATGIRL?!
HAAAHAHAHAAAHAAA!!
I BROUGHT HER TO THE ULTIMATE END, AS IS MY ROLE!
YOU LIE!
THE ONLY WAY TO SEE HER AGAIN IS THROUGH ME!
MANIAC...!
PERHAPS WHEN WE'RE DONE HERE I SHALL FINALLY GO ABROAD...
...AND VISIT GOTHAM CITY!
NEVER!!!
WHAT WERE YOU SAYING ABOUT DEFINING CONCEPTS, BATMAN?
I THINK I MAY HAVE TURNED DOWN A DIFFERENT TUNNEL.

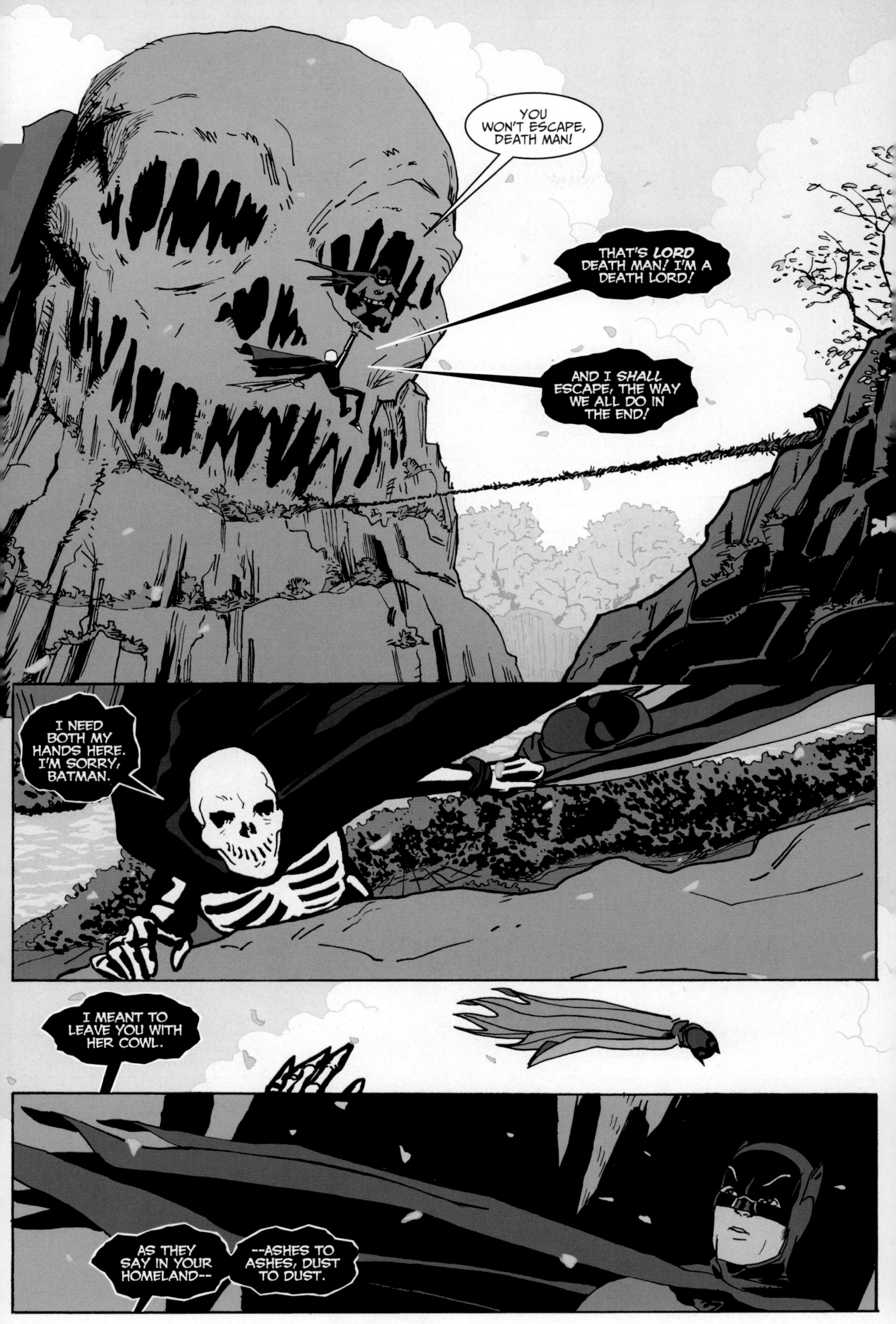
YOU WON'T ESCAPE, DEATH MAN!
THAT'S LORD DEATH MAN! I'M A DEATH LORD!
AND I SHALL ESCAPE, THE WAY WE ALL DO IN THE END!
I NEED BOTH MY HANDS HERE. I'M SORRY, BATMAN.
I MEANT TO LEAVE YOU WITH HER COWL.
AS THEY SAY IN YOUR HOMELAND--
--ASHES TO ASHES, DUST TO DUST.

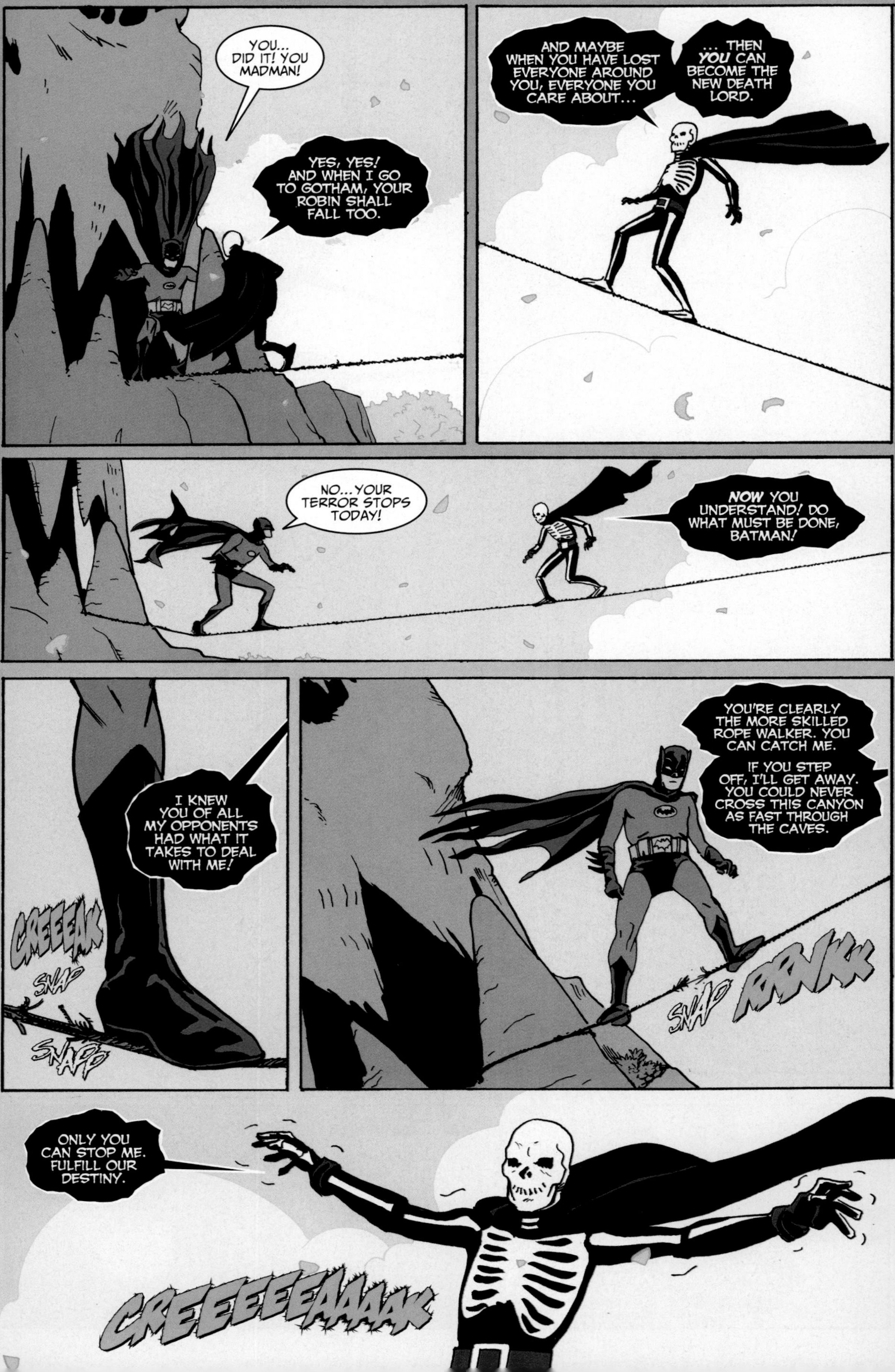
YOU... DID IT! YOU MADMAN!
YES, YES! AND WHEN I GO TO GOTHAM, YOUR ROBIN SHALL FALL TOO.
AND MAYBE WHEN YOU HAVE LOST EVERYONE AROUND YOU, EVERYONE YOU CARE ABOUT...
... THEN YOU CAN BECOME THE NEW DEATH LORD.
NO...YOUR TERROR STOPS TODAY!
NOW YOU UNDERSTAND! DO WHAT MUST BE DONE, BATMAN!
I KNEW YOU OF ALL MY OPPONENTS HAD WHAT IT TAKES TO DEAL WITH ME!
CREEEAK
SNAP
SNAPP
YOU'RE CLEARLY THE MORE SKILLED ROPE WALKER. YOU CAN CATCH ME.
IF YOU STEP OFF, I'LL GET AWAY. YOU COULD NEVER CROSS THIS CANYON AS FAST THROUGH THE CAVES.
SNAP
KRRNKK
ONLY YOU CAN STOP ME. FULFILL OUR DESTINY.
CREEEEEAAAAK

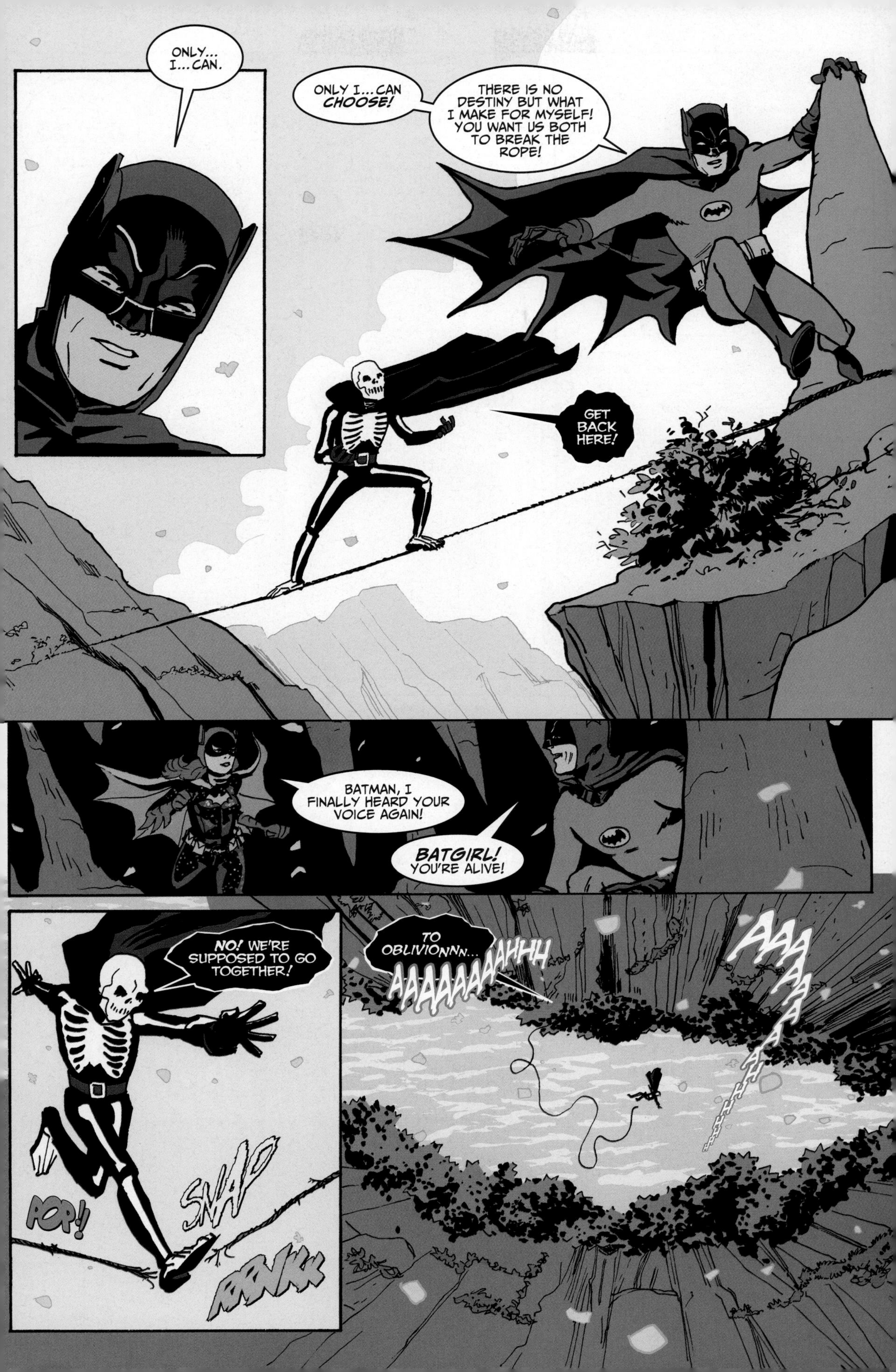
ONLY... I...CAN.
ONLY I...CAN CHOOSE!
THERE IS NO DESTINY BUT WHAT I MAKE FOR MYSELF! YOU WANT US BOTH TO BREAK THE ROPE!
GET BACK HERE!
BATMAN, I FINALLY HEARD YOUR VOICE AGAIN!
BATGIRL! YOU'RE ALIVE!
NO! WE'RE SUPPOSED TO GO TOGETHER!
POP!
SNAP
TO OBLIVIONNN...AAAAAAAAAHHH
AAAAAAAAAAHHHHH

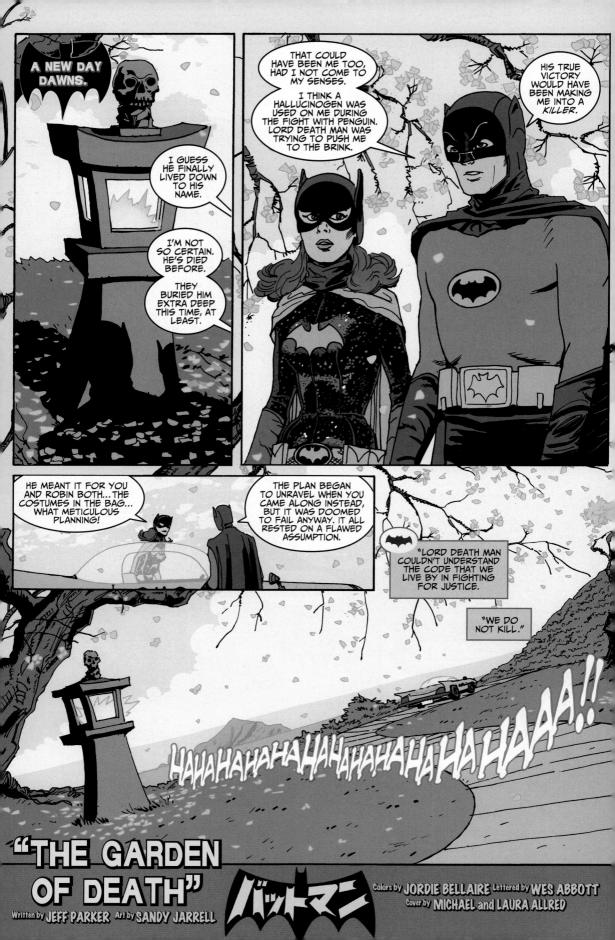

A NEW DAY DAWNS.

I GUESS HE FINALLY LIVED DOWN TO HIS NAME.

I'M NOT SO CERTAIN. HE'S DIED BEFORE.

THEY BURIED HIM EXTRA DEEP THIS TIME, AT LEAST.

THAT COULD HAVE BEEN ME TOO, HAD I NOT COME TO MY SENSES.

I THINK A HALLUCINOGEN WAS USED ON ME DURING THE FIGHT WITH PENGUIN. LORD DEATH MAN WAS TRYING TO PUSH ME TO THE BRINK.

HIS TRUE VICTORY WOULD HAVE BEEN MAKING ME INTO A KILLER.

HE MEANT IT FOR YOU AND ROBIN BOTH... THE COSTUMES IN THE BAG... WHAT METICULOUS PLANNING!

THE PLAN BEGAN TO UNRAVEL WHEN YOU CAME ALONG INSTEAD, BUT IT WAS DOOMED TO FAIL ANYWAY. IT ALL RESTED ON A FLAWED ASSUMPTION.

"LORD DEATH MAN COULDN'T UNDERSTAND THE CODE THAT WE LIVE BY IN FIGHTING FOR JUSTICE.

"WE DO NOT KILL."

HAHAHAHAHAHAHAHAHAHAHA HA HAAA!!!

"THE GARDEN OF DEATH"

バットマン

Written by JEFF PARKER Art by SANDY JARRELL

Colors by JORDIE BELLAIRE Lettered by WES ABBOTT
Cover by MICHAEL and LAURA ALLRED

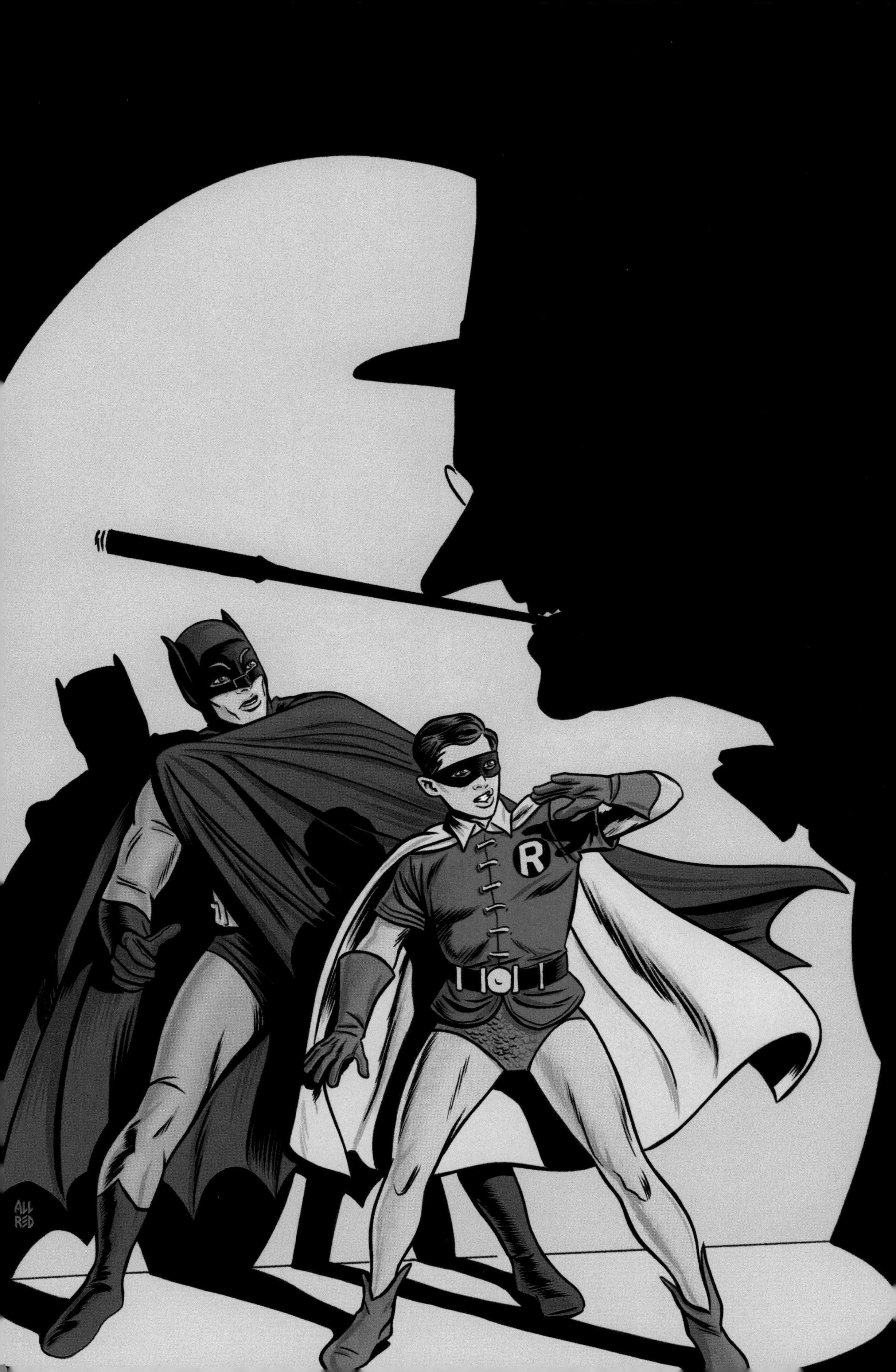
ALL
RED

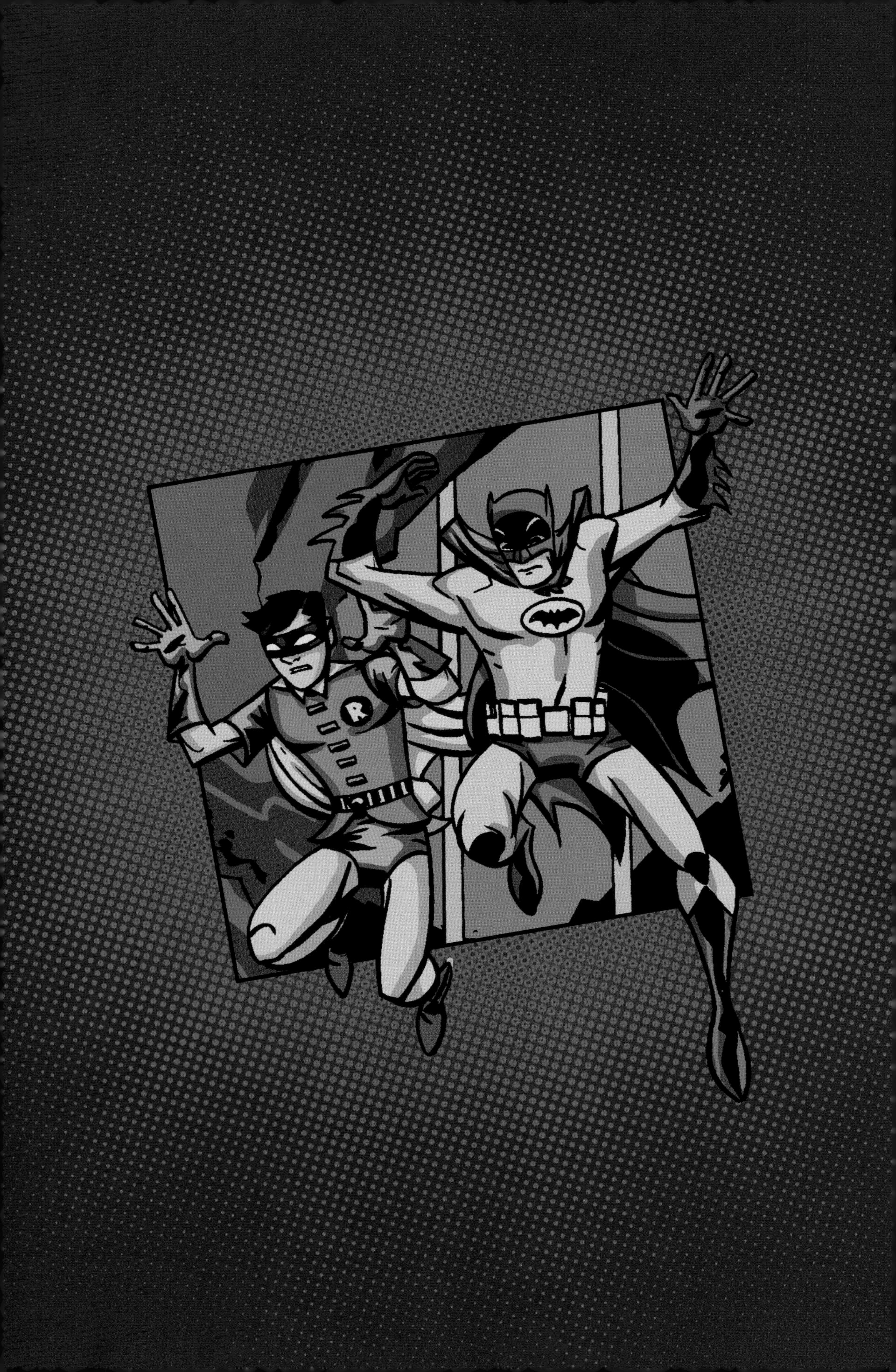

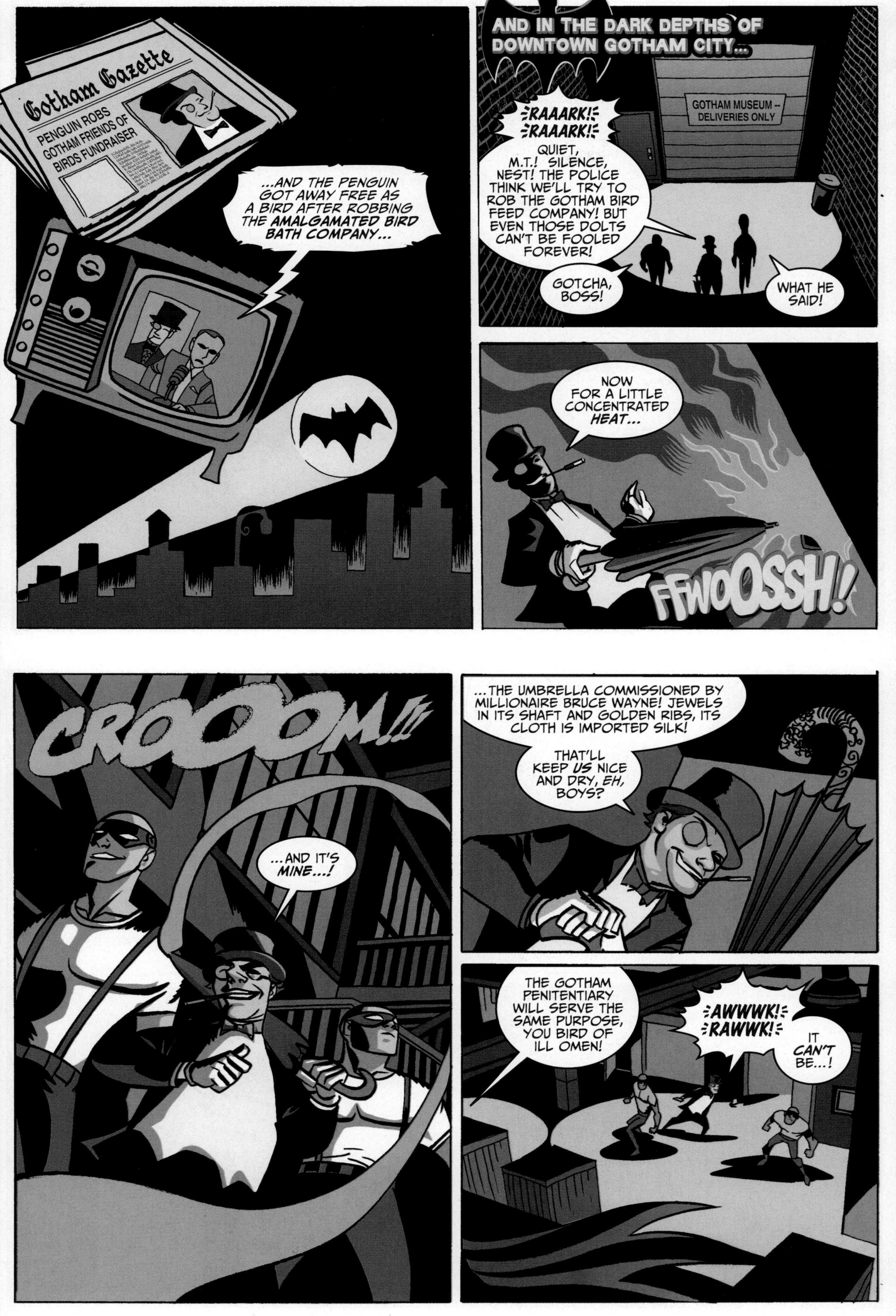
Gotham Gazette
PENGUIN ROBS GOTHAM FRIENDS OF BIRDS FUNDRAISER
...AND THE PENGUIN GOT AWAY FREE AS A BIRD AFTER ROBBING THE AMALGAMATED BIRD BATH COMPANY...
AND IN THE DARK DEPTHS OF DOWNTOWN GOTHAM CITY...
GOTHAM MUSEUM -- DELIVERIES ONLY
RAAARK! RAAARK!
QUIET, M.T.! SILENCE, NEST! THE POLICE THINK WE'LL TRY TO ROB THE GOTHAM BIRD FEED COMPANY! BUT EVEN THOSE DOLTS CAN'T BE FOOLED FOREVER!
GOTCHA, BOSS!
WHAT HE SAID!
NOW FOR A LITTLE CONCENTRATED HEAT...
FFWOOSSH!!
CROOOM!!!
...AND IT'S MINE...!
...THE UMBRELLA COMMISSIONED BY MILLIONAIRE BRUCE WAYNE! JEWELS IN ITS SHAFT AND GOLDEN RIBS, ITS CLOTH IS IMPORTED SILK!
THAT'LL KEEP US NICE AND DRY, EH, BOYS?
THE GOTHAM PENITENTIARY WILL SERVE THE SAME PURPOSE, YOU BIRD OF ILL OMEN!
AWWWK! RAWWK!
IT CAN'T BE...!

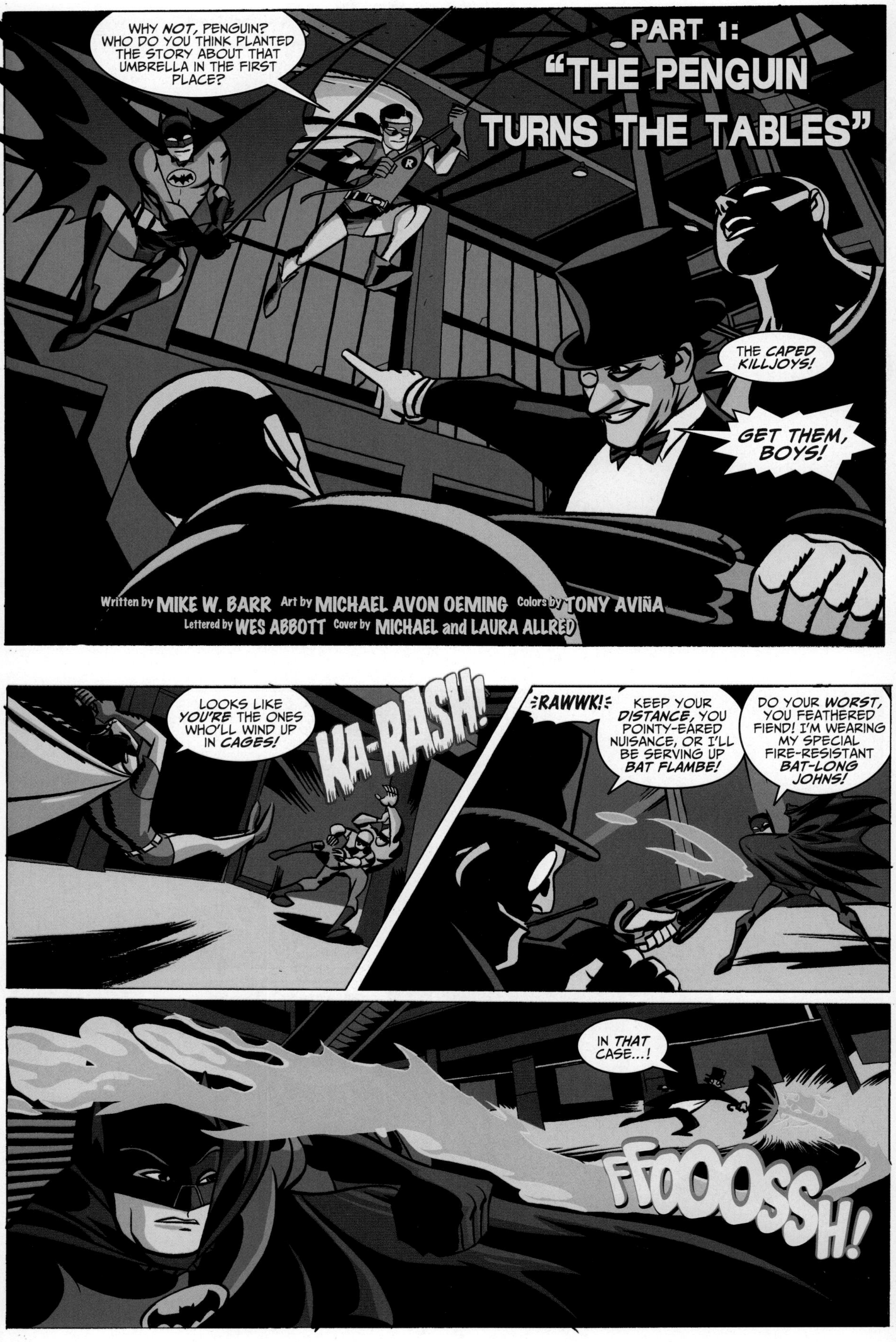

WHY NOT, PENGUIN? WHO DO YOU THINK PLANTED THE STORY ABOUT THAT UMBRELLA IN THE FIRST PLACE?
PART 1:
"THE PENGUIN TURNS THE TABLES"
THE CAPED KILLJOYS!
GET THEM, BOYS!
Written by MIKE W. BARR Art by MICHAEL AVON OEMING Colors by TONY AVIÑA
Lettered by WES ABBOTT Cover by MICHAEL and LAURA ALLRED
LOOKS LIKE YOU'RE THE ONES WHO'LL WIND UP IN CAGES!
KA-RASH!
RAWWK!
KEEP YOUR DISTANCE, YOU POINTY-EARED NUISANCE, OR I'LL BE SERVING UP BAT FLAMBE!
DO YOUR WORST, YOU FEATHERED FIEND! I'M WEARING MY SPECIAL FIRE-RESISTANT BAT-LONG JOHNS!
IN THAT CASE...!
FFOOOSSH!

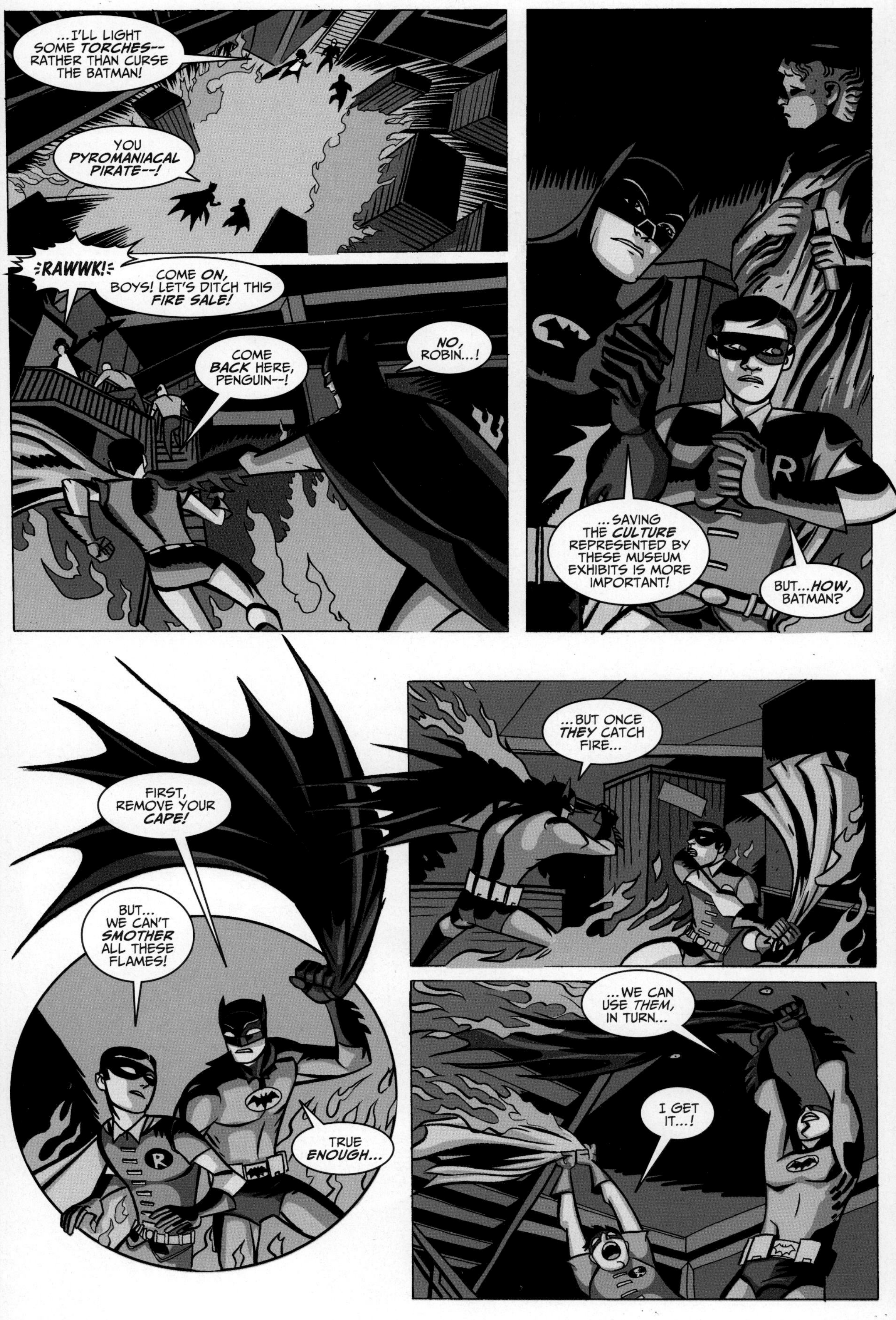
...I'LL LIGHT SOME TORCHES-- RATHER THAN CURSE THE BATMAN!
YOU PYROMANIACAL PIRATE--!
RAWWK!
COME ON, BOYS! LET'S DITCH THIS FIRE SALE!
COME BACK HERE, PENGUIN--!
NO, ROBIN...!
...SAVING THE CULTURE REPRESENTED BY THESE MUSEUM EXHIBITS IS MORE IMPORTANT!
BUT...HOW, BATMAN?
FIRST, REMOVE YOUR CAPE!
BUT... WE CAN'T SMOTHER ALL THESE FLAMES!
TRUE ENOUGH...
...BUT ONCE THEY CATCH FIRE...
...WE CAN USE THEM, IN TURN...
I GET IT...!

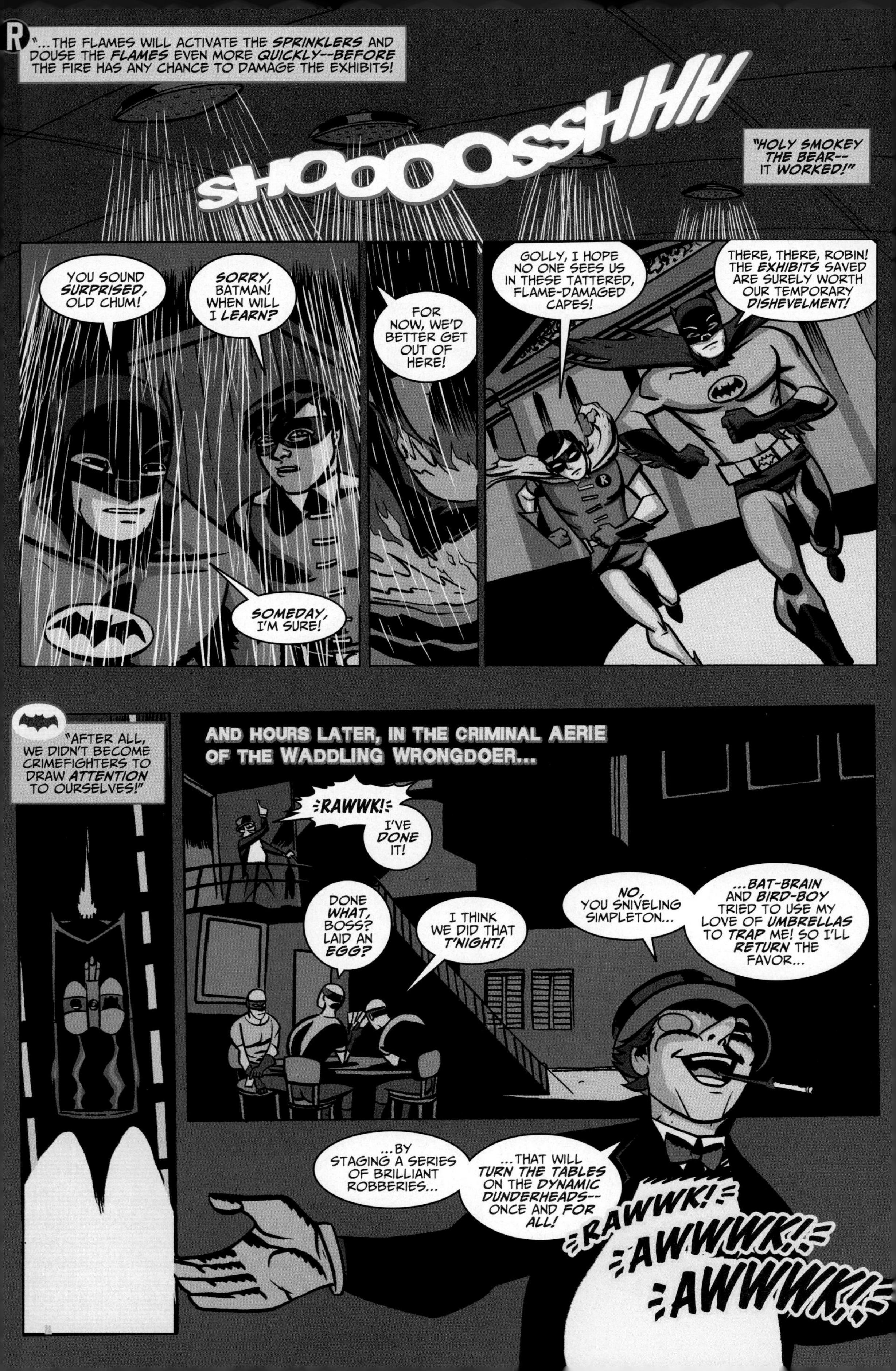
"...THE FLAMES WILL ACTIVATE THE SPRINKLERS AND DOUSE THE FLAMES EVEN MORE QUICKLY--BEFORE THE FIRE HAS ANY CHANCE TO DAMAGE THE EXHIBITS!
SHOOOOOSSHHHH
"HOLY SMOKEY THE BEAR-- IT WORKED!"
YOU SOUND SURPRISED, OLD CHUM!
SORRY, BATMAN! WHEN WILL I LEARN?
SOMEDAY, I'M SURE!
FOR NOW, WE'D BETTER GET OUT OF HERE!
GOLLY, I HOPE NO ONE SEES US IN THESE TATTERED, FLAME-DAMAGED CAPES!
THERE, THERE, ROBIN! THE EXHIBITS SAVED ARE SURELY WORTH OUR TEMPORARY DISHEVELMENT!
"AFTER ALL, WE DIDN'T BECOME CRIMEFIGHTERS TO DRAW ATTENTION TO OURSELVES!"
AND HOURS LATER, IN THE CRIMINAL AERIE OF THE WADDLING WRONGDOER...
RAWWK! I'VE DONE IT!
DONE WHAT, BOSS? LAID AN EGG?
I THINK WE DID THAT T'NIGHT!
NO, YOU SNIVELING SIMPLETON...
...BAT-BRAIN AND BIRD-BOY TRIED TO USE MY LOVE OF UMBRELLAS TO TRAP ME! SO I'LL RETURN THE FAVOR...
...BY STAGING A SERIES OF BRILLIANT ROBBERIES...
...THAT WILL TURN THE TABLES ON THE DYNAMIC DUNDERHEADS-- ONCE AND FOR ALL!
RAWWK! AWWWK! AWWWK!

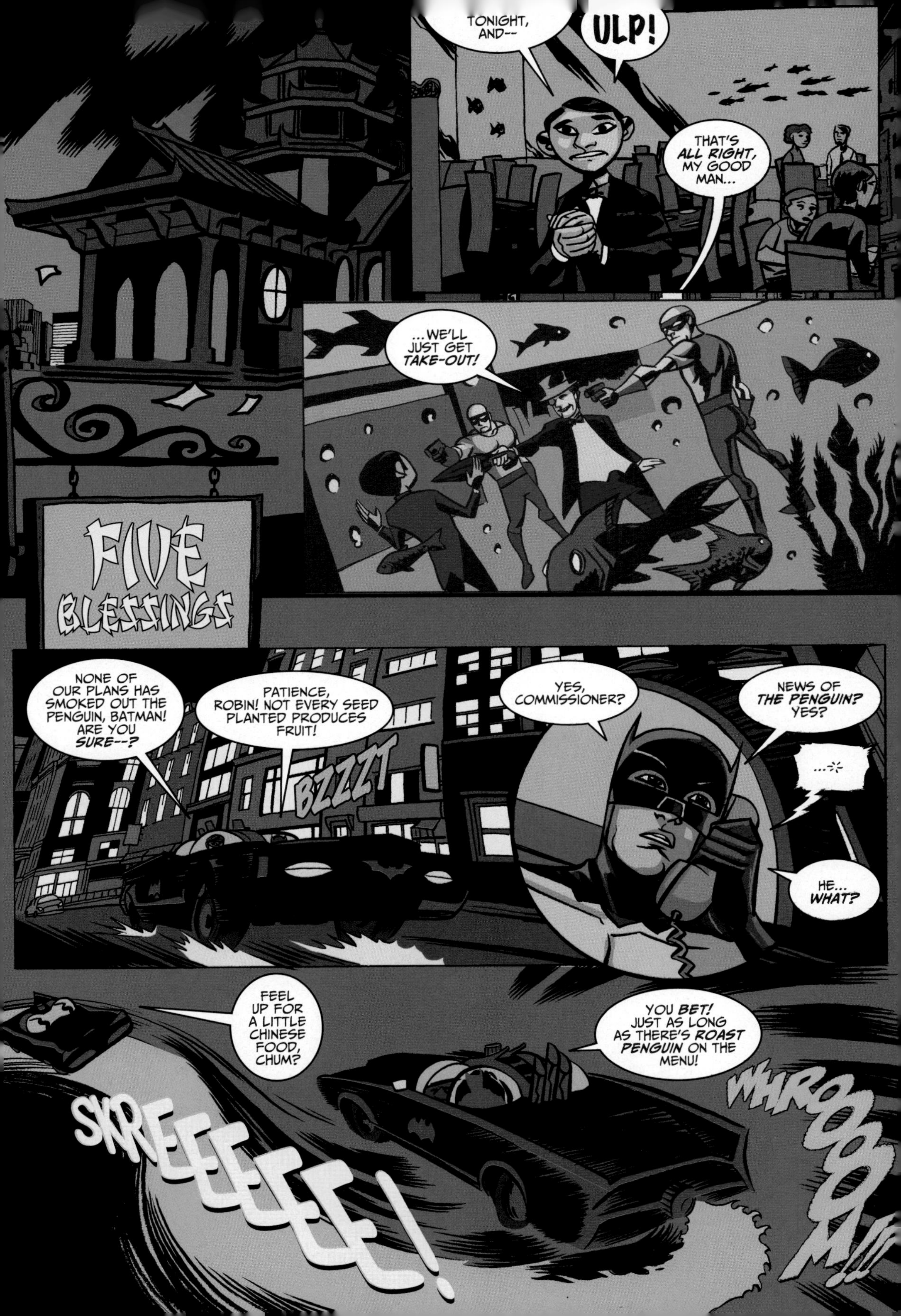
FIVE BLESSINGS
TONIGHT, AND--
ULP!
THAT'S ALL RIGHT, MY GOOD MAN...
...WE'LL JUST GET TAKE-OUT!
NONE OF OUR PLANS HAS SMOKED OUT THE PENGUIN, BATMAN! ARE YOU SURE--?
PATIENCE, ROBIN! NOT EVERY SEED PLANTED PRODUCES FRUIT!
BZZZT
YES, COMMISSIONER?
NEWS OF THE PENGUIN? YES?
...
HE... WHAT?
FEEL UP FOR A LITTLE CHINESE FOOD, CHUM?
YOU BET! JUST AS LONG AS THERE'S ROAST PENGUIN ON THE MENU!
SKREEEEEEEE!
WHROOOOM!!

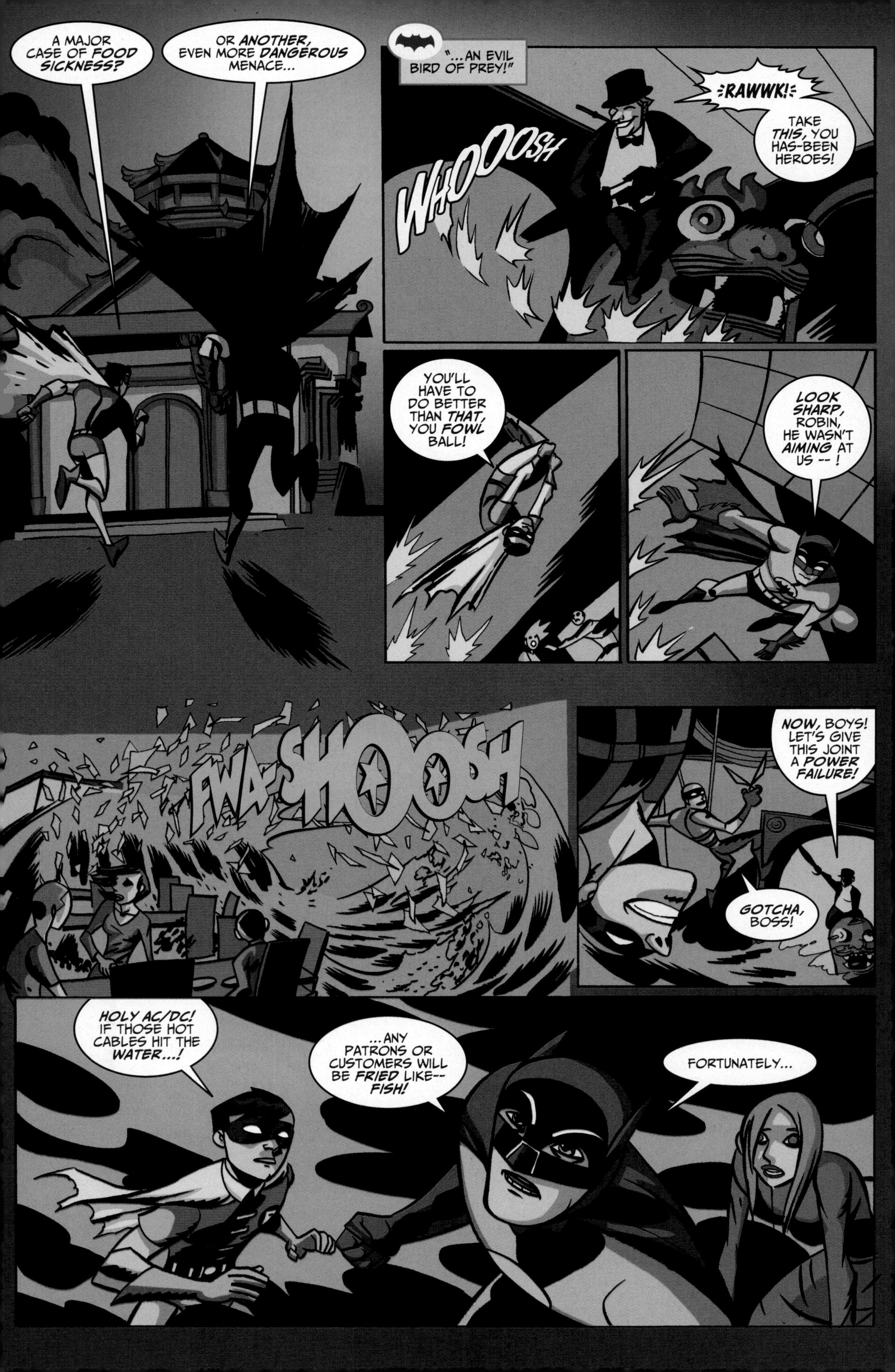
A MAJOR CASE OF FOOD SICKNESS?
OR ANOTHER, EVEN MORE DANGEROUS MENACE...
"...AN EVIL BIRD OF PREY!"
WHOOOSH
RAWWK!
TAKE THIS, YOU HAS-BEEN HEROES!
YOU'LL HAVE TO DO BETTER THAN THAT, YOU FOWL BALL!
LOOK SHARP, ROBIN, HE WASN'T AIMING AT US -- !
FWA-SHOOOSH
NOW, BOYS! LET'S GIVE THIS JOINT A POWER FAILURE!
GOTCHA, BOSS!
HOLY AC/DC! IF THOSE HOT CABLES HIT THE WATER...!
...ANY PATRONS OR CUSTOMERS WILL BE FRIED LIKE-- FISH!
FORTUNATELY...

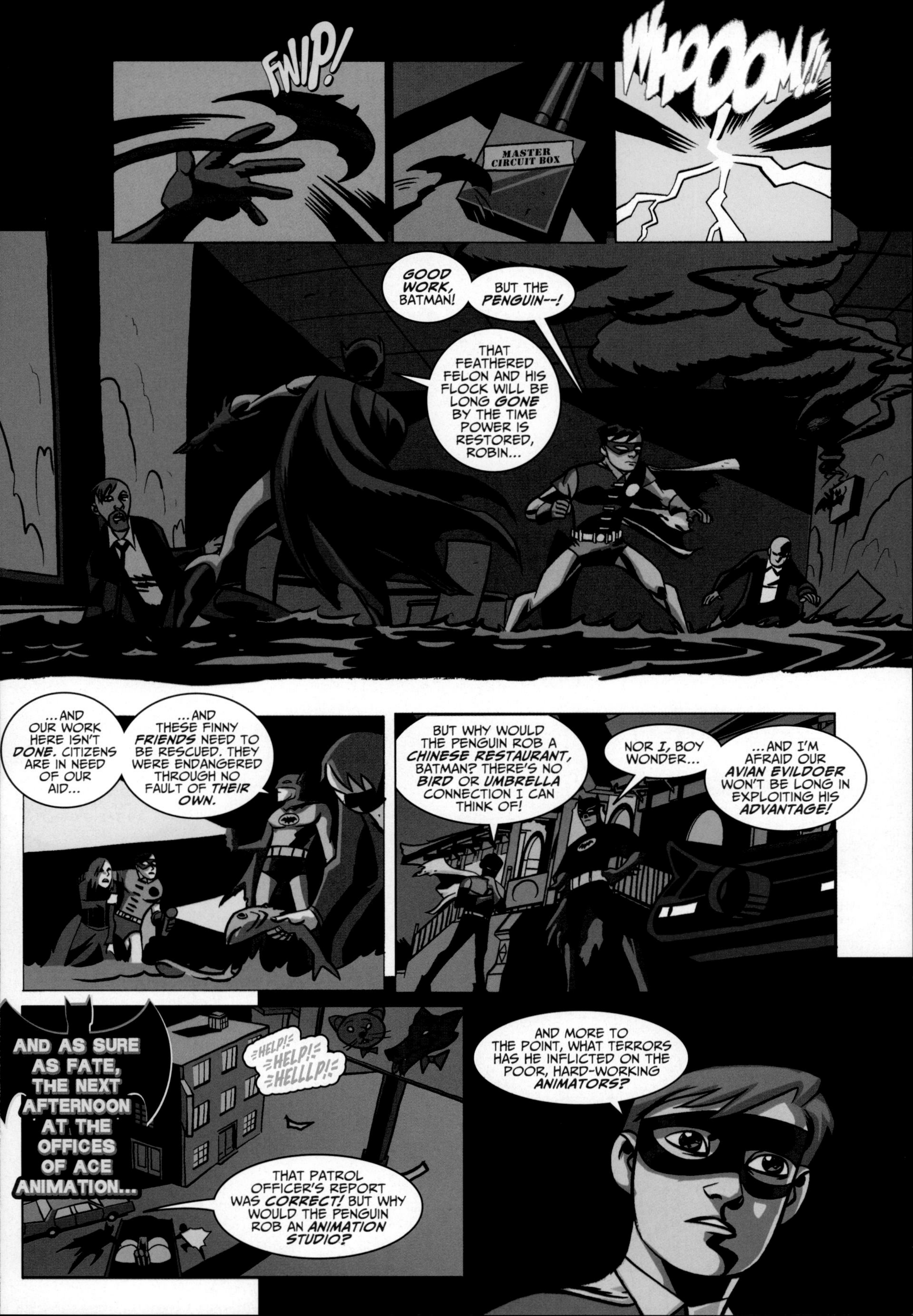

FWIP!
MASTER CIRCUIT BOX
WHOOOM!!!
GOOD WORK, BATMAN!
BUT THE PENGUIN--!
THAT FEATHERED FELON AND HIS FLOCK WILL BE LONG GONE BY THE TIME POWER IS RESTORED, ROBIN...
...AND OUR WORK HERE ISN'T DONE. CITIZENS ARE IN NEED OF OUR AID...
...AND THESE FINNY FRIENDS NEED TO BE RESCUED. THEY WERE ENDANGERED THROUGH NO FAULT OF THEIR OWN.
BUT WHY WOULD THE PENGUIN ROB A CHINESE RESTAURANT, BATMAN? THERE'S NO BIRD OR UMBRELLA CONNECTION I CAN THINK OF!
NOR I, BOY WONDER...
...AND I'M AFRAID OUR AVIAN EVILDOER WON'T BE LONG IN EXPLOITING HIS ADVANTAGE!
AND AS SURE AS FATE, THE NEXT AFTERNOON AT THE OFFICES OF ACE ANIMATION...
HELP! HELP! HELLLP!
THAT PATROL OFFICER'S REPORT WAS CORRECT! BUT WHY WOULD THE PENGUIN ROB AN ANIMATION STUDIO?
AND MORE TO THE POINT, WHAT TERRORS HAS HE INFLICTED ON THE POOR, HARD-WORKING ANIMATORS?

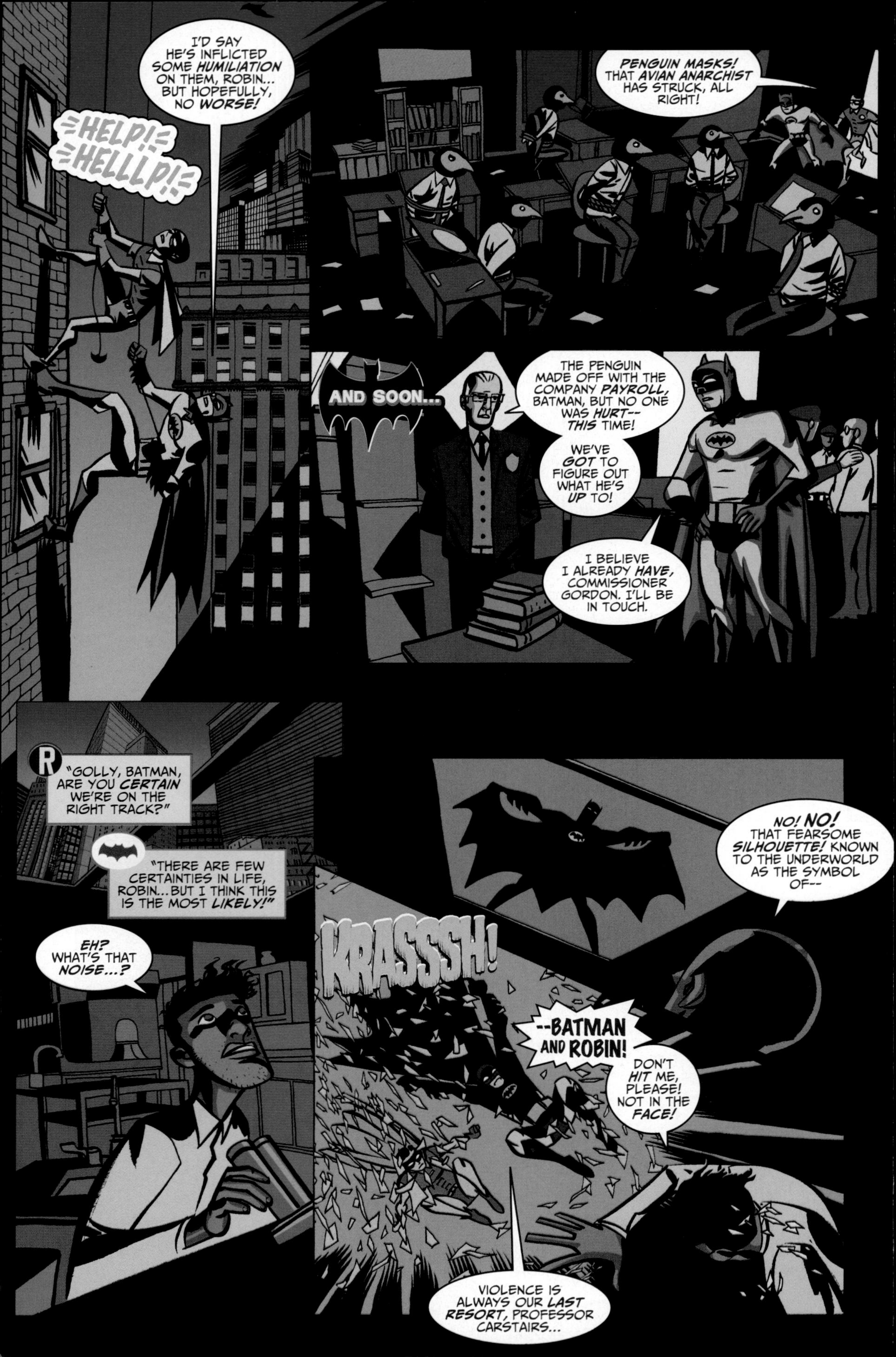
I'D SAY HE'S INFLICTED SOME HUMILIATION ON THEM, ROBIN... BUT HOPEFULLY, NO WORSE!
HELP! HELLLP!
PENGUIN MASKS! THAT AVIAN ANARCHIST HAS STRUCK, ALL RIGHT!
AND SOON...
THE PENGUIN MADE OFF WITH THE COMPANY PAYROLL, BATMAN, BUT NO ONE WAS HURT-- THIS TIME!
WE'VE GOT TO FIGURE OUT WHAT HE'S UP TO!
I BELIEVE I ALREADY HAVE, COMMISSIONER GORDON. I'LL BE IN TOUCH.
"GOLLY, BATMAN, ARE YOU CERTAIN WE'RE ON THE RIGHT TRACK?"
"THERE ARE FEW CERTAINTIES IN LIFE, ROBIN... BUT I THINK THIS IS THE MOST LIKELY!"
EH? WHAT'S THAT NOISE...?
NO! NO! THAT FEARSOME SILHOUETTE! KNOWN TO THE UNDERWORLD AS THE SYMBOL OF--
KRASSSH!
--BATMAN AND ROBIN!
DON'T HIT ME, PLEASE! NOT IN THE FACE!
VIOLENCE IS ALWAYS OUR LAST RESORT, PROFESSOR CARSTAIRS...

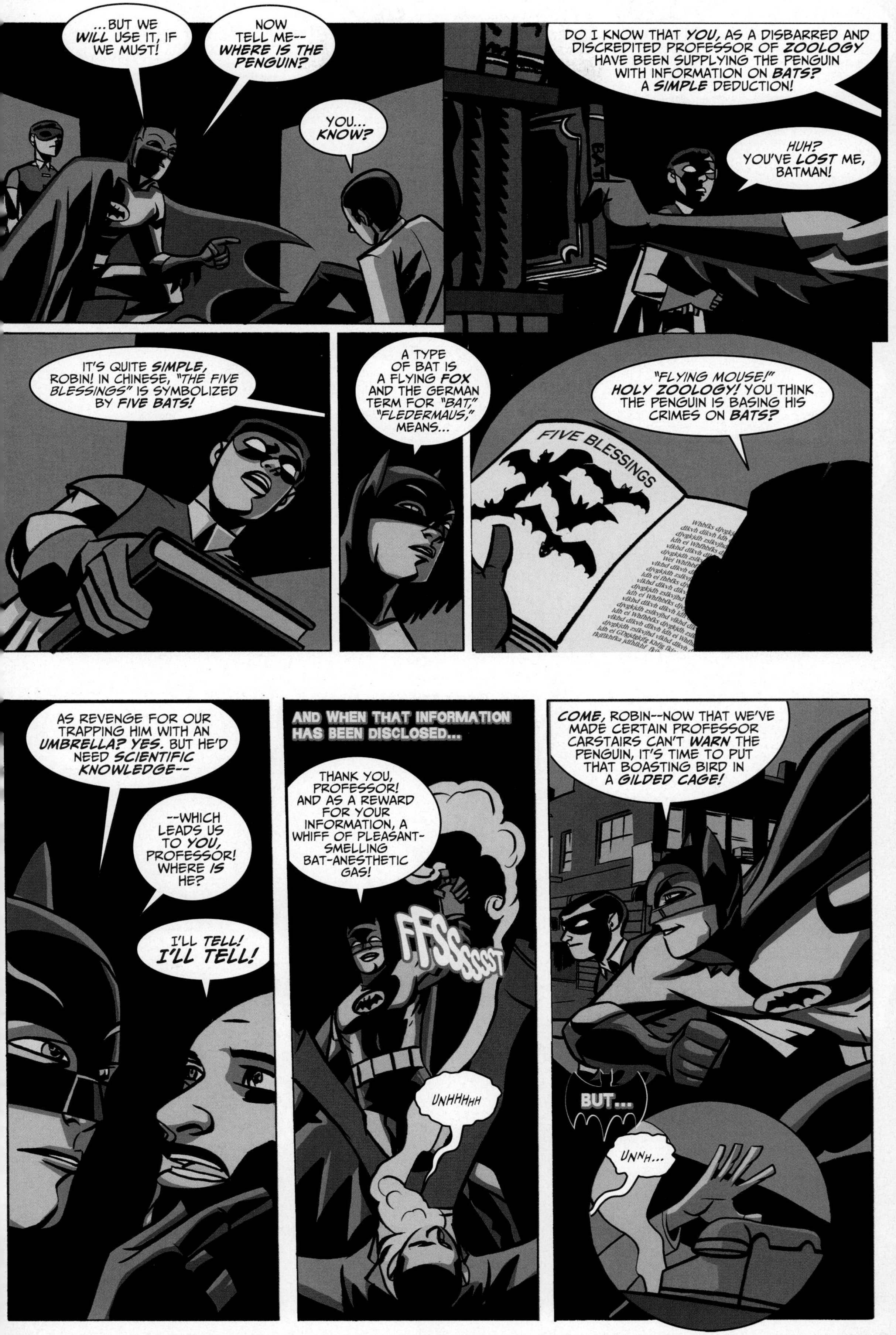
...BUT WE WILL USE IT, IF WE MUST!
NOW TELL ME-- WHERE IS THE PENGUIN?
YOU... KNOW?
DO I KNOW THAT YOU, AS A DISBARRED AND DISCREDITED PROFESSOR OF ZOOLOGY HAVE BEEN SUPPLYING THE PENGUIN WITH INFORMATION ON BATS? A SIMPLE DEDUCTION!
HUH? YOU'VE LOST ME, BATMAN!
IT'S QUITE SIMPLE, ROBIN! IN CHINESE, "THE FIVE BLESSINGS" IS SYMBOLIZED BY FIVE BATS!
A TYPE OF BAT IS A FLYING FOX AND THE GERMAN TERM FOR "BAT," "FLEDERMAUS," MEANS...
"FLYING MOUSE!" HOLY ZOOLOGY! YOU THINK THE PENGUIN IS BASING HIS CRIMES ON BATS?
FIVE BLESSINGS
AS REVENGE FOR OUR TRAPPING HIM WITH AN UMBRELLA? YES. BUT HE'D NEED SCIENTIFIC KNOWLEDGE--
--WHICH LEADS US TO YOU, PROFESSOR! WHERE IS HE?
I'LL TELL! I'LL TELL!
AND WHEN THAT INFORMATION HAS BEEN DISCLOSED...
THANK YOU, PROFESSOR! AND AS A REWARD FOR YOUR INFORMATION, A WHIFF OF PLEASANT-SMELLING BAT-ANESTHETIC GAS!
FFSSSSSST
UNHHHHH
COME, ROBIN--NOW THAT WE'VE MADE CERTAIN PROFESSOR CARSTAIRS CAN'T WARN THE PENGUIN, IT'S TIME TO PUT THAT BOASTING BIRD IN A GILDED CAGE!
BUT...
UNNH...

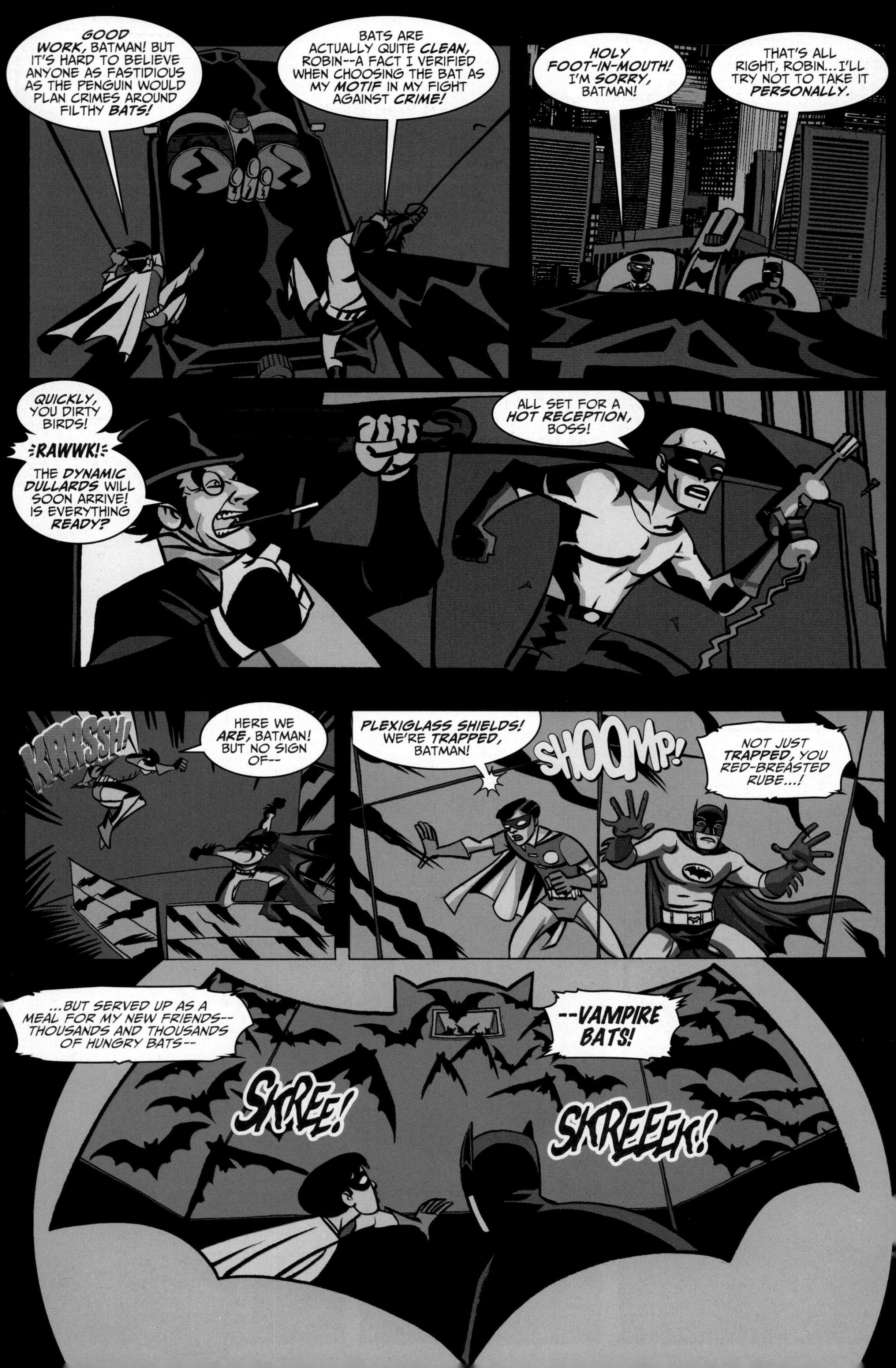
GOOD WORK, BATMAN! BUT IT'S HARD TO BELIEVE ANYONE AS FASTIDIOUS AS THE PENGUIN WOULD PLAN CRIMES AROUND FILTHY BATS!
BATS ARE ACTUALLY QUITE CLEAN, ROBIN--A FACT I VERIFIED WHEN CHOOSING THE BAT AS MY MOTIF IN MY FIGHT AGAINST CRIME!
HOLY FOOT-IN-MOUTH! I'M SORRY, BATMAN!
THAT'S ALL RIGHT, ROBIN...I'LL TRY NOT TO TAKE IT PERSONALLY.
QUICKLY, YOU DIRTY BIRDS!
RAWWK!
THE DYNAMIC DULLARDS WILL SOON ARRIVE! IS EVERYTHING READY?
ALL SET FOR A HOT RECEPTION, BOSS!
KRRSSH!
HERE WE ARE, BATMAN! BUT NO SIGN OF--
PLEXIGLASS SHIELDS! WE'RE TRAPPED, BATMAN!
SHOOMP!
NOT JUST TRAPPED, YOU RED-BREASTED RUBE...!
...BUT SERVED UP AS A MEAL FOR MY NEW FRIENDS--THOUSANDS AND THOUSANDS OF HUNGRY BATS--
--VAMPIRE BATS!
SKREE!
SKREEEK!

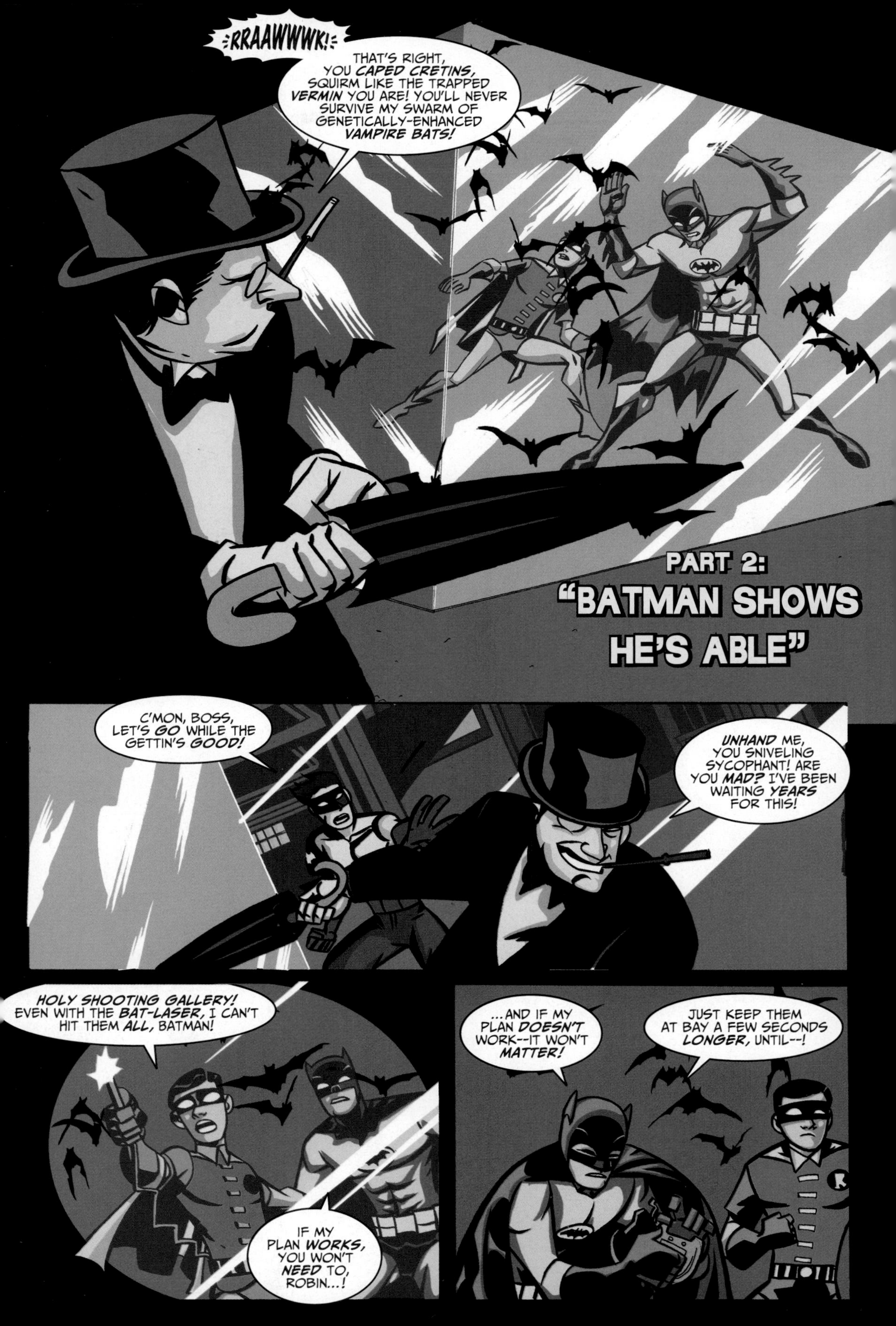
RRAAWWWK!
THAT'S RIGHT, YOU CAPED CRETINS, SQUIRM LIKE THE TRAPPED VERMIN YOU ARE! YOU'LL NEVER SURVIVE MY SWARM OF GENETICALLY-ENHANCED VAMPIRE BATS!
PART 2:
"BATMAN SHOWS HE'S ABLE"
C'MON, BOSS, LET'S GO WHILE THE GETTIN'S GOOD!
UNHAND ME, YOU SNIVELING SYCOPHANT! ARE YOU MAD? I'VE BEEN WAITING YEARS FOR THIS!
HOLY SHOOTING GALLERY! EVEN WITH THE BAT-LASER, I CAN'T HIT THEM ALL, BATMAN!
IF MY PLAN WORKS, YOU WON'T NEED TO, ROBIN...!
...AND IF MY PLAN DOESN'T WORK--IT WON'T MATTER!
JUST KEEP THEM AT BAY A FEW SECONDS LONGER, UNTIL--!

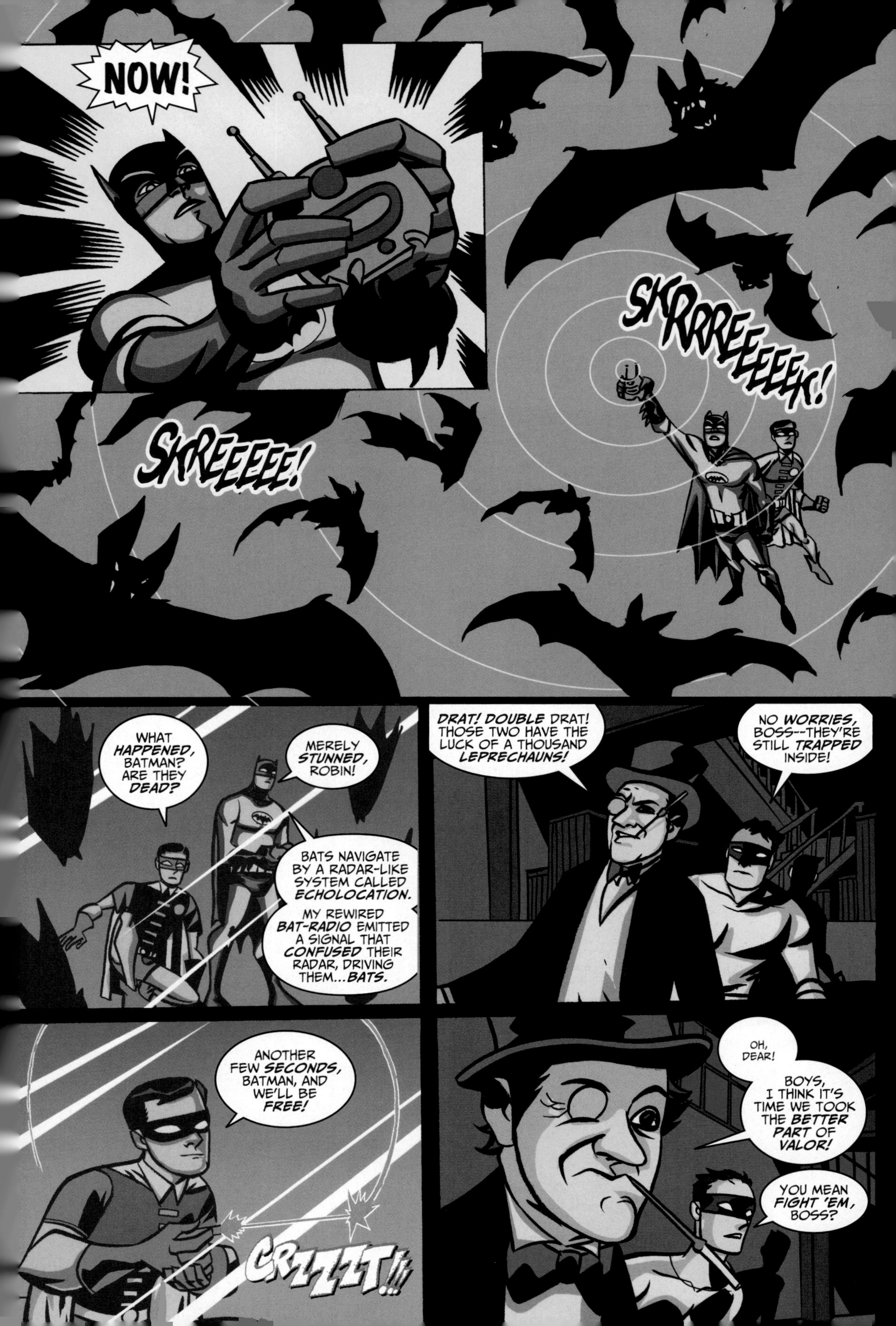
NOW!
SKRRRREEEEEEK!
SKREEEEEE!
WHAT HAPPENED, BATMAN? ARE THEY DEAD?
MERELY STUNNED, ROBIN!
BATS NAVIGATE BY A RADAR-LIKE SYSTEM CALLED ECHOLOCATION.
MY REWIRED BAT-RADIO EMITTED A SIGNAL THAT CONFUSED THEIR RADAR, DRIVING THEM...BATS.
DRAT! DOUBLE DRAT! THOSE TWO HAVE THE LUCK OF A THOUSAND LEPRECHAUNS!
NO WORRIES, BOSS--THEY'RE STILL TRAPPED INSIDE!
ANOTHER FEW SECONDS, BATMAN, AND WE'LL BE FREE!
CRZZZT!!!
OH, DEAR!
BOYS, I THINK IT'S TIME WE TOOK THE BETTER PART OF VALOR!
YOU MEAN FIGHT 'EM, BOSS?

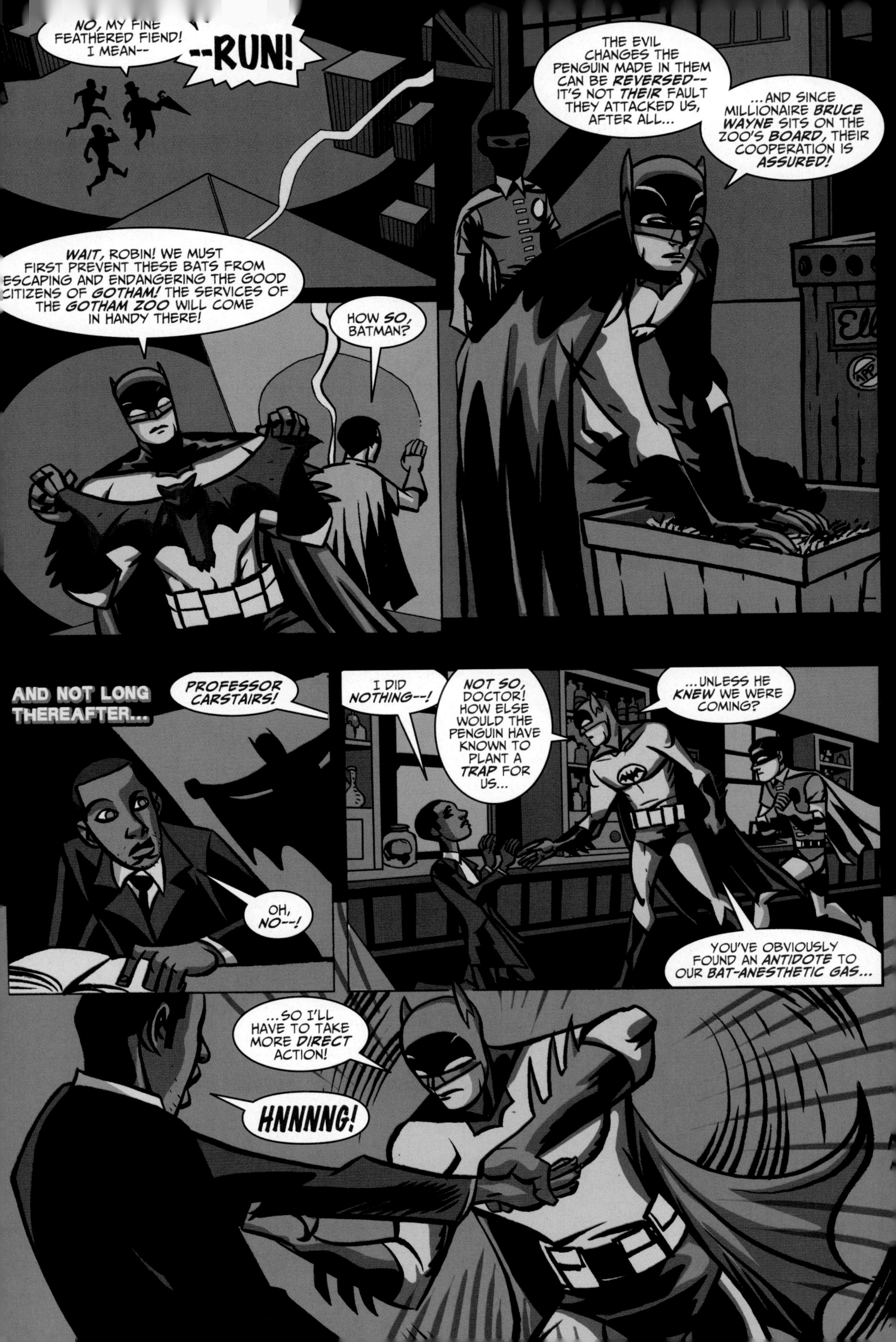
NO, MY FINE FEATHERED FIEND! I MEAN--
--RUN!
THE EVIL CHANGES THE PENGUIN MADE IN THEM CAN BE REVERSED-- IT'S NOT THEIR FAULT THEY ATTACKED US, AFTER ALL...
...AND SINCE MILLIONAIRE BRUCE WAYNE SITS ON THE ZOO'S BOARD, THEIR COOPERATION IS ASSURED!
WAIT, ROBIN! WE MUST FIRST PREVENT THESE BATS FROM ESCAPING AND ENDANGERING THE GOOD CITIZENS OF GOTHAM! THE SERVICES OF THE GOTHAM ZOO WILL COME IN HANDY THERE!
HOW SO, BATMAN?
AND NOT LONG THEREAFTER...
PROFESSOR CARSTAIRS!
OH, NO--!
I DID NOTHING--!
NOT SO, DOCTOR! HOW ELSE WOULD THE PENGUIN HAVE KNOWN TO PLANT A TRAP FOR US...
...UNLESS HE KNEW WE WERE COMING?
YOU'VE OBVIOUSLY FOUND AN ANTIDOTE TO OUR BAT-ANESTHETIC GAS...
...SO I'LL HAVE TO TAKE MORE DIRECT ACTION!
HNNNNG!

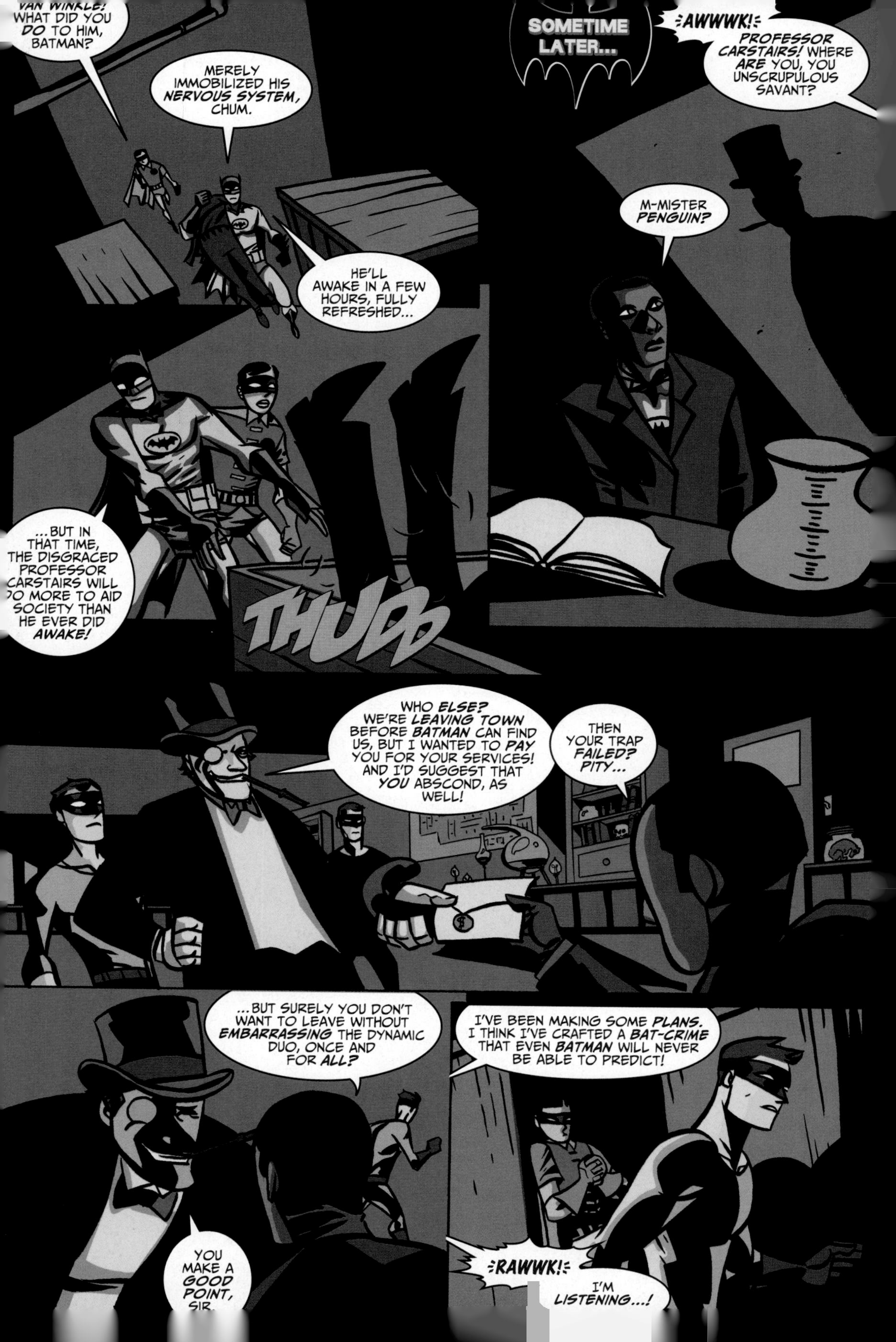
VAN WINKLE! WHAT DID YOU DO TO HIM, BATMAN?
MERELY IMMOBILIZED HIS NERVOUS SYSTEM, CHUM.
HE'LL AWAKE IN A FEW HOURS, FULLY REFRESHED...
...BUT IN THAT TIME, THE DISGRACED PROFESSOR CARSTAIRS WILL DO MORE TO AID SOCIETY THAN HE EVER DID AWAKE!
THUDD
SOMETIME LATER...
AWWWK!
PROFESSOR CARSTAIRS! WHERE ARE YOU, YOU UNSCRUPULOUS SAVANT?
M-MISTER PENGUIN?
WHO ELSE? WE'RE LEAVING TOWN BEFORE BATMAN CAN FIND US, BUT I WANTED TO PAY YOU FOR YOUR SERVICES! AND I'D SUGGEST THAT YOU ABSCOND, AS WELL!
THEN YOUR TRAP FAILED? PITY...
...BUT SURELY YOU DON'T WANT TO LEAVE WITHOUT EMBARRASSING THE DYNAMIC DUO, ONCE AND FOR ALL?
YOU MAKE A GOOD POINT, SIR.
I'VE BEEN MAKING SOME PLANS. I THINK I'VE CRAFTED A BAT-CRIME THAT EVEN BATMAN WILL NEVER BE ABLE TO PREDICT!
RAWWK!
I'M LISTENING...!

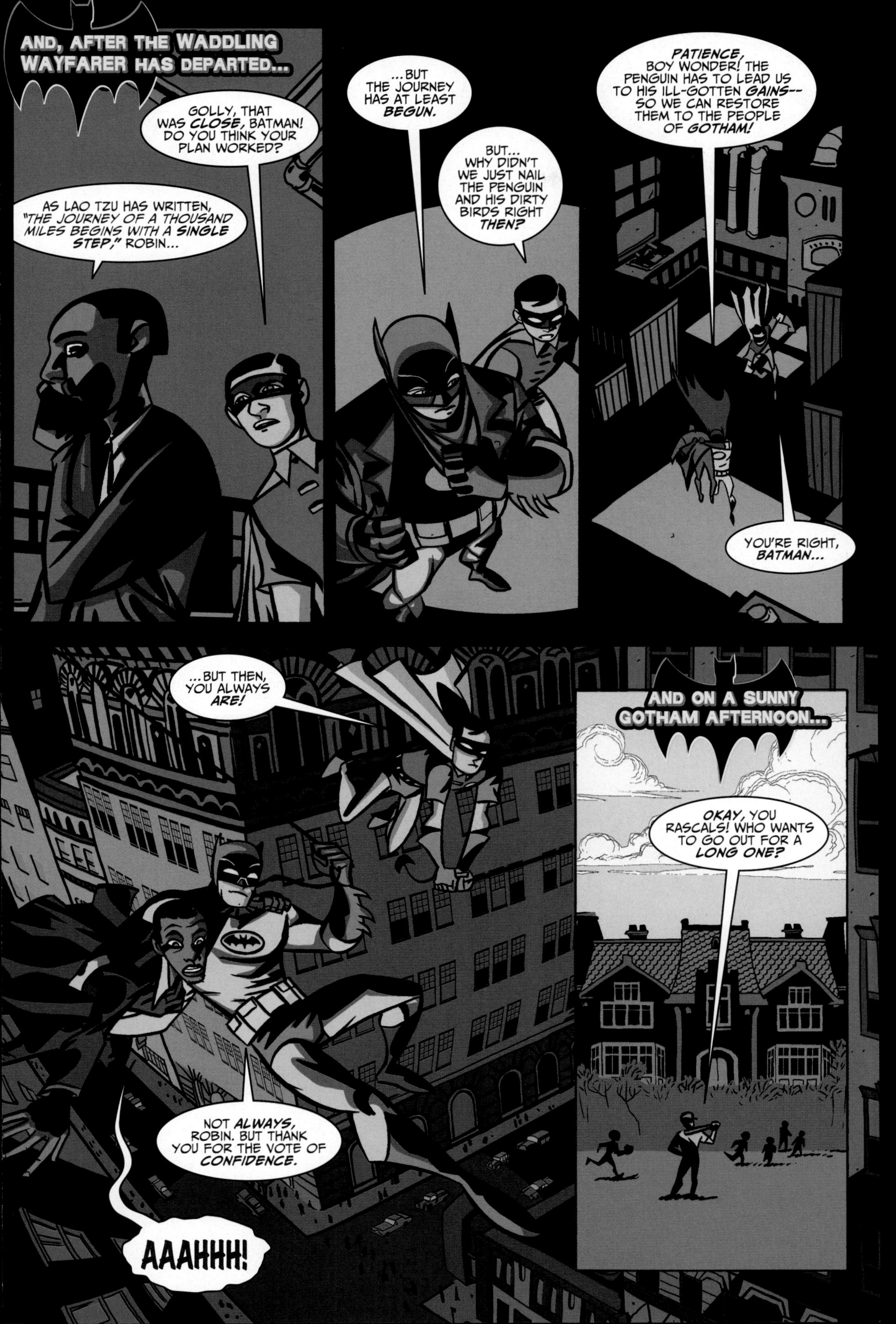

AND, AFTER THE WADDLING WAYFARER HAS DEPARTED...
GOLLY, THAT WAS CLOSE, BATMAN! DO YOU THINK YOUR PLAN WORKED?
AS LAO TZU HAS WRITTEN, "THE JOURNEY OF A THOUSAND MILES BEGINS WITH A SINGLE STEP," ROBIN...
...BUT THE JOURNEY HAS AT LEAST BEGUN.
BUT... WHY DIDN'T WE JUST NAIL THE PENGUIN AND HIS DIRTY BIRDS RIGHT THEN?
PATIENCE, BOY WONDER! THE PENGUIN HAS TO LEAD US TO HIS ILL-GOTTEN GAINS-- SO WE CAN RESTORE THEM TO THE PEOPLE OF GOTHAM!
YOU'RE RIGHT, BATMAN...
...BUT THEN, YOU ALWAYS ARE!
NOT ALWAYS, ROBIN. BUT THANK YOU FOR THE VOTE OF CONFIDENCE.
AAAHHH!
AND ON A SUNNY GOTHAM AFTERNOON...
OKAY, YOU RASCALS! WHO WANTS TO GO OUT FOR A LONG ONE?

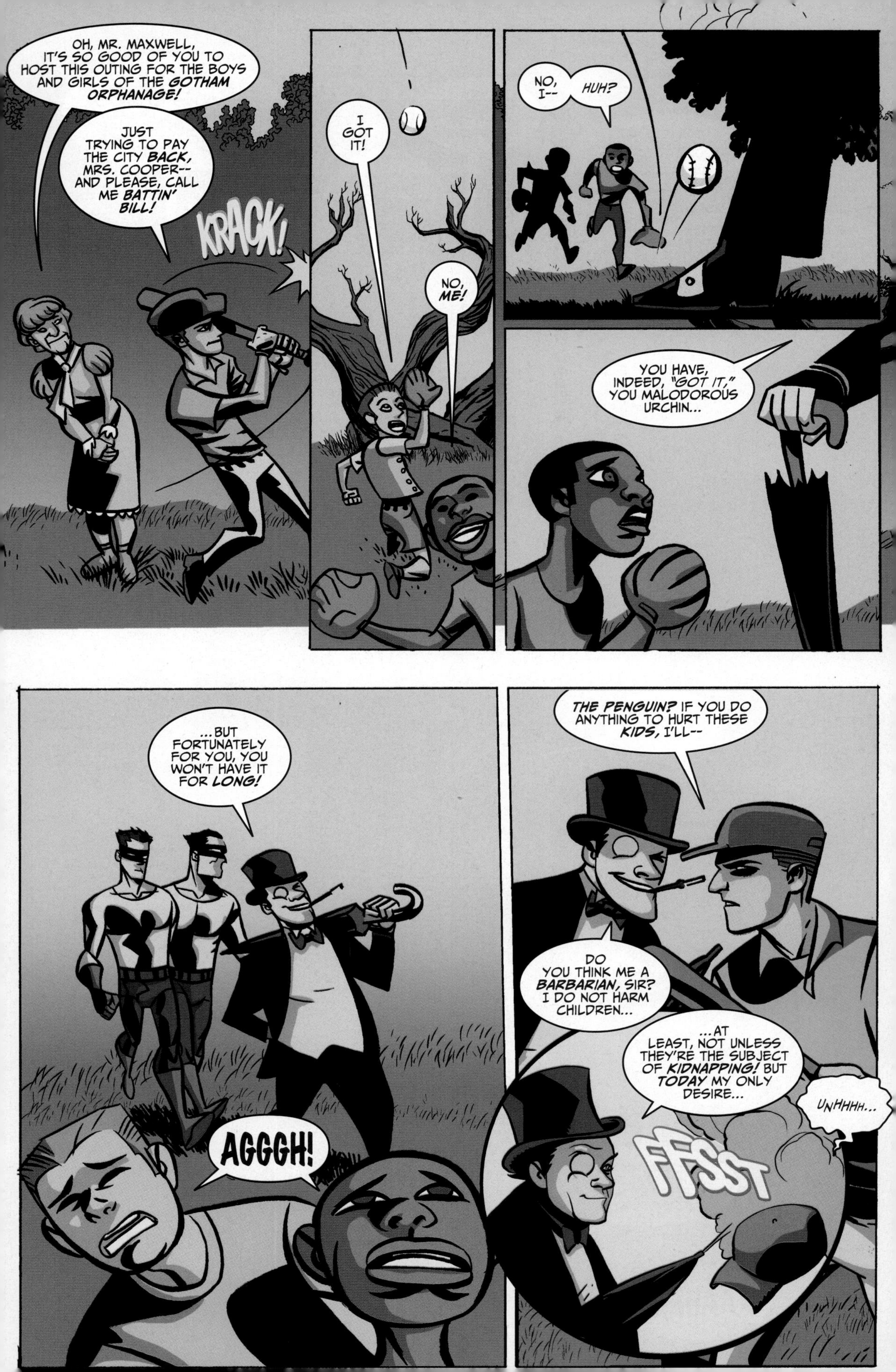
OH, MR. MAXWELL, IT'S SO GOOD OF YOU TO HOST THIS OUTING FOR THE BOYS AND GIRLS OF THE GOTHAM ORPHANAGE!
JUST TRYING TO PAY THE CITY BACK, MRS. COOPER-- AND PLEASE, CALL ME BATTIN' BILL!
KRACK!
I GOT IT!
NO, ME!
NO, I--
HUH?
YOU HAVE, INDEED, "GOT IT," YOU MALODOROUS URCHIN...
...BUT FORTUNATELY FOR YOU, YOU WON'T HAVE IT FOR LONG!
AGGGH!
THE PENGUIN? IF YOU DO ANYTHING TO HURT THESE KIDS, I'LL--
DO YOU THINK ME A BARBARIAN, SIR? I DO NOT HARM CHILDREN...
...AT LEAST, NOT UNLESS THEY'RE THE SUBJECT OF KIDNAPPING! BUT TODAY MY ONLY DESIRE...
FFSST
UNHHHH...

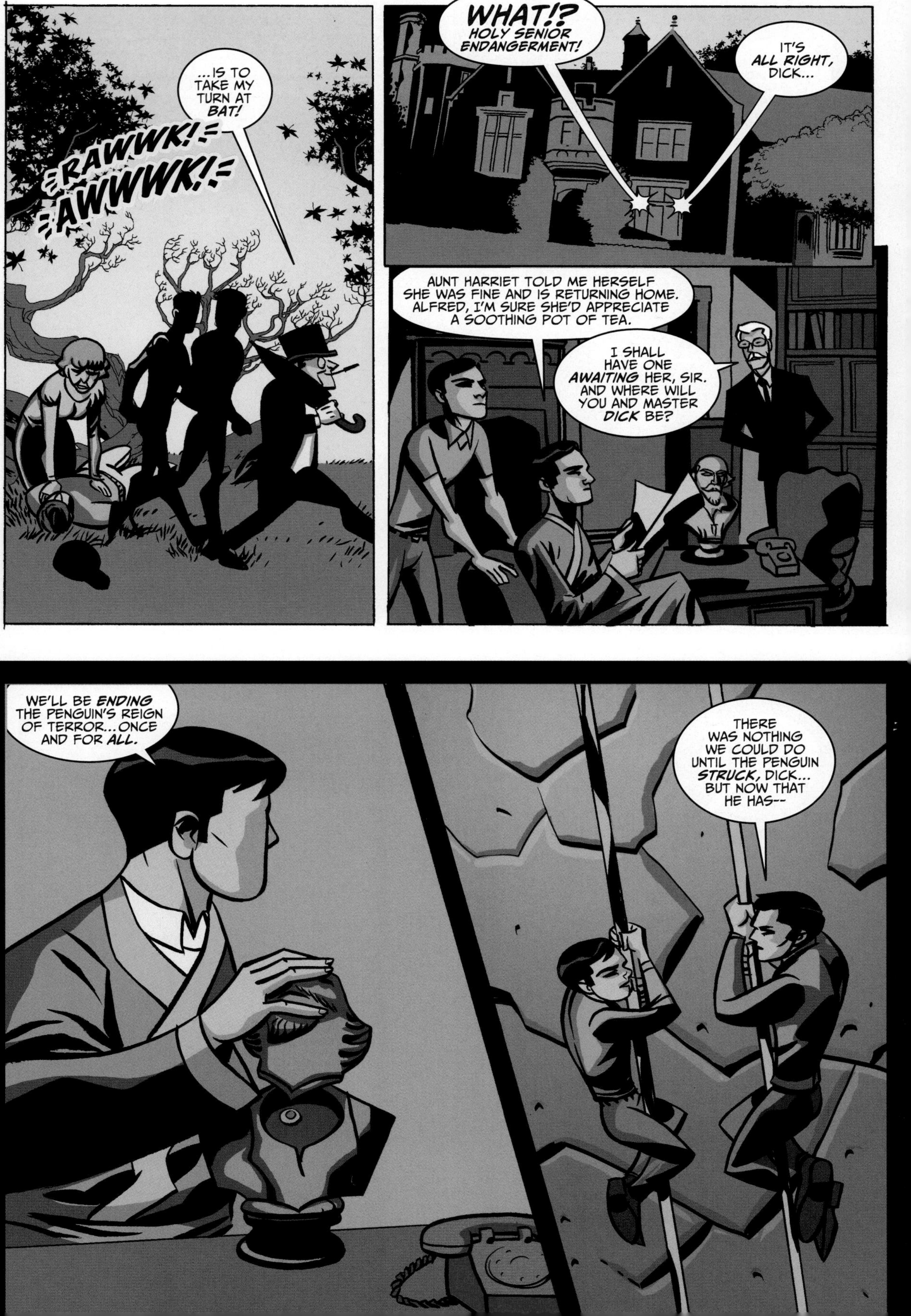
...IS TO TAKE MY TURN AT BAT!
RAWWK! AWWWK!
WHAT!? HOLY SENIOR ENDANGERMENT!
IT'S ALL RIGHT, DICK...
AUNT HARRIET TOLD ME HERSELF SHE WAS FINE AND IS RETURNING HOME. ALFRED, I'M SURE SHE'D APPRECIATE A SOOTHING POT OF TEA.
I SHALL HAVE ONE AWAITING HER, SIR. AND WHERE WILL YOU AND MASTER DICK BE?
WE'LL BE ENDING THE PENGUIN'S REIGN OF TERROR...ONCE AND FOR ALL.
THERE WAS NOTHING WE COULD DO UNTIL THE PENGUIN STRUCK, DICK... BUT NOW THAT HE HAS--

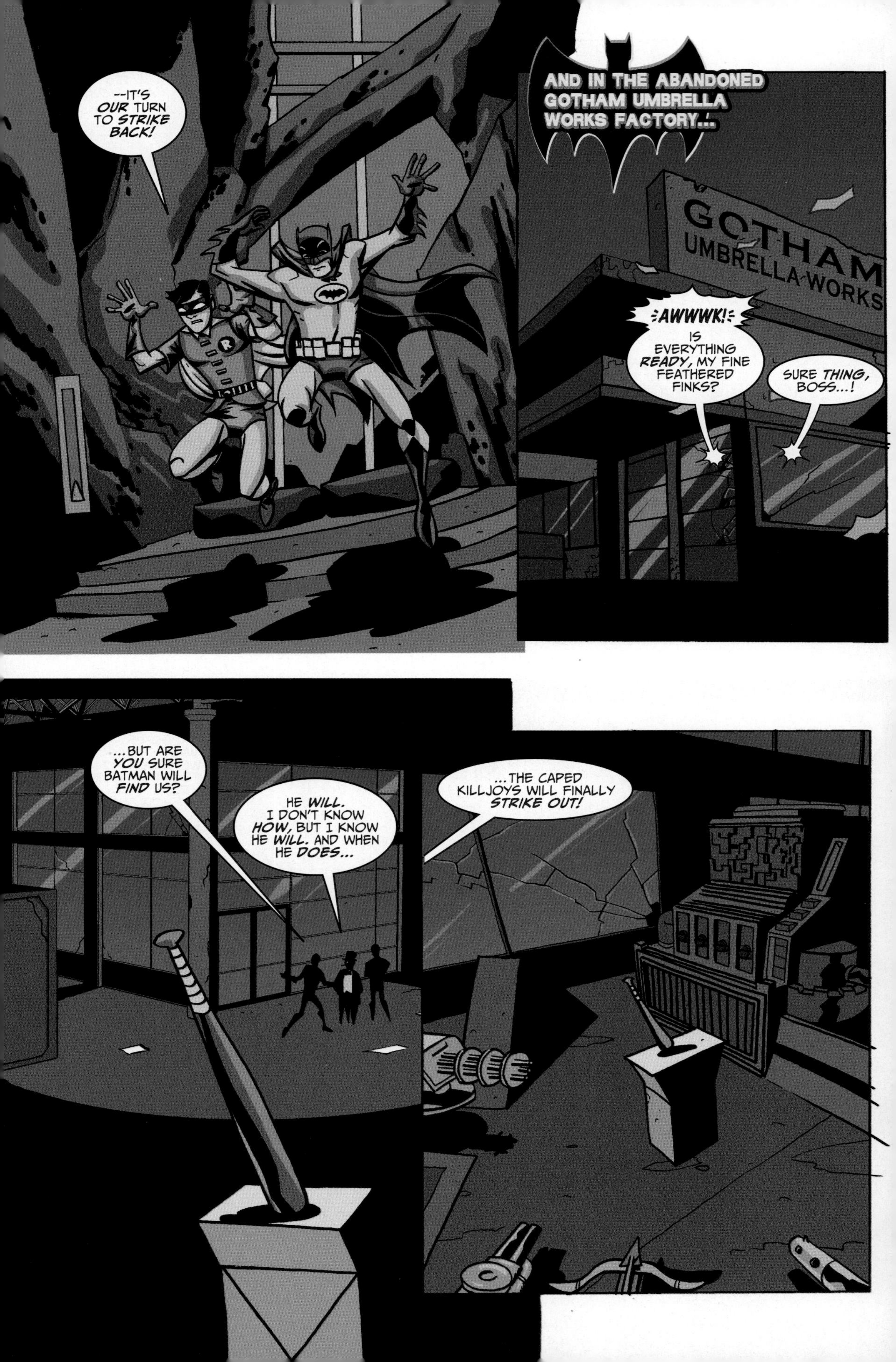

--IT'S OUR TURN TO STRIKE BACK!
AND IN THE ABANDONED GOTHAM UMBRELLA WORKS FACTORY...
GOTHAM UMBRELLA WORKS
AWWWK! IS EVERYTHING READY, MY FINE FEATHERED FINKS?
SURE THING, BOSS...!
...BUT ARE YOU SURE BATMAN WILL FIND US?
HE WILL. I DON'T KNOW HOW, BUT I KNOW HE WILL. AND WHEN HE DOES...
...THE CAPED KILLJOYS WILL FINALLY STRIKE OUT!

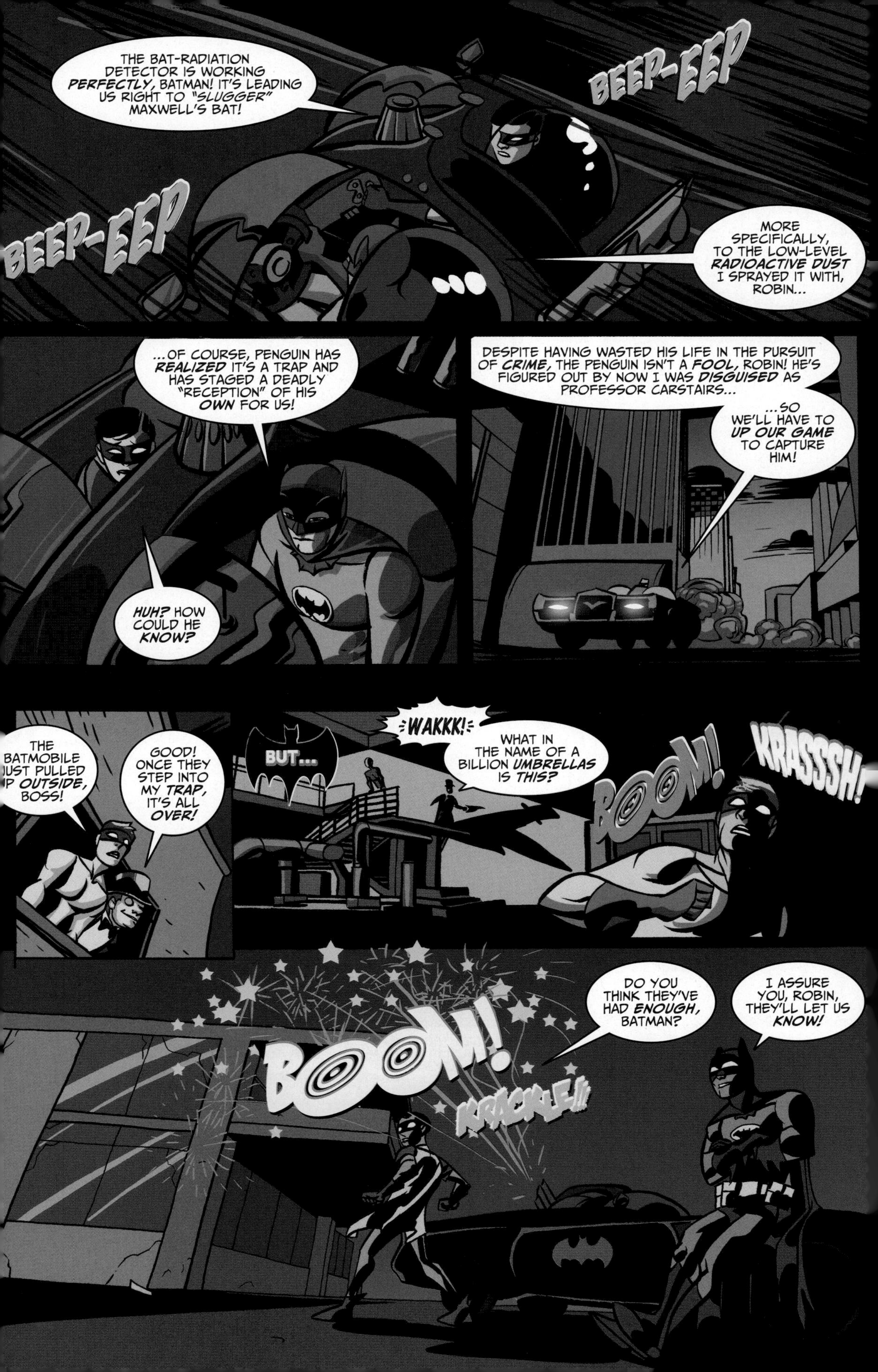

THE BAT-RADIATION DETECTOR IS WORKING PERFECTLY, BATMAN! IT'S LEADING US RIGHT TO "SLUGGER" MAXWELL'S BAT!
BEEP-EEP
BEEP-EEP
MORE SPECIFICALLY, TO THE LOW-LEVEL RADIOACTIVE DUST I SPRAYED IT WITH, ROBIN...
...OF COURSE, PENGUIN HAS REALIZED IT'S A TRAP AND HAS STAGED A DEADLY "RECEPTION" OF HIS OWN FOR US!
HUH? HOW COULD HE KNOW?
DESPITE HAVING WASTED HIS LIFE IN THE PURSUIT OF CRIME, THE PENGUIN ISN'T A FOOL, ROBIN! HE'S FIGURED OUT BY NOW I WAS DISGUISED AS PROFESSOR CARSTAIRS...
...SO WE'LL HAVE TO UP OUR GAME TO CAPTURE HIM!
THE BATMOBILE JUST PULLED UP OUTSIDE, BOSS!
GOOD! ONCE THEY STEP INTO MY TRAP, IT'S ALL OVER!
BUT...
WAKKK!
WHAT IN THE NAME OF A BILLION UMBRELLAS IS THIS?
BOOM!
KRASSSH!
BOOM!
KRACKLE!!!
DO YOU THINK THEY'VE HAD ENOUGH, BATMAN?
I ASSURE YOU, ROBIN, THEY'LL LET US KNOW!

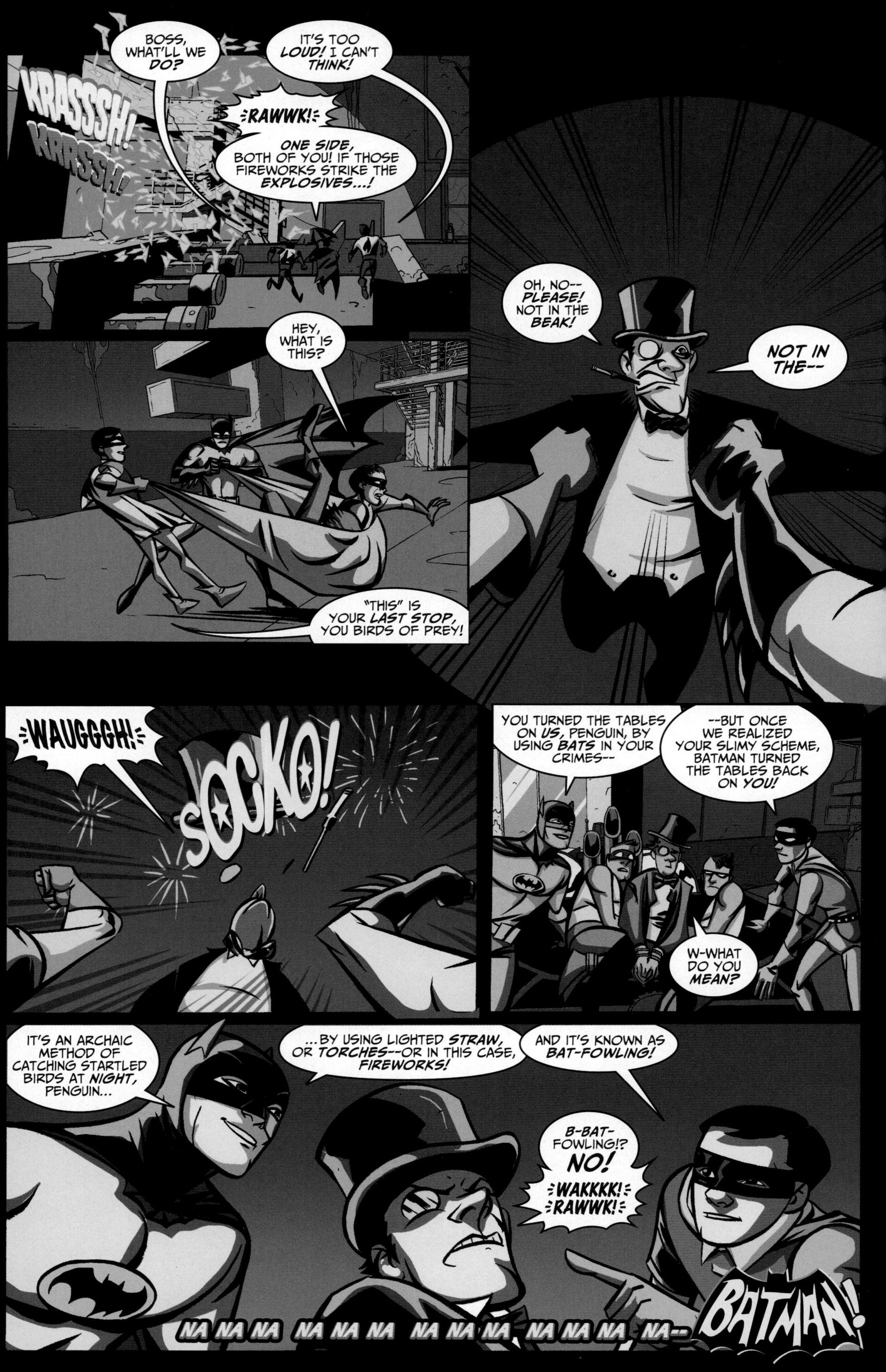
KRASSSH!
KRRSSSH!
BOSS, WHAT'LL WE DO?
IT'S TOO LOUD! I CAN'T THINK!
RAWWK!
ONE SIDE, BOTH OF YOU! IF THOSE FIREWORKS STRIKE THE EXPLOSIVES...!
HEY, WHAT IS THIS?
"THIS" IS YOUR LAST STOP, YOU BIRDS OF PREY!
OH, NO-- PLEASE! NOT IN THE BEAK!
NOT IN THE--
WAUGGGH!
SOCKO!
YOU TURNED THE TABLES ON US, PENGUIN, BY USING BATS IN YOUR CRIMES--
--BUT ONCE WE REALIZED YOUR SLIMY SCHEME, BATMAN TURNED THE TABLES BACK ON YOU!
W-WHAT DO YOU MEAN?
IT'S AN ARCHAIC METHOD OF CATCHING STARTLED BIRDS AT NIGHT, PENGUIN...
...BY USING LIGHTED STRAW, OR TORCHES--OR IN THIS CASE, FIREWORKS!
AND IT'S KNOWN AS BAT-FOWLING!
B-BAT-FOWLING!? NO!
WAKKKK! RAWWK!
NA NA NA NA NA NA NA NA NA NA NA NA NA-- BATMAN!

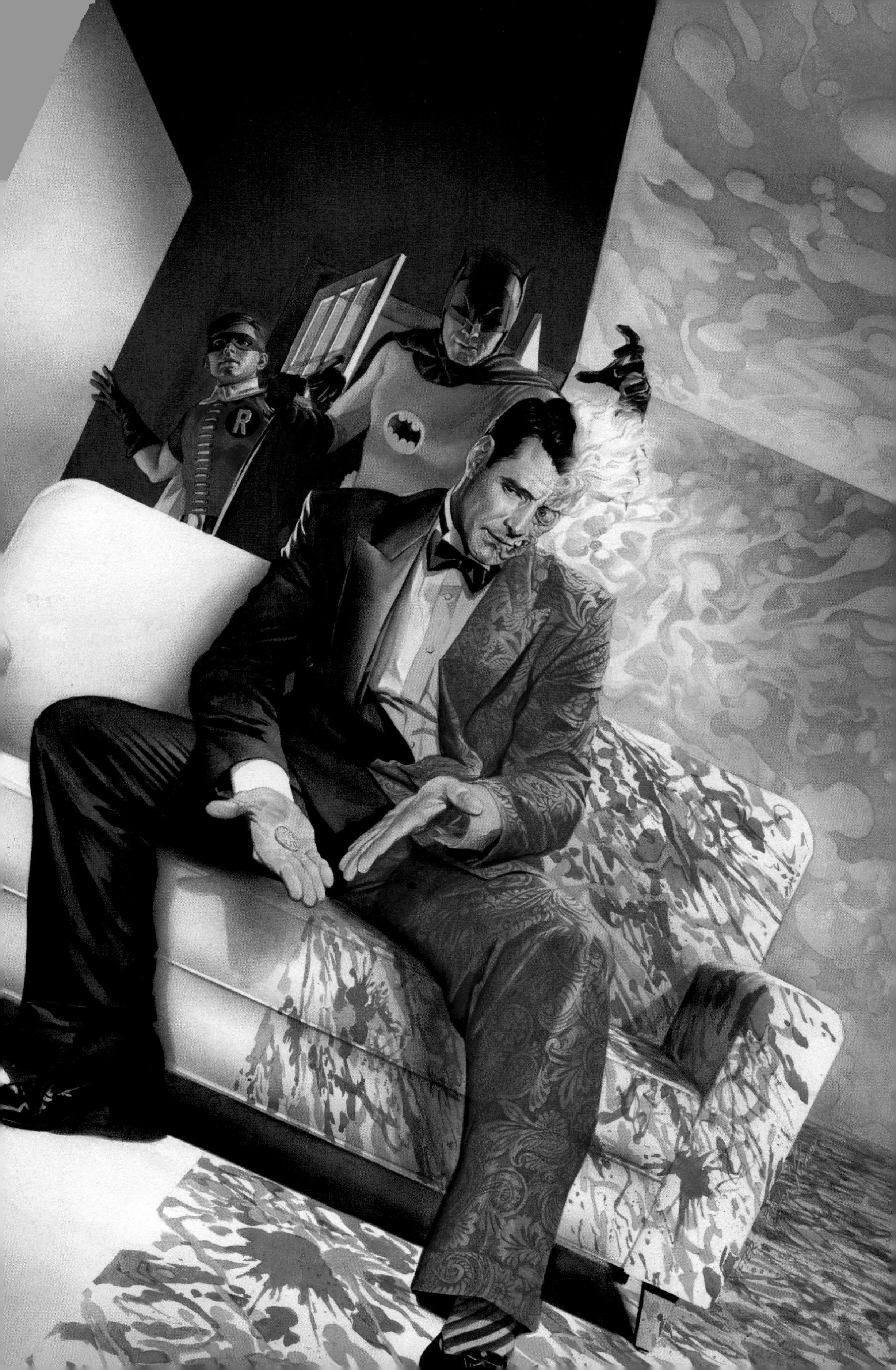

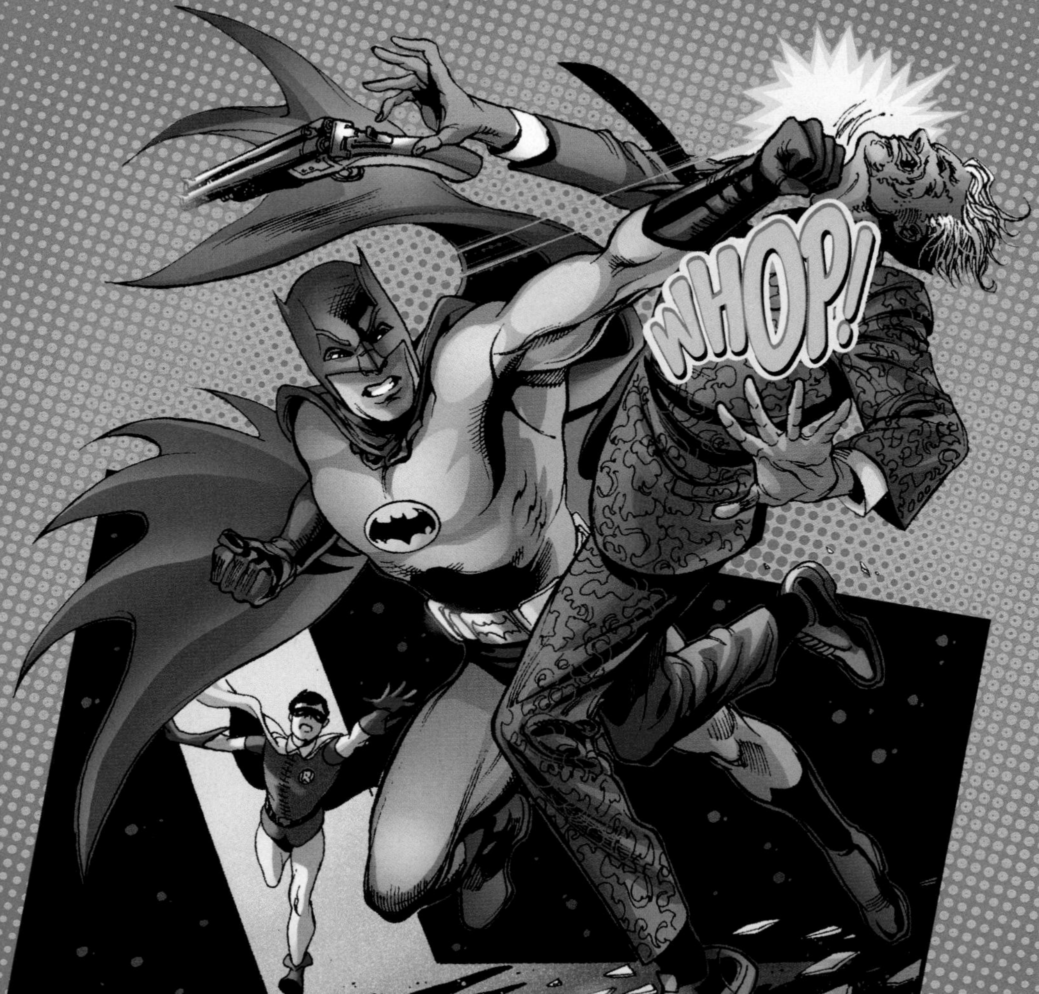
WHOP!

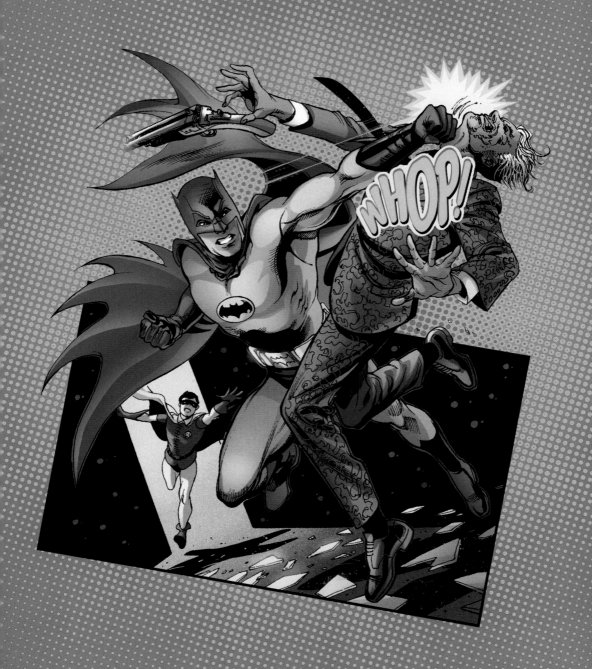

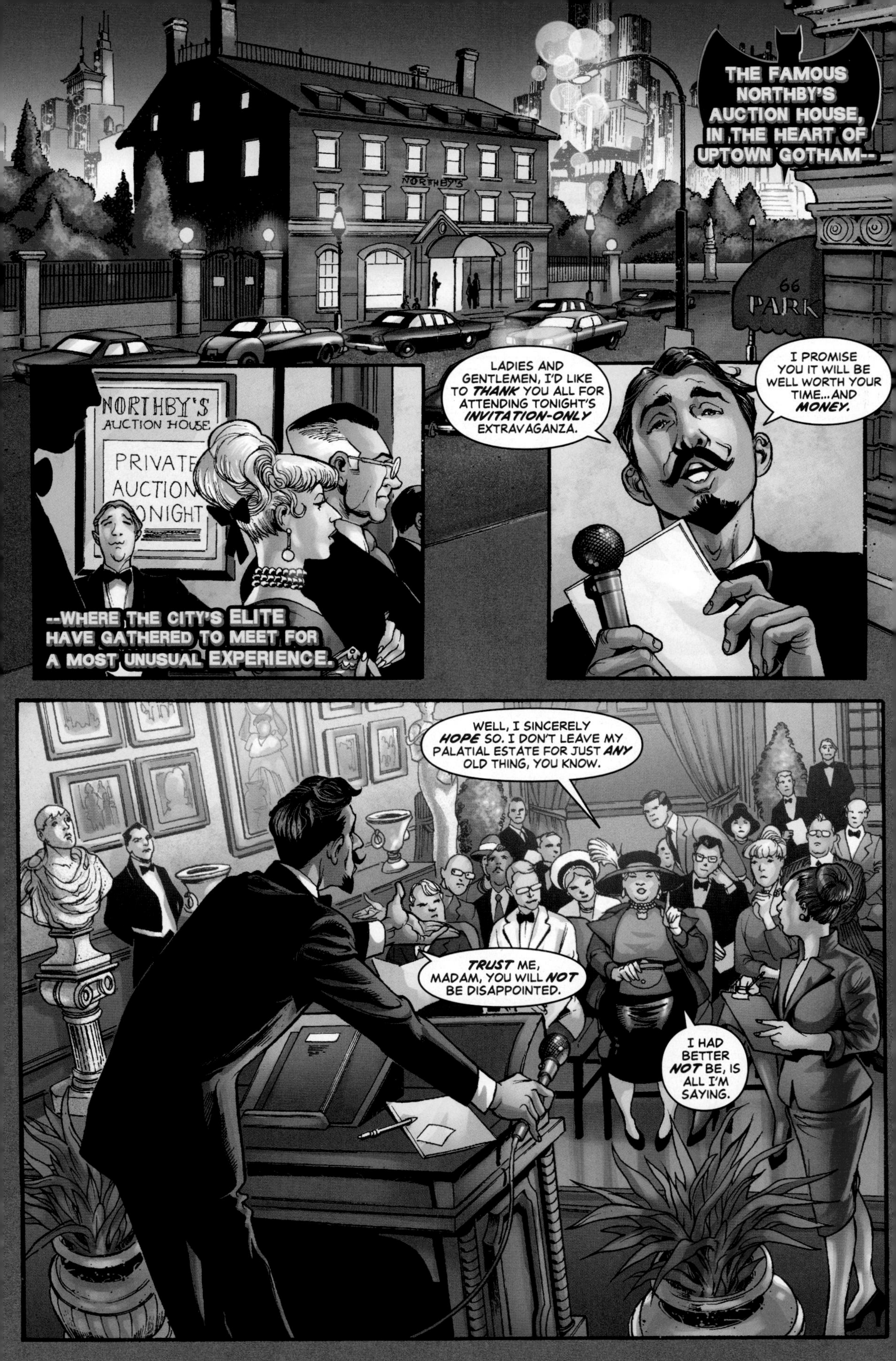
THE FAMOUS NORTHBY'S AUCTION HOUSE, IN THE HEART OF UPTOWN GOTHAM--
NORTHBY'S
66 PARK
NORTHBY'S AUCTION HOUSE
PRIVATE AUCTION TONIGHT
--WHERE THE CITY'S ELITE HAVE GATHERED TO MEET FOR A MOST UNUSUAL EXPERIENCE.
LADIES AND GENTLEMEN, I'D LIKE TO THANK YOU ALL FOR ATTENDING TONIGHT'S INVITATION-ONLY EXTRAVAGANZA.
I PROMISE YOU IT WILL BE WELL WORTH YOUR TIME...AND MONEY.
WELL, I SINCERELY HOPE SO. I DON'T LEAVE MY PALATIAL ESTATE FOR JUST ANY OLD THING, YOU KNOW.
TRUST ME, MADAM, YOU WILL NOT BE DISAPPOINTED.
I HAD BETTER NOT BE, IS ALL I'M SAYING.

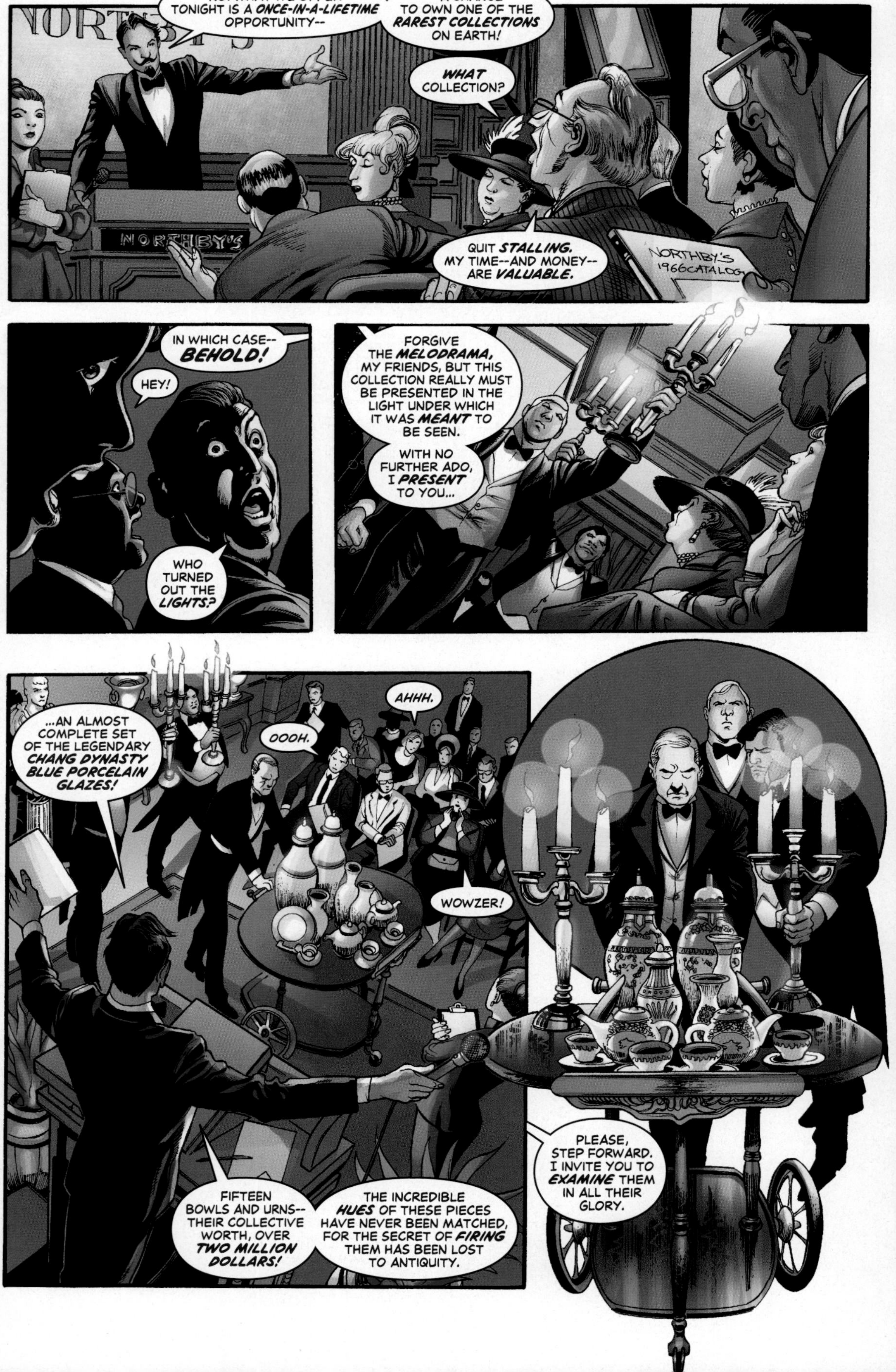
NORTHBY'S
NO. WHAT WE OFFER TONIGHT IS A ONCE-IN-A-LIFETIME OPPORTUNITY--
--A CHANCE TO OWN ONE OF THE RAREST COLLECTIONS ON EARTH!
WHAT COLLECTION?
NORTHBY'S
QUIT STALLING. MY TIME--AND MONEY--ARE VALUABLE.
NORTHBY'S 1966 CATALOG
IN WHICH CASE-- BEHOLD!
HEY!
WHO TURNED OUT THE LIGHTS?
FORGIVE THE MELODRAMA, MY FRIENDS, BUT THIS COLLECTION REALLY MUST BE PRESENTED IN THE LIGHT UNDER WHICH IT WAS MEANT TO BE SEEN.
WITH NO FURTHER ADO, I PRESENT TO YOU...
...AN ALMOST COMPLETE SET OF THE LEGENDARY CHANG DYNASTY BLUE PORCELAIN GLAZES!
AHHH.
OOOH.
WOWZER!
FIFTEEN BOWLS AND URNS-- THEIR COLLECTIVE WORTH, OVER TWO MILLION DOLLARS!
THE INCREDIBLE HUES OF THESE PIECES HAVE NEVER BEEN MATCHED, FOR THE SECRET OF FIRING THEM HAS BEEN LOST TO ANTIQUITY.
PLEASE, STEP FORWARD. I INVITE YOU TO EXAMINE THEM IN ALL THEIR GLORY.

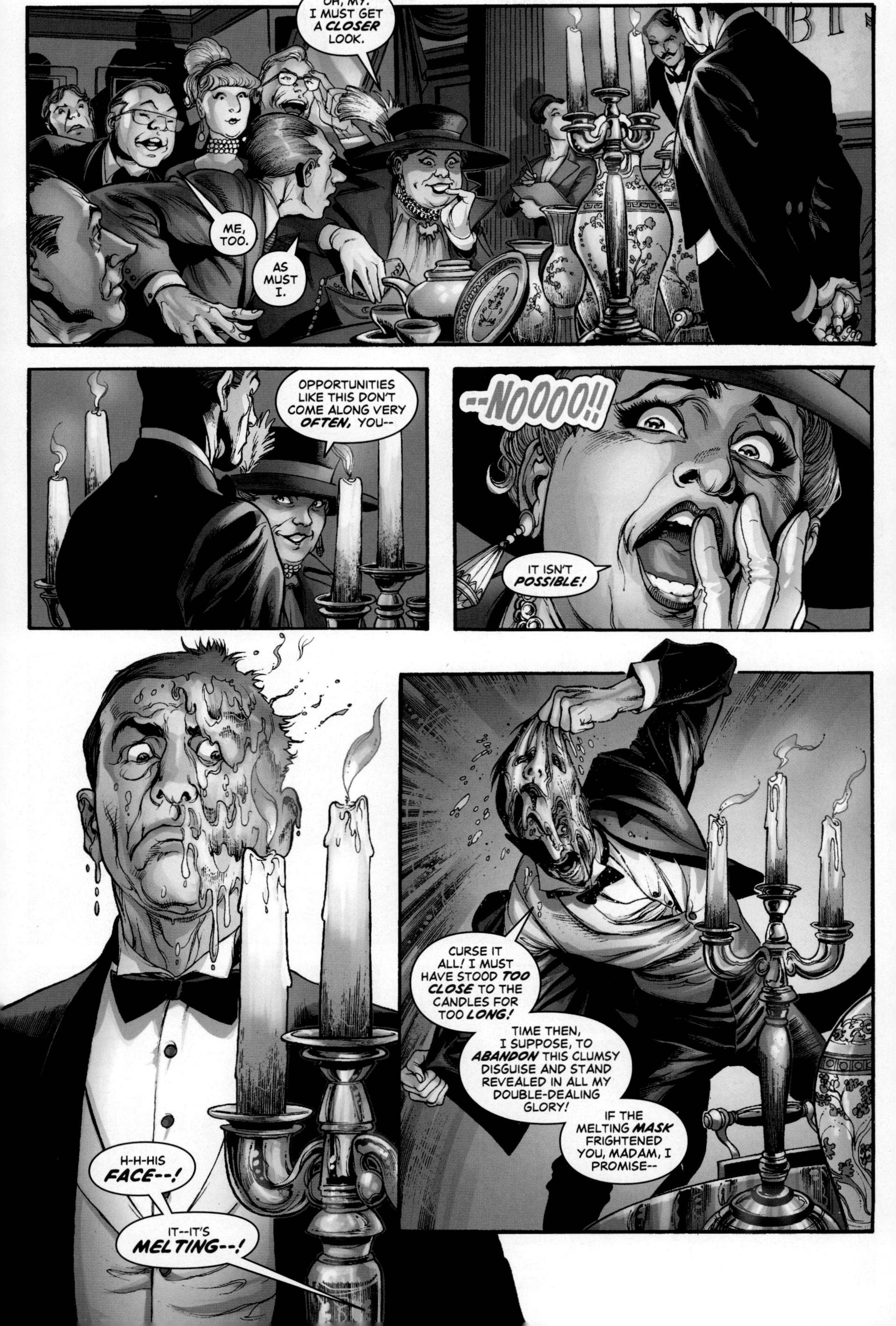
OH, MY. I MUST GET A CLOSER LOOK.
ME, TOO.
AS MUST I.
OPPORTUNITIES LIKE THIS DON'T COME ALONG VERY OFTEN, YOU--
--NOOOO!!
IT ISN'T POSSIBLE!
H-H-HIS FACE--!
IT--IT'S MELTING--!
CURSE IT ALL! I MUST HAVE STOOD TOO CLOSE TO THE CANDLES FOR TOO LONG!
TIME THEN, I SUPPOSE, TO ABANDON THIS CLUMSY DISGUISE AND STAND REVEALED IN ALL MY DOUBLE-DEALING GLORY!
IF THE MELTING MASK FRIGHTENED YOU, MADAM, I PROMISE--

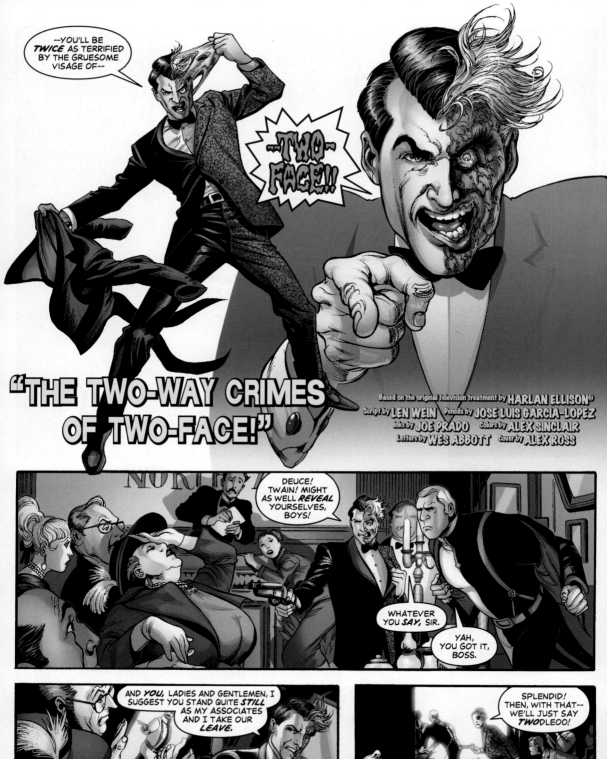

--YOU'LL BE *TWICE* AS TERRIFIED BY THE GRUESOME VISAGE OF--

~TWO~ FACE!!

"THE TWO-WAY CRIMES OF TWO-FACE!"

Based on the original television treatment by **HARLAN ELLISON**©
Script by **LEN WEIN** Pencils by **JOSE LUIS GARCIA-LOPEZ**
Inks by **JOE PRADO** Colors by **ALEX SINCLAIR**
Letters by **WES ABBOTT** Cover by **ALEX ROSS**

DEUCE! TWAIN! MIGHT AS WELL *REVEAL* YOURSELVES, BOYS!

WHATEVER YOU *SAY*, SIR.

YAH, YOU GOT IT, BOSS.

AND *YOU*, LADIES AND GENTLEMEN, I SUGGEST YOU STAND QUITE *STILL* AS MY ASSOCIATES AND I TAKE OUR *LEAVE*.

AFTER ALL, YOU WOULDN'T WANT TO MAKE MY DOUBLE-BARRELED BUDDY HERE *ANGRY* NOW, WOULD YOU?

N-N-NO!

N-NOT AT ALL!

SPLENDID! THEN, WITH THAT-- WE'LL JUST SAY *TWO*DLEOO!

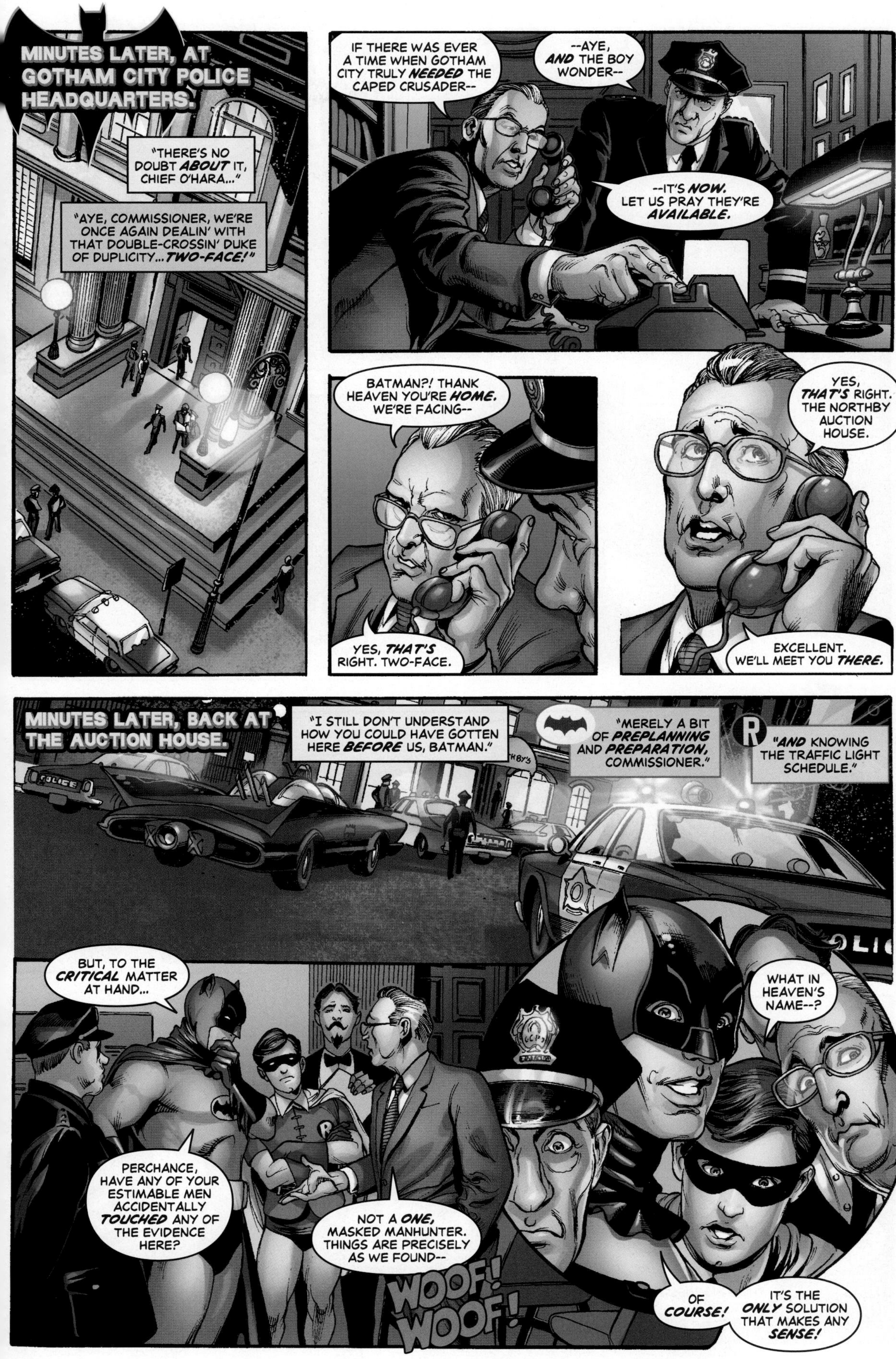

MINUTES LATER, AT GOTHAM CITY POLICE HEADQUARTERS.
"THERE'S NO DOUBT ABOUT IT, CHIEF O'HARA..."
"AYE, COMMISSIONER, WE'RE ONCE AGAIN DEALIN' WITH THAT DOUBLE-CROSSIN' DUKE OF DUPLICITY...TWO-FACE!"
IF THERE WAS EVER A TIME WHEN GOTHAM CITY TRULY NEEDED THE CAPED CRUSADER--
--AYE, AND THE BOY WONDER--
--IT'S NOW. LET US PRAY THEY'RE AVAILABLE.
BATMAN?! THANK HEAVEN YOU'RE HOME. WE'RE FACING--
YES, THAT'S RIGHT. TWO-FACE.
YES, THAT'S RIGHT. THE NORTHBY AUCTION HOUSE.
EXCELLENT. WE'LL MEET YOU THERE.
MINUTES LATER, BACK AT THE AUCTION HOUSE.
"I STILL DON'T UNDERSTAND HOW YOU COULD HAVE GOTTEN HERE BEFORE US, BATMAN."
"MERELY A BIT OF PREPLANNING AND PREPARATION, COMMISSIONER."
"AND KNOWING THE TRAFFIC LIGHT SCHEDULE."
BUT, TO THE CRITICAL MATTER AT HAND...
PERCHANCE, HAVE ANY OF YOUR ESTIMABLE MEN ACCIDENTALLY TOUCHED ANY OF THE EVIDENCE HERE?
NOT A ONE, MASKED MANHUNTER. THINGS ARE PRECISELY AS WE FOUND--
WOOF! WOOF!
WHAT IN HEAVEN'S NAME--?
OF COURSE!
IT'S THE ONLY SOLUTION THAT MAKES ANY SENSE!

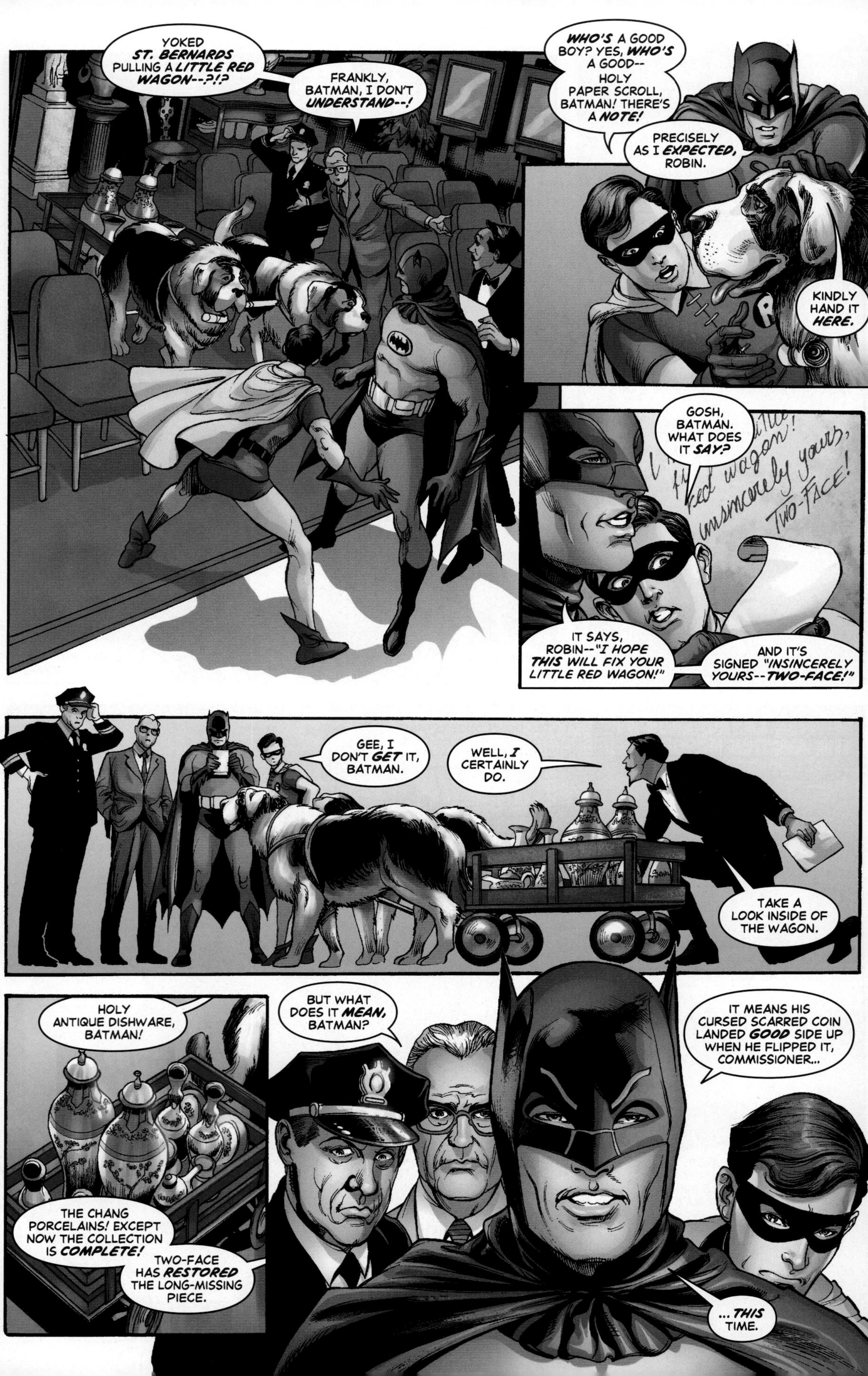

YOKED **ST. BERNARDS** PULLING A ***LITTLE RED WAGON***--?!?
FRANKLY, BATMAN, I DON'T ***UNDERSTAND***--!
WHO'S A GOOD BOY? YES, ***WHO'S*** A GOOD-- HOLY PAPER SCROLL, BATMAN! THERE'S A ***NOTE!***
PRECISELY AS I ***EXPECTED,*** ROBIN.
KINDLY HAND IT ***HERE.***
GOSH, BATMAN. WHAT DOES IT ***SAY?***
IT SAYS, ROBIN--"*I HOPE* ***THIS*** *WILL FIX YOUR LITTLE RED WAGON!*"
AND IT'S SIGNED "***INSINCERELY YOURS--TWO-FACE!***"
GEE, I DON'T ***GET*** IT, BATMAN.
WELL, ***I*** CERTAINLY DO.
TAKE A LOOK INSIDE OF THE WAGON.
HOLY ANTIQUE DISHWARE, BATMAN!
THE CHANG PORCELAINS! EXCEPT NOW THE COLLECTION IS ***COMPLETE!***
TWO-FACE HAS ***RESTORED*** THE LONG-MISSING PIECE.
BUT WHAT DOES IT ***MEAN,*** BATMAN?
IT MEANS HIS CURSED SCARRED COIN LANDED ***GOOD*** SIDE UP WHEN HE FLIPPED IT, COMMISSIONER...
...***THIS*** TIME.

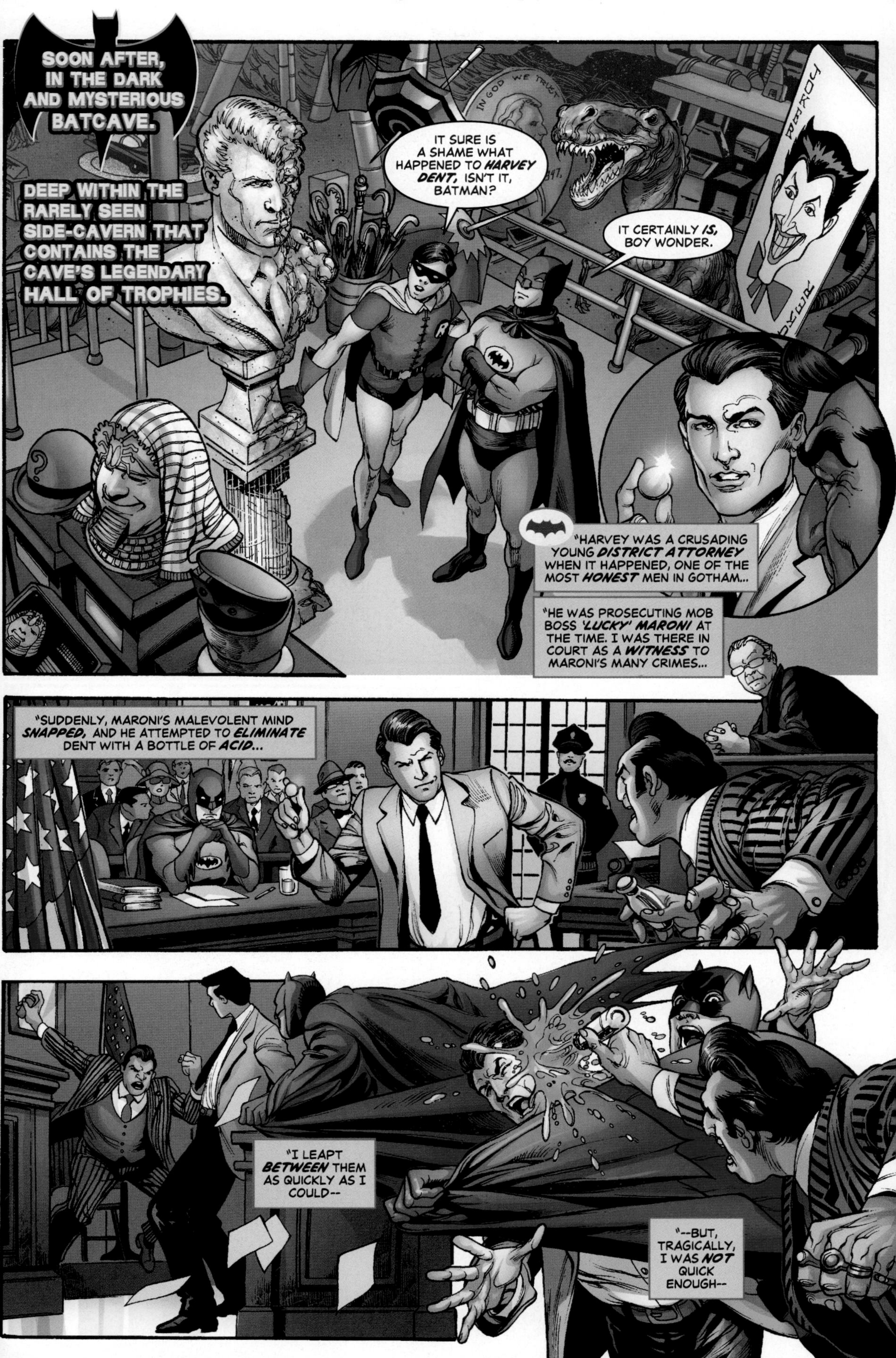
SOON AFTER, IN THE DARK AND MYSTERIOUS BATCAVE.
DEEP WITHIN THE RARELY SEEN SIDE-CAVERN THAT CONTAINS THE CAVE'S LEGENDARY HALL OF TROPHIES.
IT SURE IS A SHAME WHAT HAPPENED TO HARVEY DENT, ISN'T IT, BATMAN?
IT CERTAINLY IS, BOY WONDER.
"HARVEY WAS A CRUSADING YOUNG DISTRICT ATTORNEY WHEN IT HAPPENED, ONE OF THE MOST HONEST MEN IN GOTHAM...
"HE WAS PROSECUTING MOB BOSS 'LUCKY' MARONI AT THE TIME. I WAS THERE IN COURT AS A WITNESS TO MARONI'S MANY CRIMES...
"SUDDENLY, MARONI'S MALEVOLENT MIND SNAPPED, AND HE ATTEMPTED TO ELIMINATE DENT WITH A BOTTLE OF ACID...
"I LEAPT BETWEEN THEM AS QUICKLY AS I COULD--
"--BUT, TRAGICALLY, I WAS NOT QUICK ENOUGH--

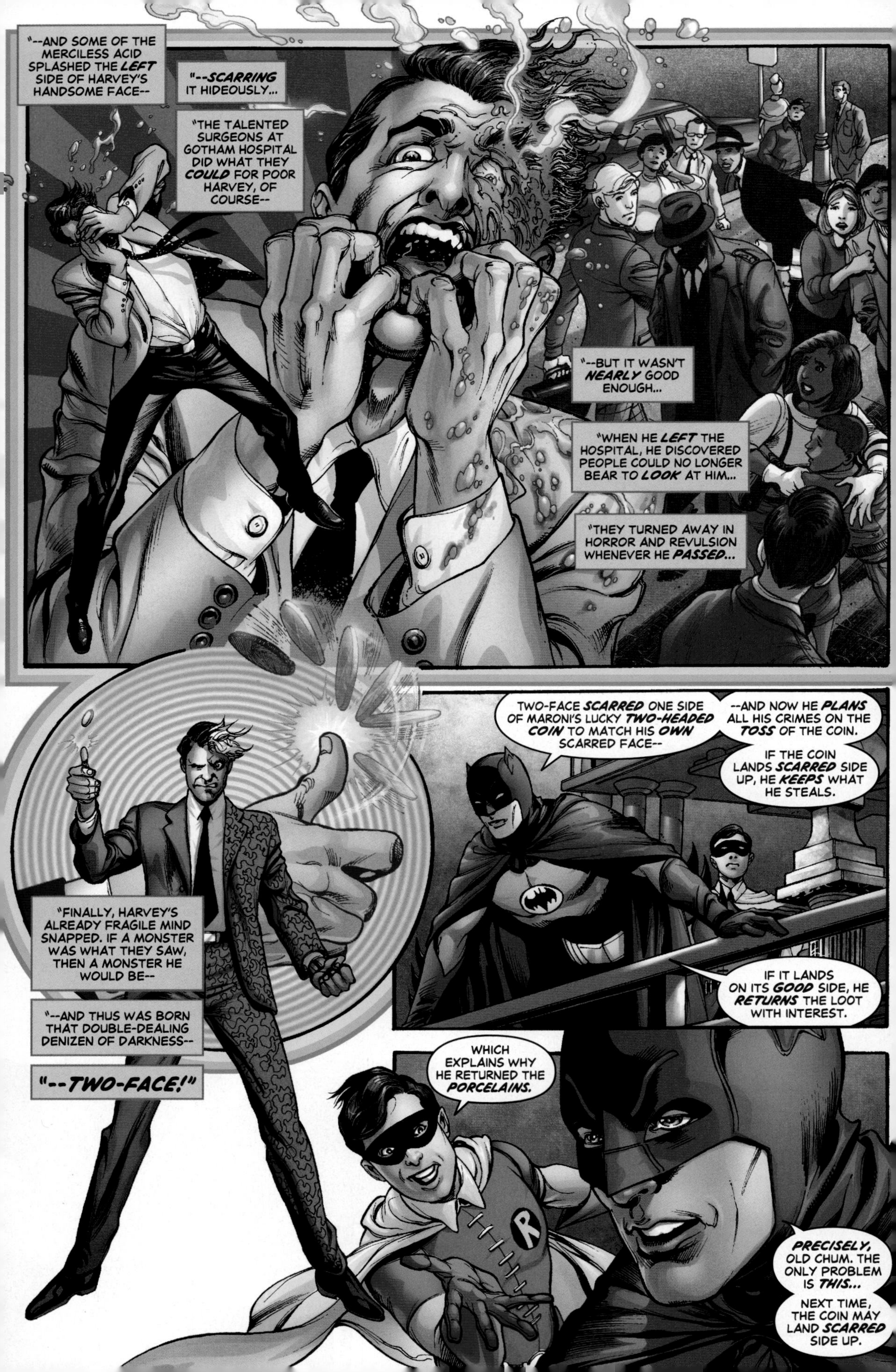
"--AND SOME OF THE MERCILESS ACID SPLASHED THE LEFT SIDE OF HARVEY'S HANDSOME FACE--
"--SCARRING IT HIDEOUSLY...
"THE TALENTED SURGEONS AT GOTHAM HOSPITAL DID WHAT THEY COULD FOR POOR HARVEY, OF COURSE--
"--BUT IT WASN'T NEARLY GOOD ENOUGH...
"WHEN HE LEFT THE HOSPITAL, HE DISCOVERED PEOPLE COULD NO LONGER BEAR TO LOOK AT HIM...
"THEY TURNED AWAY IN HORROR AND REVULSION WHENEVER HE PASSED...
"FINALLY, HARVEY'S ALREADY FRAGILE MIND SNAPPED. IF A MONSTER WAS WHAT THEY SAW, THEN A MONSTER HE WOULD BE--
"--AND THUS WAS BORN THAT DOUBLE-DEALING DENIZEN OF DARKNESS--
"--TWO-FACE!"
TWO-FACE SCARRED ONE SIDE OF MARONI'S LUCKY TWO-HEADED COIN TO MATCH HIS OWN SCARRED FACE--
--AND NOW HE PLANS ALL HIS CRIMES ON THE TOSS OF THE COIN.
IF THE COIN LANDS SCARRED SIDE UP, HE KEEPS WHAT HE STEALS.
IF IT LANDS ON ITS GOOD SIDE, HE RETURNS THE LOOT WITH INTEREST.
WHICH EXPLAINS WHY HE RETURNED THE PORCELAINS.
PRECISELY, OLD CHUM. THE ONLY PROBLEM IS THIS...
NEXT TIME, THE COIN MAY LAND SCARRED SIDE UP.

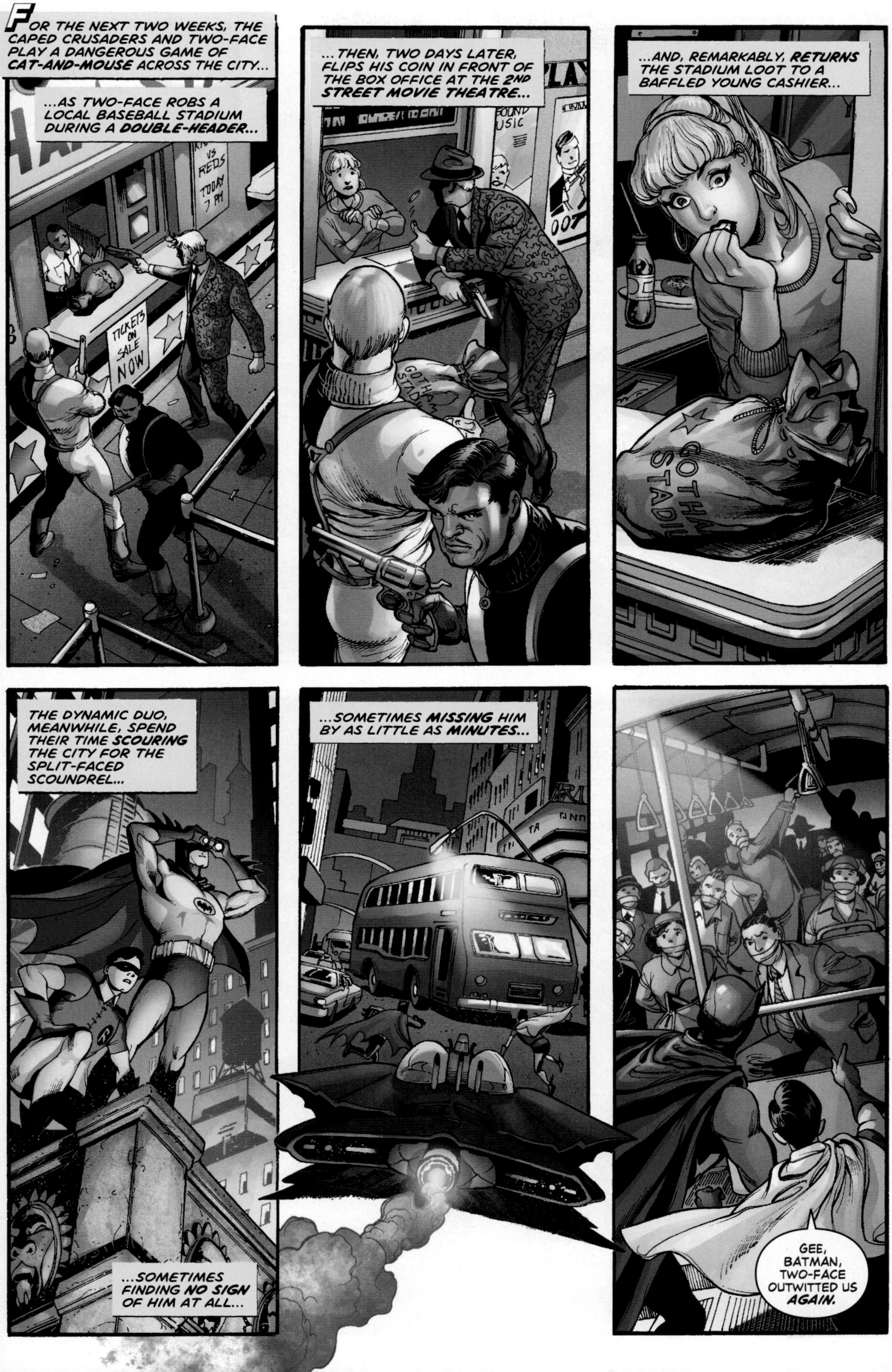
FOR THE NEXT TWO WEEKS, THE CAPED CRUSADERS AND TWO-FACE PLAY A DANGEROUS GAME OF CAT-AND-MOUSE ACROSS THE CITY...
...AS TWO-FACE ROBS A LOCAL BASEBALL STADIUM DURING A DOUBLE-HEADER...
TICKETS ON SALE NOW
...THEN, TWO DAYS LATER, FLIPS HIS COIN IN FRONT OF THE BOX OFFICE AT THE 2ND STREET MOVIE THEATRE...
...AND, REMARKABLY, RETURNS THE STADIUM LOOT TO A BAFFLED YOUNG CASHIER...
THE DYNAMIC DUO, MEANWHILE, SPEND THEIR TIME SCOURING THE CITY FOR THE SPLIT-FACED SCOUNDREL...
...SOMETIMES FINDING NO SIGN OF HIM AT ALL...
...SOMETIMES MISSING HIM BY AS LITTLE AS MINUTES...
GEE, BATMAN, TWO-FACE OUTWITTED US AGAIN.

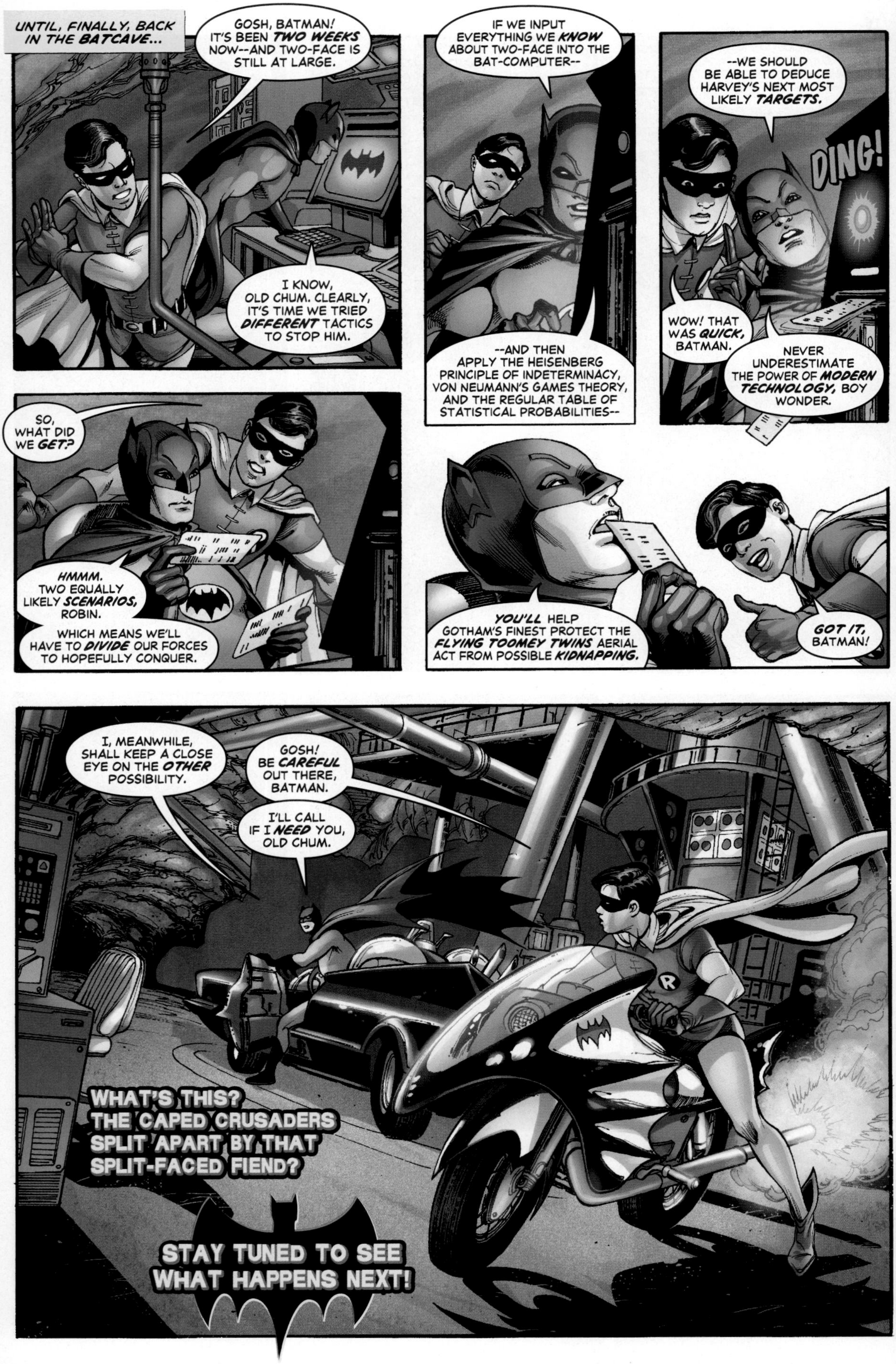
UNTIL, FINALLY, BACK IN THE BATCAVE...
GOSH, BATMAN! IT'S BEEN TWO WEEKS NOW--AND TWO-FACE IS STILL AT LARGE.
I KNOW, OLD CHUM. CLEARLY, IT'S TIME WE TRIED DIFFERENT TACTICS TO STOP HIM.
IF WE INPUT EVERYTHING WE KNOW ABOUT TWO-FACE INTO THE BAT-COMPUTER--
--AND THEN APPLY THE HEISENBERG PRINCIPLE OF INDETERMINACY, VON NEUMANN'S GAMES THEORY, AND THE REGULAR TABLE OF STATISTICAL PROBABILITIES--
--WE SHOULD BE ABLE TO DEDUCE HARVEY'S NEXT MOST LIKELY TARGETS.
DING!
WOW! THAT WAS QUICK, BATMAN.
NEVER UNDERESTIMATE THE POWER OF MODERN TECHNOLOGY, BOY WONDER.
SO, WHAT DID WE GET?
HMMM. TWO EQUALLY LIKELY SCENARIOS, ROBIN.
WHICH MEANS WE'LL HAVE TO DIVIDE OUR FORCES TO HOPEFULLY CONQUER.
YOU'LL HELP GOTHAM'S FINEST PROTECT THE FLYING TOOMEY TWINS AERIAL ACT FROM POSSIBLE KIDNAPPING.
GOT IT, BATMAN!
I, MEANWHILE, SHALL KEEP A CLOSE EYE ON THE OTHER POSSIBILITY.
GOSH! BE CAREFUL OUT THERE, BATMAN.
I'LL CALL IF I NEED YOU, OLD CHUM.
WHAT'S THIS? THE CAPED CRUSADERS SPLIT APART BY THAT SPLIT-FACED FIEND?
STAY TUNED TO SEE WHAT HAPPENS NEXT!

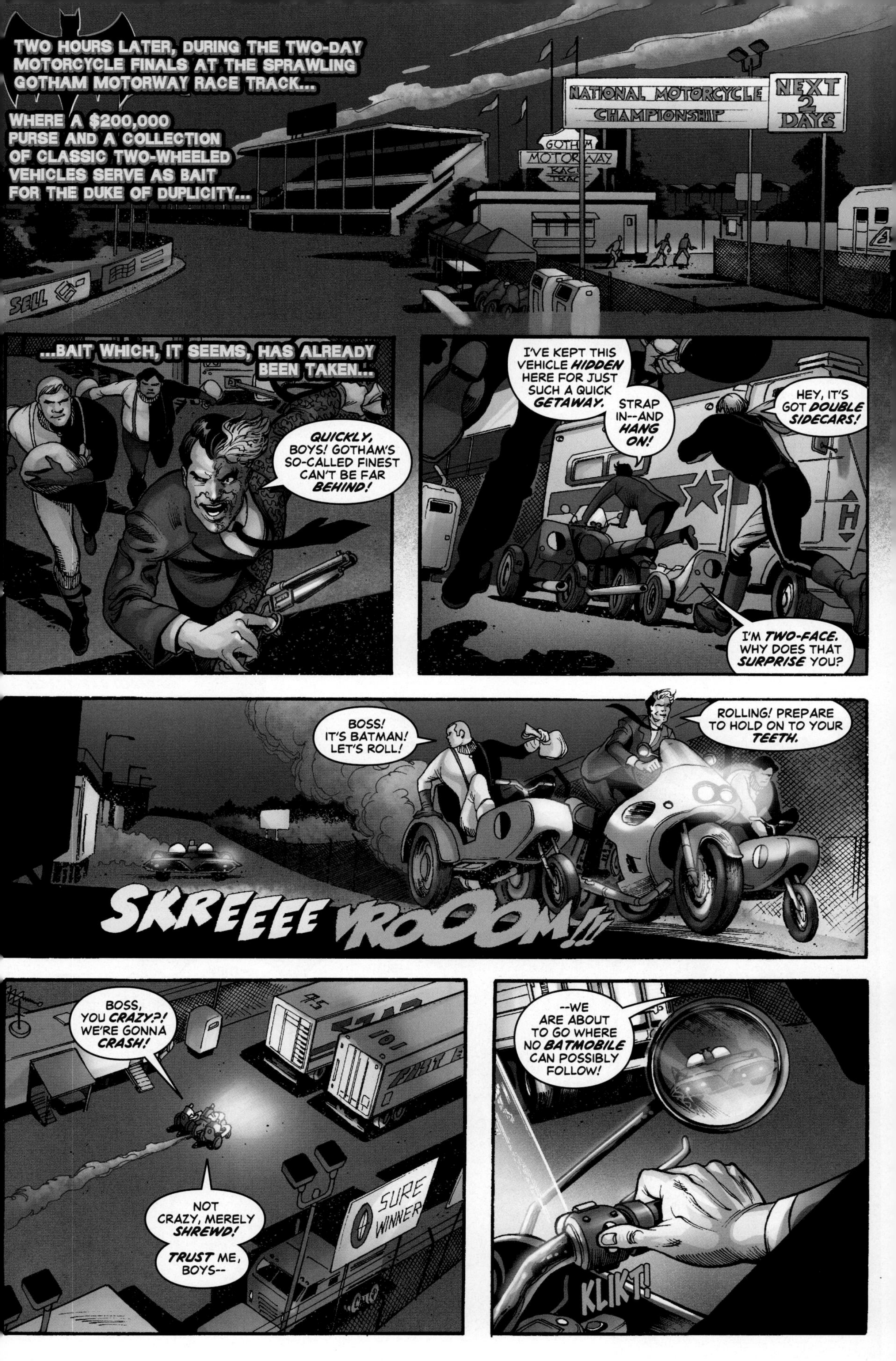
TWO HOURS LATER, DURING THE TWO-DAY MOTORCYCLE FINALS AT THE SPRAWLING GOTHAM MOTORWAY RACE TRACK...
WHERE A $200,000 PURSE AND A COLLECTION OF CLASSIC TWO-WHEELED VEHICLES SERVE AS BAIT FOR THE DUKE OF DUPLICITY...
NATIONAL MOTORCYCLE CHAMPIONSHIP
NEXT 2 DAYS
GOTHAM MOTORWAY RACE TRACK
SELL
...BAIT WHICH, IT SEEMS, HAS ALREADY BEEN TAKEN...
QUICKLY, BOYS! GOTHAM'S SO-CALLED FINEST CAN'T BE FAR BEHIND!
I'VE KEPT THIS VEHICLE HIDDEN HERE FOR JUST SUCH A QUICK GETAWAY.
STRAP IN--AND HANG ON!
HEY, IT'S GOT DOUBLE SIDECARS!
I'M TWO-FACE. WHY DOES THAT SURPRISE YOU?
BOSS! IT'S BATMAN! LET'S ROLL!
ROLLING! PREPARE TO HOLD ON TO YOUR TEETH.
SKREEEEE VROOOOM!!!
BOSS, YOU CRAZY?! WE'RE GONNA CRASH!
NOT CRAZY, MERELY SHREWD!
TRUST ME, BOYS--
SURE WINNER
--WE ARE ABOUT TO GO WHERE NO BATMOBILE CAN POSSIBLY FOLLOW!
KLIKT!

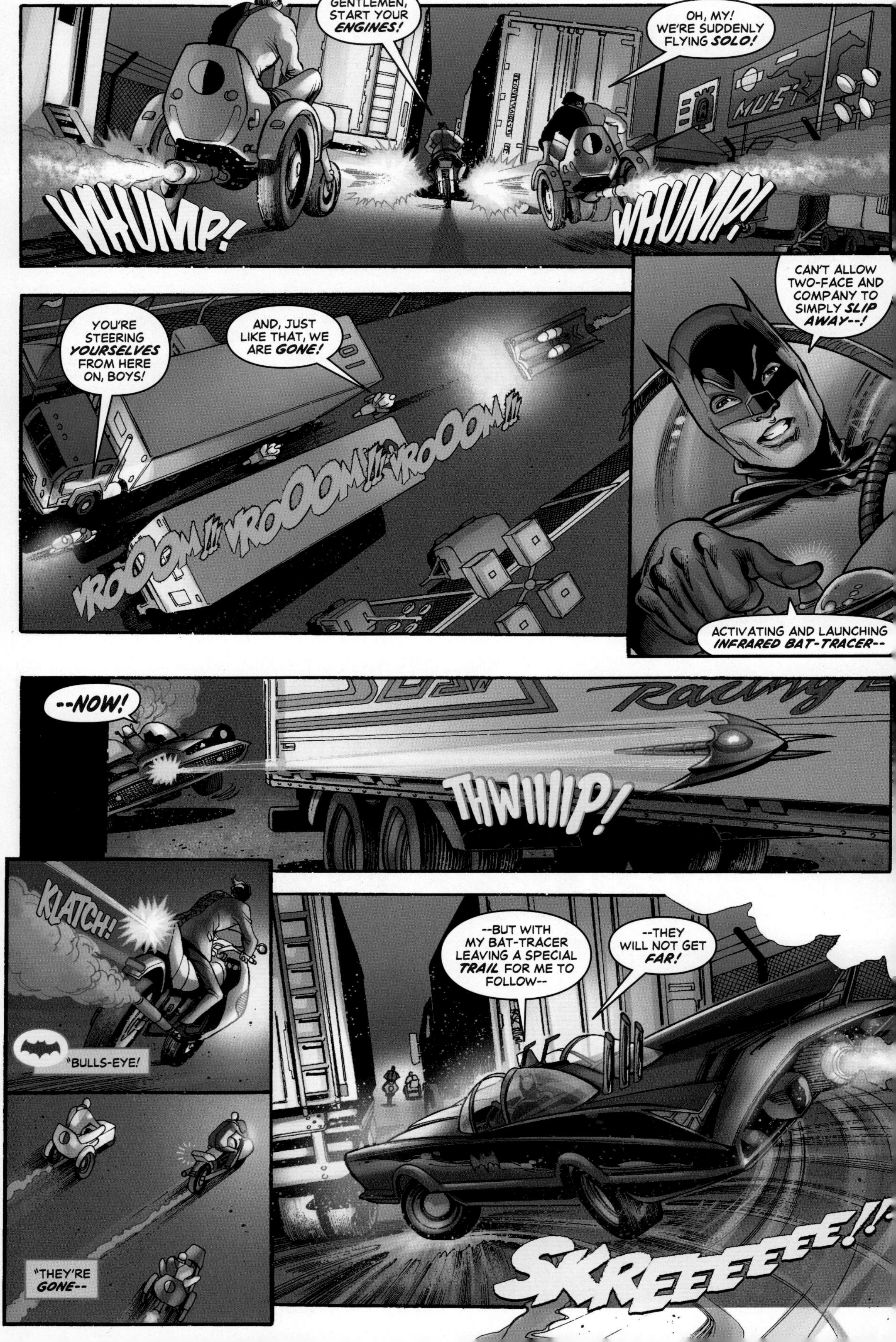
GENTLEMEN, START YOUR ENGINES!
OH, MY! WE'RE SUDDENLY FLYING SOLO!
WHUMP!
WHUMP!
YOU'RE STEERING YOURSELVES FROM HERE ON, BOYS!
AND, JUST LIKE THAT, WE ARE GONE!
VROOOM!!! VROOOM!!! VROOOM!!!
CAN'T ALLOW TWO-FACE AND COMPANY TO SIMPLY SLIP AWAY--!
ACTIVATING AND LAUNCHING INFRARED BAT-TRACER--
--NOW!
THWIIIIP!
KLATCH!
"BULLS-EYE!
"THEY'RE GONE--
--BUT WITH MY BAT-TRACER LEAVING A SPECIAL TRAIL FOR ME TO FOLLOW--
--THEY WILL NOT GET FAR!
SKREEEEEEE!!

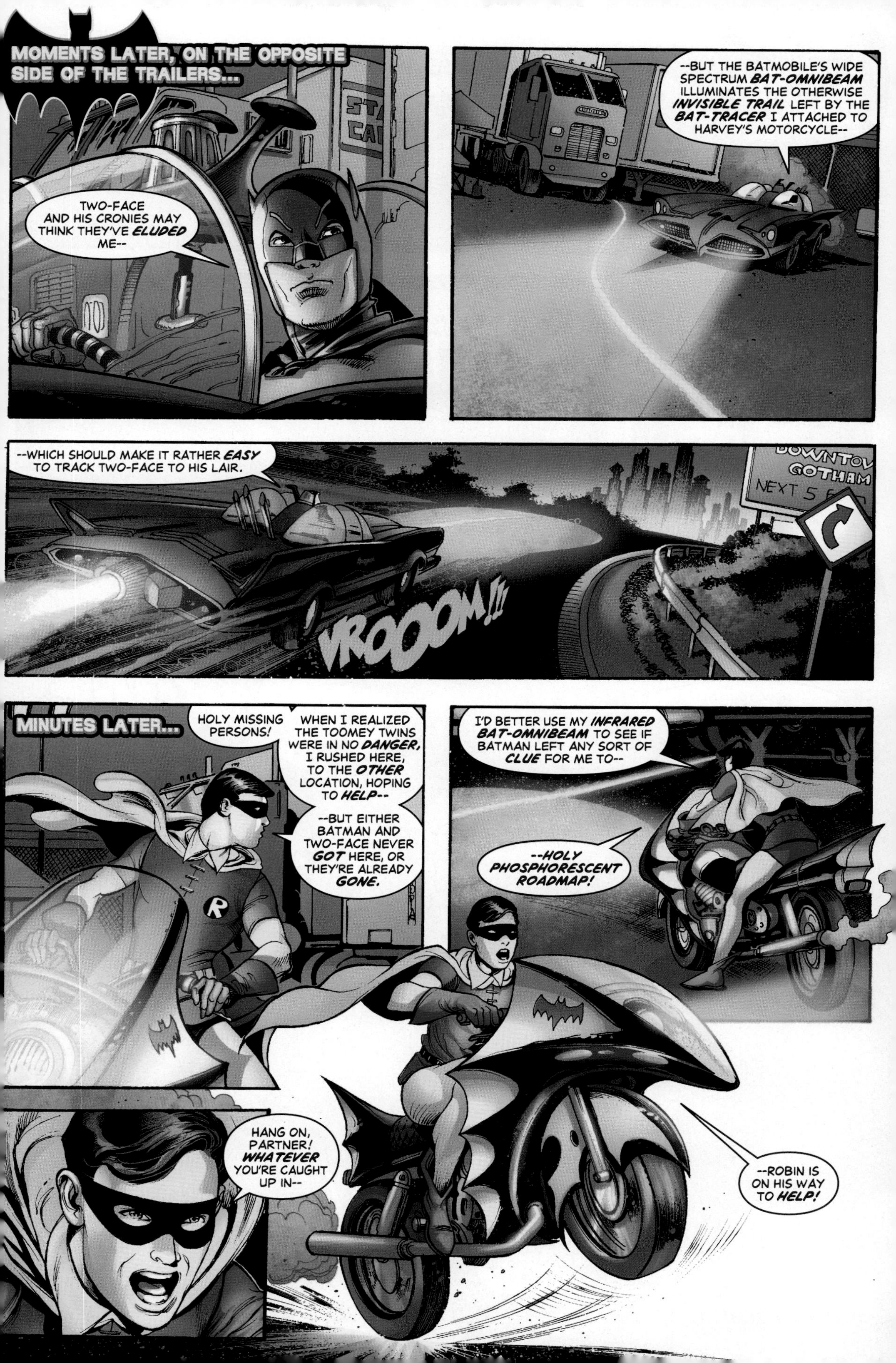
MOMENTS LATER, ON THE OPPOSITE SIDE OF THE TRAILERS...
TWO-FACE AND HIS CRONIES MAY THINK THEY'VE ELUDED ME--
--BUT THE BATMOBILE'S WIDE SPECTRUM BAT-OMNIBEAM ILLUMINATES THE OTHERWISE INVISIBLE TRAIL LEFT BY THE BAT-TRACER I ATTACHED TO HARVEY'S MOTORCYCLE--
--WHICH SHOULD MAKE IT RATHER EASY TO TRACK TWO-FACE TO HIS LAIR.
GOTHAM
VROOOM!!!
MINUTES LATER...
HOLY MISSING PERSONS!
WHEN I REALIZED THE TOOMEY TWINS WERE IN NO DANGER, I RUSHED HERE, TO THE OTHER LOCATION, HOPING TO HELP--
--BUT EITHER BATMAN AND TWO-FACE NEVER GOT HERE, OR THEY'RE ALREADY GONE.
I'D BETTER USE MY INFRARED BAT-OMNIBEAM TO SEE IF BATMAN LEFT ANY SORT OF CLUE FOR ME TO--
--HOLY PHOSPHORESCENT ROADMAP!
HANG ON, PARTNER! WHATEVER YOU'RE CAUGHT UP IN--
--ROBIN IS ON HIS WAY TO HELP!

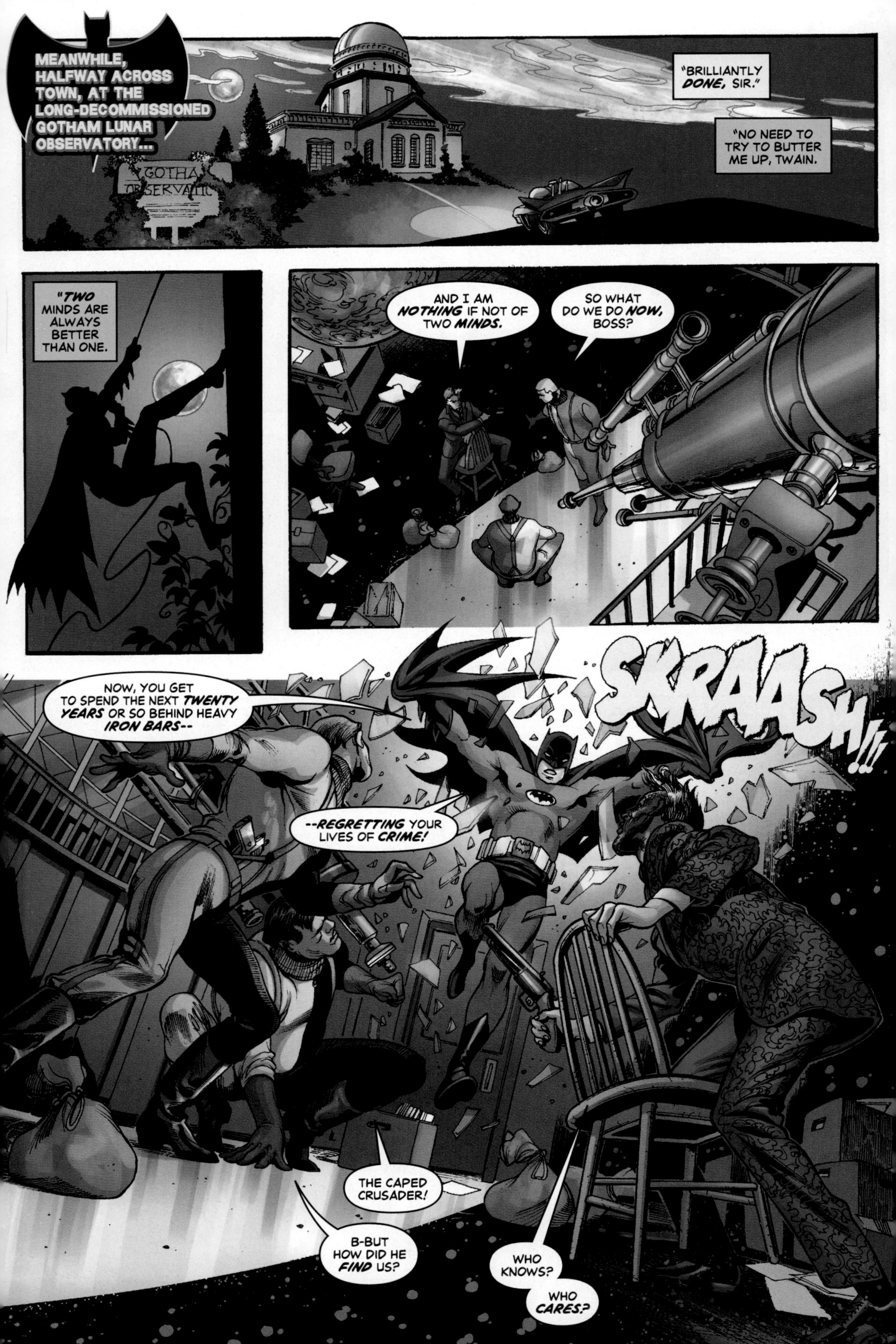

MEANWHILE, HALFWAY ACROSS TOWN, AT THE LONG-DECOMMISSIONED GOTHAM LUNAR OBSERVATORY...
"BRILLIANTLY DONE, SIR."
"NO NEED TO TRY TO BUTTER ME UP, TWAIN.
"TWO MINDS ARE ALWAYS BETTER THAN ONE.
AND I AM NOTHING IF NOT OF TWO MINDS.
SO WHAT DO WE DO NOW, BOSS?
SKRAASH!!!
NOW, YOU GET TO SPEND THE NEXT TWENTY YEARS OR SO BEHIND HEAVY IRON BARS--
--REGRETTING YOUR LIVES OF CRIME!
THE CAPED CRUSADER!
B-BUT HOW DID HE FIND US?
WHO KNOWS?
WHO CARES?

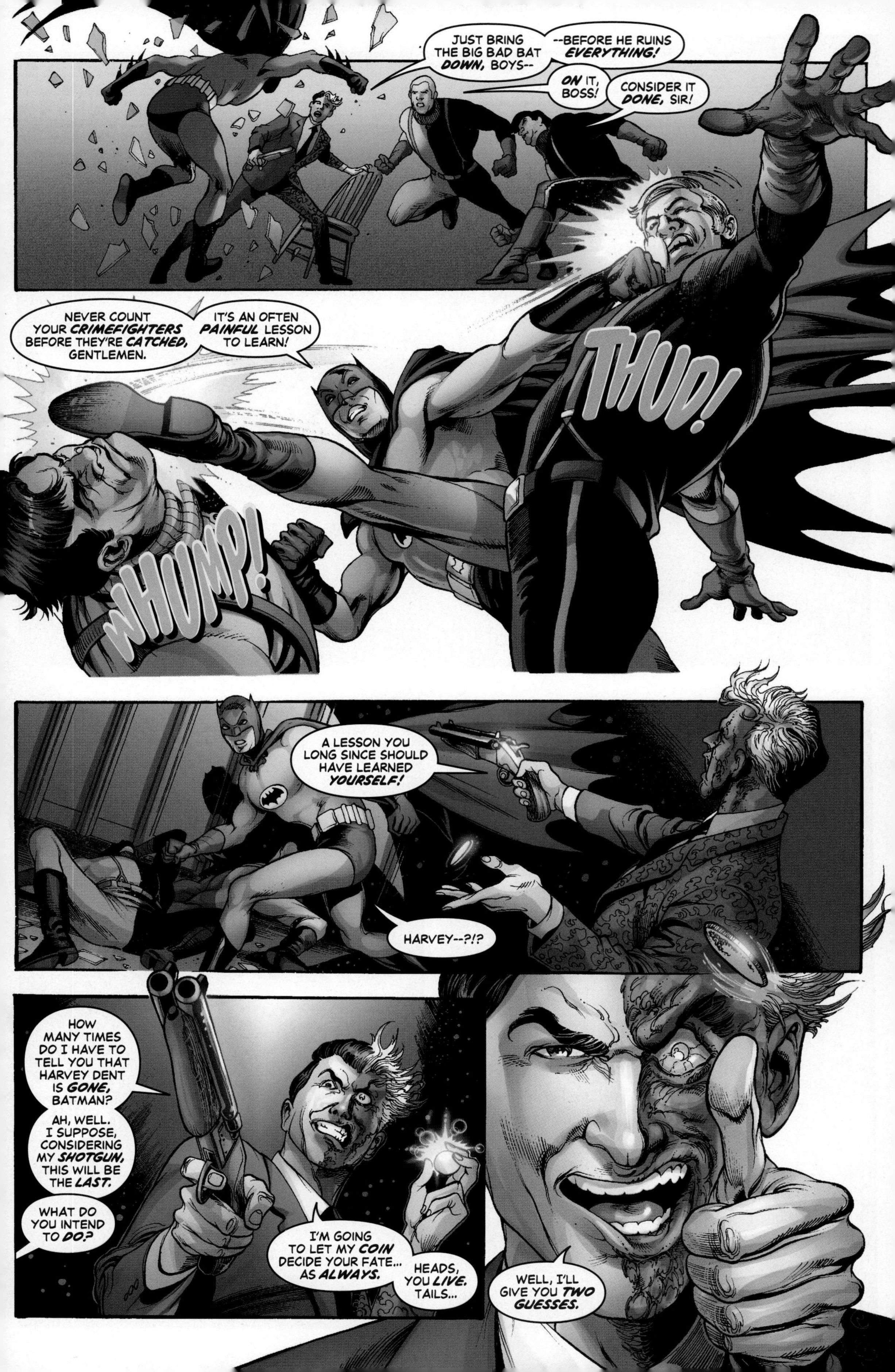
JUST BRING THE BIG BAD BAT DOWN, BOYS--
--BEFORE HE RUINS EVERYTHING!
ON IT, BOSS!
CONSIDER IT DONE, SIR!
NEVER COUNT YOUR CRIMEFIGHTERS BEFORE THEY'RE CATCHED, GENTLEMEN.
IT'S AN OFTEN PAINFUL LESSON TO LEARN!
THUD!
WHUMP!
A LESSON YOU LONG SINCE SHOULD HAVE LEARNED YOURSELF!
HARVEY--?!?
HOW MANY TIMES DO I HAVE TO TELL YOU THAT HARVEY DENT IS GONE, BATMAN?
AH, WELL. I SUPPOSE, CONSIDERING MY SHOTGUN, THIS WILL BE THE LAST.
WHAT DO YOU INTEND TO DO?
I'M GOING TO LET MY COIN DECIDE YOUR FATE... AS ALWAYS.
HEADS, YOU LIVE. TAILS...
WELL, I'LL GIVE YOU TWO GUESSES.

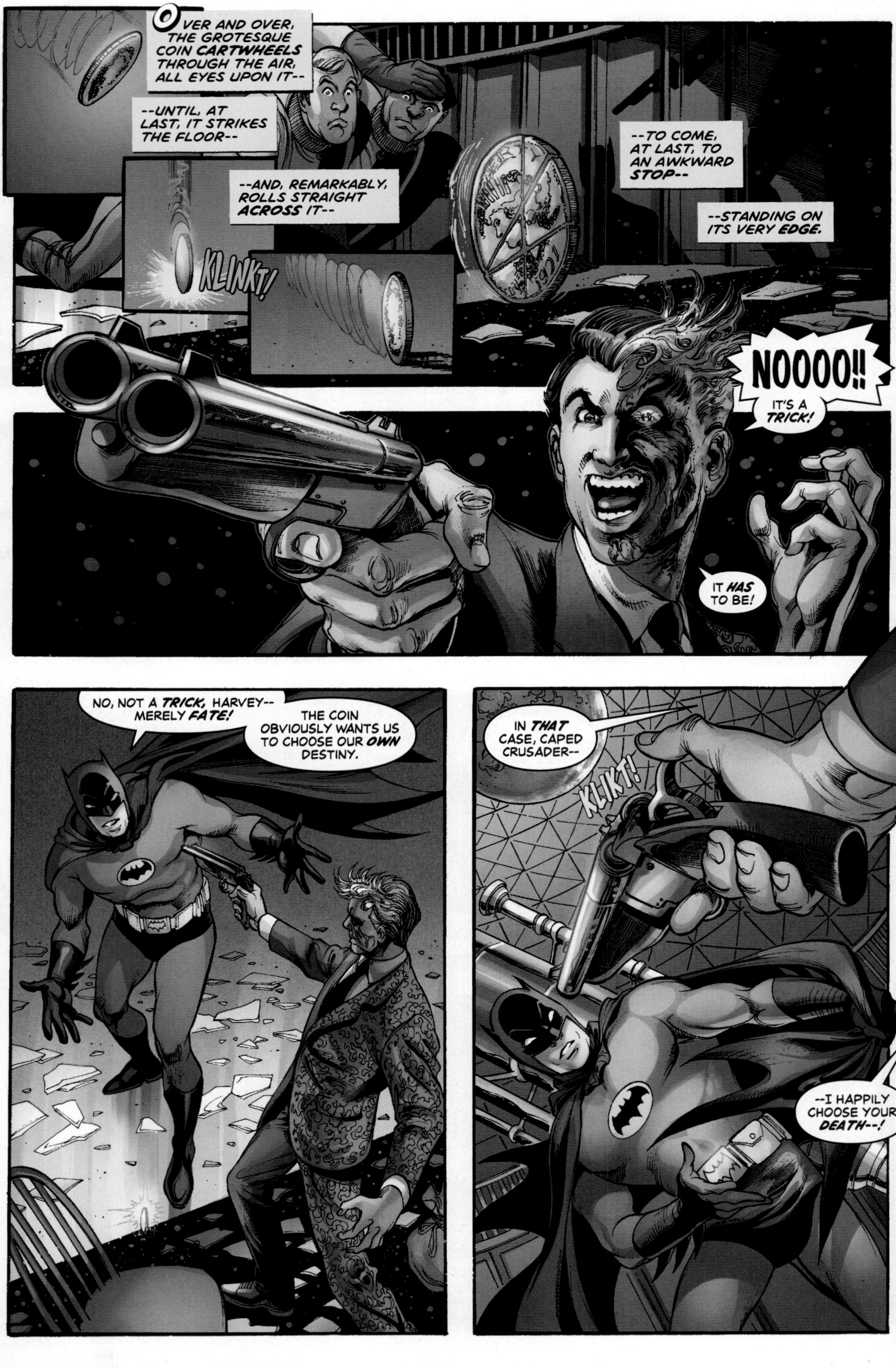
OVER AND OVER, THE GROTESQUE COIN CARTWHEELS THROUGH THE AIR, ALL EYES UPON IT--
--UNTIL, AT LAST, IT STRIKES THE FLOOR--
--AND, REMARKABLY, ROLLS STRAIGHT ACROSS IT--
KLINKT!
--TO COME, AT LAST, TO AN AWKWARD STOP--
--STANDING ON ITS VERY EDGE.
NOOOO!! IT'S A TRICK!
IT HAS TO BE!
NO, NOT A TRICK, HARVEY-- MERELY FATE!
THE COIN OBVIOUSLY WANTS US TO CHOOSE OUR OWN DESTINY.
IN THAT CASE, CAPED CRUSADER--
KLIKT!
--I HAPPILY CHOOSE YOUR DEATH--!

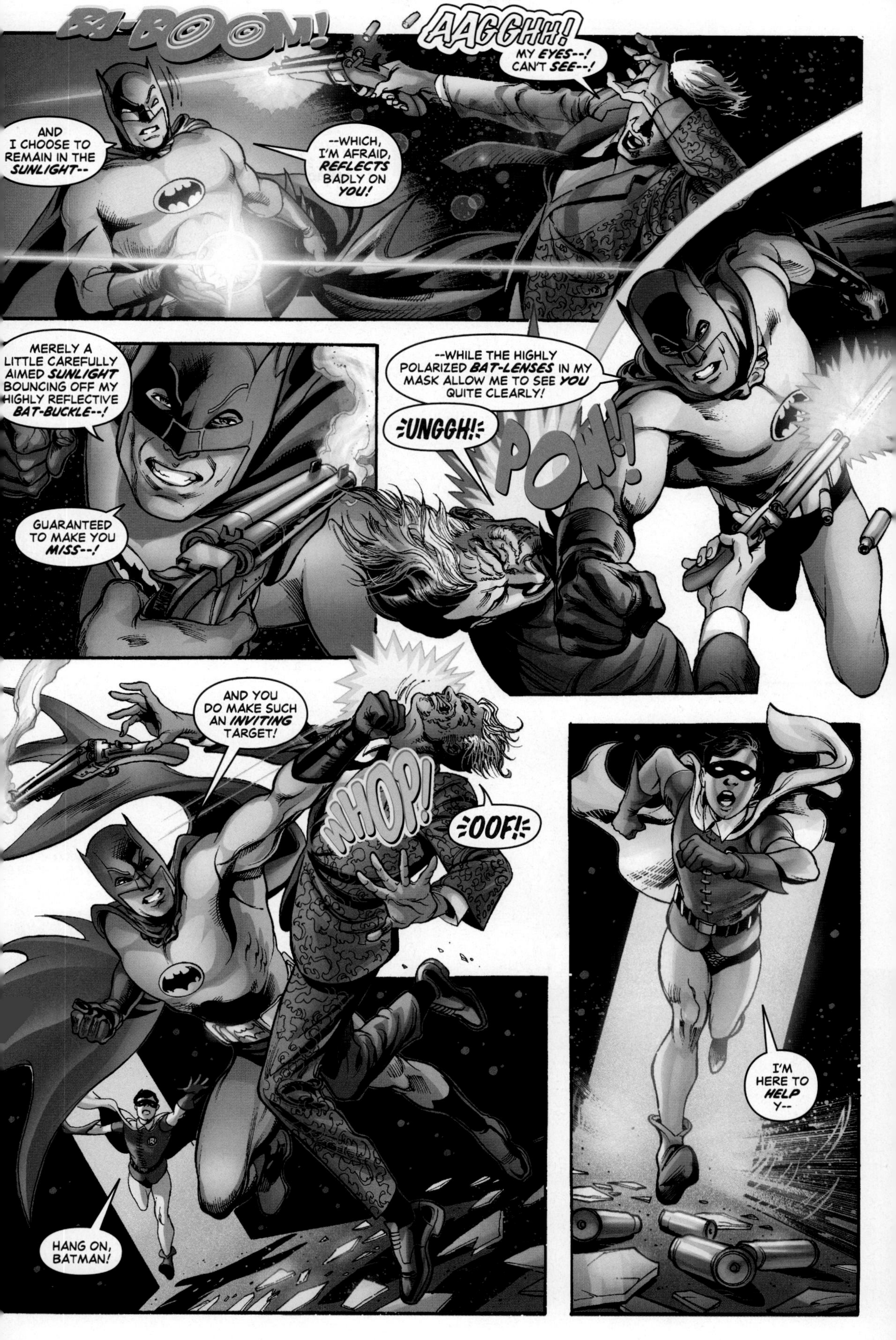

BA-BOOM!
AAGGHH!
MY EYES--! CAN'T SEE--!
AND I CHOOSE TO REMAIN IN THE SUNLIGHT--
--WHICH, I'M AFRAID, REFLECTS BADLY ON YOU!
MERELY A LITTLE CAREFULLY AIMED SUNLIGHT BOUNCING OFF MY HIGHLY REFLECTIVE BAT-BUCKLE--!
GUARANTEED TO MAKE YOU MISS--!
--WHILE THE HIGHLY POLARIZED BAT-LENSES IN MY MASK ALLOW ME TO SEE YOU QUITE CLEARLY!
UNGGH!
POW!!
AND YOU DO MAKE SUCH AN INVITING TARGET!
WHOP!
OOF!
HANG ON, BATMAN!
I'M HERE TO HELP Y--

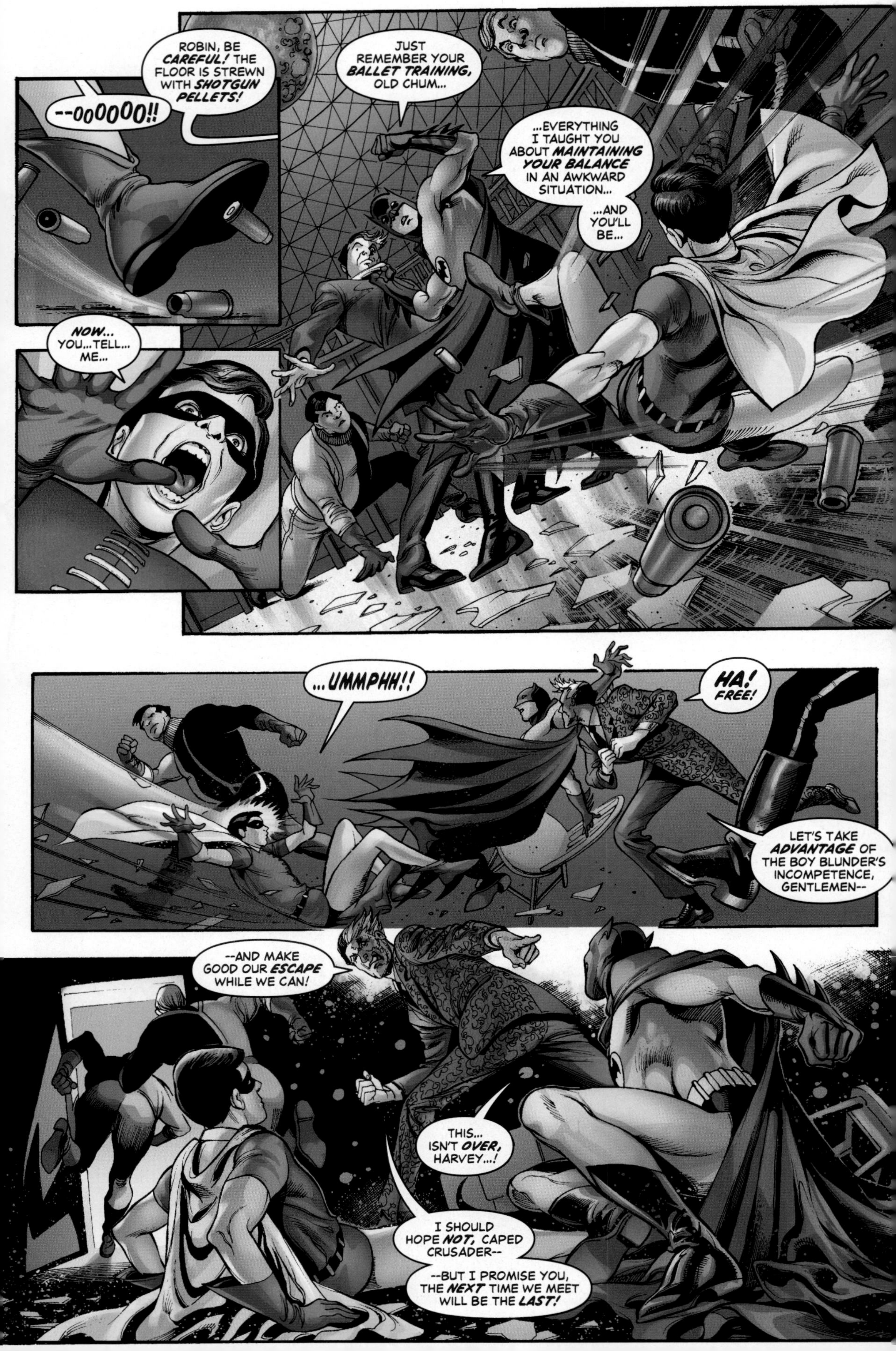

--OOOOOO!!
ROBIN, BE CAREFUL! THE FLOOR IS STREWN WITH SHOTGUN PELLETS!
JUST REMEMBER YOUR BALLET TRAINING, OLD CHUM...
...EVERYTHING I TAUGHT YOU ABOUT MAINTAINING YOUR BALANCE IN AN AWKWARD SITUATION...
...AND YOU'LL BE...
NOW... YOU...TELL... ME...
...UMMPHH!!
HA! FREE!
LET'S TAKE ADVANTAGE OF THE BOY BLUNDER'S INCOMPETENCE, GENTLEMEN--
--AND MAKE GOOD OUR ESCAPE WHILE WE CAN!
THIS... ISN'T OVER, HARVEY...!
I SHOULD HOPE NOT, CAPED CRUSADER--
--BUT I PROMISE YOU, THE NEXT TIME WE MEET WILL BE THE LAST!

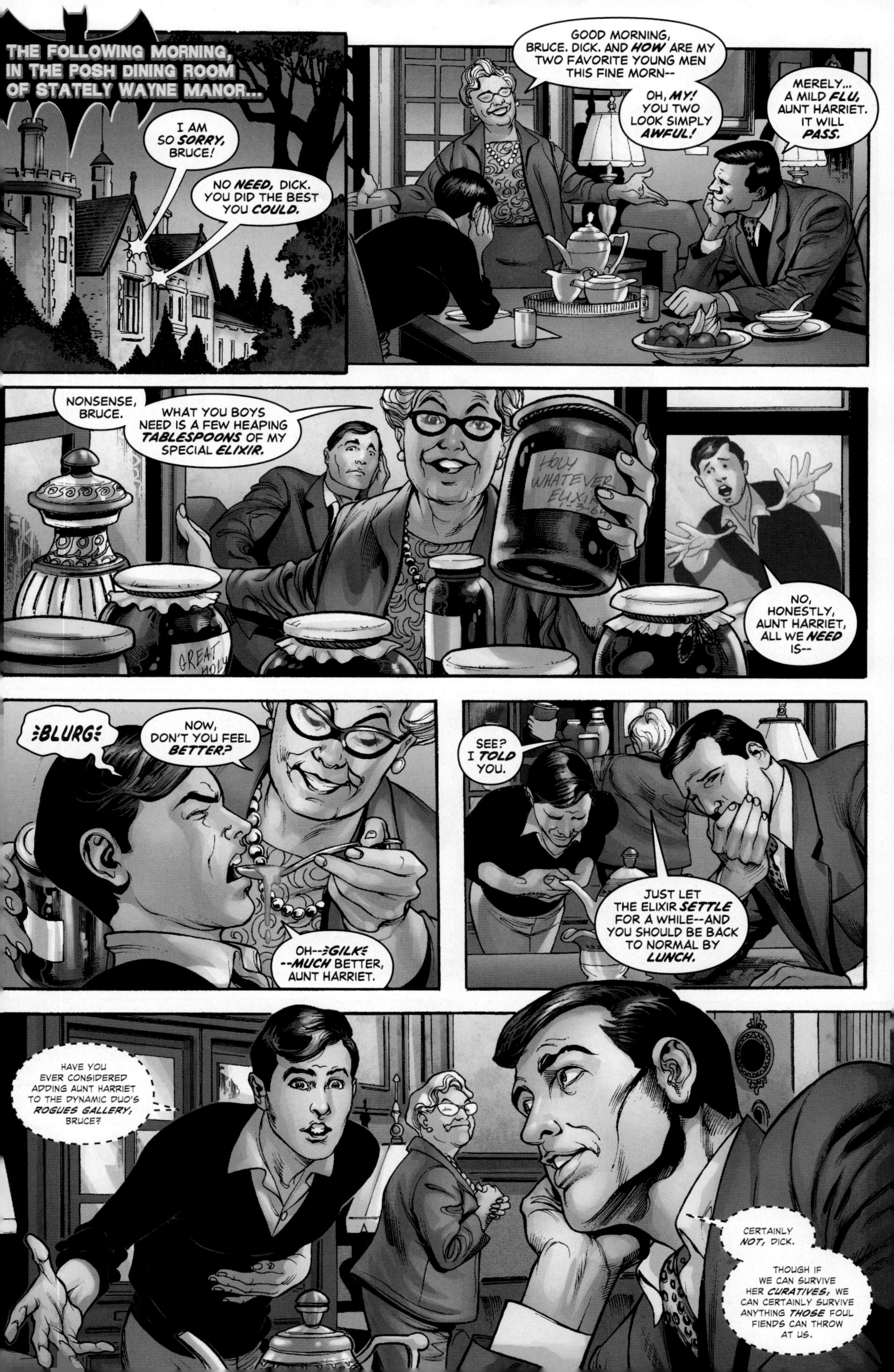

THE FOLLOWING MORNING, IN THE POSH DINING ROOM OF STATELY WAYNE MANOR...
I AM SO SORRY, BRUCE!
NO NEED, DICK. YOU DID THE BEST YOU COULD.
GOOD MORNING, BRUCE. DICK. AND HOW ARE MY TWO FAVORITE YOUNG MEN THIS FINE MORN--
OH, MY! YOU TWO LOOK SIMPLY AWFUL!
MERELY... A MILD FLU, AUNT HARRIET. IT WILL PASS.
NONSENSE, BRUCE.
WHAT YOU BOYS NEED IS A FEW HEAPING TABLESPOONS OF MY SPECIAL ELIXIR.
HOLY WHATEVER ELIXIR 1-3-64
NO, HONESTLY, AUNT HARRIET, ALL WE NEED IS--
GREAT HOLY
BLURG
NOW, DON'T YOU FEEL BETTER?
OH-- GILK --MUCH BETTER, AUNT HARRIET.
SEE? I TOLD YOU.
JUST LET THE ELIXIR SETTLE FOR A WHILE--AND YOU SHOULD BE BACK TO NORMAL BY LUNCH.
HAVE YOU EVER CONSIDERED ADDING AUNT HARRIET TO THE DYNAMIC DUO'S ROGUES GALLERY, BRUCE?
CERTAINLY NOT, DICK.
THOUGH IF WE CAN SURVIVE HER CURATIVES, WE CAN CERTAINLY SURVIVE ANYTHING THOSE FOUL FIENDS CAN THROW AT US.

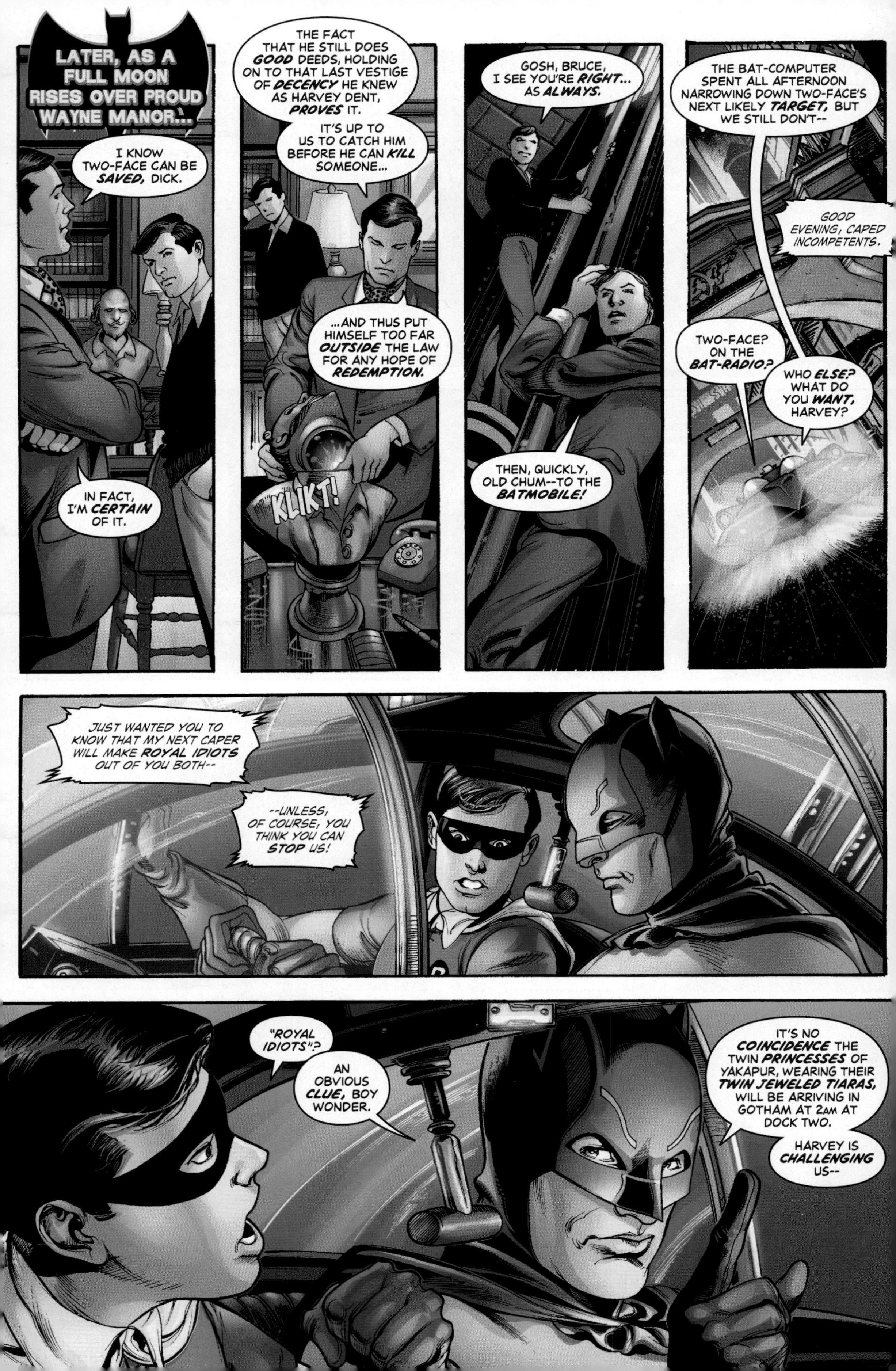
LATER, AS A FULL MOON RISES OVER PROUD WAYNE MANOR...
I KNOW TWO-FACE CAN BE SAVED, DICK.
IN FACT, I'M CERTAIN OF IT.
THE FACT THAT HE STILL DOES GOOD DEEDS, HOLDING ON TO THAT LAST VESTIGE OF DECENCY HE KNEW AS HARVEY DENT, PROVES IT.
IT'S UP TO US TO CATCH HIM BEFORE HE CAN KILL SOMEONE...
...AND THUS PUT HIMSELF TOO FAR OUTSIDE THE LAW FOR ANY HOPE OF REDEMPTION.
KLIKT!
GOSH, BRUCE, I SEE YOU'RE RIGHT... AS ALWAYS.
THEN, QUICKLY, OLD CHUM--TO THE BATMOBILE!
THE BAT-COMPUTER SPENT ALL AFTERNOON NARROWING DOWN TWO-FACE'S NEXT LIKELY TARGET, BUT WE STILL DON'T--
GOOD EVENING, CAPED INCOMPETENTS.
TWO-FACE? ON THE BAT-RADIO?
WHO ELSE? WHAT DO YOU WANT, HARVEY?
JUST WANTED YOU TO KNOW THAT MY NEXT CAPER WILL MAKE ROYAL IDIOTS OUT OF YOU BOTH--
--UNLESS, OF COURSE, YOU THINK YOU CAN STOP US!
"ROYAL IDIOTS"?
AN OBVIOUS CLUE, BOY WONDER.
IT'S NO COINCIDENCE THE TWIN PRINCESSES OF YAKAPUR, WEARING THEIR TWIN JEWELED TIARAS, WILL BE ARRIVING IN GOTHAM AT 2AM AT DOCK TWO.
HARVEY IS CHALLENGING US--

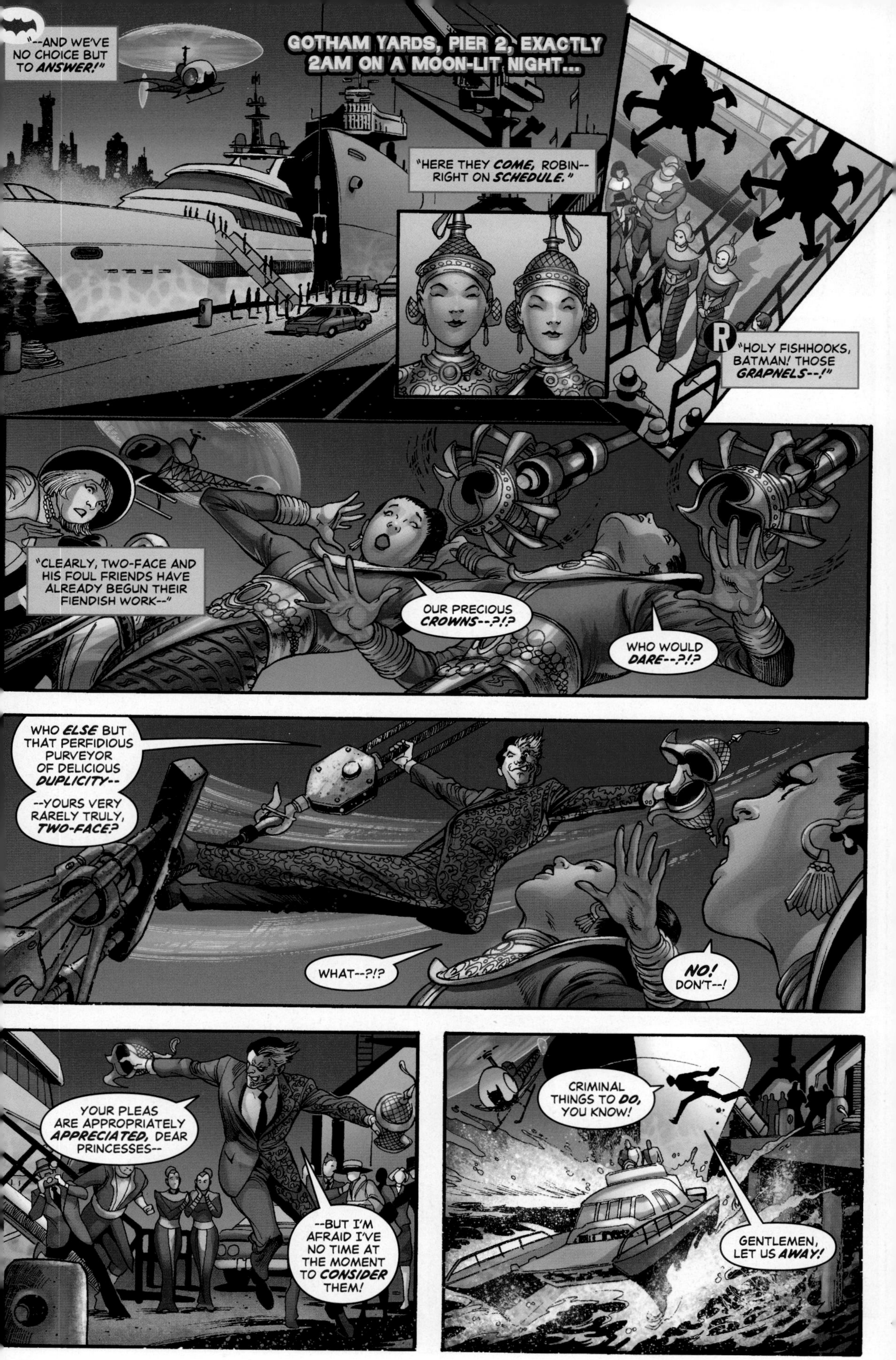
"--AND WE'VE NO CHOICE BUT TO ANSWER!"
GOTHAM YARDS, PIER 2, EXACTLY 2AM ON A MOON-LIT NIGHT...
"HERE THEY COME, ROBIN-- RIGHT ON SCHEDULE."
"HOLY FISHHOOKS, BATMAN! THOSE GRAPNELS--!"
"CLEARLY, TWO-FACE AND HIS FOUL FRIENDS HAVE ALREADY BEGUN THEIR FIENDISH WORK--"
OUR PRECIOUS CROWNS--?!?
WHO WOULD DARE--?!?
WHO ELSE BUT THAT PERFIDIOUS PURVEYOR OF DELICIOUS DUPLICITY--
--YOURS VERY RARELY TRULY, TWO-FACE?
WHAT--?!?
NO! DON'T--!
YOUR PLEAS ARE APPROPRIATELY APPRECIATED, DEAR PRINCESSES--
--BUT I'M AFRAID I'VE NO TIME AT THE MOMENT TO CONSIDER THEM!
CRIMINAL THINGS TO DO, YOU KNOW!
GENTLEMEN, LET US AWAY!

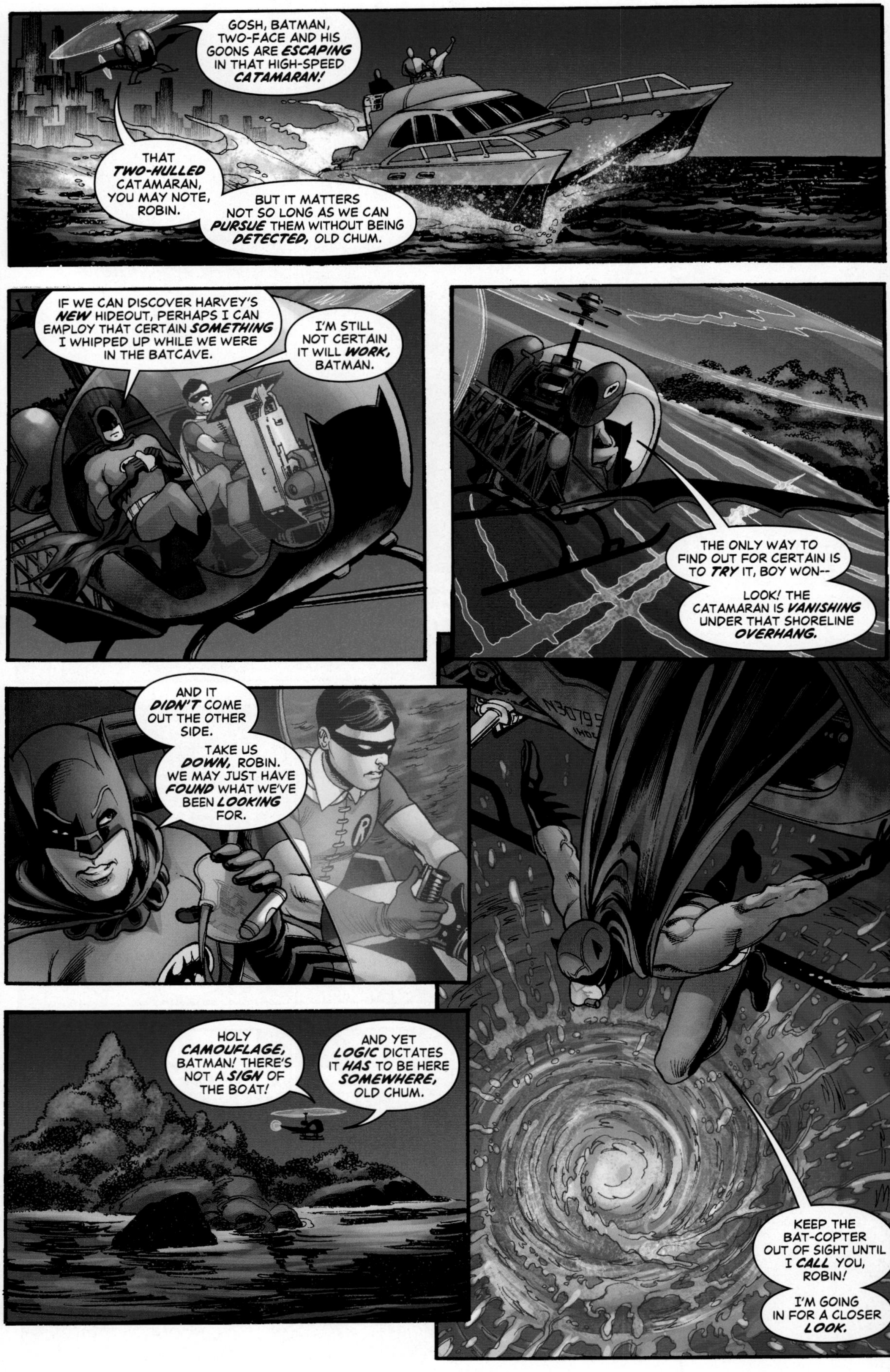

GOSH, BATMAN, TWO-FACE AND HIS GOONS ARE ESCAPING IN THAT HIGH-SPEED CATAMARAN!
THAT TWO-HULLED CATAMARAN, YOU MAY NOTE, ROBIN.
BUT IT MATTERS NOT SO LONG AS WE CAN PURSUE THEM WITHOUT BEING DETECTED, OLD CHUM.
IF WE CAN DISCOVER HARVEY'S NEW HIDEOUT, PERHAPS I CAN EMPLOY THAT CERTAIN SOMETHING I WHIPPED UP WHILE WE WERE IN THE BATCAVE.
I'M STILL NOT CERTAIN IT WILL WORK, BATMAN.
THE ONLY WAY TO FIND OUT FOR CERTAIN IS TO TRY IT, BOY WON--
LOOK! THE CATAMARAN IS VANISHING UNDER THAT SHORELINE OVERHANG.
AND IT DIDN'T COME OUT THE OTHER SIDE.
TAKE US DOWN, ROBIN. WE MAY JUST HAVE FOUND WHAT WE'VE BEEN LOOKING FOR.
HOLY CAMOUFLAGE, BATMAN! THERE'S NOT A SIGN OF THE BOAT!
AND YET LOGIC DICTATES IT HAS TO BE HERE SOMEWHERE, OLD CHUM.
KEEP THE BAT-COPTER OUT OF SIGHT UNTIL I CALL YOU, ROBIN!
I'M GOING IN FOR A CLOSER LOOK.

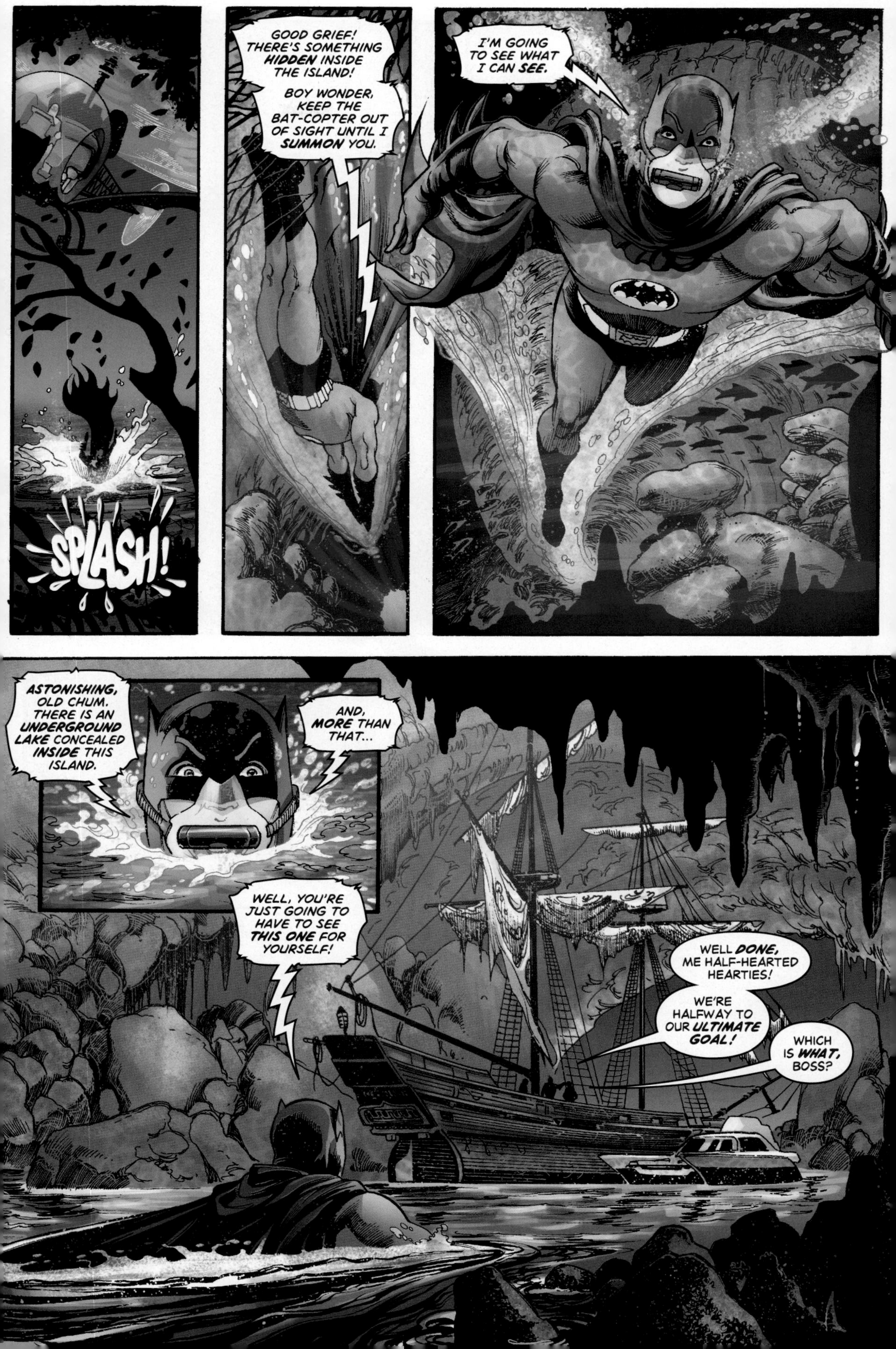
SPLASH!
GOOD GRIEF! THERE'S SOMETHING HIDDEN INSIDE THE ISLAND!
BOY WONDER, KEEP THE BAT-COPTER OUT OF SIGHT UNTIL I SUMMON YOU.
I'M GOING TO SEE WHAT I CAN SEE.
ASTONISHING, OLD CHUM. THERE IS AN UNDERGROUND LAKE CONCEALED INSIDE THIS ISLAND.
AND, MORE THAN THAT...
WELL, YOU'RE JUST GOING TO HAVE TO SEE THIS ONE FOR YOURSELF!
WELL DONE, ME HALF-HEARTED HEARTIES!
WE'RE HALFWAY TO OUR ULTIMATE GOAL!
WHICH IS WHAT, BOSS?

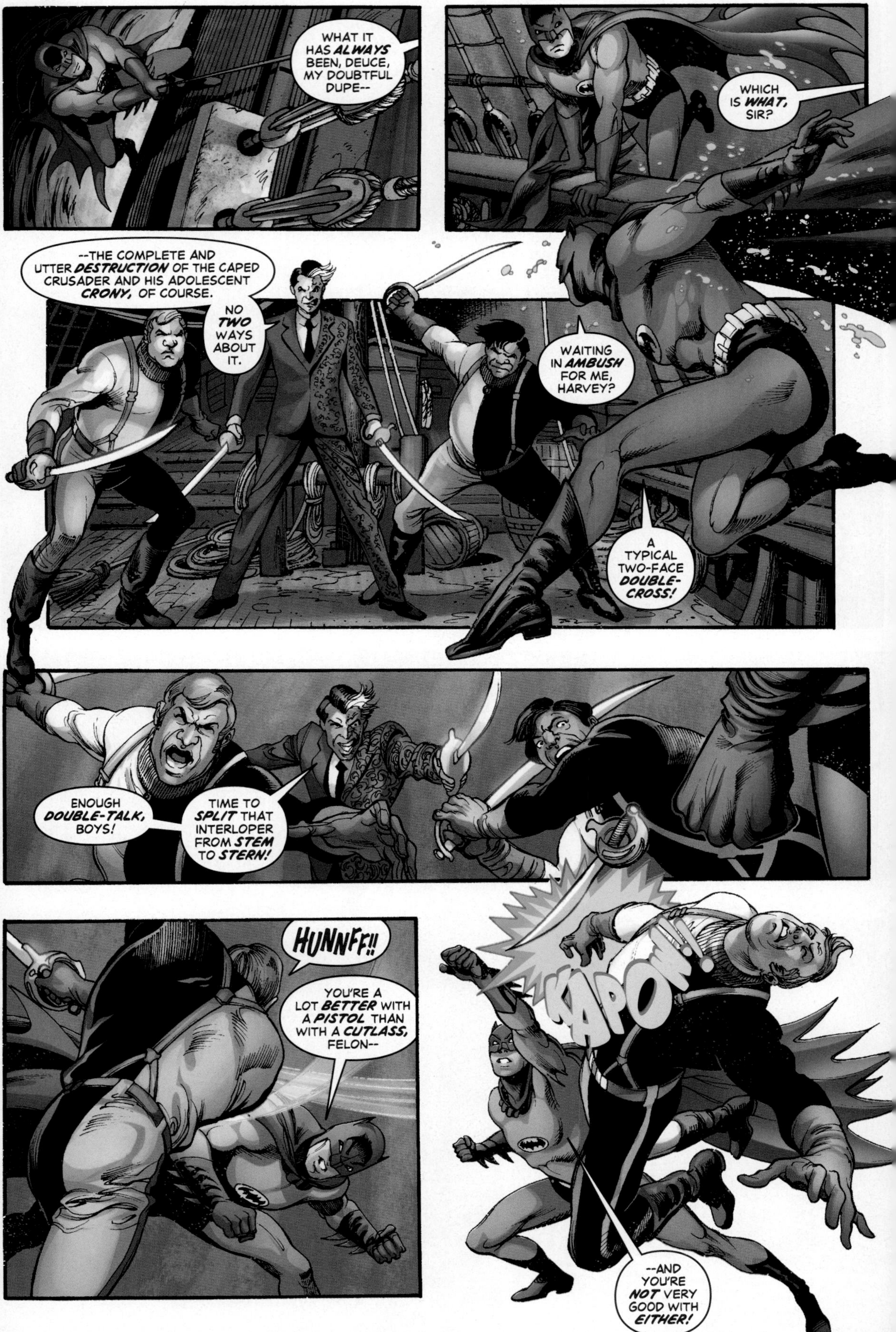
WHAT IT HAS ALWAYS BEEN, DEUCE, MY DOUBTFUL DUPE--
WHICH IS WHAT, SIR?
--THE COMPLETE AND UTTER DESTRUCTION OF THE CAPED CRUSADER AND HIS ADOLESCENT CRONY, OF COURSE.
NO TWO WAYS ABOUT IT.
WAITING IN AMBUSH FOR ME, HARVEY?
A TYPICAL TWO-FACE DOUBLE-CROSS!
ENOUGH DOUBLE-TALK, BOYS!
TIME TO SPLIT THAT INTERLOPER FROM STEM TO STERN!
HUNNFF!!
YOU'RE A LOT BETTER WITH A PISTOL THAN WITH A CUTLASS, FELON--
KAPOW!!
--AND YOU'RE NOT VERY GOOD WITH EITHER!

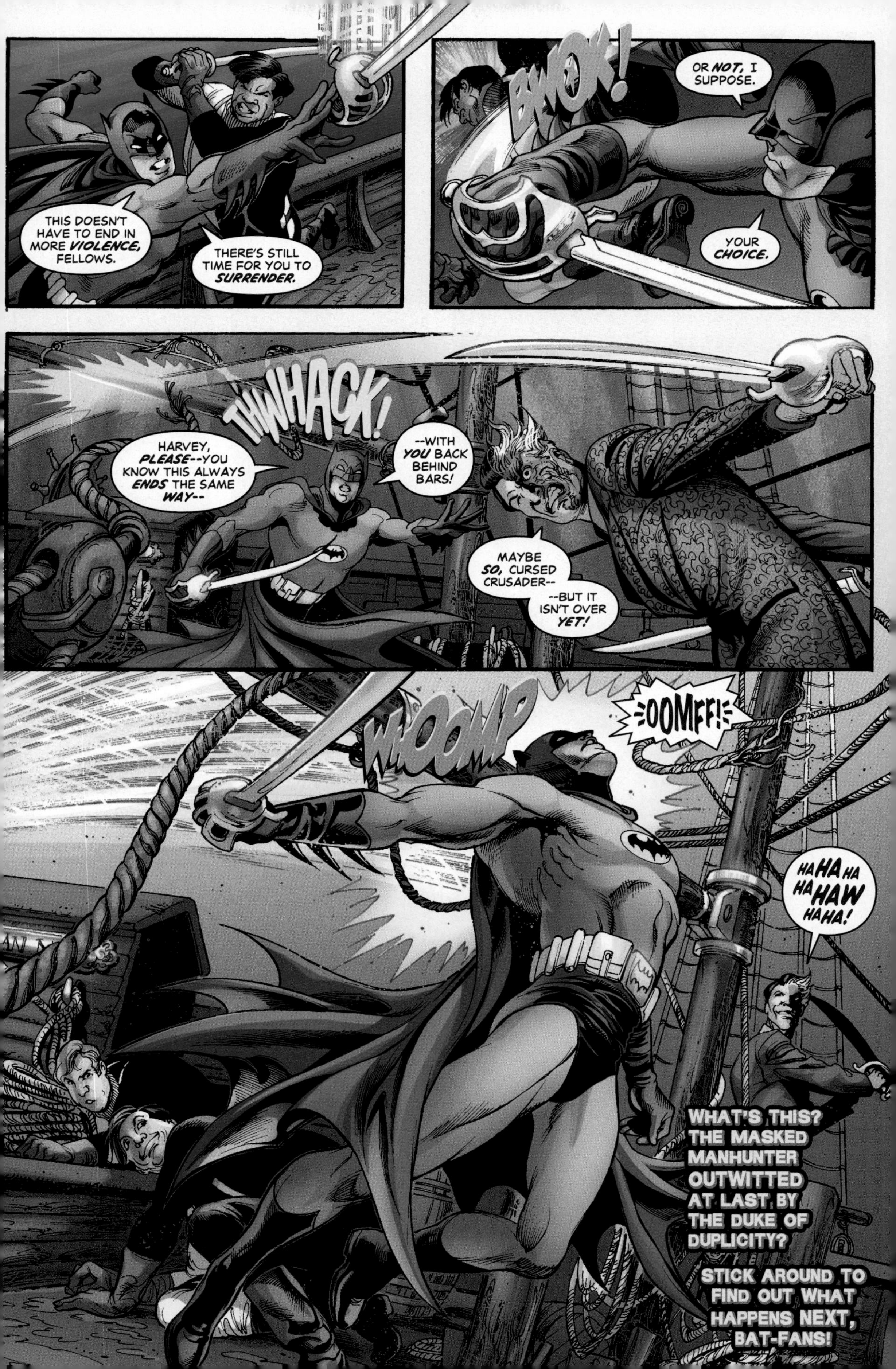
THIS DOESN'T HAVE TO END IN MORE VIOLENCE, FELLOWS.
THERE'S STILL TIME FOR YOU TO SURRENDER.
BWOK!
OR NOT, I SUPPOSE.
YOUR CHOICE.
THWHACK!
HARVEY, PLEASE--YOU KNOW THIS ALWAYS ENDS THE SAME WAY--
--WITH YOU BACK BEHIND BARS!
MAYBE SO, CURSED CRUSADER--
--BUT IT ISN'T OVER YET!
WHOOMP
OOMFF!
HAHAHA HAHAW HAHA!
WHAT'S THIS? THE MASKED MANHUNTER OUTWITTED AT LAST BY THE DUKE OF DUPLICITY?
STICK AROUND TO FIND OUT WHAT HAPPENS NEXT, BAT-FANS!

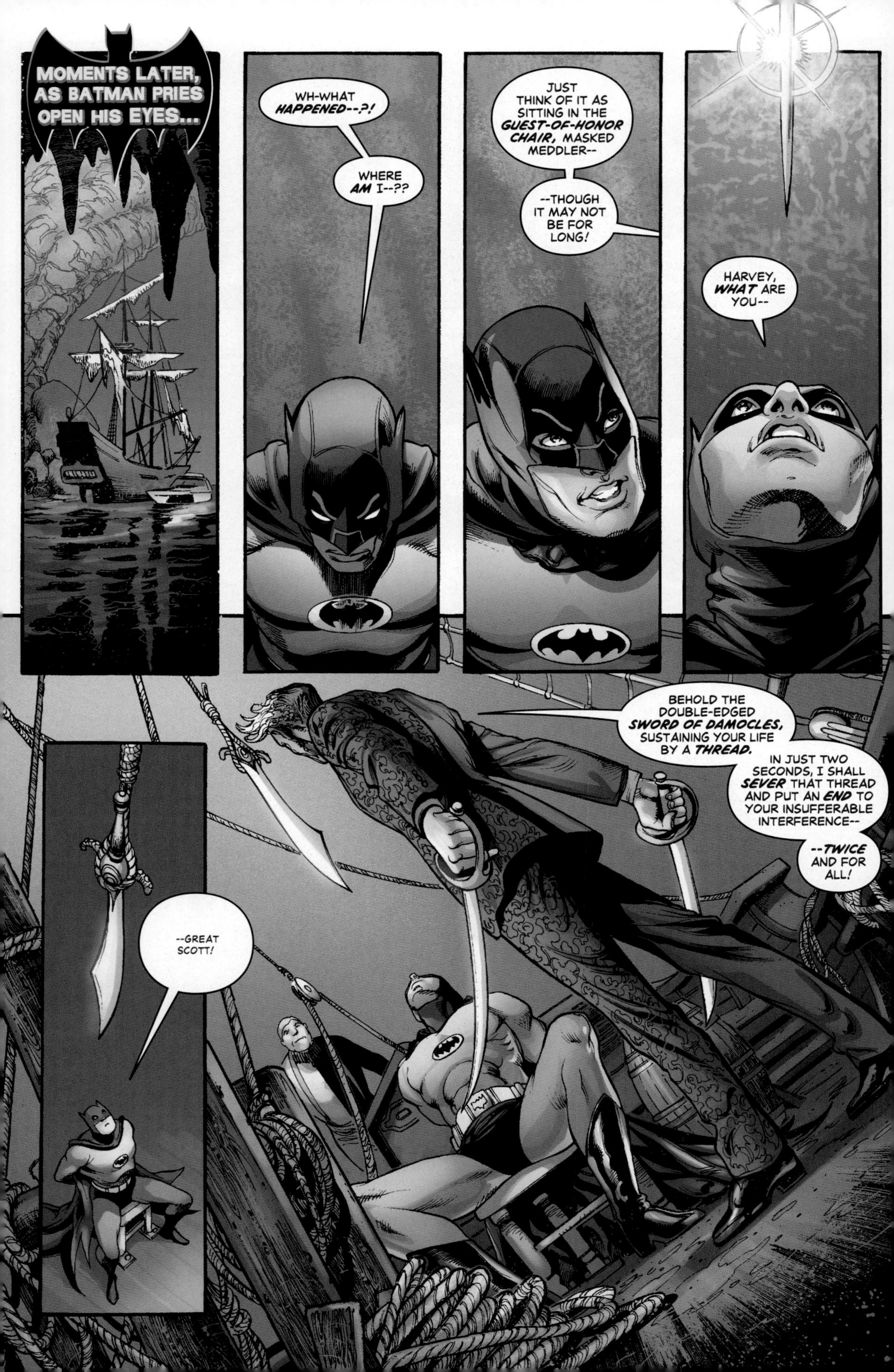
MOMENTS LATER, AS BATMAN PRIES OPEN HIS EYES...
WH-WHAT HAPPENED--?!
WHERE AM I--??
JUST THINK OF IT AS SITTING IN THE GUEST-OF-HONOR CHAIR, MASKED MEDDLER--
--THOUGH IT MAY NOT BE FOR LONG!
HARVEY, WHAT ARE YOU--
--GREAT SCOTT!
BEHOLD THE DOUBLE-EDGED SWORD OF DAMOCLES, SUSTAINING YOUR LIFE BY A THREAD.
IN JUST TWO SECONDS, I SHALL SEVER THAT THREAD AND PUT AN END TO YOUR INSUFFERABLE INTERFERENCE--
--TWICE AND FOR ALL!

OKAY NOW, ON THE *COUNT* OF...WELL, YOU *KNOW*.

...ONE...

HARVEY, YOU ARE A TREMENDOUS *DISAPPOINTMENT* TO ME.

WHAT? *HOW?*

AREN'T YOU *SWORN* TO MAKE ALL THE MAJOR *DECISIONS* OF YOUR LIFE BASED ON THE TOSS OF YOUR *COIN?*

AND YET, HERE YOU ARE, ABOUT TO *DISPOSE* OF YOUR GREATEST *FOE*--AND THERE'S NO COIN IN *SIGHT.*

YES. OF COURSE, BATMAN. YOU'RE QUITE *CORRECT.*

OKAY, HERE'S THE NEW DEAL...

COIN COMES UP *HEADS*, I DROP THE SWORD, AND YOU DIE *QUICKLY.*

TAILS, I'LL HAVE YOU *KEELHAULED* UNDER THE SHIP, WHICH IS A MUCH SLOWER, MUCH MORE PAINFUL WAY TO PERISH.

AND, IF IT LANDS ON ITS *EDGE* AGAIN, YOU *SURRENDER.* AGREED?

IMPOSSIBLE. DO YOU REALIZE THE *ODDS* OF--

FINE. *AGREED.*

CAIMAN NOIR

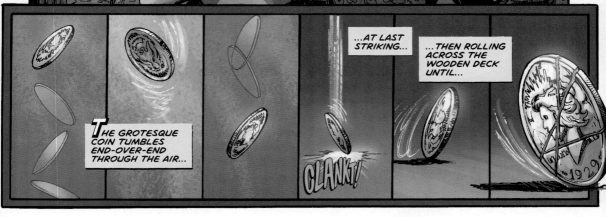

THE GROTESQUE COIN TUMBLES END-OVER-END THROUGH THE AIR...

...AT LAST STRIKING...

...THEN ROLLING ACROSS THE WOODEN DECK UNTIL...

CLANKT!

1929

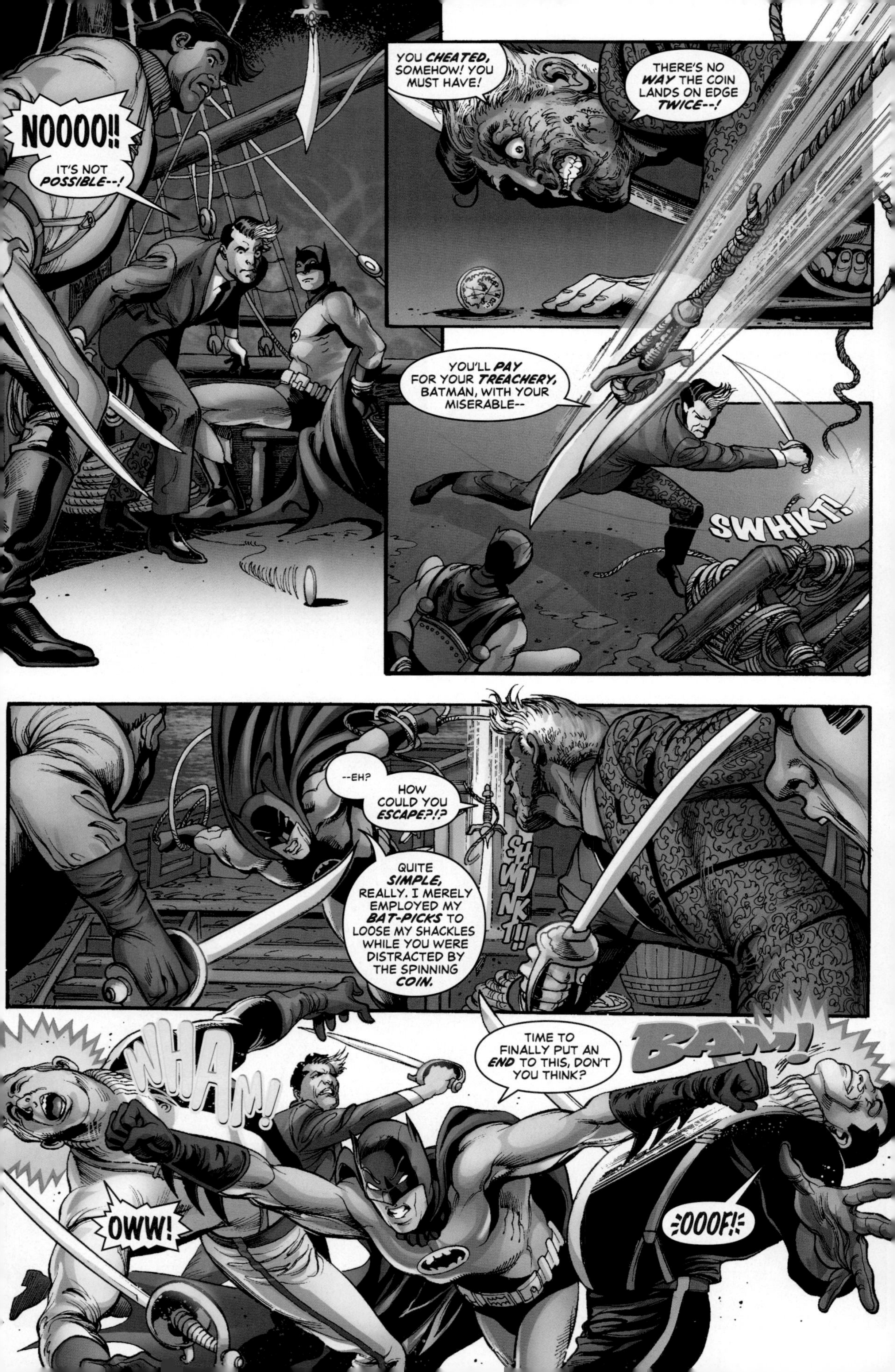
NOOOO!!
IT'S NOT POSSIBLE--!
YOU CHEATED, SOMEHOW! YOU MUST HAVE!
THERE'S NO WAY THE COIN LANDS ON EDGE TWICE--!
YOU'LL PAY FOR YOUR TREACHERY, BATMAN, WITH YOUR MISERABLE--
SWHIKT!
--EH?
HOW COULD YOU ESCAPE?!?
QUITE SIMPLE, REALLY. I MERELY EMPLOYED MY BAT-PICKS TO LOOSE MY SHACKLES WHILE YOU WERE DISTRACTED BY THE SPINNING COIN.
SHWUNK!!
WHAM!
TIME TO FINALLY PUT AN END TO THIS, DON'T YOU THINK?
BAM!
OWW!
OOOF!

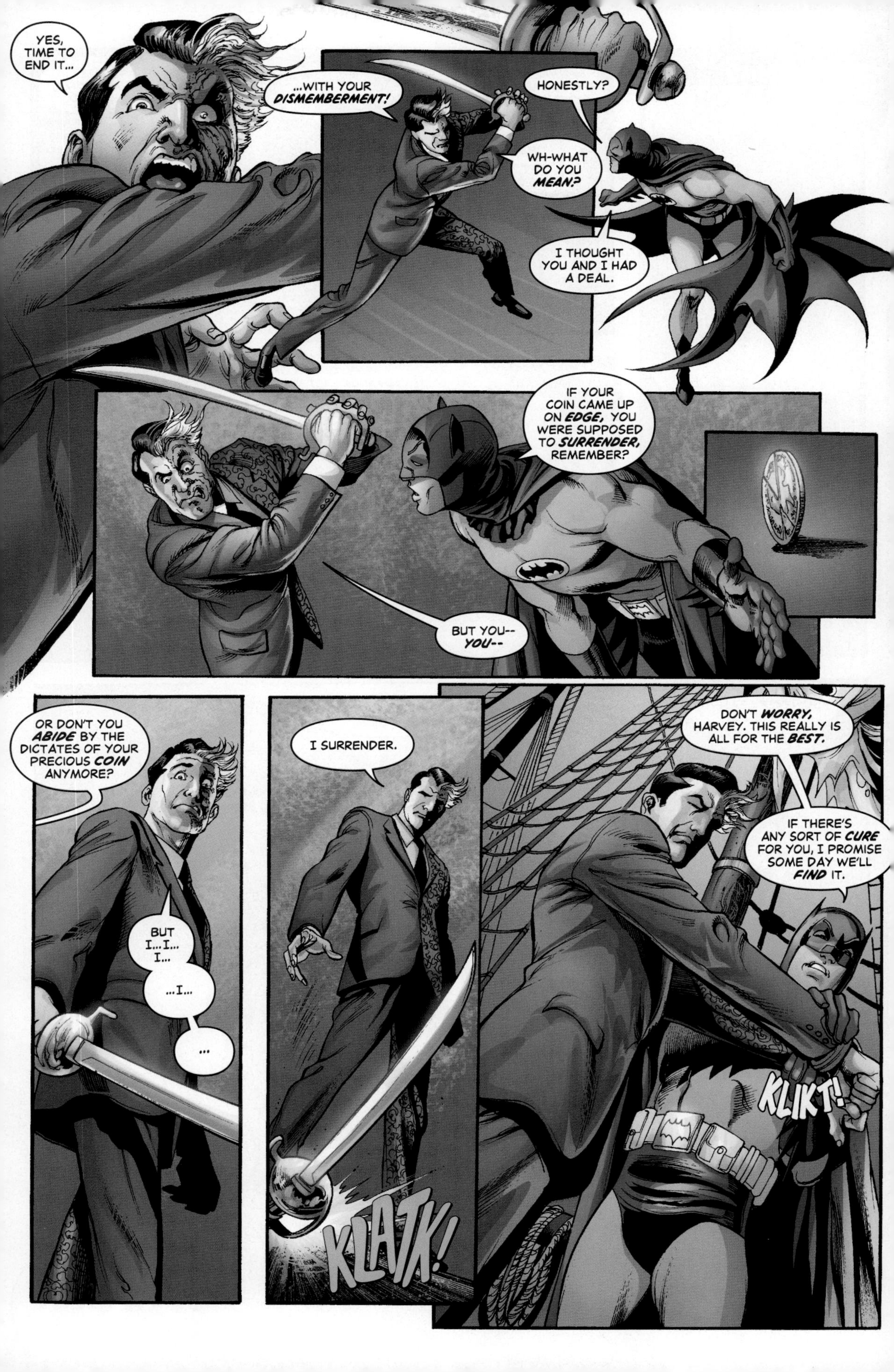
YES, TIME TO END IT...
...WITH YOUR DISMEMBERMENT!
HONESTLY?
WH-WHAT DO YOU MEAN?
I THOUGHT YOU AND I HAD A DEAL.
IF YOUR COIN CAME UP ON EDGE, YOU WERE SUPPOSED TO SURRENDER, REMEMBER?
BUT YOU-- YOU--
OR DON'T YOU ABIDE BY THE DICTATES OF YOUR PRECIOUS COIN ANYMORE?
BUT I...I... I...
...I...
...
I SURRENDER.
KLATK!
DON'T WORRY, HARVEY. THIS REALLY IS ALL FOR THE BEST.
IF THERE'S ANY SORT OF CURE FOR YOU, I PROMISE SOME DAY WE'LL FIND IT.
KLIKT!

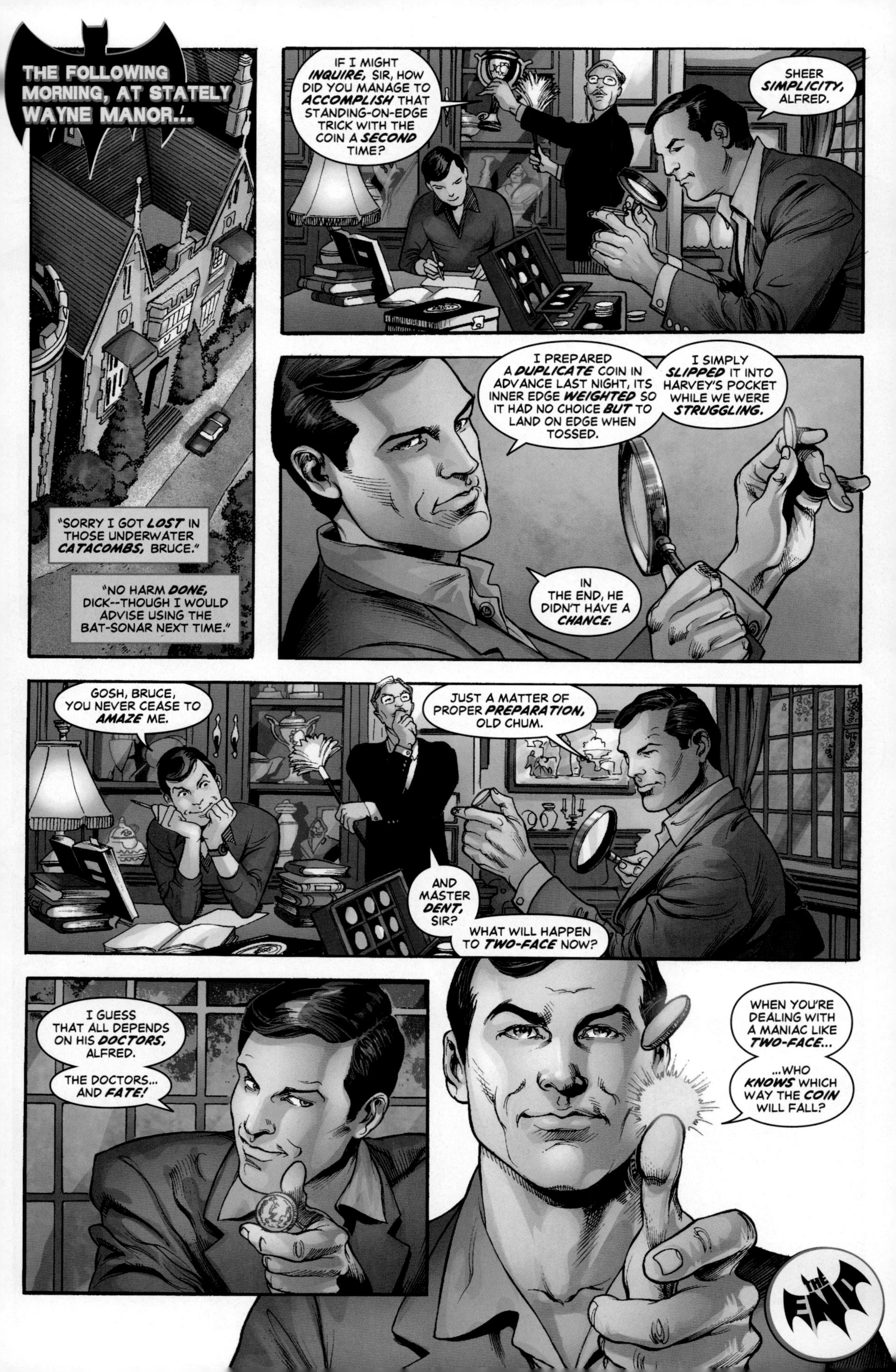
THE FOLLOWING MORNING, AT STATELY WAYNE MANOR...
"SORRY I GOT LOST IN THOSE UNDERWATER CATACOMBS, BRUCE."
"NO HARM DONE, DICK--THOUGH I WOULD ADVISE USING THE BAT-SONAR NEXT TIME."
IF I MIGHT INQUIRE, SIR, HOW DID YOU MANAGE TO ACCOMPLISH THAT STANDING-ON-EDGE TRICK WITH THE COIN A SECOND TIME?
SHEER SIMPLICITY, ALFRED.
I PREPARED A DUPLICATE COIN IN ADVANCE LAST NIGHT, ITS INNER EDGE WEIGHTED SO IT HAD NO CHOICE BUT TO LAND ON EDGE WHEN TOSSED.
I SIMPLY SLIPPED IT INTO HARVEY'S POCKET WHILE WE WERE STRUGGLING.
IN THE END, HE DIDN'T HAVE A CHANCE.
GOSH, BRUCE, YOU NEVER CEASE TO AMAZE ME.
JUST A MATTER OF PROPER PREPARATION, OLD CHUM.
AND MASTER DENT, SIR?
WHAT WILL HAPPEN TO TWO-FACE NOW?
I GUESS THAT ALL DEPENDS ON HIS DOCTORS, ALFRED.
THE DOCTORS... AND FATE!
WHEN YOU'RE DEALING WITH A MANIAC LIKE TWO-FACE...
...WHO KNOWS WHICH WAY THE COIN WILL FALL?
THE END

Batman '66: The Lost Episode

Unwrapped

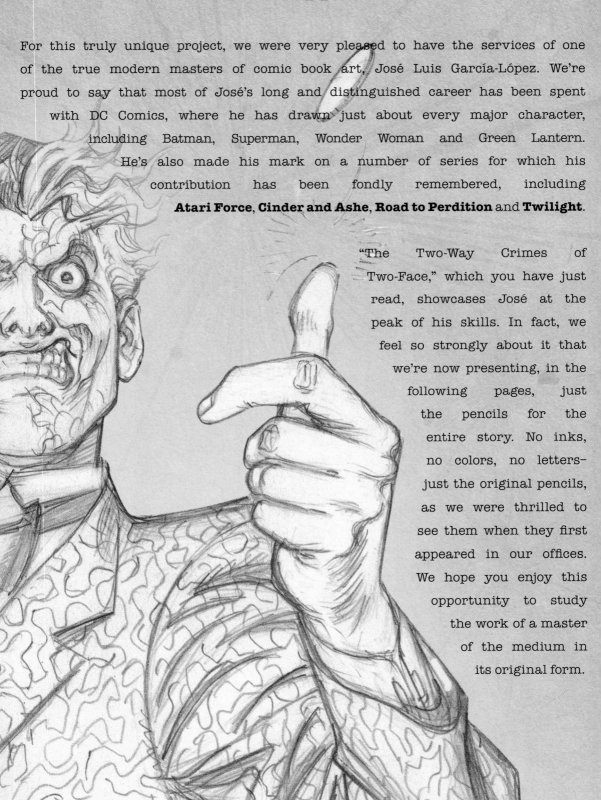

For this truly unique project, we were very pleased to have the services of one of the true modern masters of comic book art, José Luis García-López. We're proud to say that most of José's long and distinguished career has been spent with DC Comics, where he has drawn just about every major character, including Batman, Superman, Wonder Woman and Green Lantern. He's also made his mark on a number of series for which his contribution has been fondly remembered, including **Atari Force**, **Cinder and Ashe**, **Road to Perdition** and **Twilight**.

"The Two-Way Crimes of Two-Face," which you have just read, showcases José at the peak of his skills. In fact, we feel so strongly about it that we're now presenting, in the following pages, just the pencils for the entire story. No inks, no colors, no letters— just the original pencils, as we were thrilled to see them when they first appeared in our offices. We hope you enjoy this opportunity to study the work of a master of the medium in its original form.

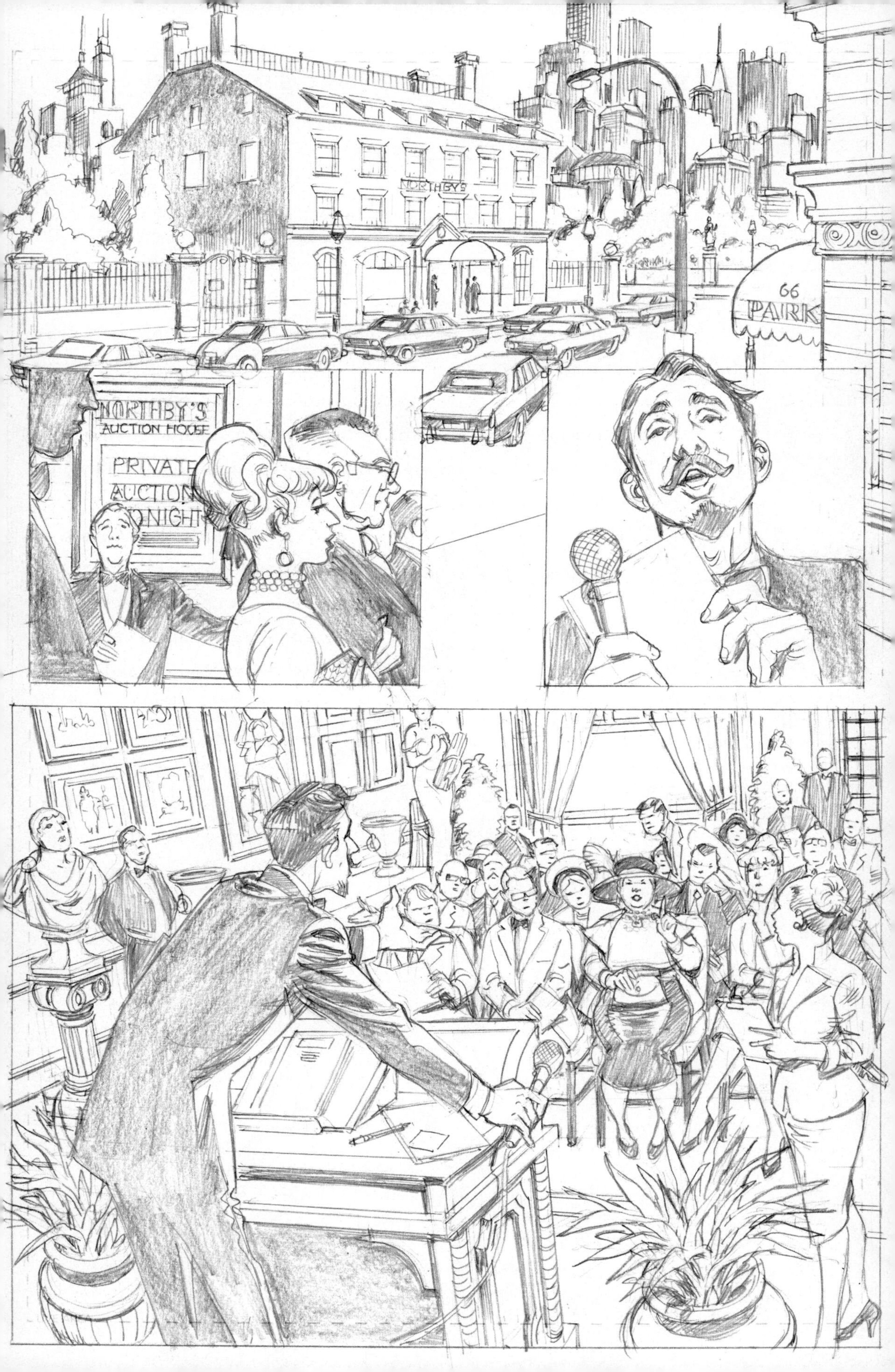
NORTHBY'S
66
PARK
NORTHBY'S
AUCTION HOUSE
PRIVATE
AUCTION

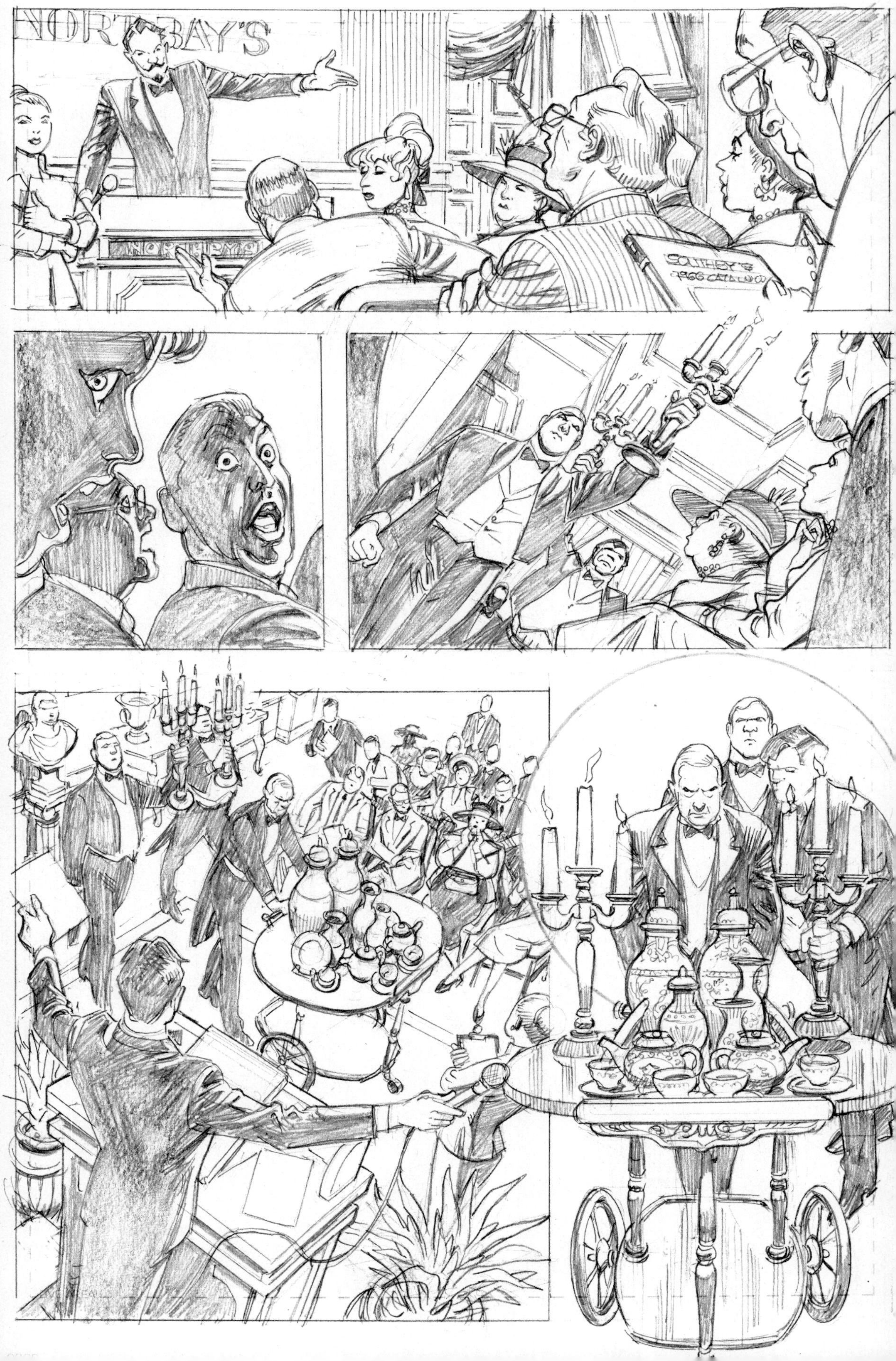
NORT BAY'S
SOUTHEY'S
1966 CATALOG

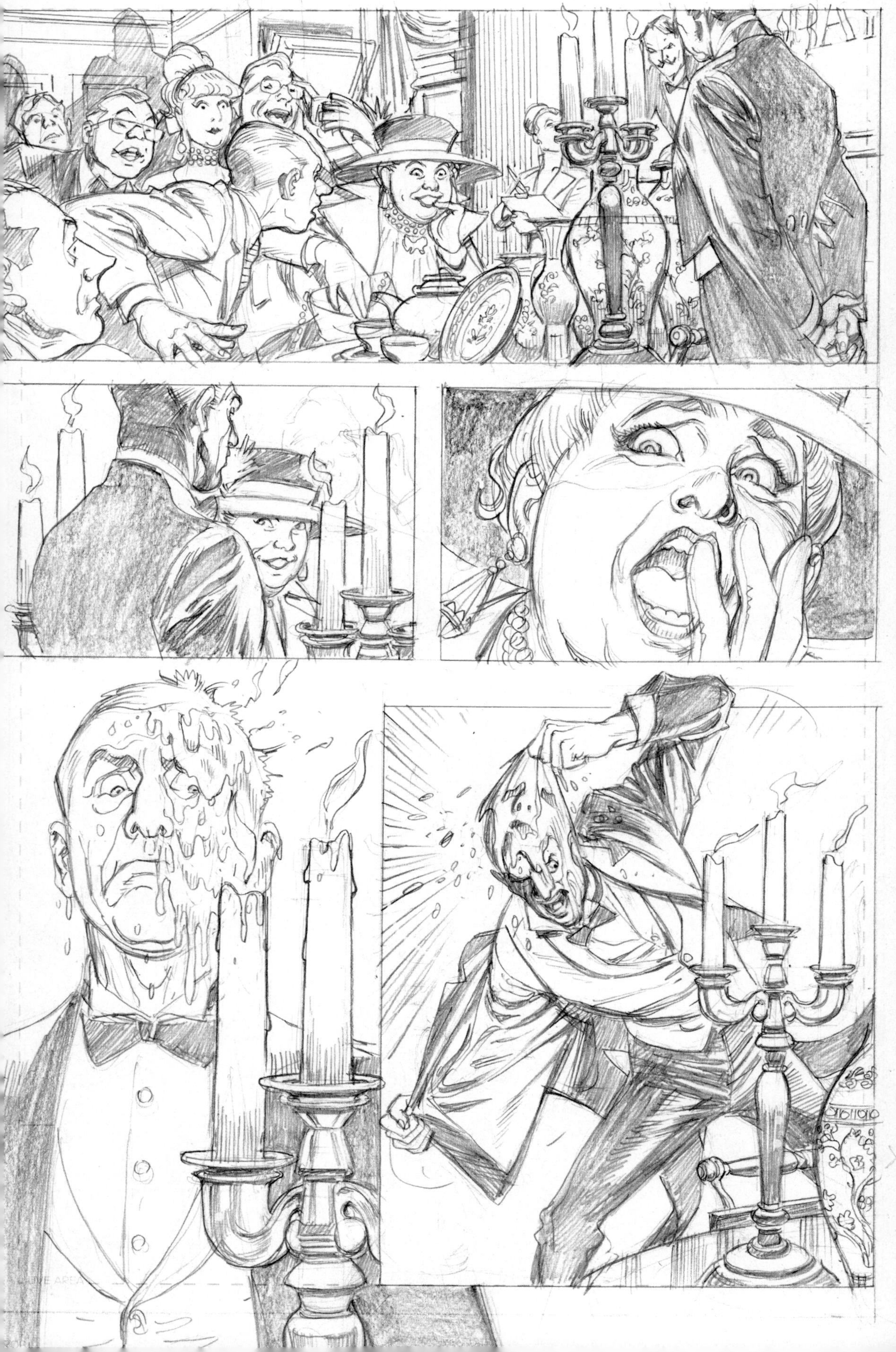

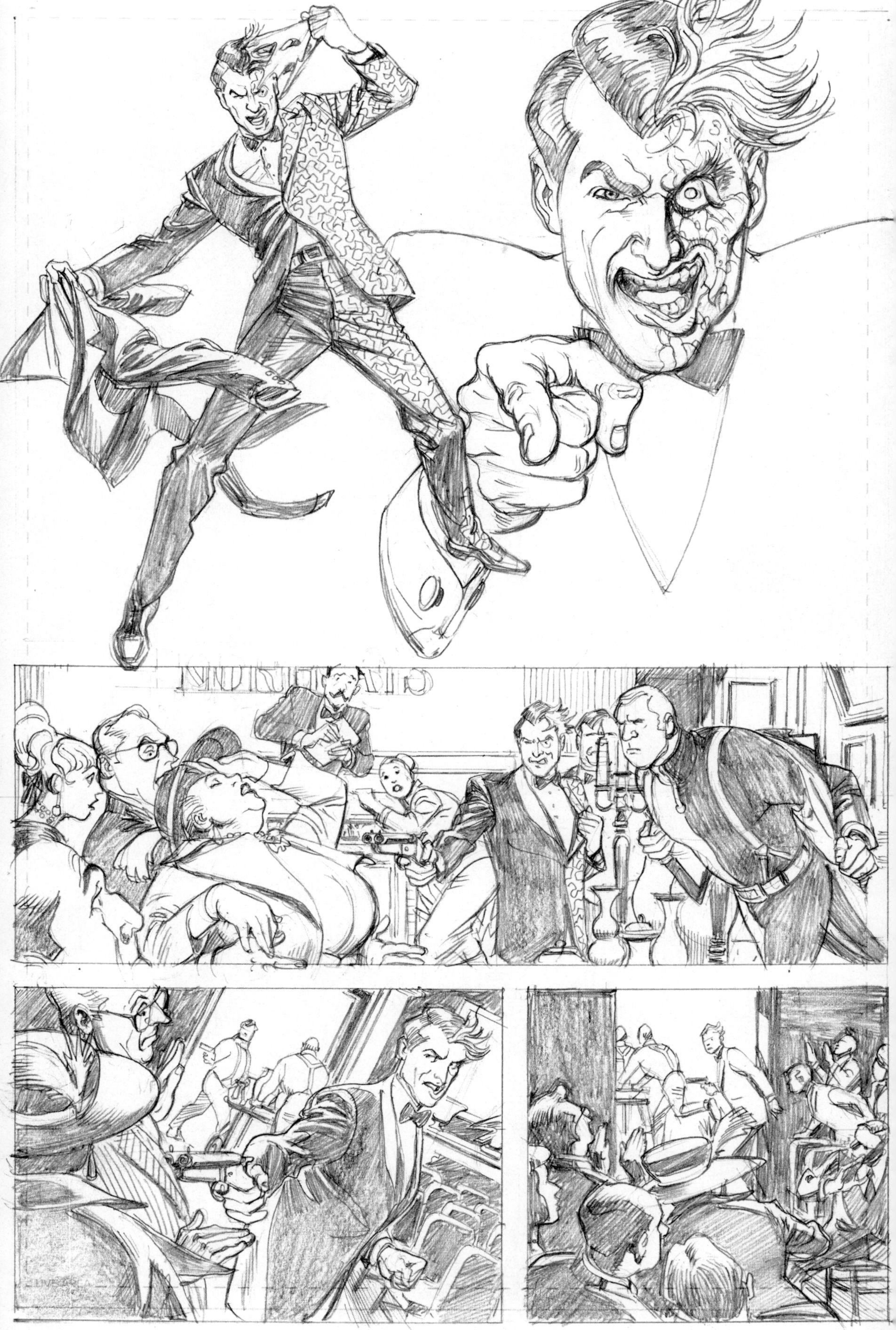

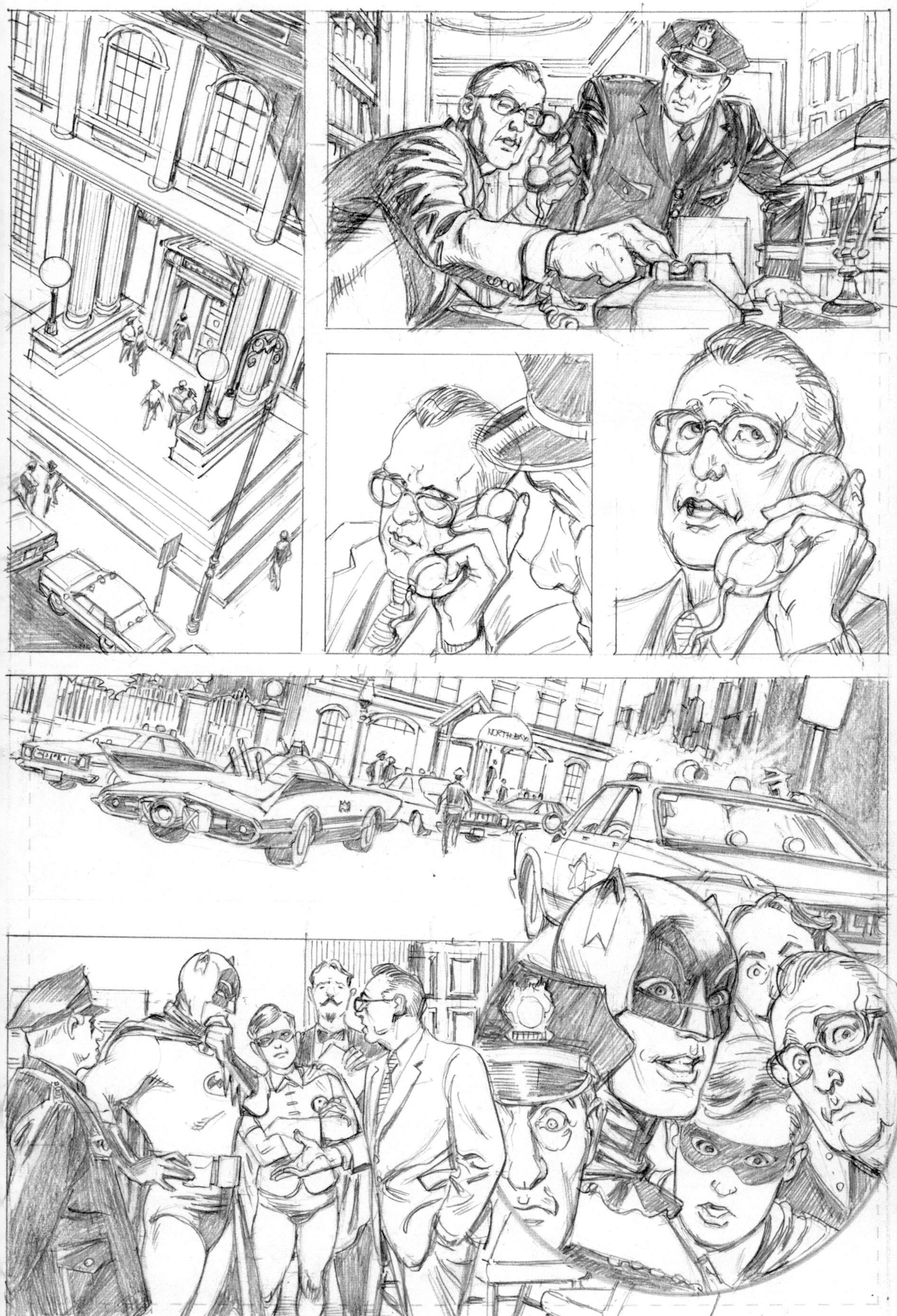

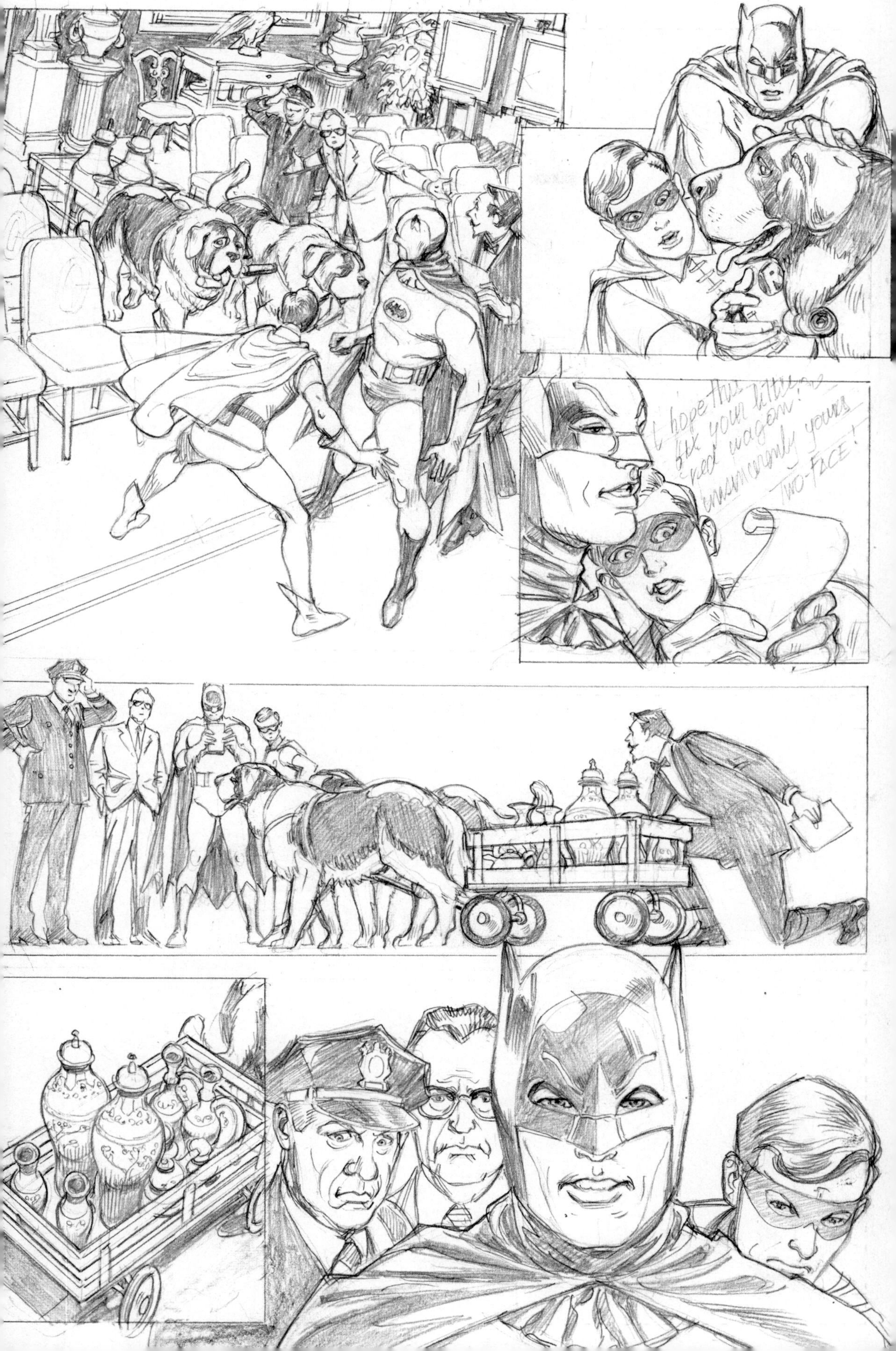

I hope this fits your little red wagon!
Unsincerely yours
TWO-FACE!

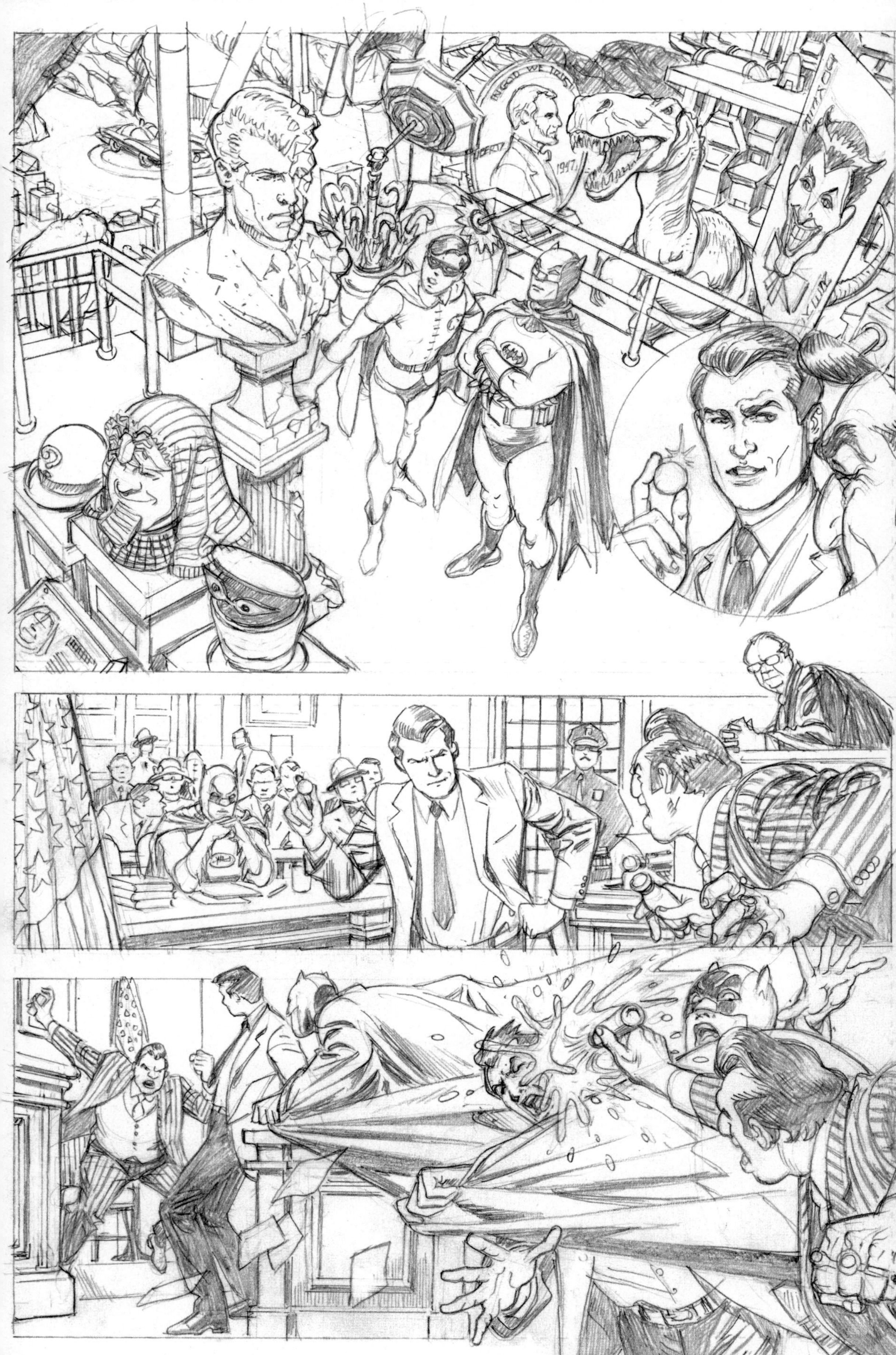

IN GOD WE TRUST
LIBERTY
1947

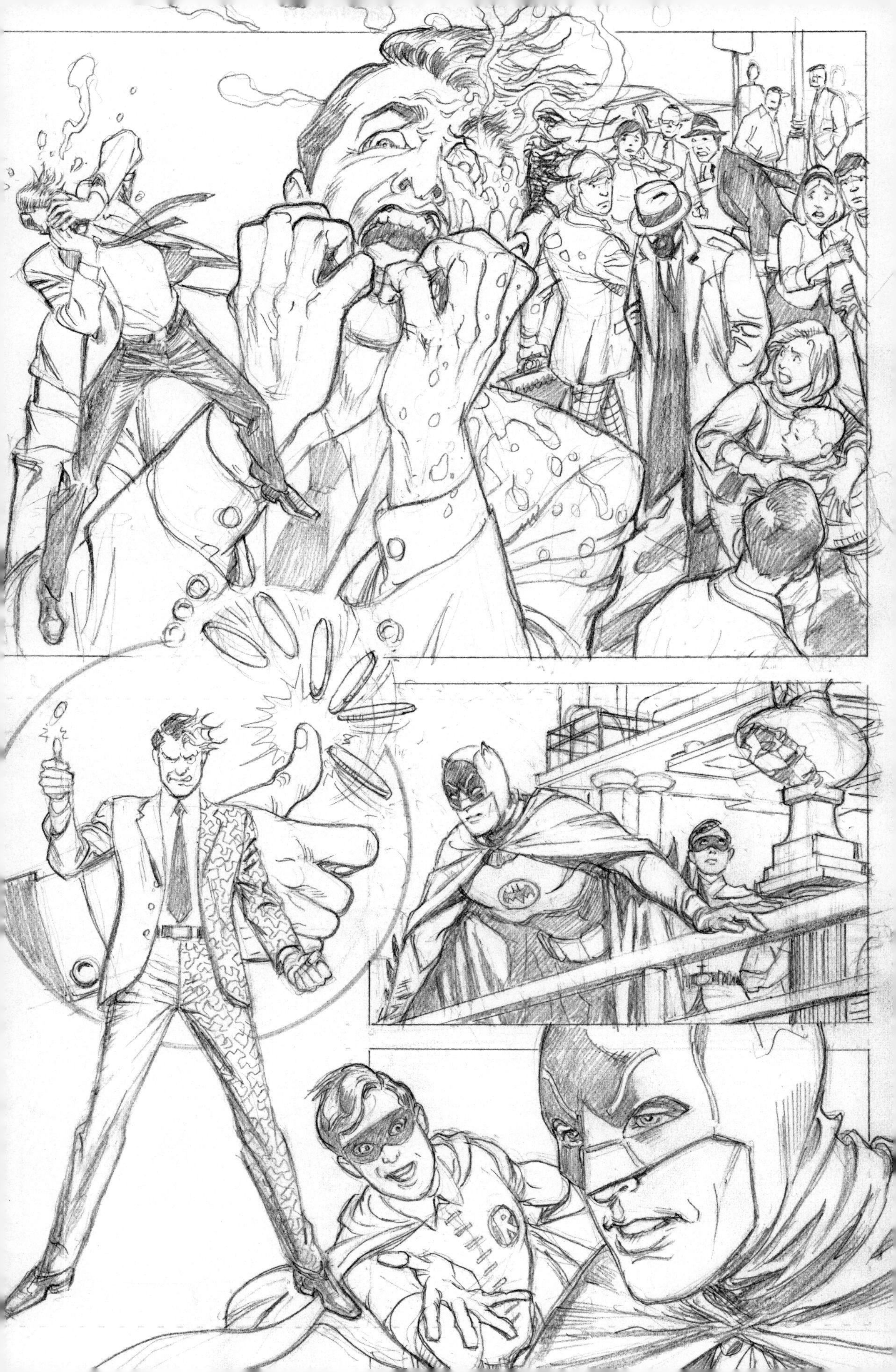

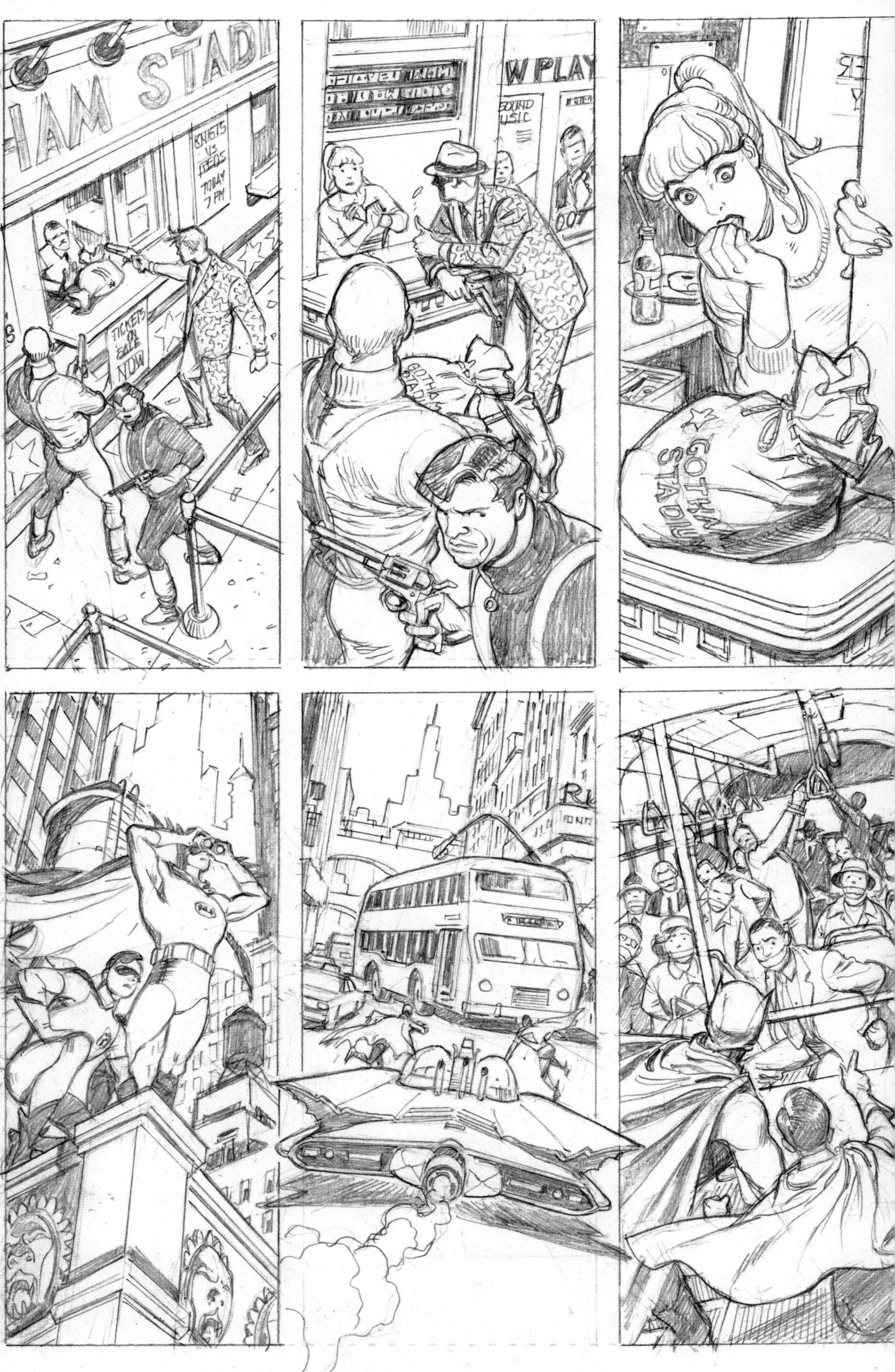

HAM STADI
TODAY 7 PM
TICKETS ON SALE NOW
W PLAY
GOTHAM STADIU

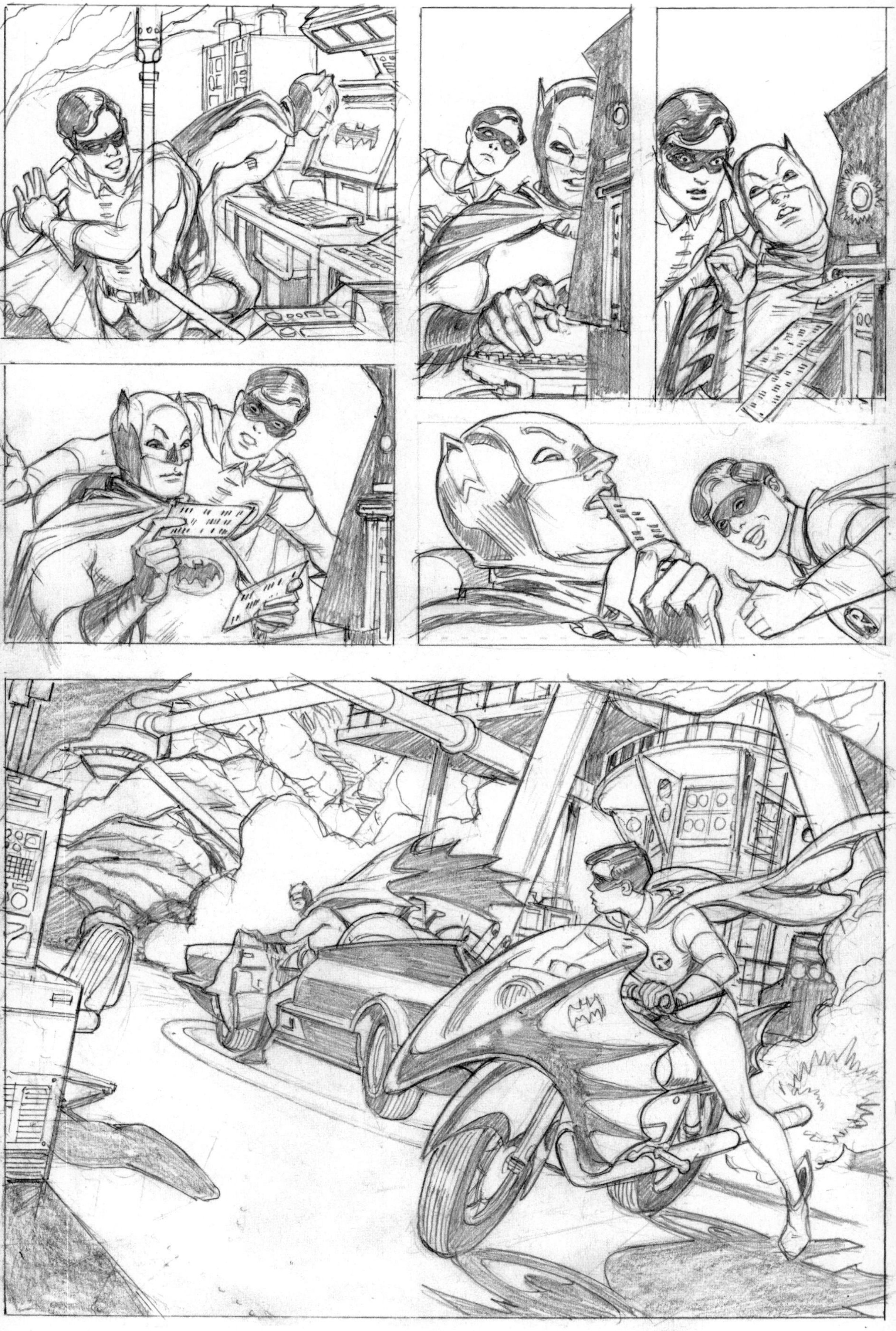

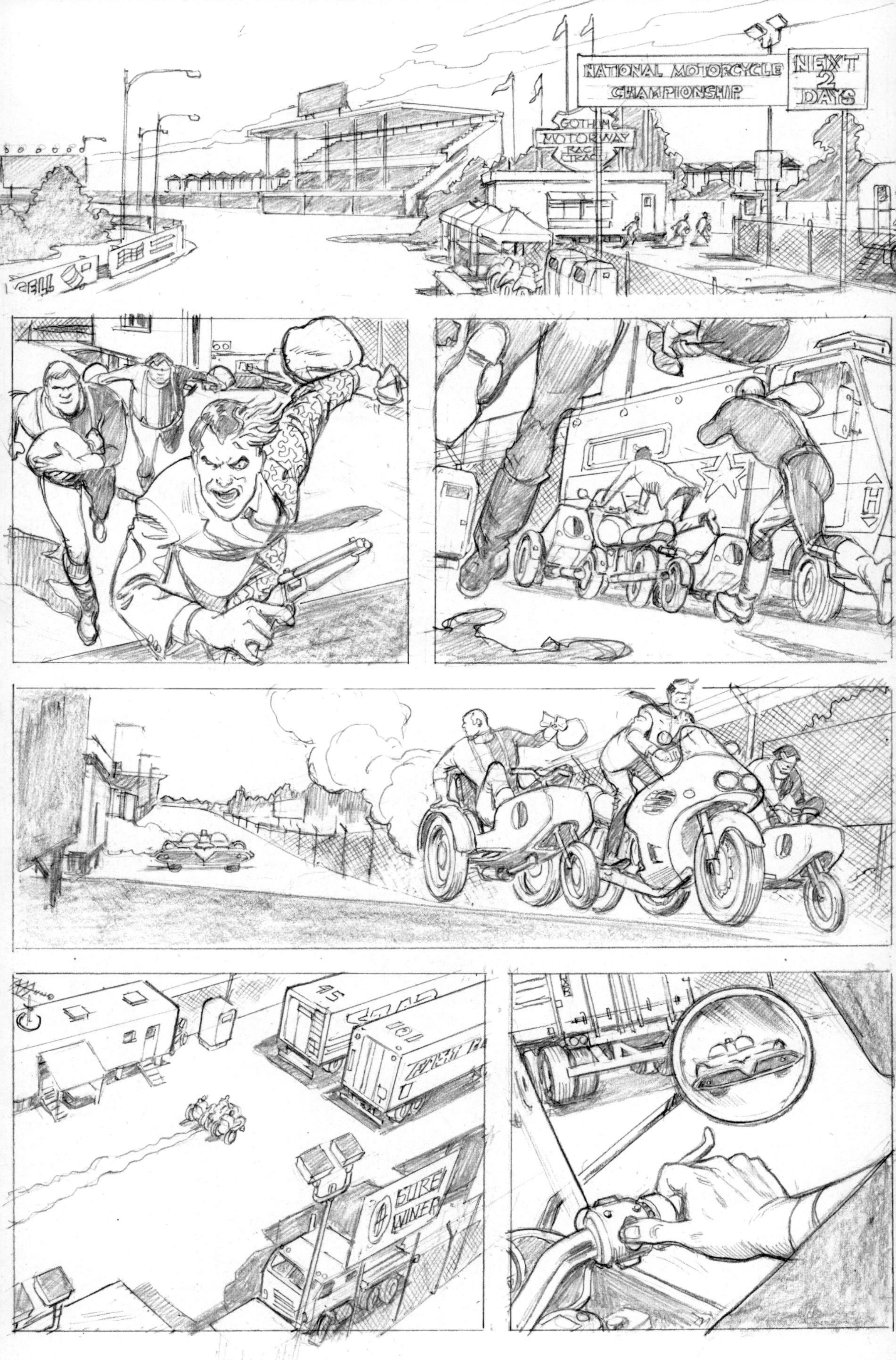
NATIONAL MOTORCYCLE CHAMPIONSHIP
NEXT 2 DAYS
GOTHAM MOTORWAY

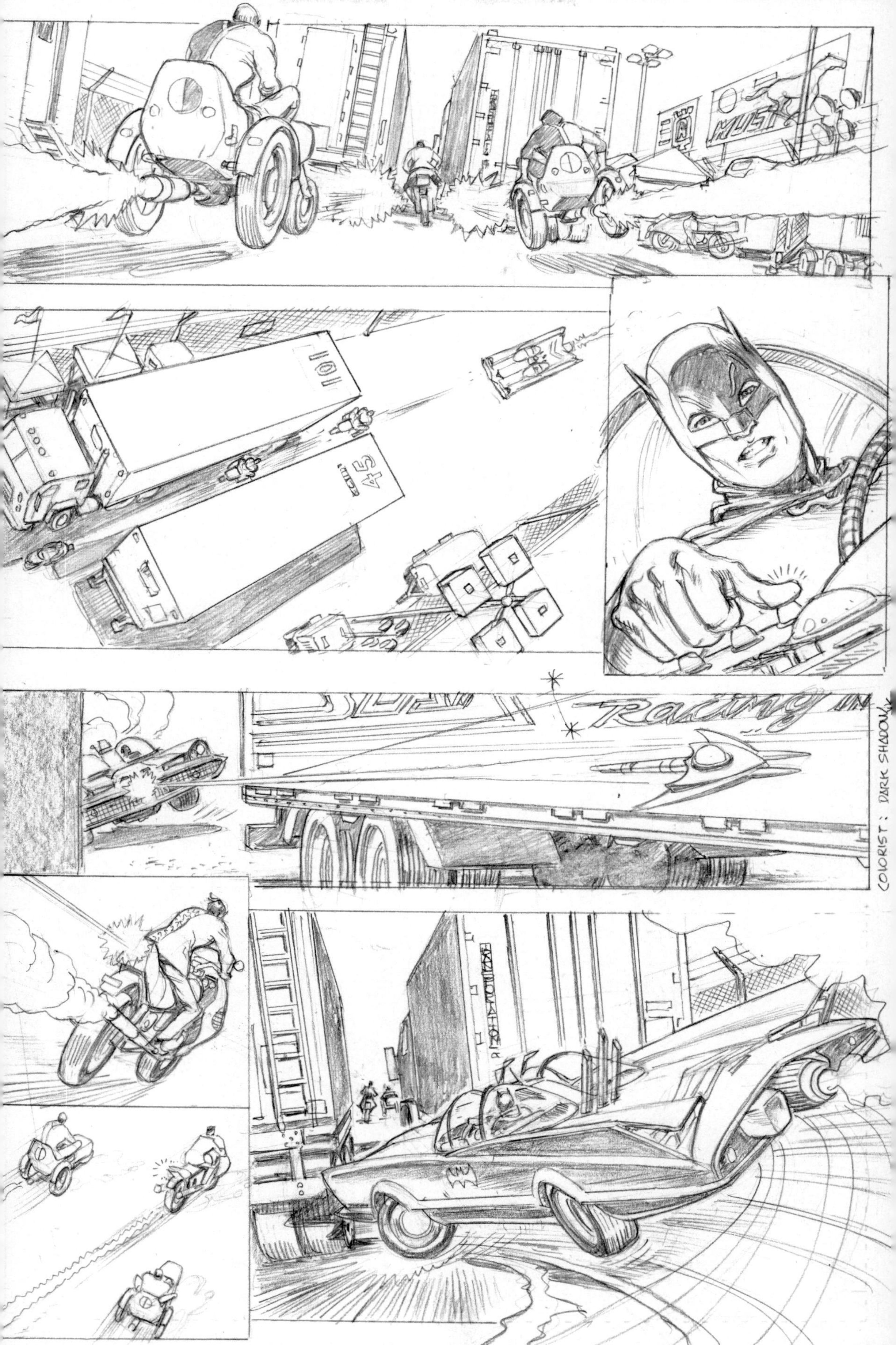
MUST
101
45
Racing
COLORIST : DARK SHADOW

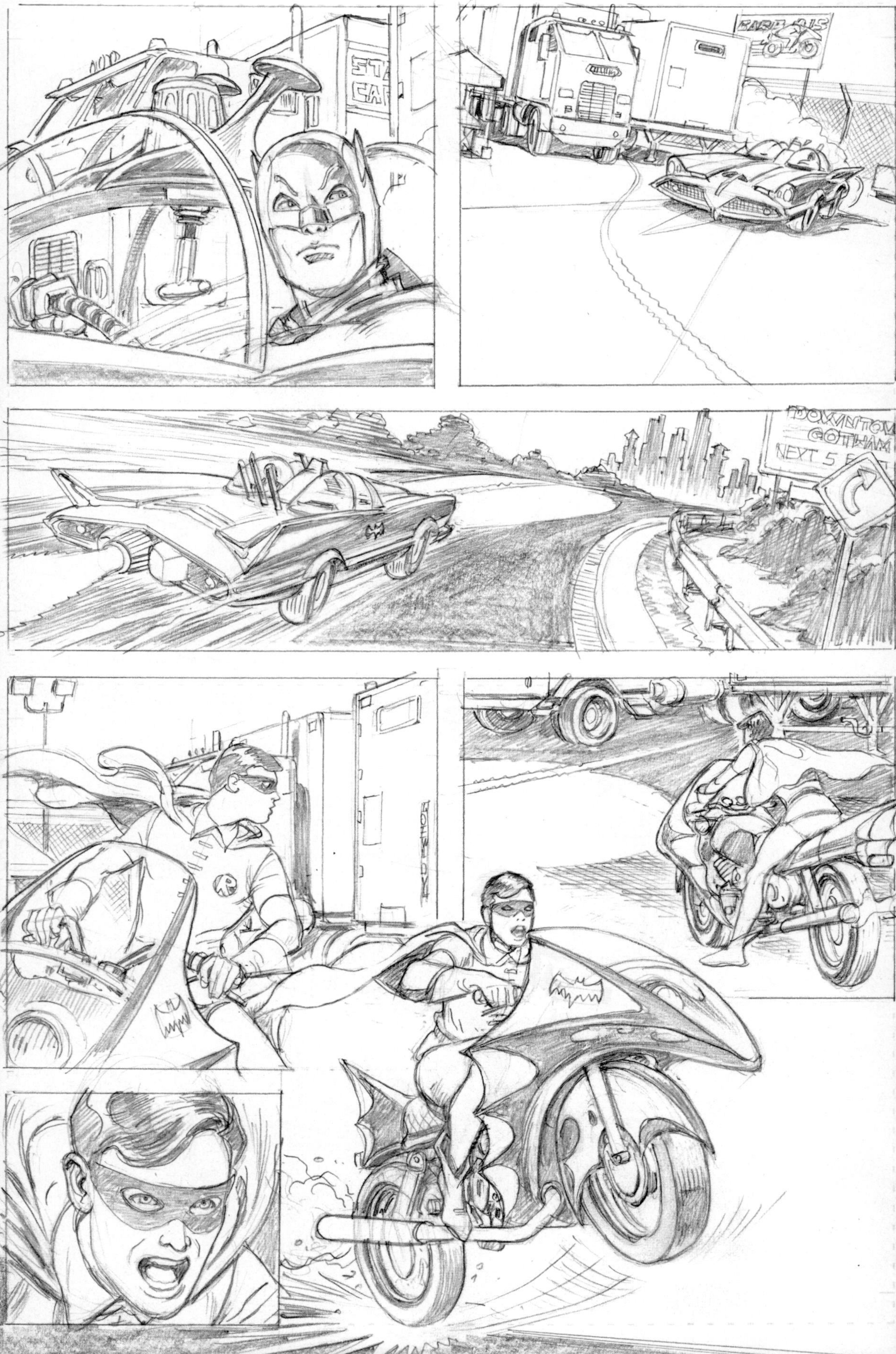
GOTHAM
NEXT 5

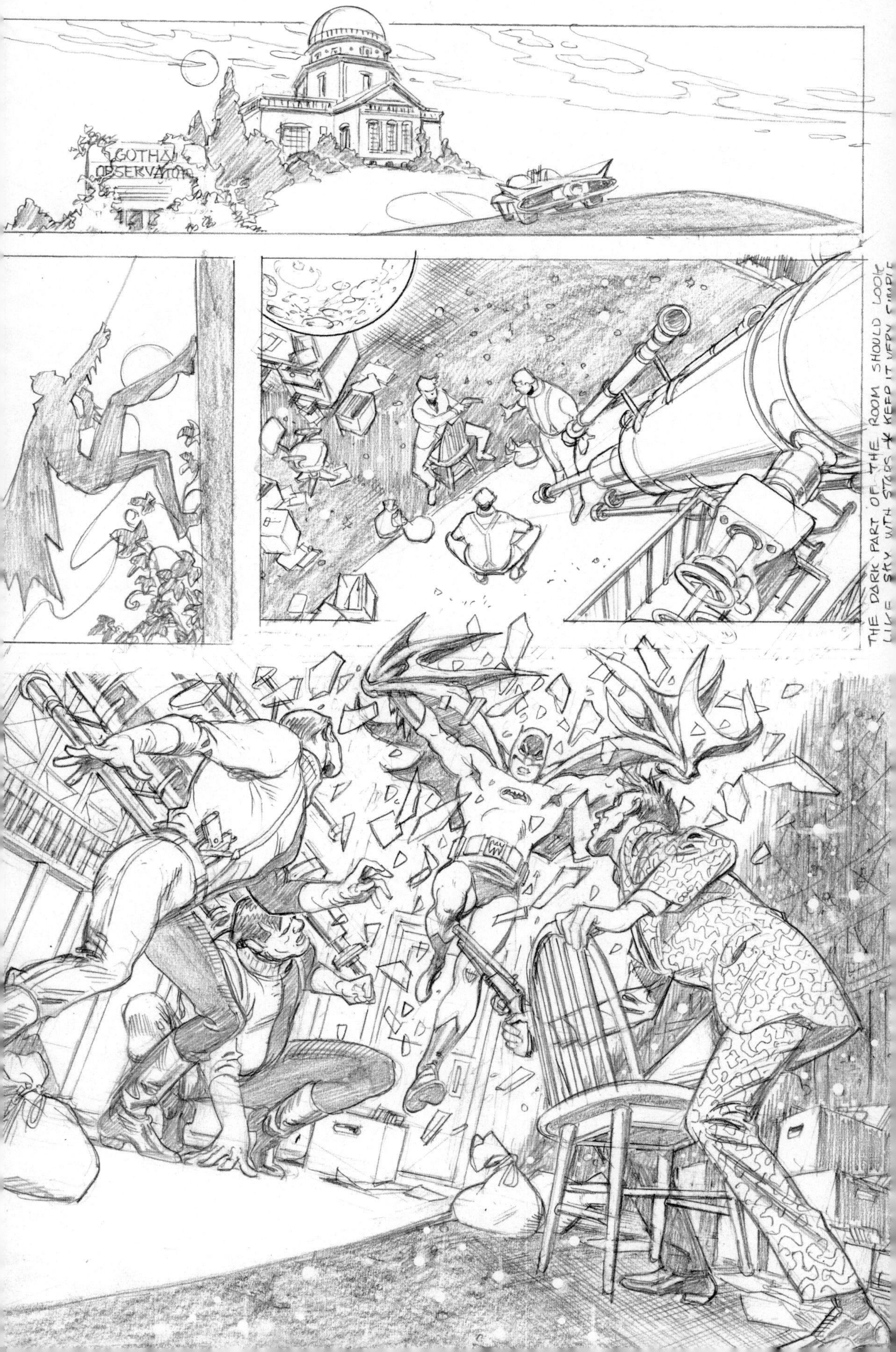
GOTHA
OBSERVATO
THE DARK PART OF THE ROOM SHOULD LOOK
LIKE SKY WITH STARS * KEEP IT VERY SIMPLE

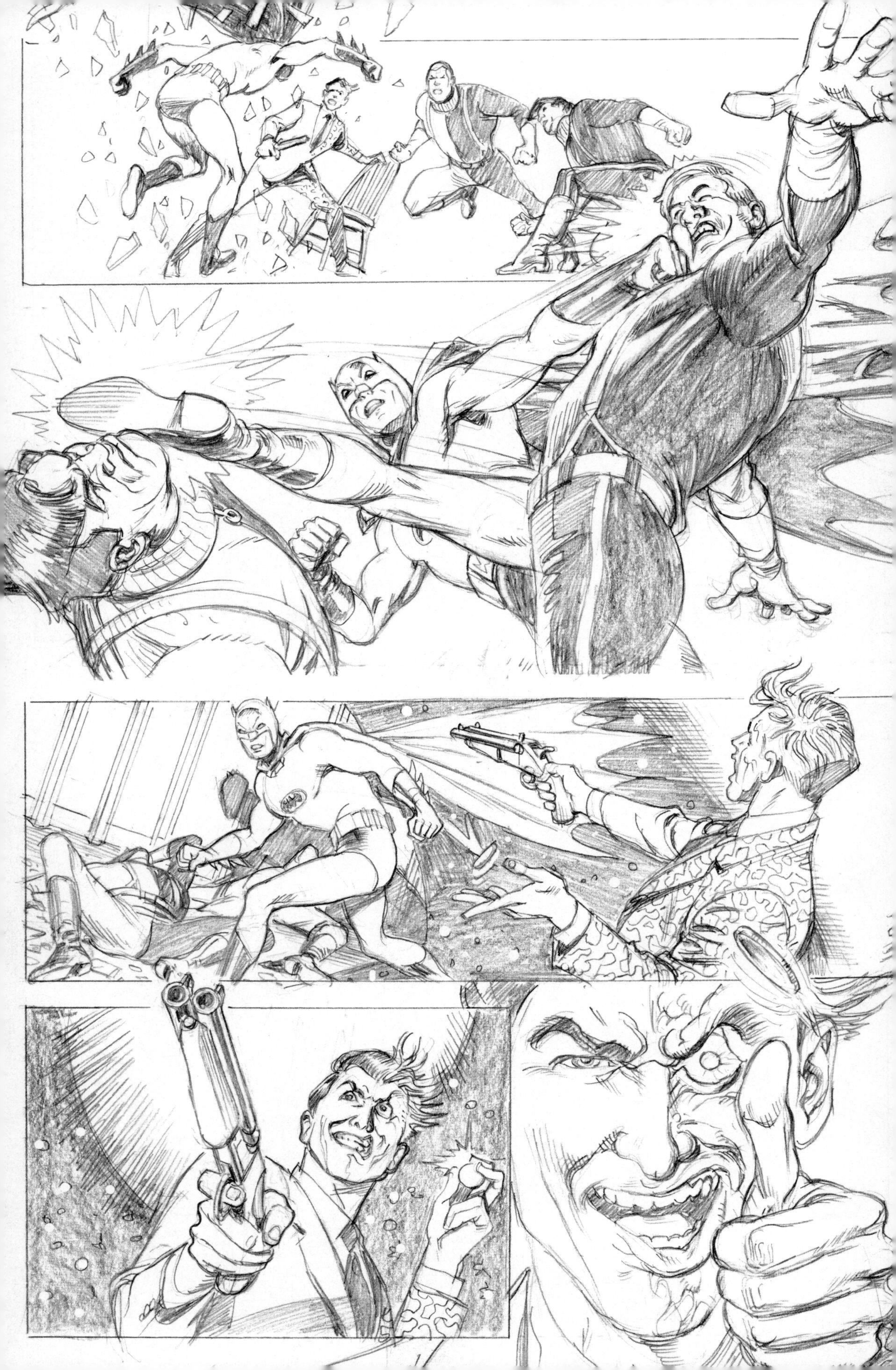

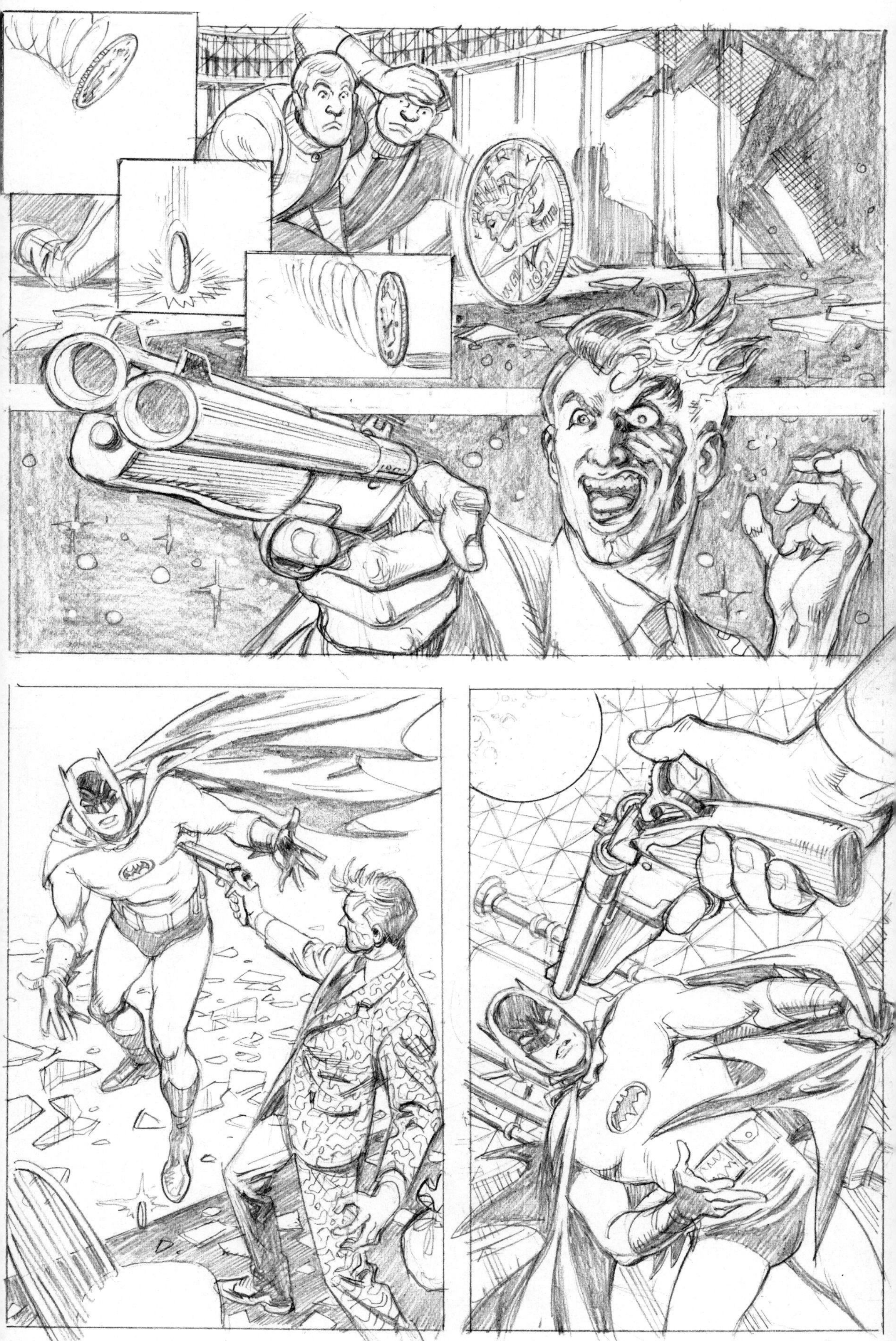

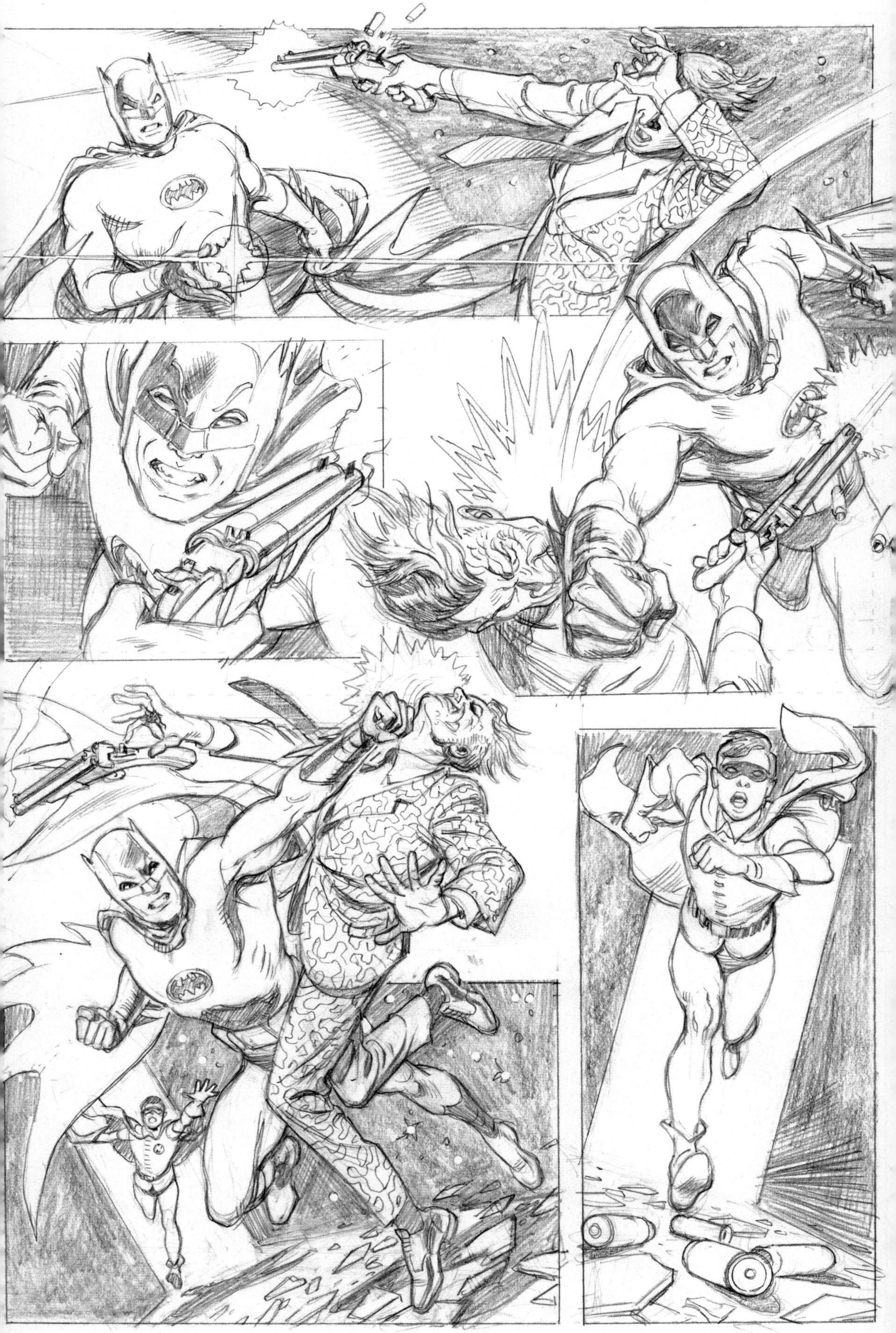

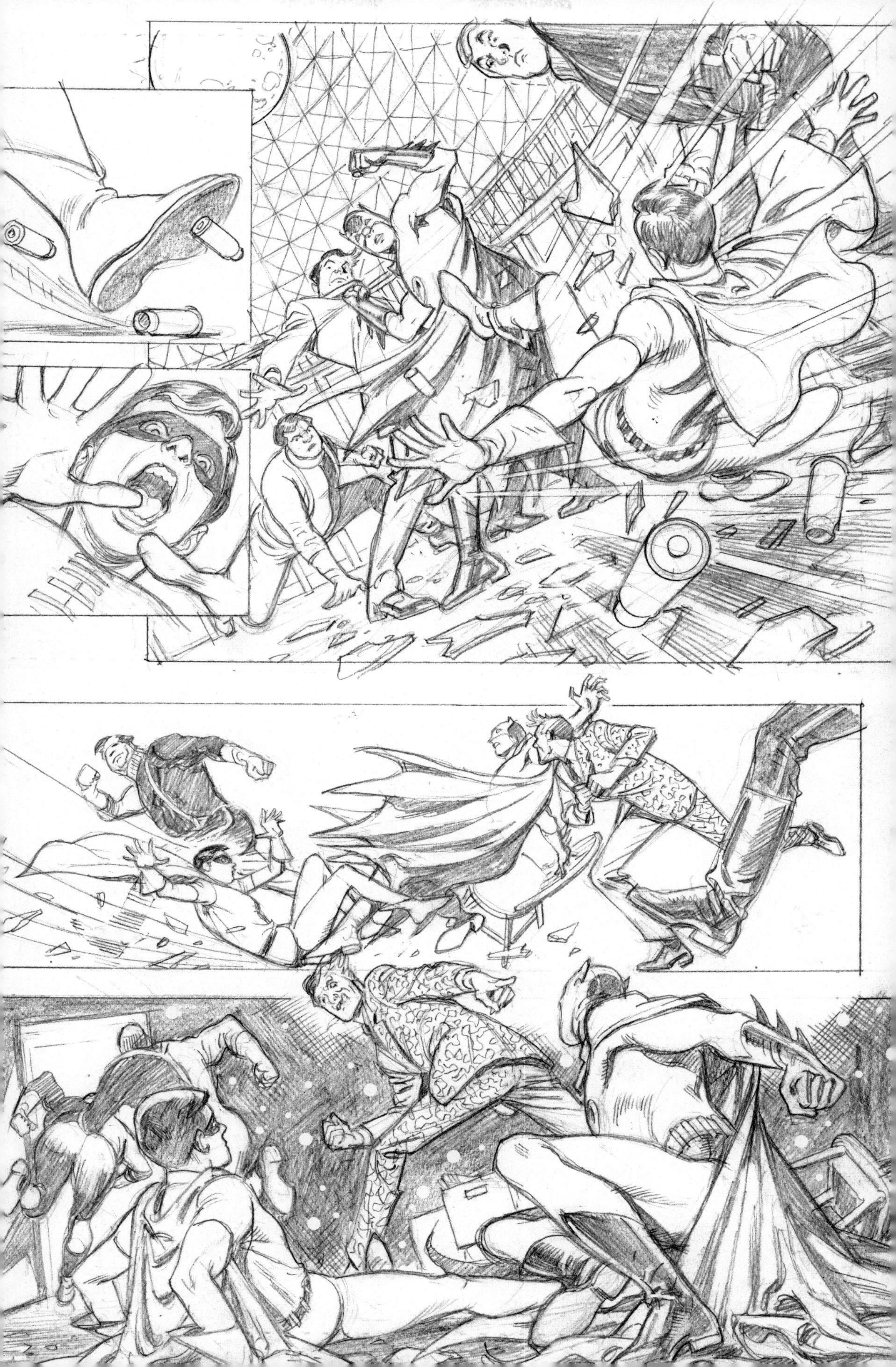

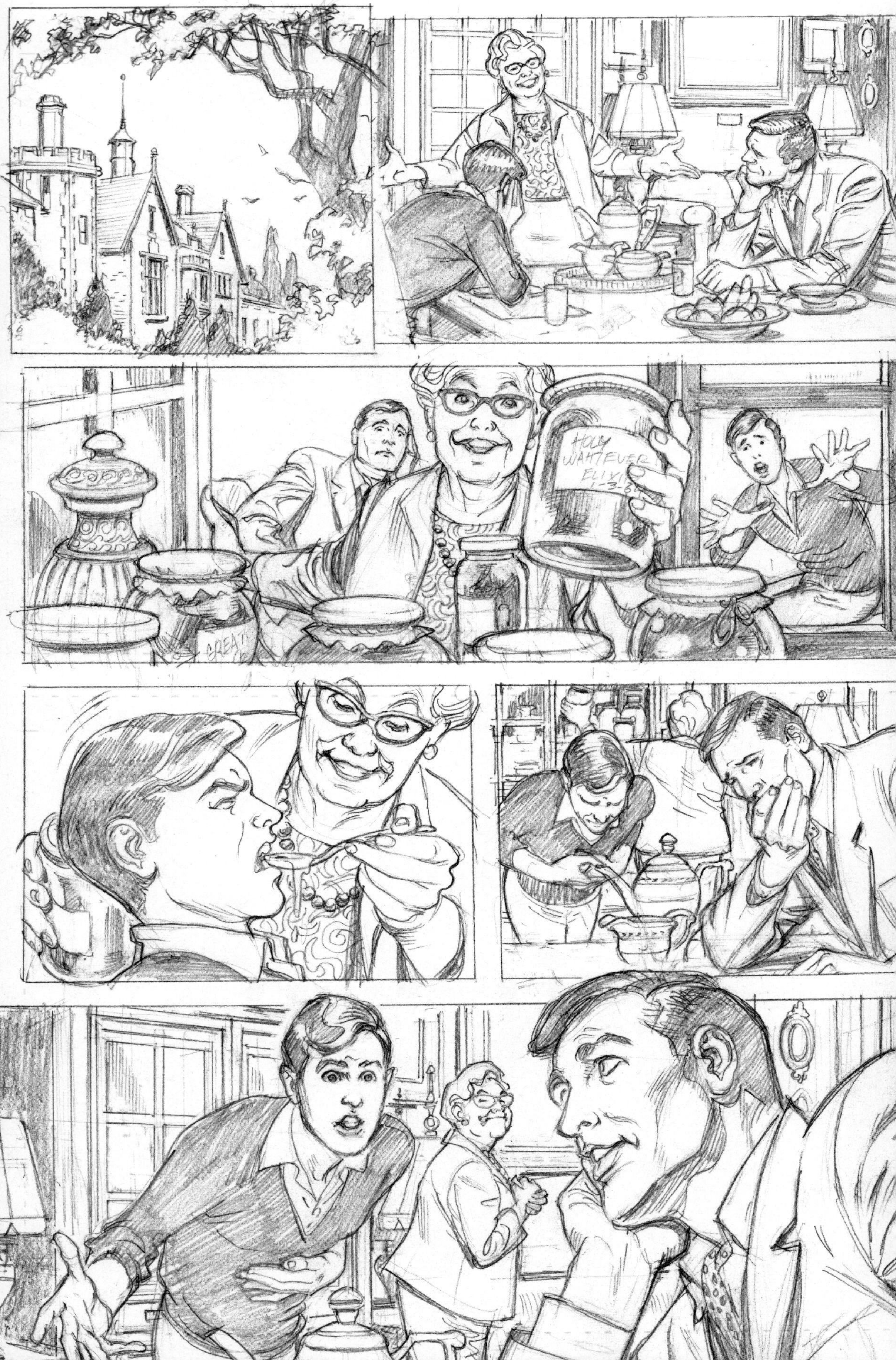
HOLY
WAHTEVER

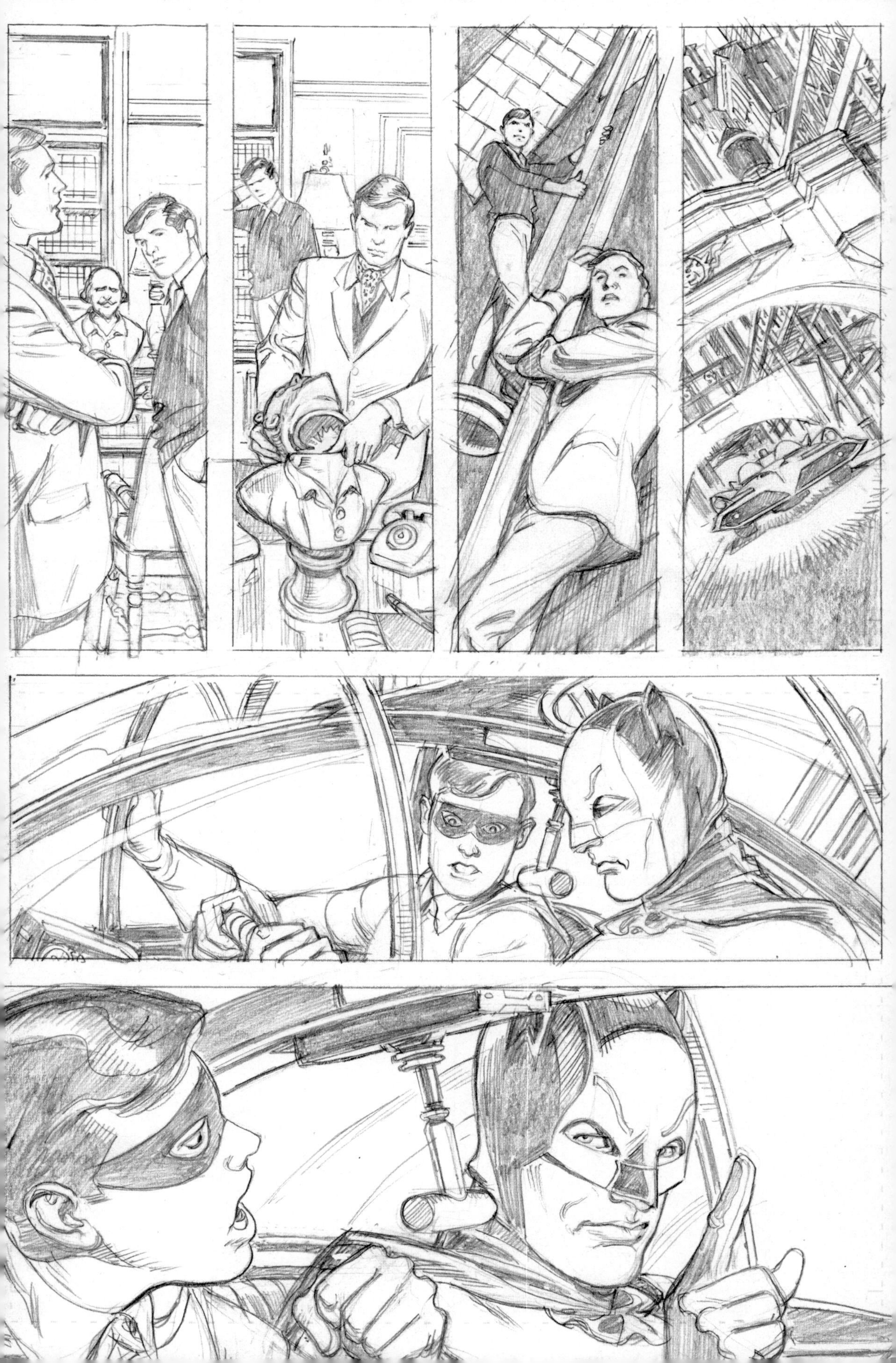

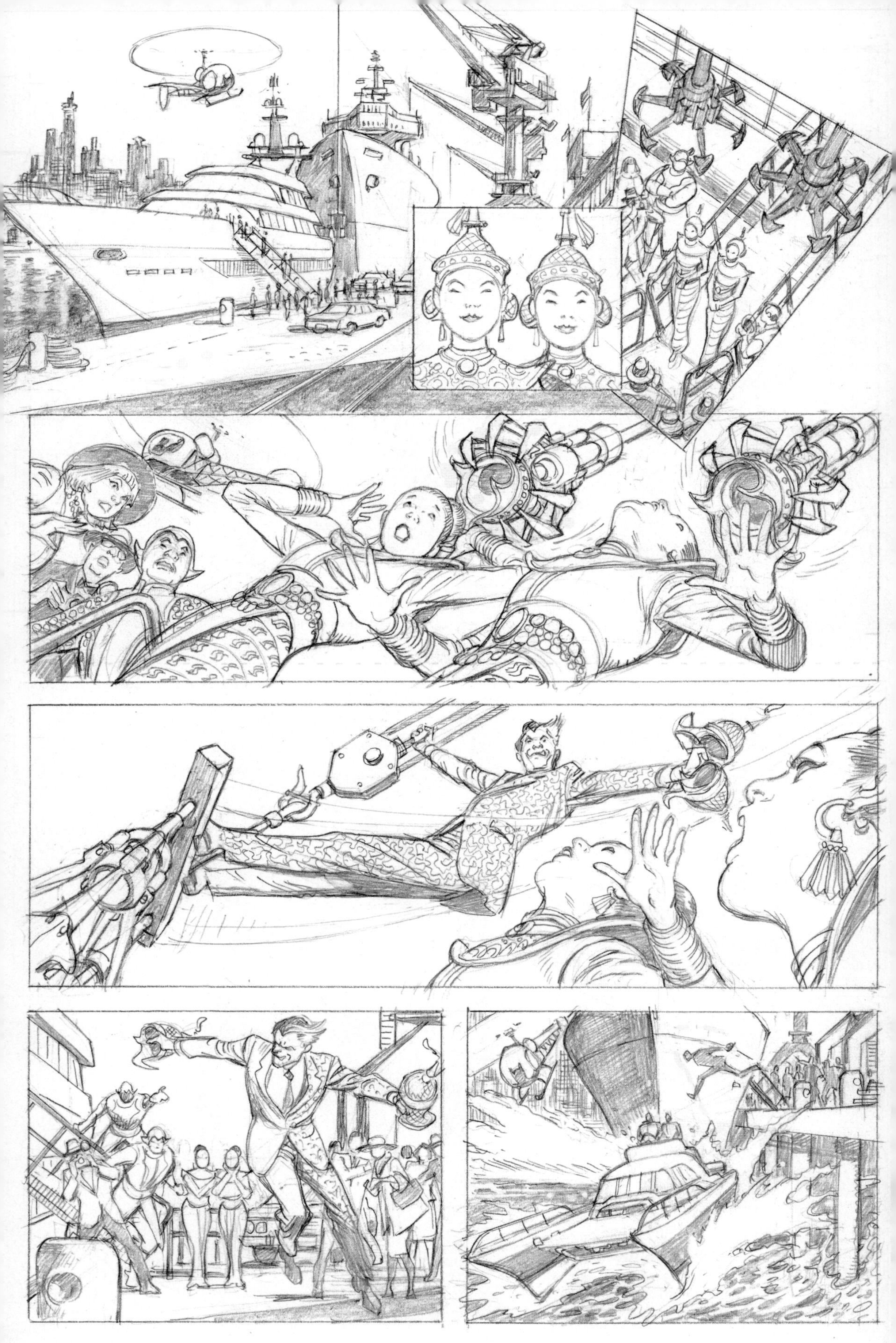

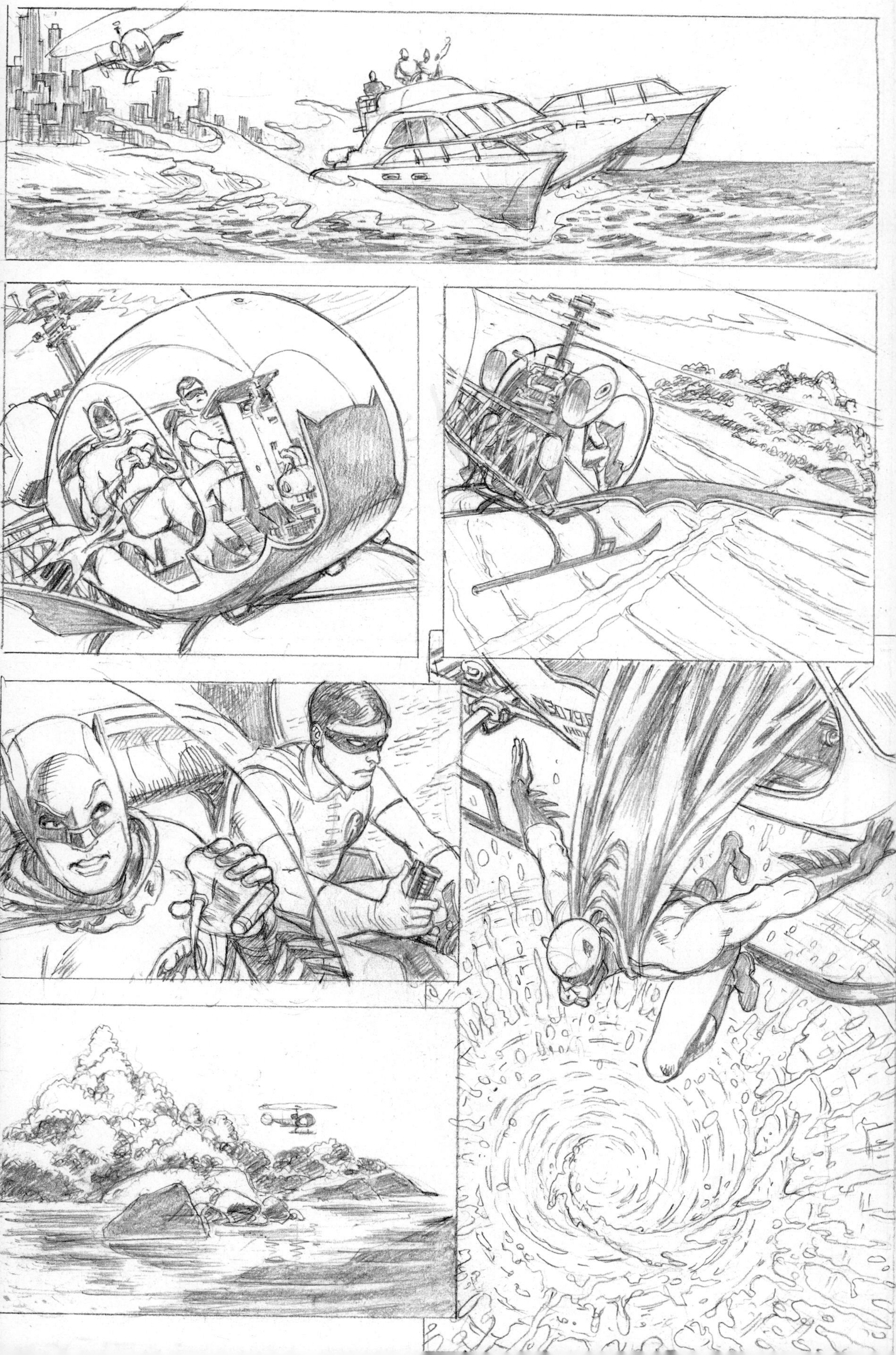

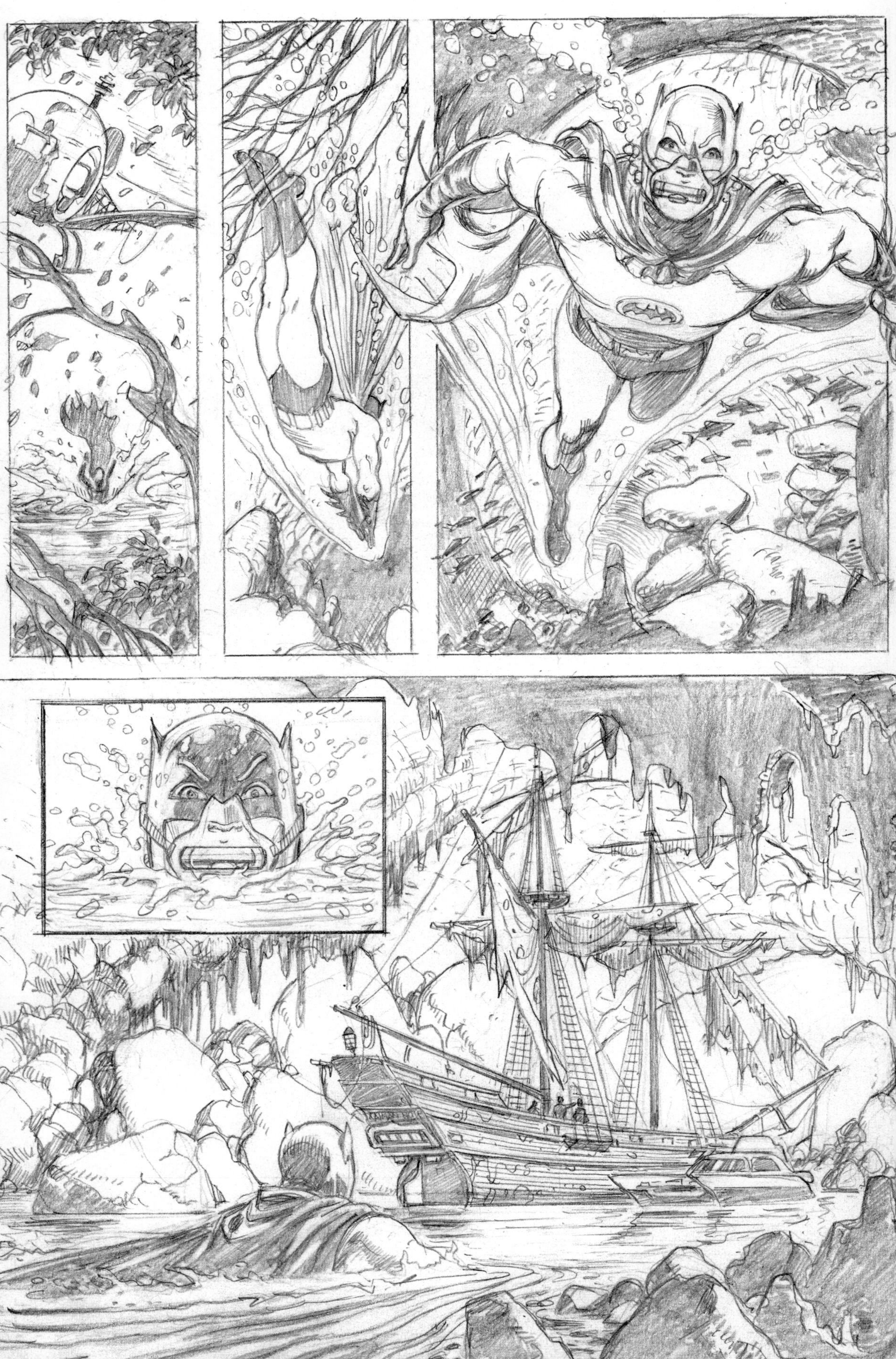

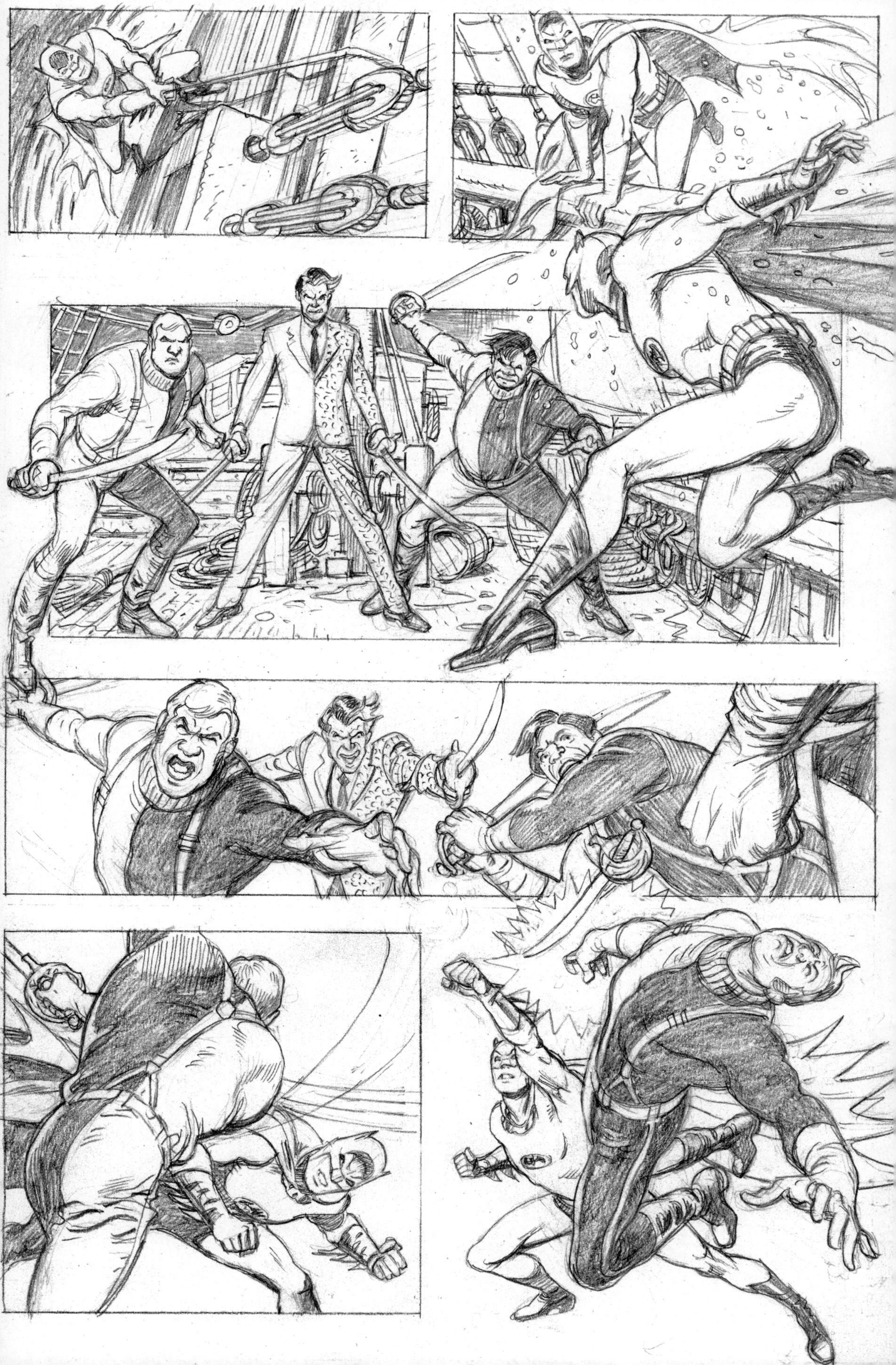

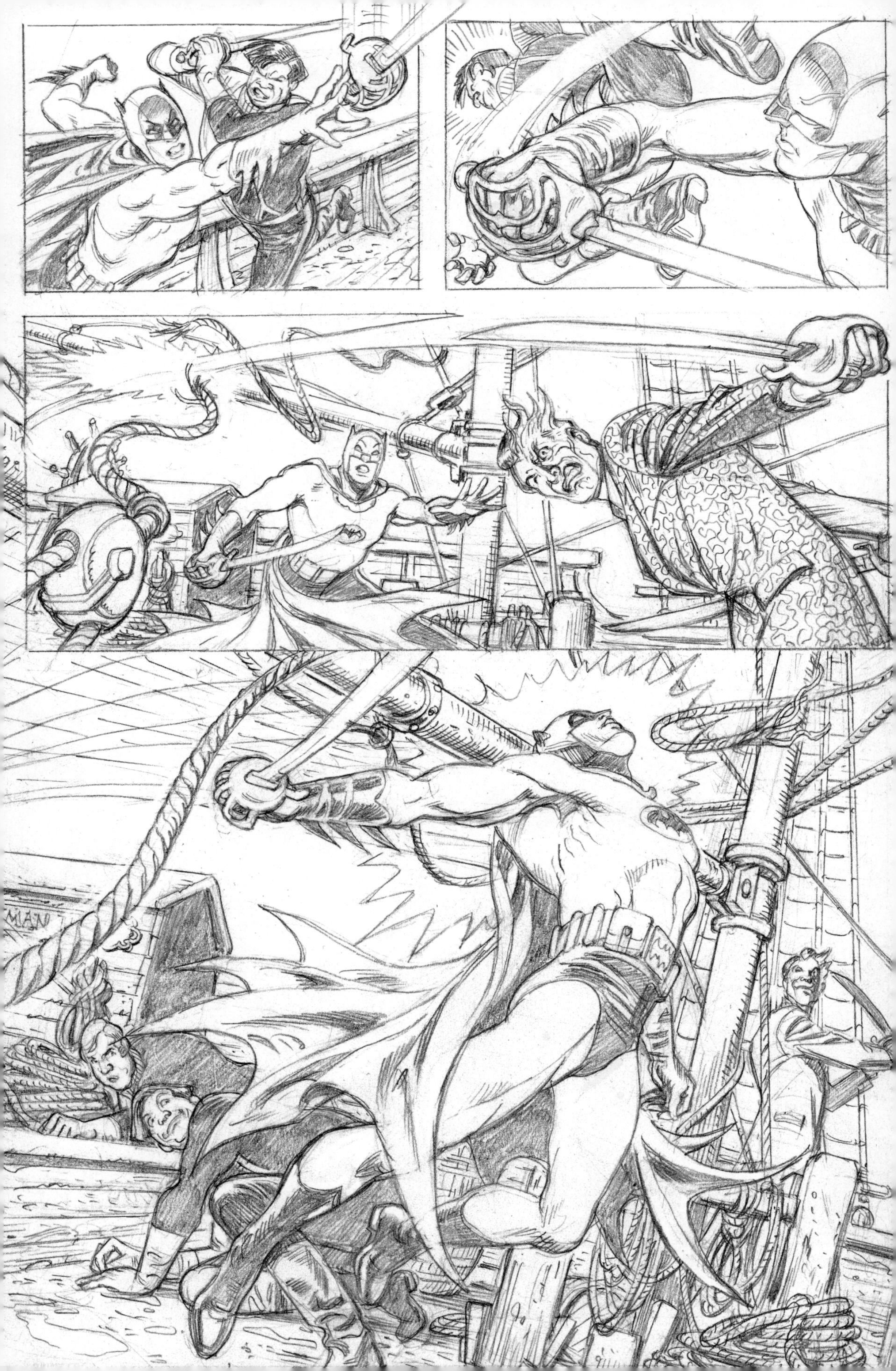

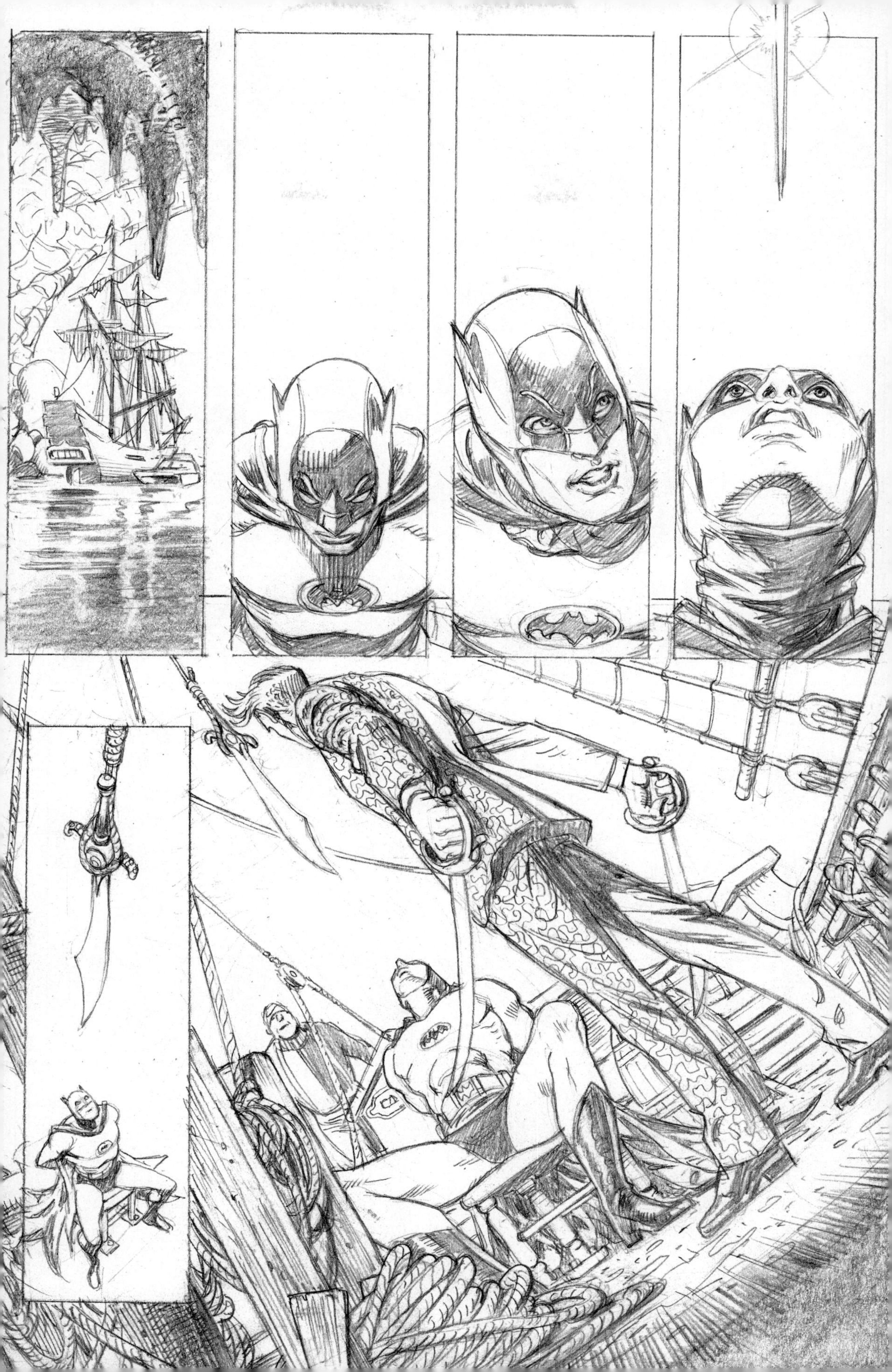

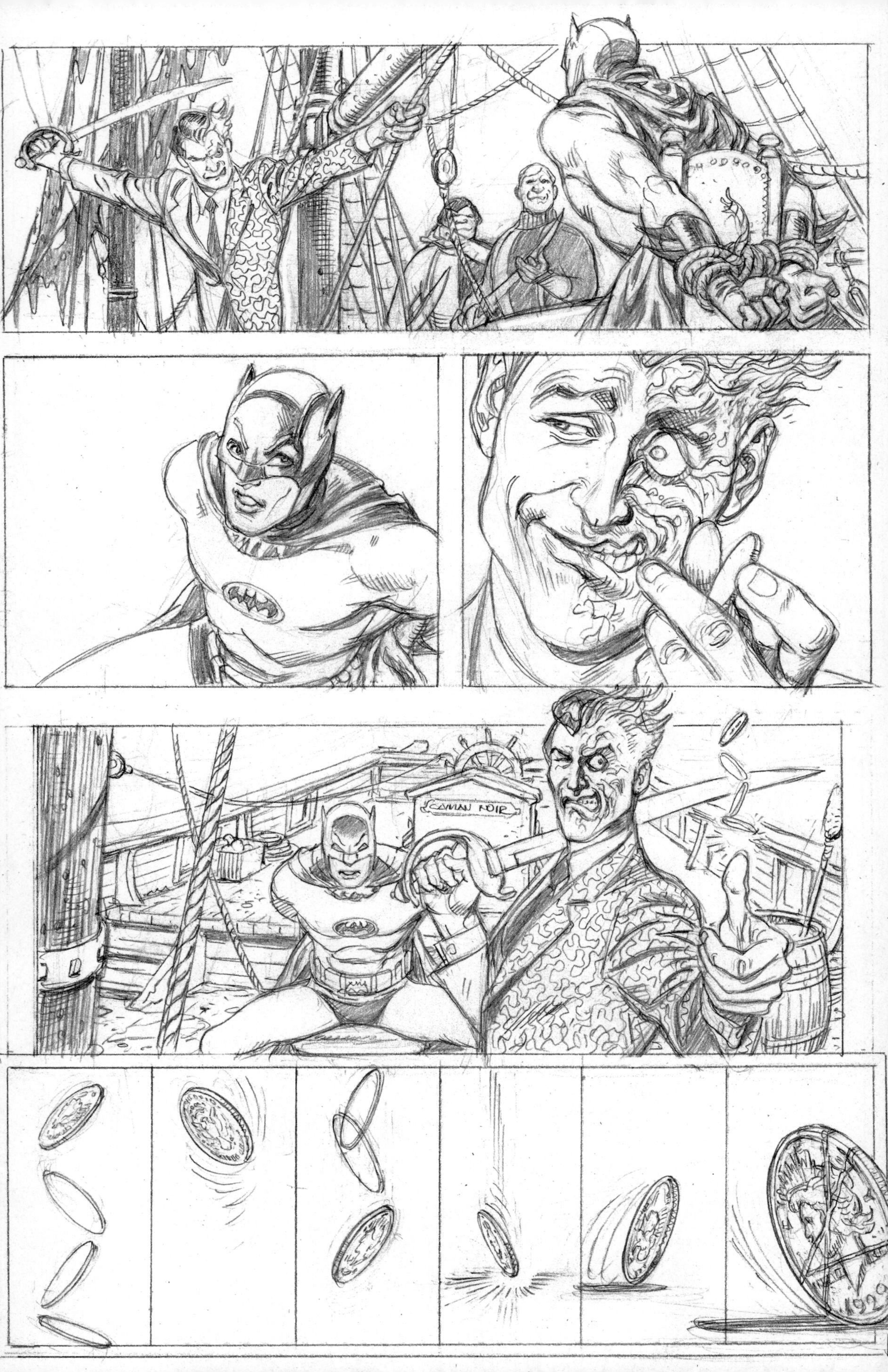
CAYMAN NOIR
1929

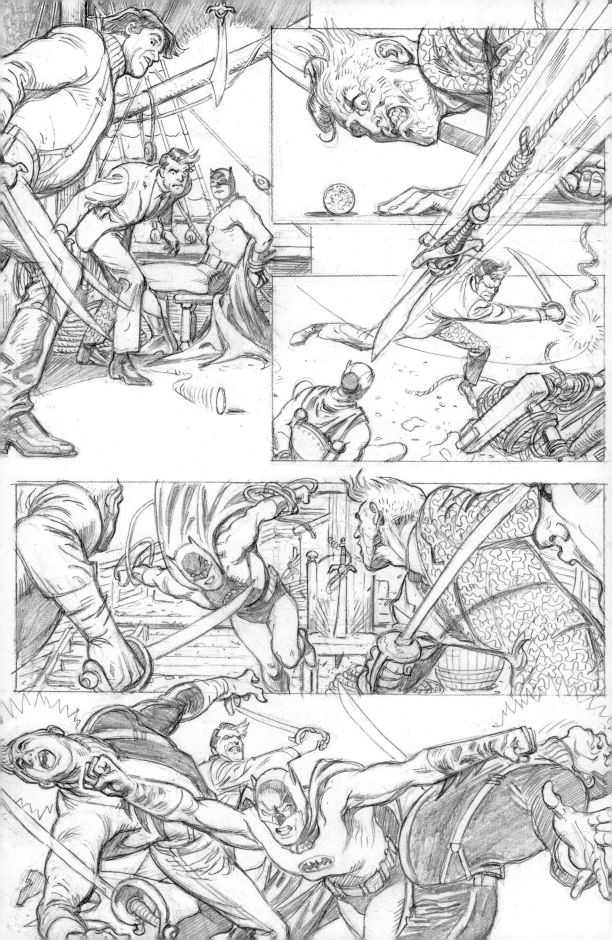

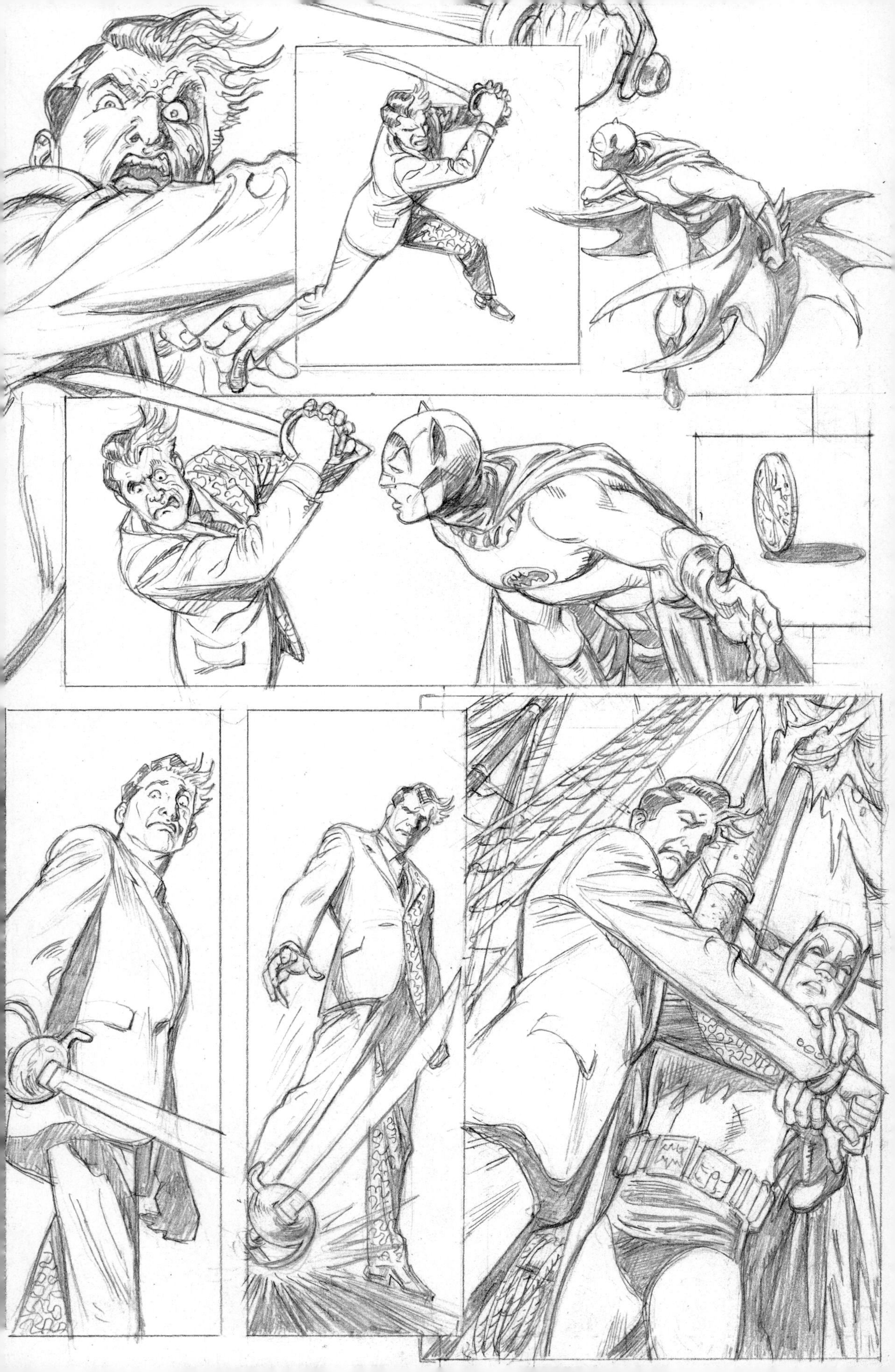

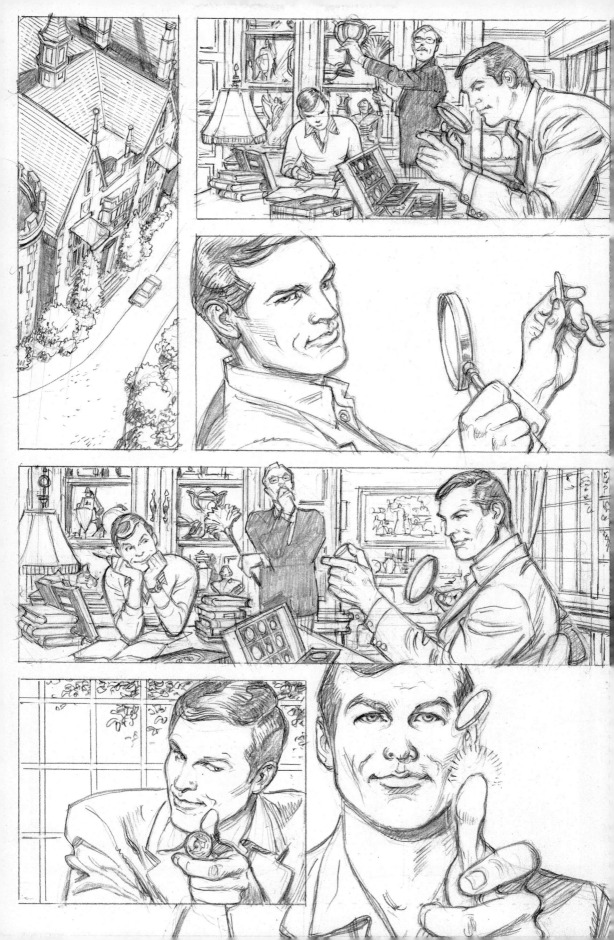

"Two-Face Sketchbook" by José Luis García-López.

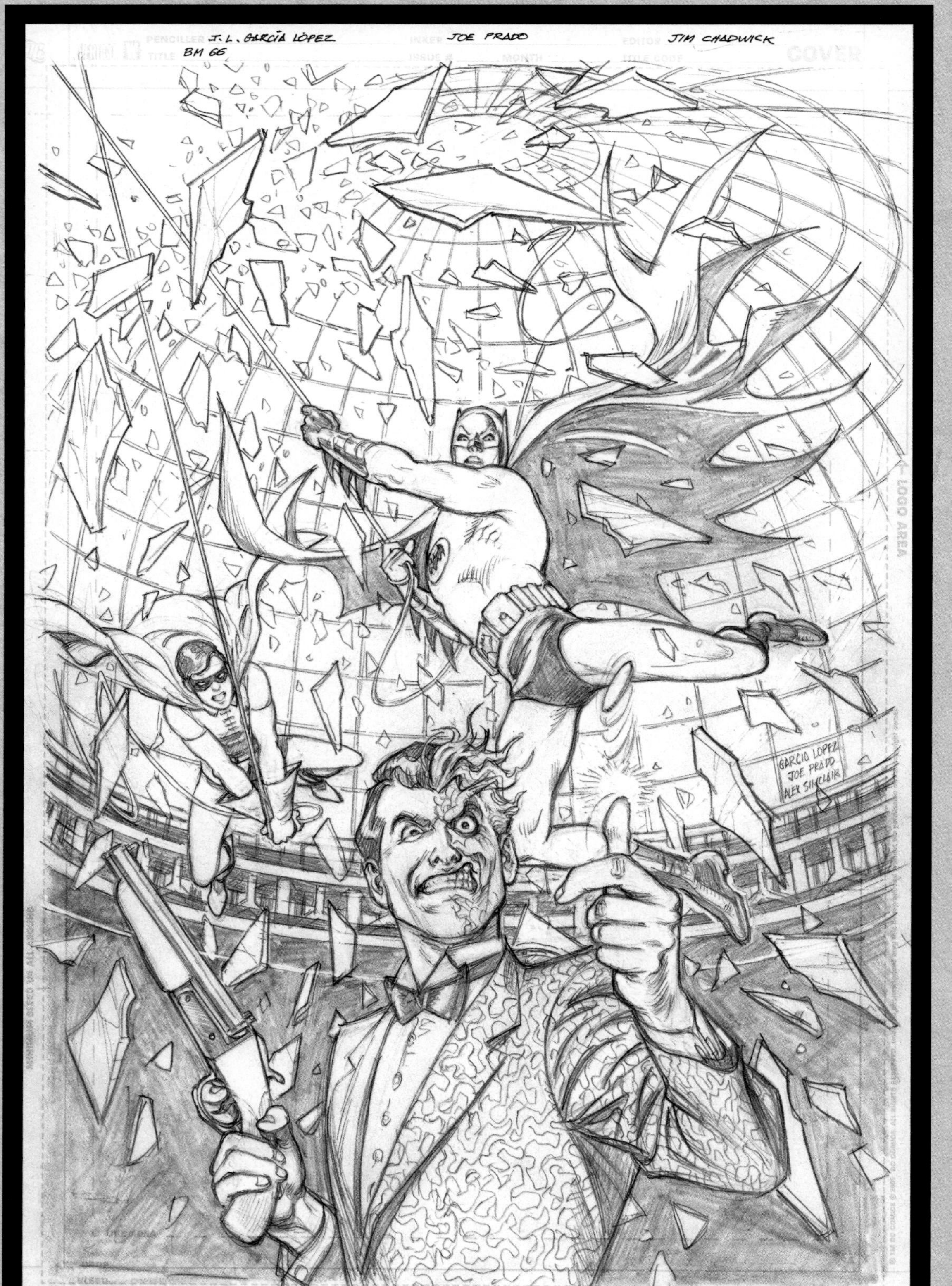
PENCILLER J. L. GARCÍA LÓPEZ
TITLE BM 66
INKER JOE PRADO
ISSUE #
MONTH
EDITOR JIM CHADWICK
TITLE CODE
COVER
LOGO AREA
GARCÍA LÓPEZ
JOE PRADO
ALEX SINCLAIR
PRINTED COVER SIZE: 6 5/8 X 10 3/16

Original pencils for the variant cover.

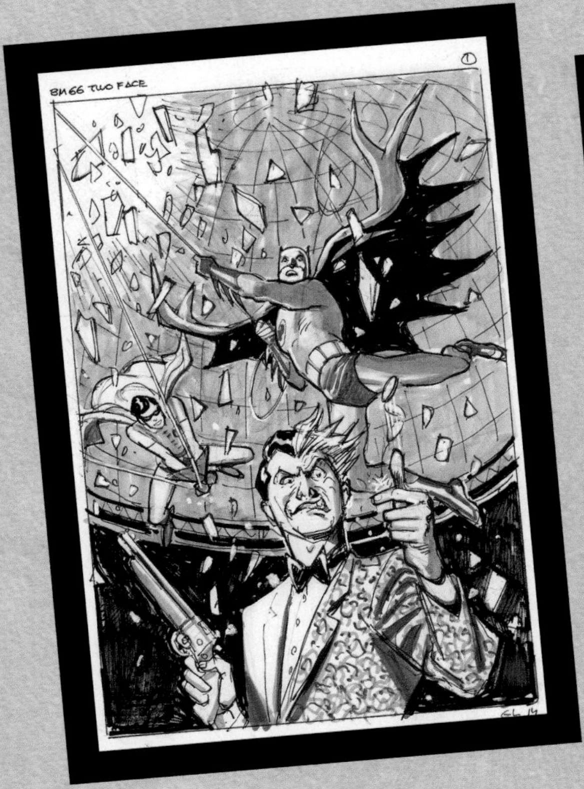
BM66 TWO FACE
1

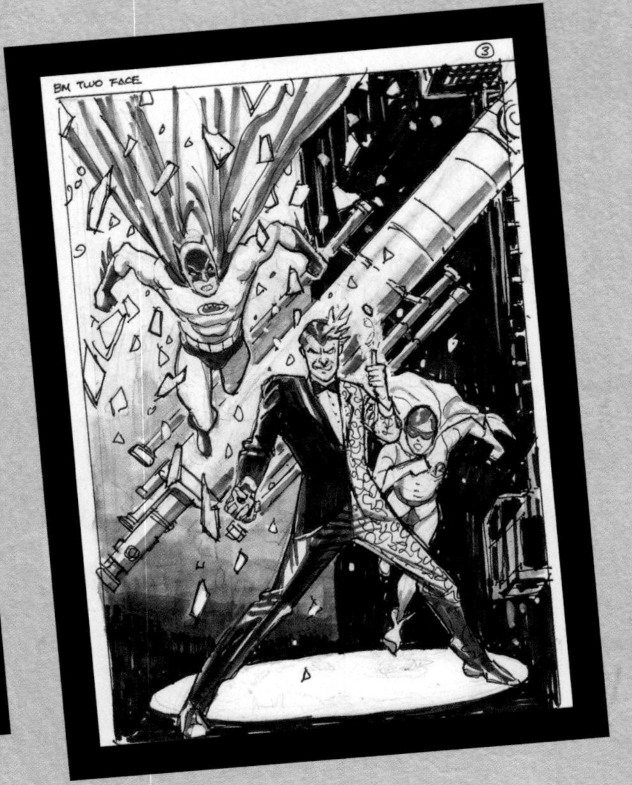
BM TWO FACE
3

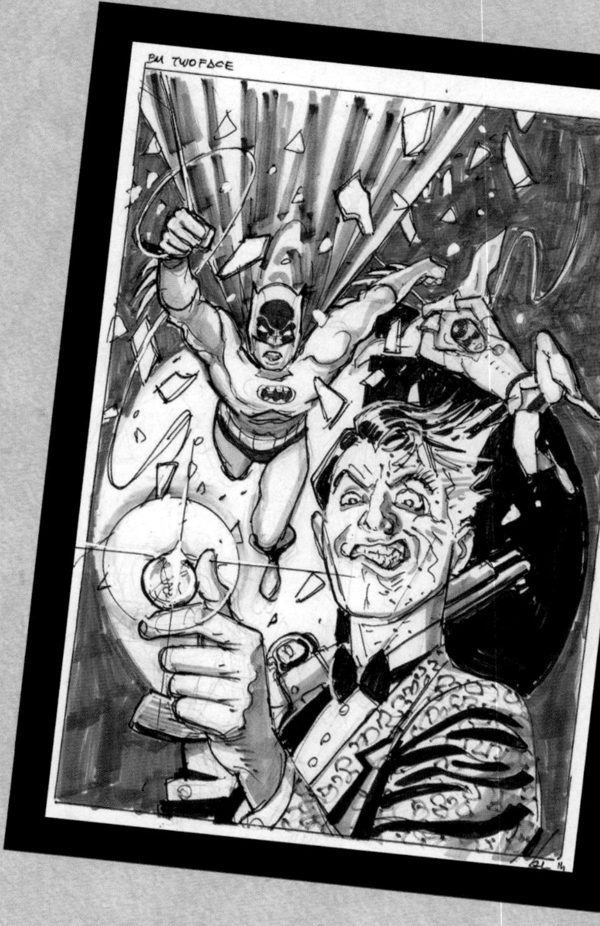
BM TWOFACE
2

Three concepts submitted by García-López for the variant cover

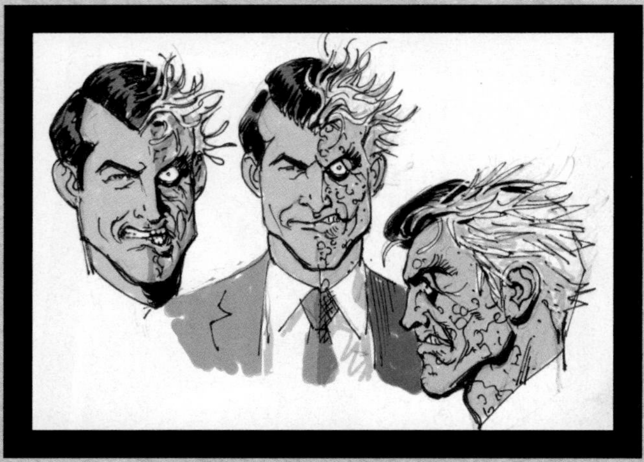

Since Two-Face never actually existed in the world of Batman '66, García-López needed to create a visual look for the character.

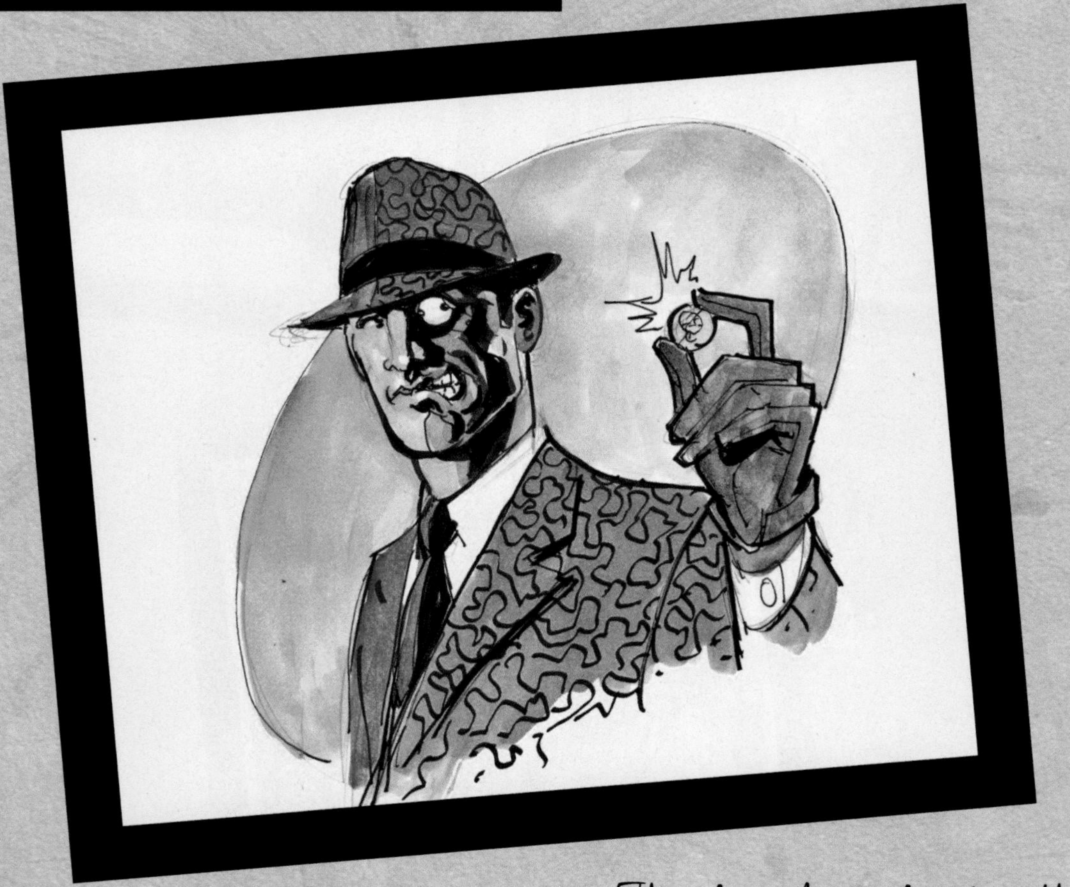

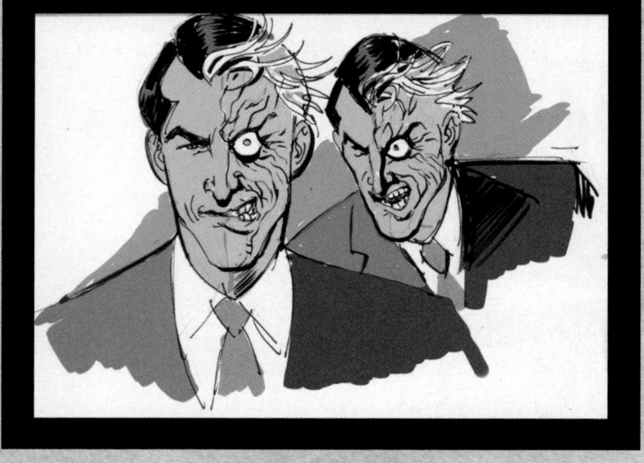

The blue skin color for the disfigured side of his face seemed too close to the version of the character on the Batman animated TV series, so the decision was made to go with green.

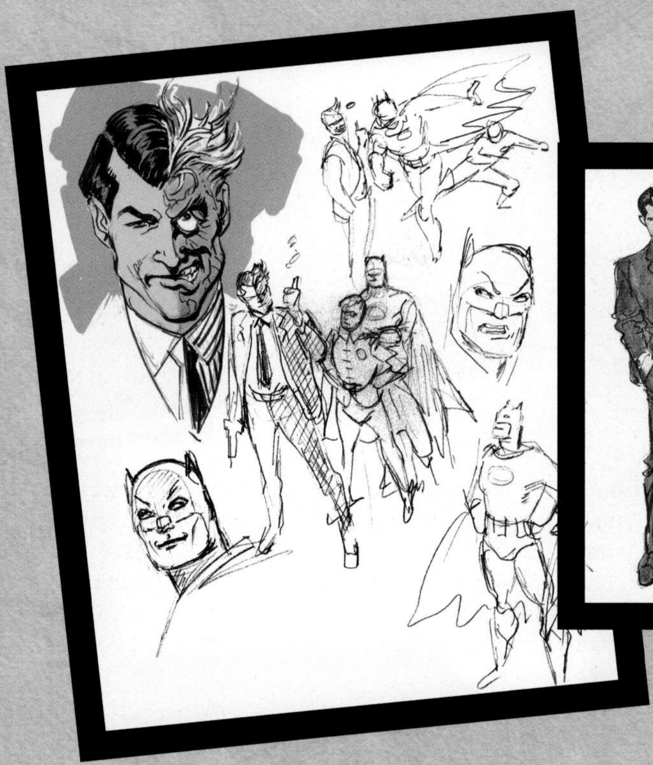

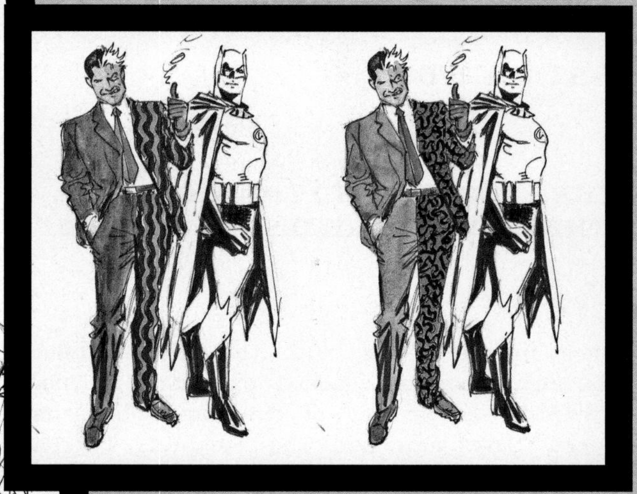

More concept drawings of Two-Face by García-López, showing scale with some full-body poses.

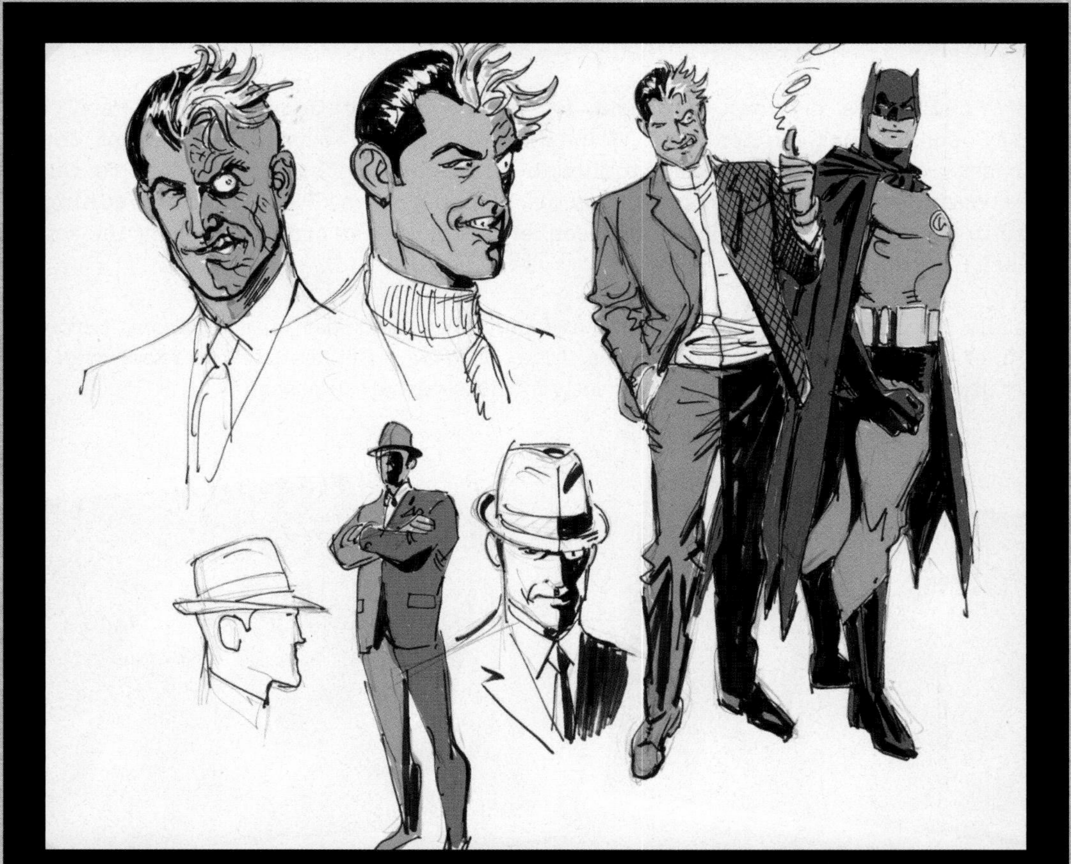

BATMAN ’66

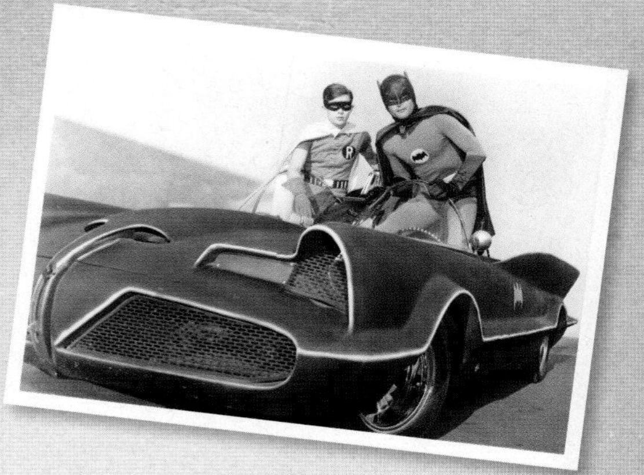

THE STORY BEHIND THE STORY OF “THE TWO-WAY CRIMES OF TWO-FACE.”

Back in the 1960s, with the Batman television series soon to hit the air, writer Harlan Ellison approached executive producer William Dozier with a story featuring Two-Face, a member of the Caped Crusader’s comic book rogues gallery. Like the Joker, Catwoman and the Penguin, Two-Face’s origins went all the way back to the early 1940s. The Two-Face story was green-lit but never made it on to the air. (A more complete accounting of events can be read in Volume 5 of Mr. Ellison’s **Brain Movies** anthology series.)

The fact that this story was never produced was unfortunate for two reasons. For one, viewers would have had an undoubtedly great episode of Batman written by Harlan Ellison, whose “The City on the Edge of Forever” is frequently regarded as the greatest episode of Star Trek, another iconic television series of that decade. For another, this would have introduced the character of Two-Face into the lineup of classic Batman TV villains. Fans love to speculate which actor of the period might have played the disfigured District Attorney turned psychopathic bad guy, Harvey Dent. Instead, the casting remains simply a fun game of “just imagine” that dedicated Batman fans continue to play.

It was Mr. Ellison’s original treatment for “The Two-Way Crimes of Two-Face” which legendary comic book writer Len Wein adapted into a comic book script for this special issue of BATMAN ’66. But we thought it might also be fun for fans to read the original treatment itself, which we present on the following pages. (Please note that editing notes included in the original manuscript have been left in the text in order to present the complete treatment.)

(The stills accompanying this feature are publicity and set photos from throughout the run of the Batman television series. “The Two-Way Crimes of Two-Face” was never actually produced, so these images are strictly for illustrative purposes.)

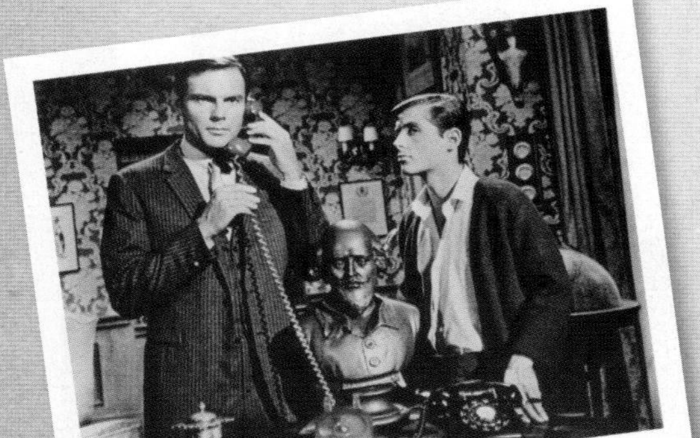

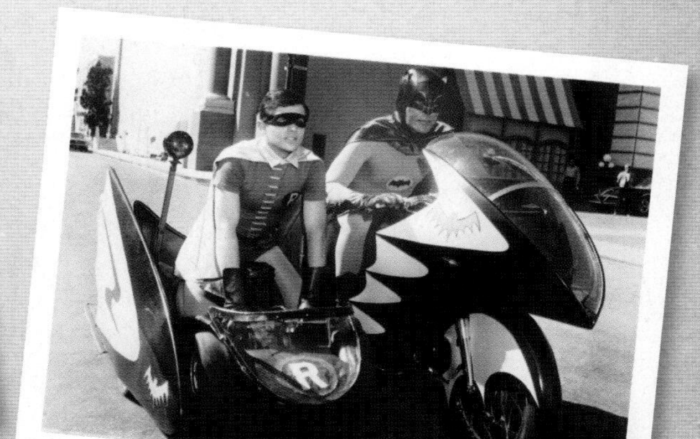

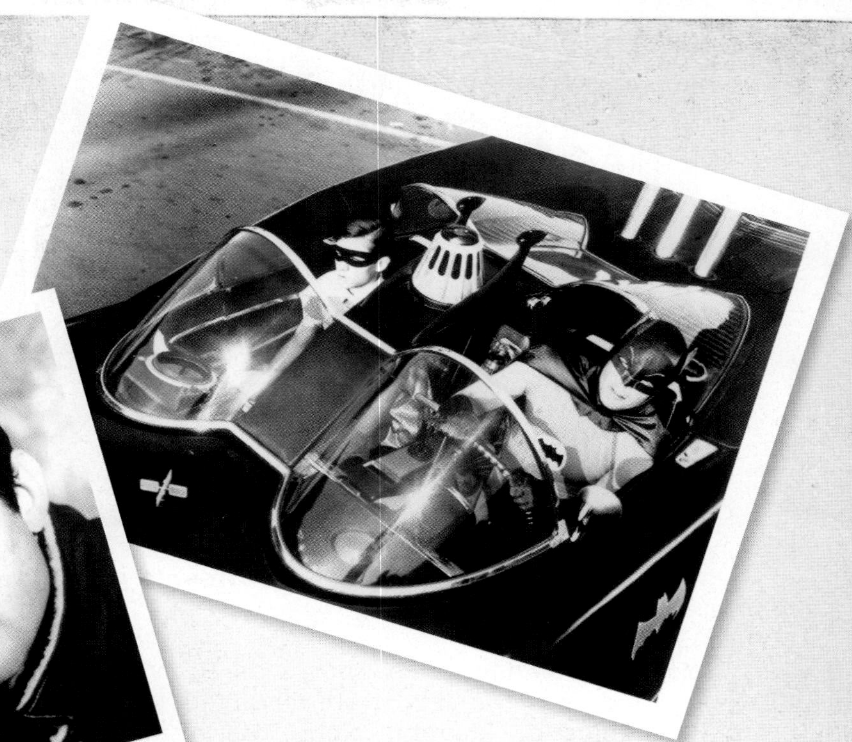

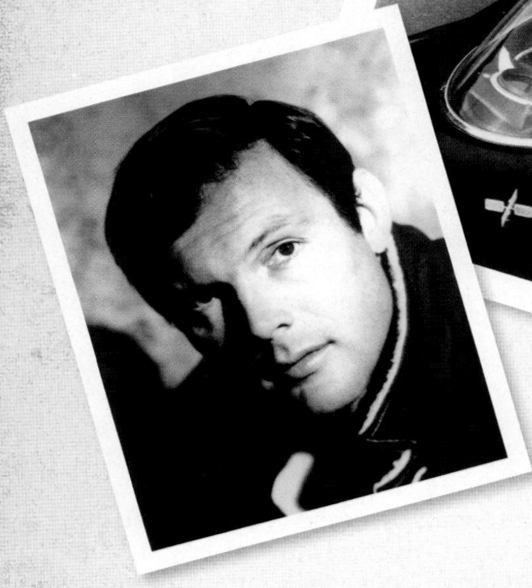

BATMAN

"The Two-Way Crimes of Two-Face"

Written by **HARLAN ELLISON®**

Presented unedited, from the original manuscript, as it appeared in Harlan Ellison's BRAIN MOVIES, volume 5.

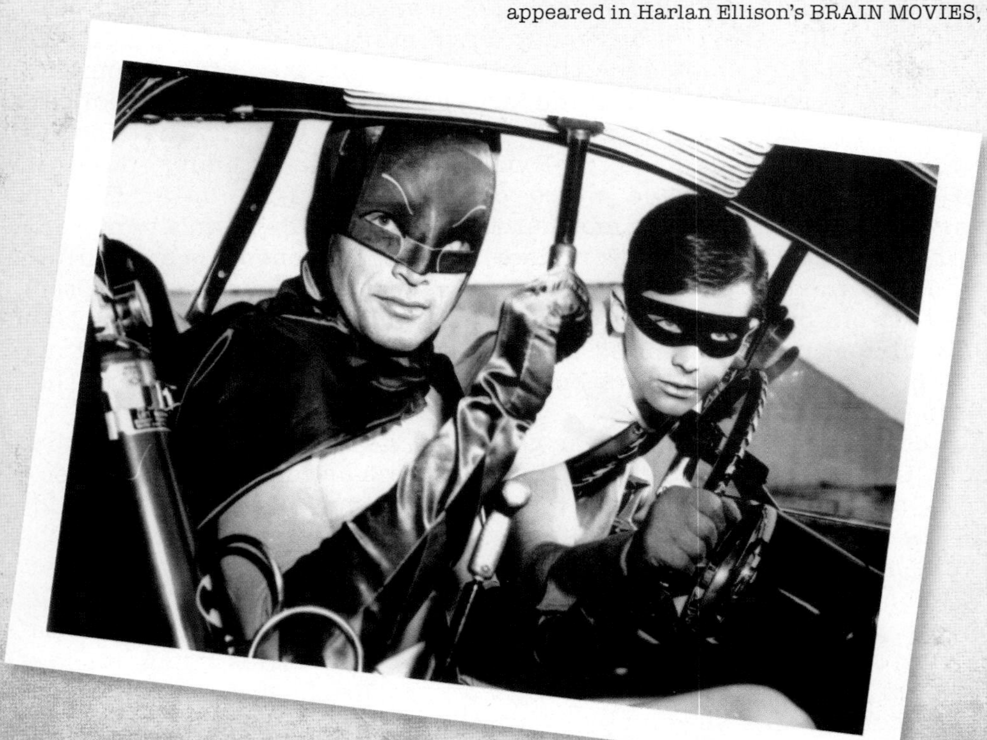

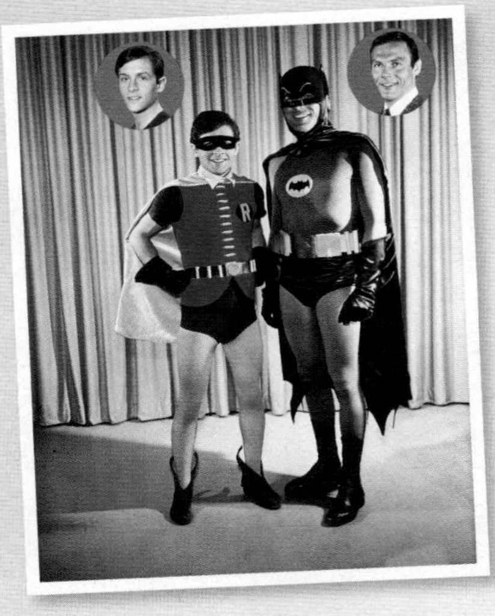

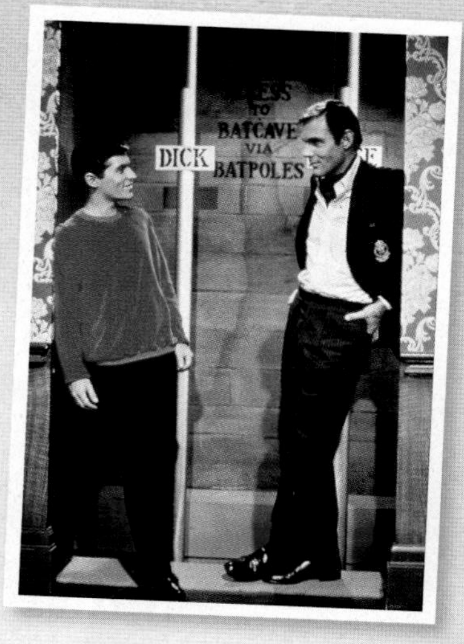
BATCAVE
VIA
BATPOLES
DICK

The deadly third banana in Batman's gallery of arch-enemies has returned! Two-Face!

(Who?)

Yeah, Two-Face, once known as Harvey Dent, District Attorney of Gotham City, but now a half-deranged criminal whose bizarre and cunning crimes all devolve upon the number 2. Dent, as prosecuting attorney in the case of "Lucky" Morony, was exhibiting the criminal's two-headed silver dollar—a well-known good luck piece for Morony—which had been found at the scene of the crime, when Morony leaped off the stand and hurled acid at Dent's face. Though Batman leaped to interpose himself, part of the acid landed on Dent, terribly disfiguring one side of his face. When plastic surgery failed, the once-handsome Dent began to brood and become schizoid. He was no longer able to practice at the bar; his appearance was repugnant to juries. He became obsessed with the dichotomy of his appearance—his right side was perfectly normal, even handsome. But his left was deformed and scarred, blue-gray from the acid. He thought Gilda, the girl he was to have married, was even against him. And finally, it sent Dent over the edge. He went mad, and from the twisted and tortured recesses of his mind came a conception of such diabolical perversity, that it could only end with the birth of...TWO-FACE! Master criminal, disciple of doubledom, Jekyll-Hyde of hoodwinkery, double-dealing dastard of banditry! Wearing a weird costume half-ugly, half-tailored, Two-Face set out on a career of crime that rivaled any of Batman's nemeses.

Yet there was still that spark of decency that had been the crusading D.A. in Two-Face, and so, torn by his own inner emotions, Two-Face adopted the two-headed coin of "Lucky" Morony as his symbol, since it had been the cause of his misfortune. He scarred and scored one side of it, leaving it as ravaged as his own face. And before he commits a crime, Two-Face flips the symbol of his personality.

If the coin comes up showing the good side, he does a good deed. If the scarred side, then the deed is evil. And so, all of his crimes are "2" crimes, double deeds; committed in daytime if good, nighttime if evil. A weird and implacable foe whose own nature is so tied to his looks that he is totally unpredictable, and so he becomes a dread threat to Batman and Robin.

But more: the cowled crusader knew Dent, sympathizes with him, wants to bring him to justice so he can be rehabilitated, perhaps undergo further surgery to restore his appearance. And with this humanitarian instinct always in Batman's thoughts, Two-Face becomes an even more deadly menace: for he has no compunctions about killing Batman!

We **FADE IN** an exclusive auction salon with a prominent sign that declares it to be a "Closed Auction Tonight." Inside, the AUCTIONEER is talking to a gathering of the most wealthy Gothamites. The items in question this night are a nearly-complete set of Chang Dynasty porcelains, the famous "Chang Blue" glazes whose incredible hues have never been matched, for the secret of firing them has been lost to antiquity for thousands of years. Fifteen porcelain jars and urns, bowls and pitchers, eight sets minus one. Worth: half a million dollars.

As the Auctioneer tells of the preciousness of these rarities, he advises the audience that to view the porcelains under precisely the proper conditions, they will be seen in the light for which they were intended: candle-light. The lights go out, and great candelabra are brought out, set along the highly polished tables.

Then an AGING PORTER wearing a smock and wrinkled with age comes out of the back bearing a tray on which are the incredibly beautiful porcelains. He moves down the tables, slowly, showing the beauties to the blue bloods. One HEFTY DOWAGER with several chins and several million dollars stays the Porter with a hand on his wrist. She wants a much closer look at those porcelains. He leans over, near the eight-candle candelabra, and she takes her time looking.

But suddenly we see an expression of horror cross the Dowager's face, and she screams. As we **REVERSE ANGLE** we get an **EXTREME CLOSEUP** on the Porter, whose face is melting! Terrifyingly, the left side of his face is running from the heat of the candles.

With a fluid motion the old man pulls out a blocky sawed-off shotgun and stands suddenly erect, not old at all. He laughs demonically as the entire assemblage is cowed in terror. "Double barrels, friends, courtesy of your two-timing guest...TWO-FACE!" And pulling off the rest of his disguise, he escapes with the porcelains.

SPIN FRAME to Commissioner Gordon calling BATMAN on the hot line. **SPIN FRAME** to Batman and ROBIN at Gordon's side, in the auction salon. As Gordon alerts Batman to the reappearance in Gotham City of Two-Face, the porcelains are returned by a pair of St. Bernard huskies pulling a little red wagon. Attached to the wagon is a note that says:

"I HOPE THIS WILL FIX YOUR LITTLE RED WAGON!"

And it is signed TWO-FACE. And when the Auctioneer counts the porcelains, he finds there are now not merely fifteen glazed items...but sixteen! Eight sets of two. The set is now complete, and incalculably more valuable.

WHAT'S THIS?

A CRIMINAL WHO DOES GOOD DEEDS?

RETURNING! MORE! THAN HE STOLE?

Camera holds on the startled faces of Batman, Robin, et al. as we **FADE OUT**.

FADE IN Act One:

The famous Hall of Trophies in the Bat-Cave. The myriad treasures and mementos of an illustrious crime-fighting career. Among the strange objects, a huge bust of Harvey Dent, alias Two-Face. One half of the bust has been terribly disfigured, chipped away with a chisel. It was being done by Dent's fiancée, Gilda, when he was disfigured by acid, and when he became Two-Face, in a fury he ruined it. Now, it reposes in the Bat-Cave, as Batman recapitulates Two-Face's career with Robin (as we have done on page one of this story). Their discussion concludes with Batman's opinion that Two-Face's coin landed on the good side, for he did a good deed by returning the Chang glazes.

"But next time," Batman warns, "it may come up evil." Which leads us into a **SERIES OF MONTAGES, WIPES & SMASH-CUTS** showing Two-Face's next "two" crimes:

Two-Face robs the box office of a baseball park, where a twi-night double-header is in progress.

Two-Face robs a double-feature movie...

Two-Face kidnaps an actor who is a double for Lincoln...

Batman swinging between buildings on Bat-rope...

The Batmobile racing aimlessly through streets...

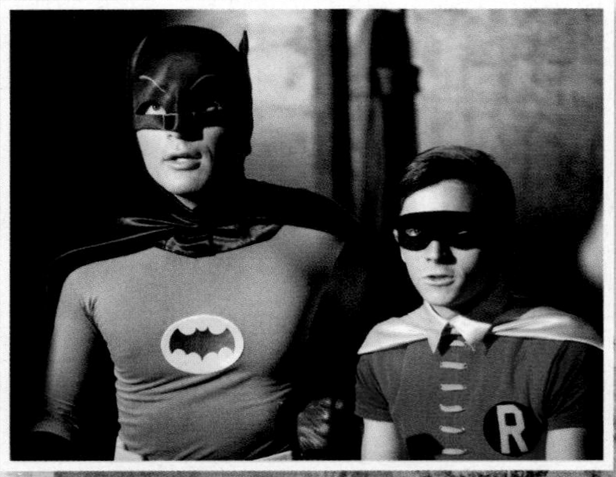

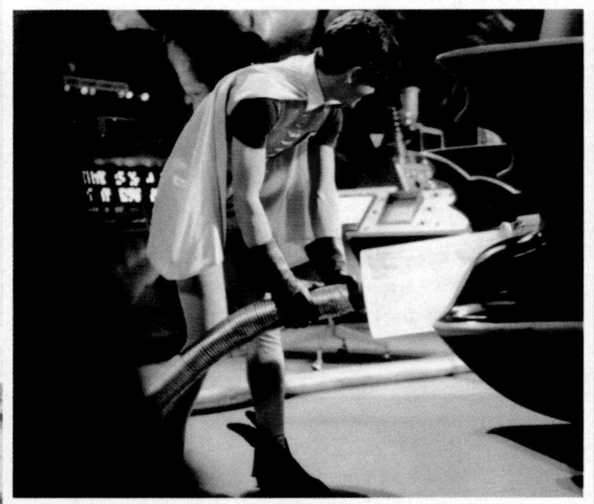

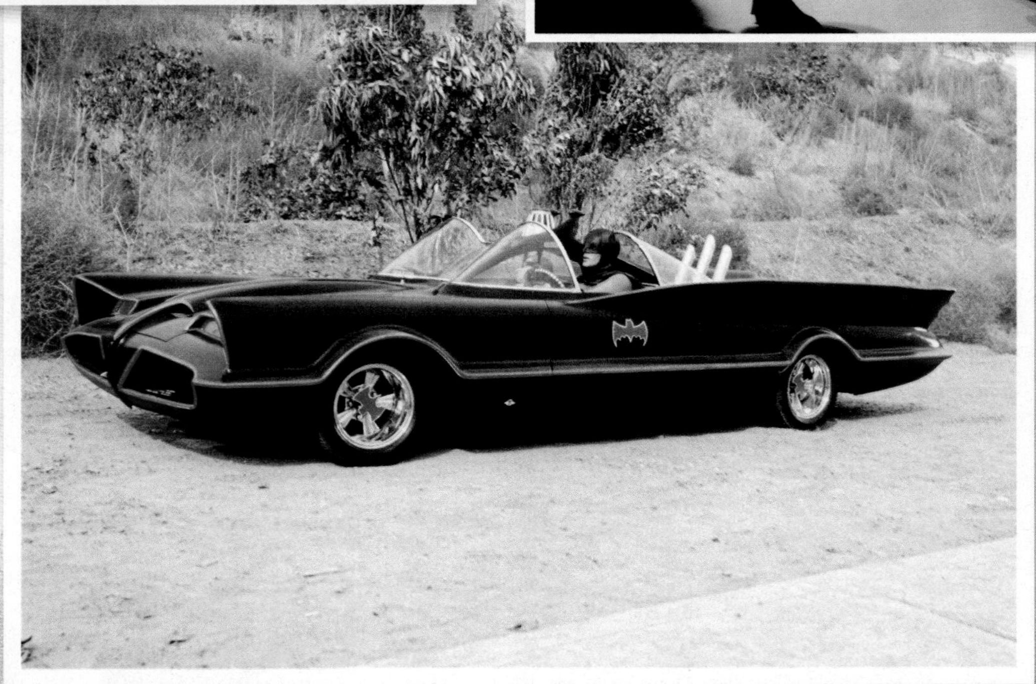

And finally, back in the Bat-Cave, with Batman and Robin forced to the conclusion that they are not going to catch Two-Face by random hunting. It has been three weeks, and he has committed good and bad deeds with seeming impunity. Batman admits the time for scientific detection has come. He and Robin punch out programming cards for the CompU-Bat VI (a super-computer built to Batman's own original and revolutionary designs like all Bat Machines) with all the data on Two-Face's crimes spree. Using the Heisenberg Principle of Indeterminacy, von Neumann's Game Theory and the Regular Table of Statistical Probabilities (not to mention some vital information from Spunky, a gambler of their acquaintance with almost an eidetic memory for gambling odds), they run the information through the computer, and compute the odds that Two-Face's next crime will be an evil one.

Batman then runs through a list of possible crimes Two-Face might commit. "He has too much self-esteem to pick a puny crime," Batman decides. "So it has to be one of these three...they're the only possibilities big enough for an arch-criminal of his capabilities."

Batman urges Commissioner Gordon to assign Chief O'Hara and his men to cover one of the crime possibilities, he sends Robin to cover the second, and he goes himself to protect the Annual Motorcycle Championships—a contest for two-wheeled vehicles.

Two-Face strikes at the cycle races, and when Batman chases him, Two-Face tries to escape with the gate receipts, using a motorcycle; fitting for a double-dealing villain, the use of a two-wheeled getaway. Batman takes up the chase using a chariot yoked behind twin cycles. But Two-Face gets away by riding the narrow cycle between two buildings, while the wider transportation Batman has employed crashes.

Ah! But not before Batman has whipped from his Utility Belt a thin tear-gas-type rod filled with phosphorescent spray, and sprayed the escaping Desperado of Duality.

The crash knocks Batman unconscious, and when he comes to, he goes looking for Two-Face. When Robin gets to the scene of the crime, Batman is gone, but he finds the discarded spray rod, and also follows the trail.

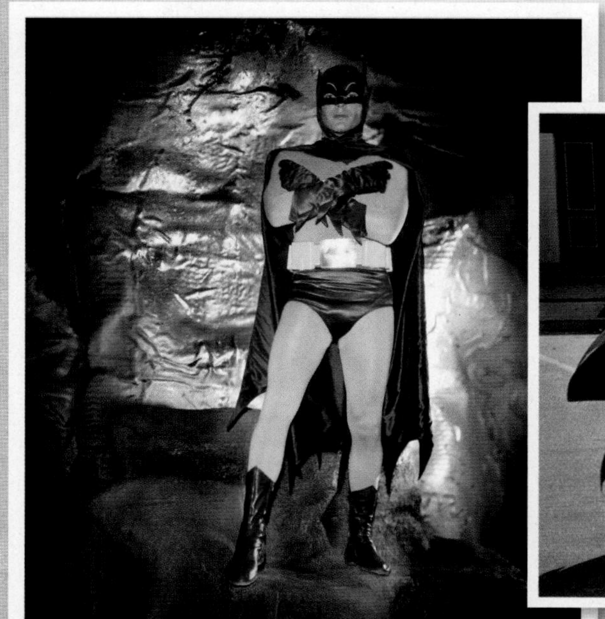

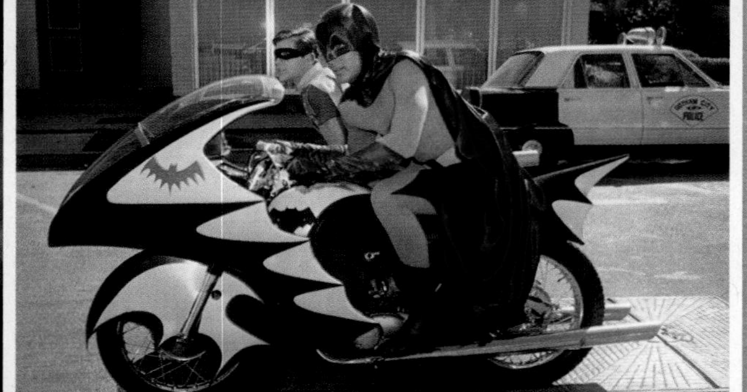

Meanwhile...

Batman has tracked Two-Face to his lair. An abandoned observatory. He decides to take Two-Face by surprise, and by swinging up the sheer face of the observatory on the Bat-Rope, he drops down through the sky-panel.

But Two-Face has been expecting him! It was a trap!

There in the "Moon Room," an exact replica of the surface of Luna, Batman finds himself trapped by Two-Face. Half the room is in daylight, just as Earth's satellite keeps its one face always to Terra.

Batman stands in daylight, and Two-Face in night, and levels a machine gun at the Cowled Crusader.

"I've been waiting for you, Batman," Two-Face taunts him. "How fitting your attack on me should turn double-cross. Now I will flip my coin. If it comes up with the unscarred side showing, I'll let you go...if it's the evil side, you'll die! Get ready, Batman, the gods of chance are shooting craps for your life."

He flips the coin into the air and as it spins up and up and begins to come down we **FREEZE FRAME** and
FADE OUT!

FADE IN Act Two:
 The coin comes down and wedges itself between the floorboards at the edge of the day/night division of the Moon Room. On edge. A pathetic indeterminacy overcomes Two-Face. He can neither stay nor go; kill nor release. His finger trembles on the trigger.
 Batman watches.
 Two-Face bites his lip.
 Batman's eyes narrow.
 Two-Face looks helpless, torn.
 Batman takes the decision out of his hands by suddenly moving his body slightly so that the "sun" that produces daylight on his half of the room reflects off the Bat-Glass in his Utility Belt, and when Two-Face reels back from the blinding light, Batman charges him. Two-Face sprays the room, and they tangle and fight there half in day, half in night.
 But just as Batman is about to capture Two-Face, Robin (who has been trailing his imperiled partner) bursts in, slips on the mass of exploded shell casings from the machine gun, and reels into Batman. They tumble in a heap, and Two-Face manages to get away.

Later, at the Wayne mansion, Aunt Harriet cannot understand why Bruce and Dick Grayson, his ward, are despondent. She suggests a vitamin deficiency, and forces both of them to take a heaping tablespoon-ful of her old family elixir. Bruce and Dick look as though they are going to be ill, but Aunt Harriet goes up to bed secure in the knowledge that she has attended to what ails them.

But what troubles the Dynamic Duo is a moral problem. Two-Face can be saved, Bruce is certain of that. The fact that he still does good deeds, holding on to that last vestige of decency he knew as Harvey Dent, compels Batman to try to save Two-Face. He suggests to Dick that they make their rounds, try to get a lead on Two-Face, try to find him before he can kill someone, and put himself too far outside the Law for any hope of redemption.

WHIP-PAN to Two-Face, in his new hideout, which we cannot make out, save that it is beamed and made of wood. He rails at the night, at Fate, and most of all, at Batman! He blames Batman for his plight, as the one man who stands between him and success. He swears he will kill Batman, and decides to go out looking for him.

Then Two-Face smiles, evilly. He has the method for luring Batman into his clutches...

In the Bat-Plane, suddenly the two-way radio comes on, and Two-Face (who has jammed the Bat-frequency) taunts Batman, calling him a caped incompetent, telling him the next caper to be pulled off will make a royal boob out of Batman, and challenging Batman to stop him.

It takes the keen minds of two great crime-fighters to figure out what Two-Face meant, but working together, Batman and Robin decide the clue was "royal boob."

And coincidentally (ha! fat chance!) royalty is arriving in Gotham City! The Siamese Princesses of a tiny Hindu nation, whose jeweled crowns are duplicates of one another. Batman tells Robin that's the next two-crime of the troublesome two-timer, Two-Face, and he'll be ready.

And so, as the ship docks at Gotham Pier 9, and the two Princesses walk down the gangplank, the Bat-Copter circles overhead. Suddenly, a quayside crane begins to unreel, and double-grapnels swing down just over the two beautiful Princesses and snare their crowns, at the same time.

Then Two-Face leaps from the crane, dashes to pier side and slips into a pair of water-skis with a frame attached. He spurts away, across the bay, and the Bat-Copter follows.

Treatment revisions: 12 Nov 65

Pages 8-9

STET to final paragraph , then insert following; cut final paragraph (p. 8) and cut through to bottom fourth paragraph page 9.

Then Two-Face leaps from the crane and escapes as the Bat-Copter follows overhead; Batman knows Two-Face will lead him to his lair if only they can keep up with him. "And when I get to him, I think I can outwit him, save him, despite himself...with what I've prepared," Batman says enigmatically.

And they do stay with him, unobserved, as Two-Face races across town to an old motion picture studio, abandoned many years before. Robin lowers the Bat-Copter, and Batman hurtles down on his Bat-Rope, crashing through the dusty skylight, into the interior of the murky, eerie studio.

And there, on a full-scale set of a Mississippi riverboat—a twin-paddle, two-stack riverboat—he finds Two-Face's new hideout.

Batman skulks on board. But Two-Face had been waiting for him, has once again lured the dark champion to his doom. They grapple and Batman seems to be winning, but suddenly, almost startlingly, Two-Face slugs Batman a good WHAP! and Batman collapses.

RESUME ORIGINAL TREATMENT, beginning with fifth paragraph, page 9.

Overhead; Batman knows Two-Face will lead him to his lair if they can only keep up with him "And when I get to him, I think I can outwit him...with what I've prepared," Batman says enigmatically.

But suddenly, even as they watch, Two-Face's two-ski water-skimmer vanishes under some low-lying branches on the edge of an island, and he is gone. Batman tells Robin to circle the island, but they see nothing. Two-Face is gone.

Batman dons a frogman suit and as Robin circles low, he dives out of the Bat-Copter, hits water, and swims under the island. It was as he suspected, there is an underwater tunnel that leads to an underwater cave, and in that cave is Two-Face's new hideout...a two-masted schooner, left over from an amusement pier.

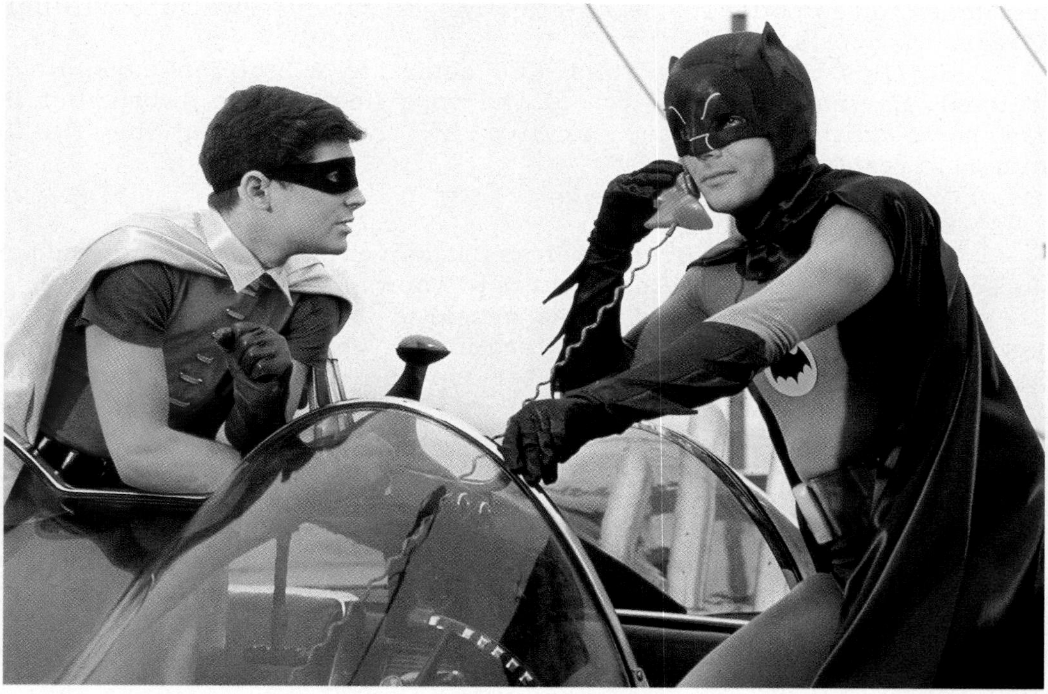

Batman climbs up the anchor chain and gets on board. But Two-Face has been waiting for him, has once again lured the dark champion to his doom. They grapple and Batman seems to be winning, but suddenly, almost startlingly, Two-Face slugs Batman a good WHAP! and Batman collapses.

When he comes to, the double-crossing demon of duality has him tied to a chair, and a two-edged sword hangs over Batman. Two-Face once again offers Batman the chance of the fates; if the coin comes up heads, then Two-Face will cut the rope holding the sword, and Batman will die quickly. If it comes up the scarred side, then he will keelhaul Batman—dragging him under the schooner with a hawser rope in the manner of old-time pirates—and it will be a slow doom. "You see, I'm being scrupulously fair," he taunts the masked lawman, "but I'm done taking chances with you."

"Wait!" Batman stops him. "What if it lands on edge again?" Two-Face laughs. The odds against it happening a second time are impossible. He says it can't happen.

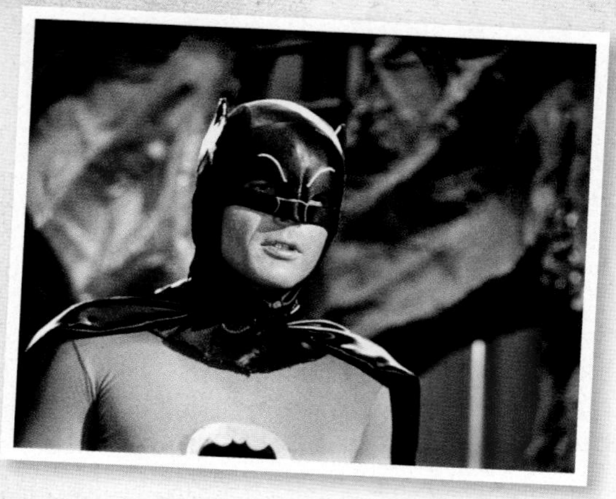

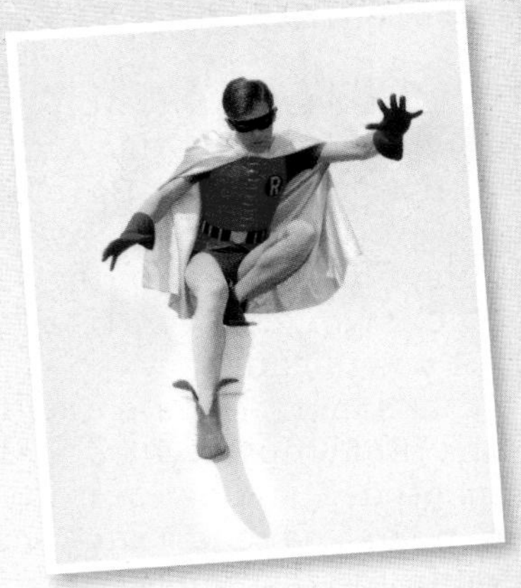

Batman suggests, if it does, though, will Two-Face release him, and surrender to the police for psychiatric rehabilitation? Two-Face willingly agrees, it is such a joke.

He flips the coin, it rolls, and comes to a stop...on edge. He is stunned. He tries to move, to cut the rope holding the sword, but he has so conditioned himself to live by the coin, that he finally slumps in resignation.

"You win, again."

Batman takes him in.

Later, Robin and Alfred listen as Batman explains what happened on the schooner. "But how—?" Robin wants to know.

"You remember I said I was prepared for him the next time we met," Batman reminds Robin. His ward nods. "Well, I wanted Two-Face to capture me, knowing he would offer me the coin-chance again. So I prepared a special silver dollar, that was loaded, like a pair of crooked dice. All the weight was in the bottom edge, so no matter how he threw it, it had to come down on edge. When we were fighting, I picked his pocket, took his own coin, and slipped my bogus copy into his pocket. Like all double-crossers, Two-Face was a sucker for his own twisted mechanics."

Robin smiles. "So you had your cake and ate it, too, Batman. You captured him, and saved him. Do you think the psychiatrists can help him back to normal?"

Batman looks disturbed "'Two-Face is out of circulation now, but only time will tell."

And on that faintly ominous note, we

FADE OUT

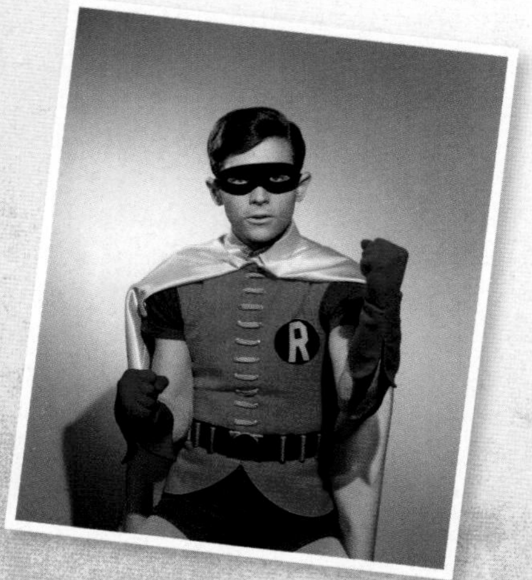

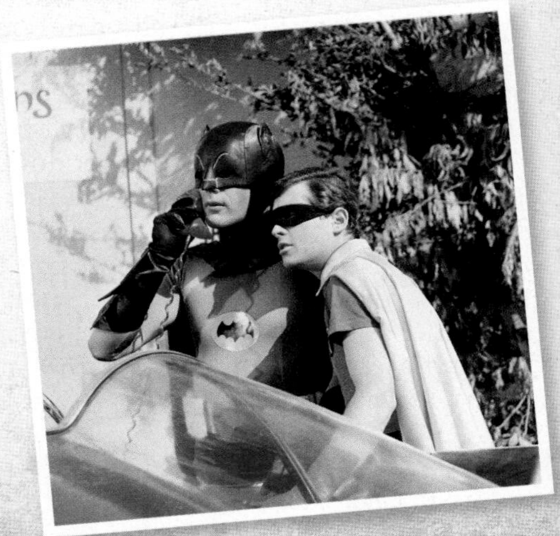

Design by: Shannon Tompros

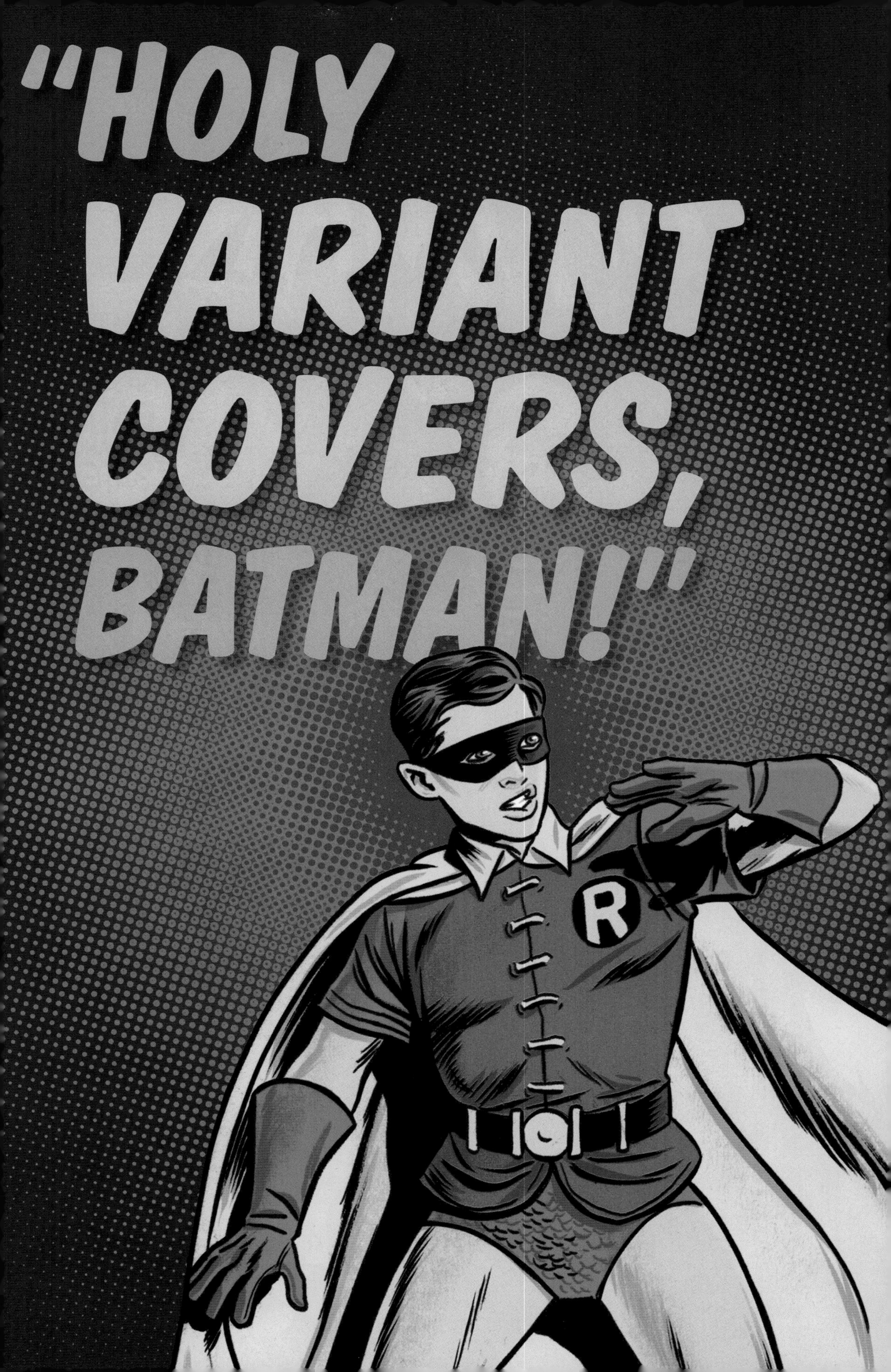
"HOLY VARIANT COVERS, BATMAN!"

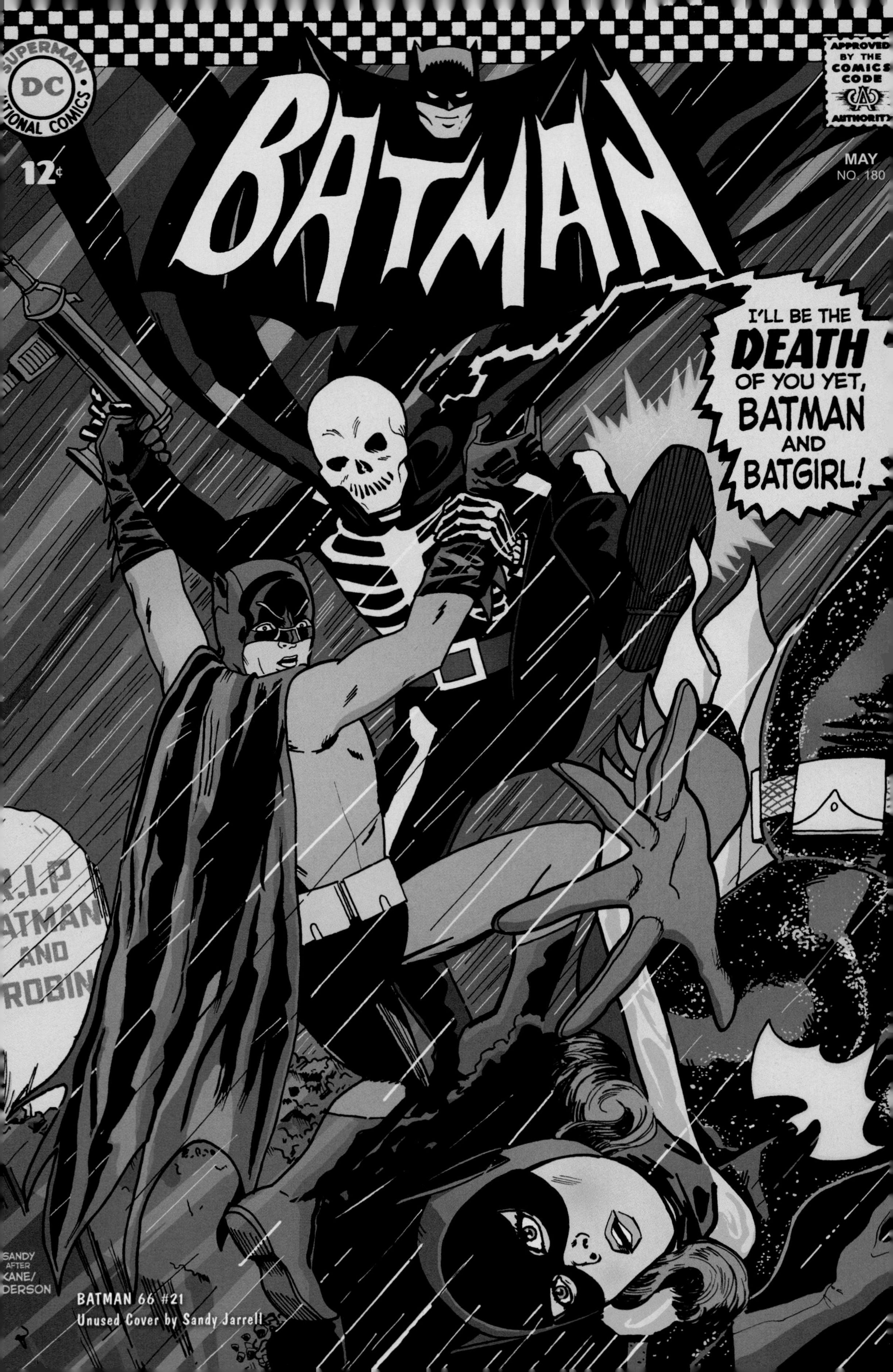

SUPERMAN
DC
ATIONAL COMICS
12¢
APPROVED BY THE COMICS CODE AUTHORITY
BATMAN
MAY
NO. 180
I'LL BE THE DEATH OF YOU YET, BATMAN AND BATGIRL!
R.I.P
ATMAN
AND
ROBIN
SANDY
AFTER
KANE/
DERSON

BATMAN 66 #21
Unused Cover by Sandy Jarrell

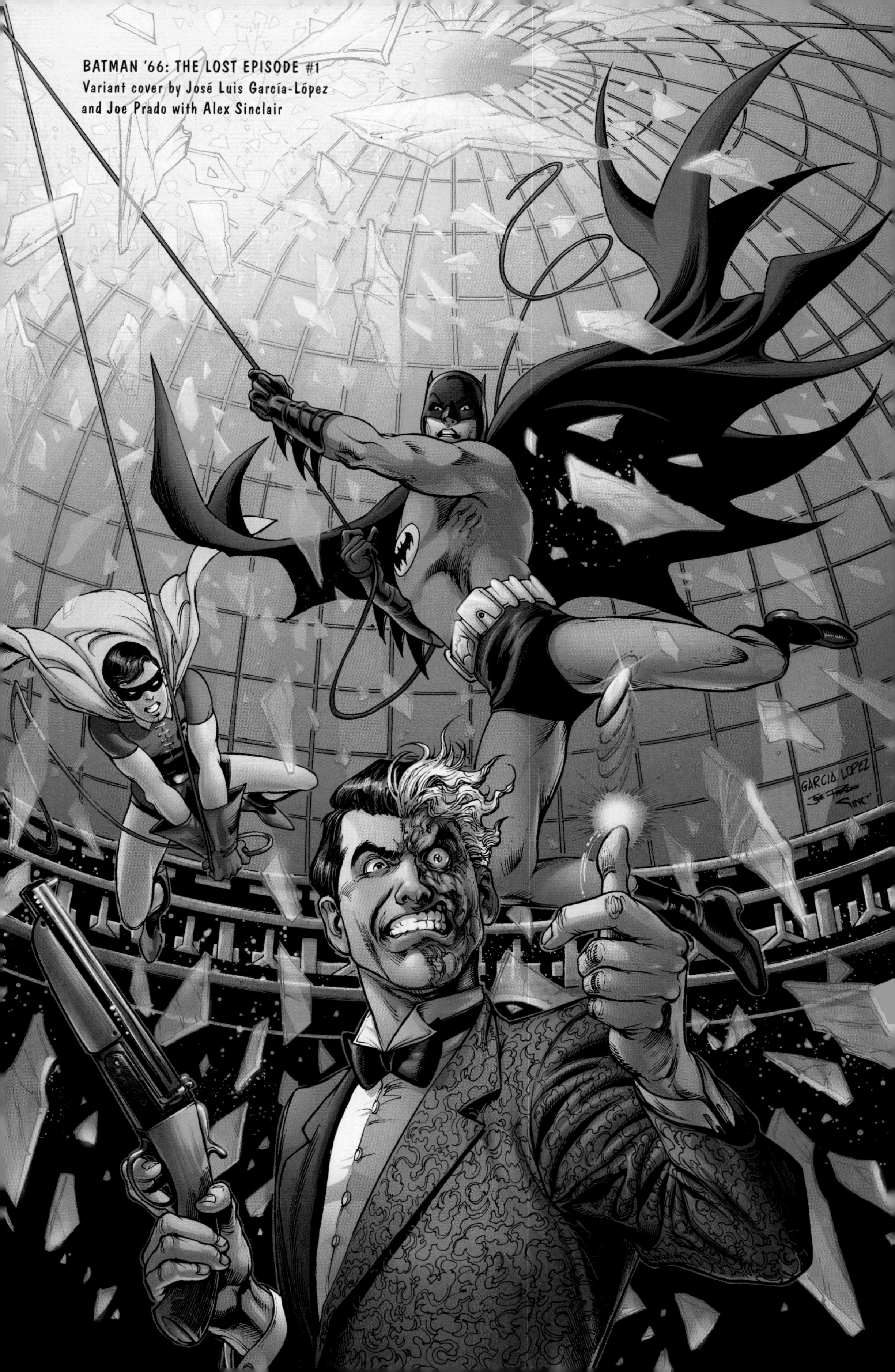
GARCIA LOPEZ

BATMAN '66: THE LOST EPISODE #1
Variant cover by José Luis García-López
and Joe Prado with Alex Sinclair

"Rock solid."—IGN

"This is the kind of Batman story I like to read: an actual mystery with an emotional hook."
—THE ONION/AV CLUB

START AT THE BEGINNING!

BATMAN & ROBIN
VOLUME 1: BORN TO KILL

**BATMAN & ROBIN
VOL. 2: PEARL**

**BATMAN & ROBIN
VOL. 3: DEATH OF THE
FAMILY**

**BATMAN
INCORPORATED
VOL. 1: DEMON STAR**

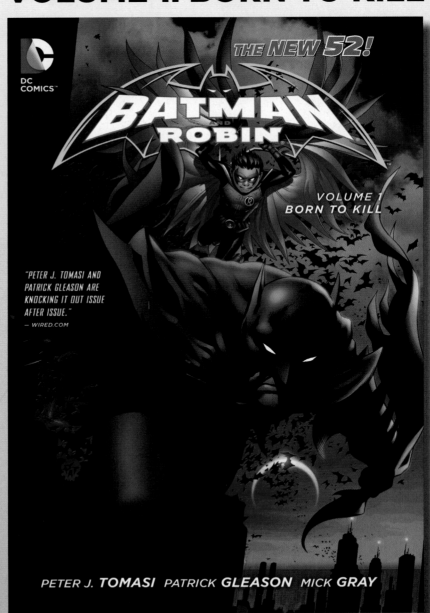

THE NEW 52!

DC COMICS™

BATMAN AND ROBIN

VOLUME 1
BORN TO KILL

"PETER J. TOMASI AND PATRICK GLEASON ARE KNOCKING IT OUT ISSUE AFTER ISSUE."
— WIRED.COM

PETER J. **TOMASI** PATRICK **GLEASON** MICK **GRAY**

"[Writer Scott Snyder] pulls from the oldest aspects of the Batman myth, combines it with sinister-comic elements from the series' best period, and gives the whole thing terrific forward-spin."—ENTERTAINMENT WEEKLY

START AT THE BEGINNING!

BATMAN VOLUME 1: THE COURT OF OWLS

BATMAN VOL. 2: THE CITY OF OWLS

with SCOTT SNYDER and GREG CAPULLO

BATMAN VOL. 3: DEATH OF THE FAMILY

with SCOTT SNYDER and GREG CAPULLO

BATMAN: NIGHT OF THE OWLS

with SCOTT SNYDER and GREG CAPULLO

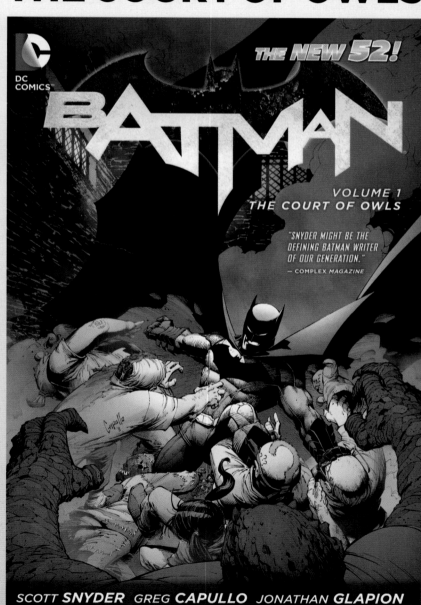

THE NEW 52!

DC COMICS

BATMAN

VOLUME 1
THE COURT OF OWLS

"SNYDER MIGHT BE THE DEFINING BATMAN WRITER OF OUR GENERATION."
— COMPLEX MAGAZINE

SCOTT SNYDER   GREG CAPULLO   JONATHAN GLAPION

DC COMICS™

"Combines the real world elements that have made the Christopher Nolan movies so successful with stylized visuals that only the comic medium can provide."
—COMPLEX MAGAZINE

MUST-READ TALES OF THE DARK KNIGHT!

BATMAN EARTH ONE: VOL. 1

GEOFF JOHNS & GARY FRANK

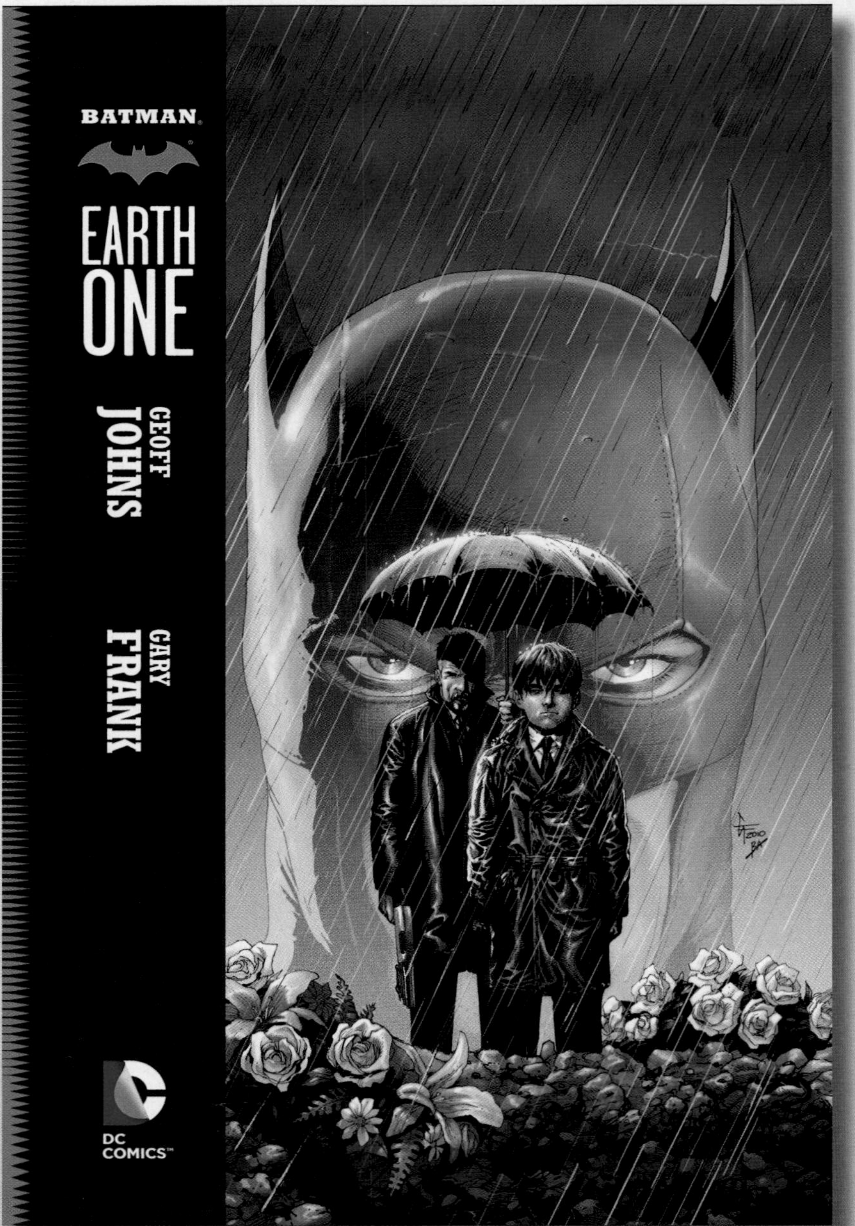
BATMAN
EARTH ONE
GEOFF JOHNS
GARY FRANK
DC COMICS™

BATMAN VOL. 3: DEATH OF THE FAMILY

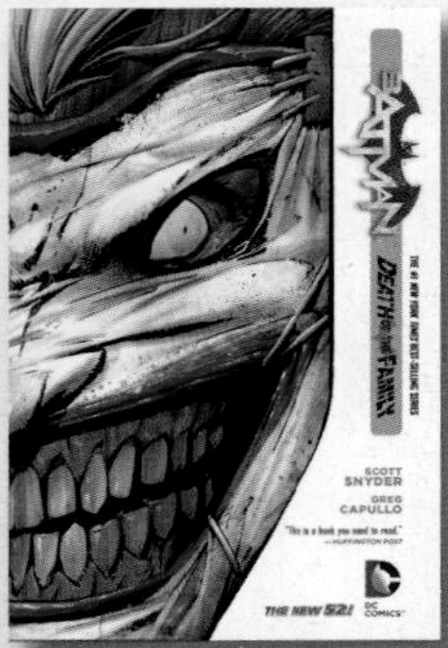
SCOTT SNYDER
GREG CAPULLO
THE NEW 52!

by SCOTT SNYDER & GREG CAPULLO

BATMAN: KNIGHTFALL VOLS. 1-3

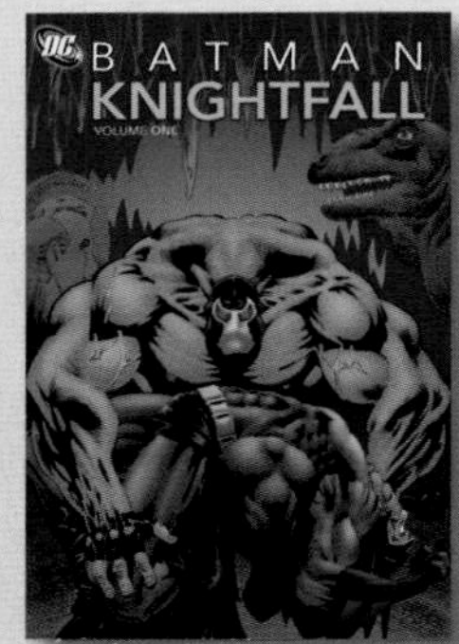
BATMAN
KNIGHTFALL
VOLUME ONE

BATMAN: NO MAN'S LAND VOLS. 1-4

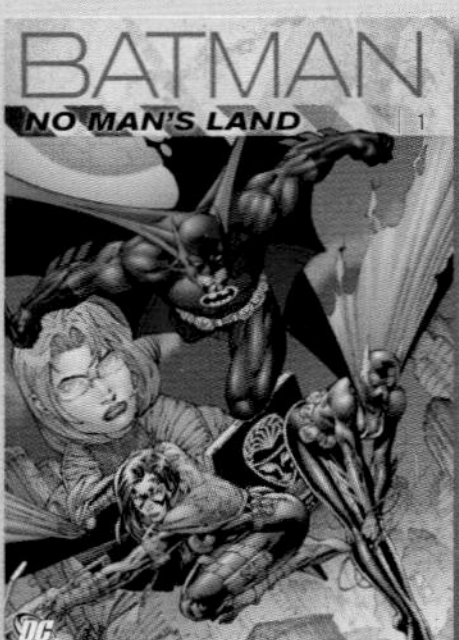
BATMAN
NO MAN'S LAND
1